Norfolk Record Society
Volume LXXII for 2008

Sir John Pettus (1549/50–1614), *vir civilis*, endower of sermons and founder of the Library in 1608. Norwich Civic Portrait 71. Artist unknown, 1612.

THE MINUTES, DONATION BOOK AND CATALOGUE OF NORWICH CITY LIBRARY, FOUNDED IN 1608

Edited by
CLIVE WILKINS-JONES

Norfolk Record Society
Volume LXXII for 2008

© The Norfolk Record Society, 2008

First published in 2008
by the Norfolk Record Society

ISBN 978-0-9556357-1-7

Produced by John Saunders Design & Production
Printed by Biddles Ltd. King's Lynn

Contents

Illustrations

Frontispiece Sir John Pettus (1549/50–1614), *vir civilis*, endower of sermons and founder of the Library in 1608. Norwich Civic Portrait 71. Artist unknown, 1612.

Between pages 18 and 19

1. Detail from an engraving by Daniel King of the south side of St Andrew's Hall showing the swordbearer's lodgings that housed the Library, 1657.

2. Title page of the Donation Book, commemorating the foundation by Sir John Pettus.

3. Dr John Collinges (1623/4–1691), chaplain to the Hobart family and librarian in 1657. Engraving by R. White, 1673.

4. The antiquary, John Kirkpatrick (1687–1728), one of the Library's most generous donors.

Preface

This book came about as a result of longstanding interest in the life and work of John Collinges, Norwich City Library's first librarian, a man who deserves a much more flattering epitaph than 'conventickling Doctor' or 'seditious infuser of ill principles'. I first came across Collinges through the work of Penelope Corfield and David Stoker and am pleased to acknowledge the influence of both those scholars on this book. Discussions over several years with Matthew Reynolds about the religous politics of the city before and after Matthew Wren have also left a lasting residue. The influence of Victor Morgan's ideas on the culture of the sermon and on very much else will also be apparent.

Thanks are also due to George Hyde for introducing me to Walter Benjamin's essay on libraries and to William Woods for many discussions about the 'strangers'. Some of the difficulties I had with translations from Latin were eased by Elizabeth Rutledge and also by my wife.

Clive Wilkins-Jones
Norwich

Acknowledgments

All three manuscripts are published by kind permission of the Norfolk County Archivist, Dr John Alban, and the frontispiece and plates by that of the Norfolk Heritage Centre, Norfolk and Norwich Millenium Library. The portrait of Sir John Pettus is reproduced by kind permission of Norfolk Museums & Archaeology Service.

A generous publication grant was received from the Trustees of the Norwich Town Close Estate Charity.

Editorial practice

Rules of transcription

Original spelling has been retained. Punctuation and capitalisation have been modernised and contractions and abbreviations expanded. Abbreviated Christian names have been extended. Dates have been standardised and are given in New Style.

Symbols and editorial conventions

italics   Editorial additions enclosed in square brackets

[word]   Missing words supplied by the editor

*   *   Insertions and interlineations by the compilers of the manuscripts

<   >   Deletions by the compilers of the manuscripts

[?]   Uncertainty about the transcription of a word

/   /   Marginal entry or annotation by the compilers of the manuscripts

Abbreviations

Blomefield	Francis Blomefield, *An Essay towards the Topographical History of the County of Norfolk*, continued by Charles Parkin, second edition, 11 vols (1805–10)
Branford	Colin Branford, 'Powers of association: aspects of elite social, cultural and political life in Norwich *c*.1680–1760' (PhD. Thesis, UEA 1993)
Cozens-Hardy	Basil Cozens-Hardy and Ernest Kent, *The Mayors of Norwich, 1403–1835* (Norwich, 1938)
d.	pence (12d. = 1s.; 240d. = £1)
Evans	John T. Evans, *Seventeenth-Century Norwich: Politics, Religion and Government 1620–1690* (Oxford, 1979).
NHC	Norfolk Heritage Centre, Norfolk and Norwich Millennium Library
NRO	Norfolk Record Office
ODNB	*Oxford Dictionary of National Biography* (Oxford, 2004).
Reynolds	Matthew Reynolds, *Godly Reformers and their Opponents in Early Modern England: Religion in Norwich, c.1560–1643* (Woodbridge, 2005)
s.	shillings (20s. = £1)
TNA	The National Archives
Venn	John Venn and J.A. Venn, *Alumni Cantabrigienses* (6 vols. Cambridge, 1922-54).

General Introduction:
Norwich City Library from 1608

In 1608 the City Assembly ordered that three rooms at the 'New Hall' that were being rented by Jerrom Goodwyne, the city swordbearer, were to be converted into a library.[1] The 'New Hall', now St. Andrew's Hall, was the former Dominican Friary, purchased for the city by Augustine Steward in 1540 at least partly to have 'a pulpitte…to preache the worde of God on Sondays and holydays, in such tymes, as when there is no sermon at the Crosse withyn the Cathedral Church'.[2] The three rooms were part of a building that stood on the site of what is now the south porch of St Andrew's Hall, rented by the city swordbearer. Erected in 1543, the building had formerly housed the chantry priest, John Kemp, whose function had been to say daily mass for the King and the city's inhabitants. Remarkably, it was still known as 'Mr Kemp's chamber' in 1608.[3]

Norwich City Library was the first library to be established by a city administration in England outside London in a building that was corporately owned. Ipswich's administration did not accommodate William Smarte's bequest in the former dormitory of the Dominican Friary they had purchased until 1614.[4] The library at Leicester, housed in St. Martin's church, was the joint responsibility of the parish and the civic administration.[5] Bury St. Edmunds' library owed its existence to the efforts of the incumbent of St. James, Miles Mosse, and was housed in the parish

[1] NRO, NCR, Case 16c/5, Norwich Assembly Book, 1565–1613, f. 296. Goodwyne's was a long way from being a grace and favour arrangement. As well as paying a rent of three pounds a year, he was responsible for all repairs and maintenance. But the swordbearer's office had a high status. Goodwyne describes himself as a gentleman when he came to draw up his will (NRO ANW 101 136, Will of Jerrom Goodwyne, 1612).

[2] H.Sutermeister, *The Norwich Blackfriars* (Norwich, 1977) p. 9. The 'sermon at the cross' is an allusion to the preaching place on the north side of the cathedral, the so-called 'green yard'. There was a pulpit surmounted by a cross along with covered seating for the mayor, aldermen and their wives and the dean, the Cathedral prebends, their wives and invited gentlemen. The remainder of the congregation either stood or sat on benches, paying a penny or a half-penny as they did at St Paul's Cross in London. (For a description of the green yard see Sir Thomas Browne's *Repertorium*, 1712, pp. 32–3).

[3] Sutermeister, *The Norwich Blackfriars*, p. 10.

[4] J. Blatchly, *The Town Library of Ipswich* (Woodbridge, 1989) p. 10. For the Ipswich Town Library see also the same author's 'Ipswich Town Library', *Book Collector*, 35 (1986) pp. 191–8.

[5] P. Lindley, *The Town Library of Leicester: a brief history* (Upton, 1975).

church.[6] Grantham Library had been established in St Wulfram's church in 1598 by Francis Trigge, rector of Welbourn, with the agreement of the alderman of Grantham. The library at Guildford, largely composed of a bequest by John Parkhurst, bishop of Norwich, was housed in the grammar school.[7] Although the construction work to house Coventry library was financed by the city administration, the library, which dated from 1601, was housed in the grammar school. Bristol Library, founded in 1615, was accommodated in a house made available to the city by Robert Redwood, a local gentleman.[8]

The context for the foundation of the library was a lobbying campaign by the clergy in Norwich to increase their stipends.[9] On 3 March 1605 the city's member of parliament, Sir John Pettus, wrote to the mayor, Thomas Sotherton, outlining his opposition to a bill – described by Sir Simonds D'Ewes as a 'Bill for the true payment of tithes'[10] – that would have introduced a property tax of two shillings in the pound on every house and shop in the city.[11] The money raised was to be used to increase the stipends of the city's clergy. Pettus thought compulsion would be 'a great disgrace' to the city and that such a tax would be 'inconvenient...for the meaner sort of the inhabitants and for such as pay great rents'. He thought that each parish should be free to raise the money 'proportionable as is fitting' – in other words the allocation of money should be based on the perceived competence of the incumbent. The Act was not passed, mainly through the influence of Sir John's friend, Sir Henry Hobart ('the more part would have consented to the passing of the Bill had not Sir Henry Hobart been there to give them to understand the inconvenience that might grow there upon'...). On 15 February 1607 the members of the Privy Council instructed the mayor to levy a 'proporcionable tax' to be paid yearly to ministers 'according to their difference in gifts, sufficiency, & diligence in their function'. Those who refused to pay were to be brought before the council 'to answer for their contempt'.[12] Although no notice seems to have been taken of this instruction (ministers were still petitioning for its enforcement in 1621), it is clear that Pettus was sympathetic to the plight of the

[6] J. Craig, *Reformation Politics and Polemics: the growth of Protestantism in East Anglian Market Towns, 1500–1610* (Aldershot, 2001) pp. 116–21, 205–19.

[7] G. Woodward and R.A. Christophers, *The Chained Library of the Royal Grammar School Guildford* (Guildford, 1972).

[8] C. Tovey, *Bristol City Library: its founders and benefactors* (1853) p. 4.

[9] See C. Cross, 'The incomes of provincial urban clergy, 1520–1645' in, R. O'Day and F.Heal (eds), *Princes and Paupers in the English Church, 1500–1800* (Leicester, 1981) p. 85.

[10] Simonds D'Ewes, *The Journals of all the Parliaments during the reign of Queen Elizabeth* (1682) p. 654.

[11] NRO, NCR, Case 17b, City Revenue and Letters Book, 1606–24, f. 1.

[12] City Revenue and Letters Book, ff. 1v-2.

clergy (he thought an increase in the ministers' wages was 'very fitten') and may have lobbied for the establishment of a library as a *quid pro quo*.

Pettus, mayor of Norwich in 1608 and a successful politician on the national stage – he obtained from William Cecil the concession that Norwich would not pay the subsidy on the new draperies – was credited with founding the library by the compiler of the donors' book. Sir John made a major contribution to the city through a series of generous gifts and charitable bequests. While alderman for Fyebridge he built fish stalls in his ward and a conduit for a spring near the bridge at Bishopgate.[13] Under the terms of his will property was bequeathed to the city to fund sermons by Suffolk preachers at the 'common preaching place' at the Cathedral and at the parish church of St. Simon and St. Jude. What is surprising is that he provided neither money nor property to fund the development of the library. Instead he donated a small collection of books: Binius' *Concilia omnia*, the *Magdeburg Centuriatores* and Cardinal Bellarmine's *Controversies*. After Sir John's death the Pettus family continued to take a proprietary interest in the library. In 1656 Sir Thomas Pettus paid Daniel King for an engraving of the south side of St. Andrew's Hall, an engraving that foregrounded 'Master Kempe's chamber' and the library and included the family coat of arms.[14]

The Library was established 'for the preachers and for a 'lodginge chamber for suche preachers who shall come to this cittie to preache'. As the wording makes plain, the arrangements were not just for the benefit of the city clergy but for preaching clergy travelling to the city from elsewhere who had to find overnight lodgings. It was for this reason that the sword-bearer was instructed to provide 'beddynge, lynnyng and other neces-saries'. It is very probable that these visiting preachers were combination lecturers, beneficed ministers who preached at the Cathedral in the 'common preaching place' or green yard in rotation.[15] On 4 May 1657 a committee of the Norwich Assembly recommended a combination of Norfolk and Suffolk preachers, each preacher to be paid twenty shillings,[16] the members of the combination to be nominated by a committee of aldermen and sheriffs.[17] Like exercises, combination lectures took place

---

[13] Blomefield, *History of Norfolk*, iii, p. 362; iv, pp. 427–8.

[14] D. King, *The Cathedrall and Conventual Churches of England and Wales, orthographically delineated* [1656]. Augustine Pettus, Sir John's son, donated a copy of Theodor Zwinger's *Theatrum humanae vitae* in 1610.

[15] Confusingly, the open space on the south side of St Andrew's Hall was also known as the green yard. On 29 April 1661 the City Assembly ordered that 'the pulpit & seates at the greene yard at the Newhall shalbe taken downe & laid into the Chapell & that the Mayor & Aldermen shall continue their going to the Cathedrall to the fore noone sermon on the Lords Daies & other daies as in times before 1642 they did' (NRO NCR Case 16d, Assembly Book, 1642–1668, f. 218v).

[16] Norwich Assembly Book, 1642–1668, f. 179v.

[17] Assembly Book, 1642–1668, f. 190.

weekly or fortnightly, drew their audiences from a wide area and were supplied by a panel or combination of preaching clergy. It was common practice for the combination to be present at each lecture and for the lecture to be followed by dinner and a clerical conference. In North Norfolk a combination lecture was delivered in Wiveton weekly from 1578 to 1593, involving almost half the beneficed clergy in an area between the rivers Stiffkey and Glaven.[18] After an interruption caused by the plague, the lectures were renewed either at Langham or Binham and continued well into the seventeenth century.[19]

Access to books was an essential prerequisite of the success of a combination, as it was for the efficacy of preaching generally. Patrick Collinson has shown how combination lectures stimulated the writing and publishing of books by those clergy who participated.[20] The Norwich preacher Nicholas Bownd's *Doctrine of the Sabboth* [sic] developed from a series of sermons on the decalogue. In the second edition of 1606 Bownd cited ninety-three sources apart from the Bible.[21] The Bury St. Edmund's lecturer Miles Mosse's *The Arraignment and Conviction of Usurie* (1595) was originally delivered in six sermons at Bury. Mosse cited one hundred and fifty seven authors.[22]

References to reading by individual clergy are not hard to find. Richard Greenham (*c.*1535 – *c.*1594), rector of Dry Drayton, Cambridgeshire, and author of a *Treatise of the Sabboth*, who thought that ministers should 'give themselves diligently to reading', woke at four o'clock every morning to study. Andrew Willett (1562–1621), rector of Barley in Hertfordshire and the author of *Synopsis Papismi* (1594), studied for eight hours a day and was known as the 'walking library'. One minister claimed that a clergyman without learning was like a 'lamp burning without light, like a nurse without milk, a bell without a clapper, a watchman without an eye'.[23]

There is plenty of evidence to suggest that the Norwich city administration was heavily involved in the organisation of sermons at the green yard. In 1608 the City Chamberlain paid Edward Wright for 'keepynge the dore' at the green yard. At the same time he paid the Cathedral sexton for

[18] A.Hassell Smith, 'Puritanism and Neighbourhood: a Case Study in Late Sixteenth and Early Seventeenth Century Norfolk' in, E. Royle (ed), *Regional Studies in the History of Religion in Britain since the Later Middle Ages* (York, 1984) pp. 80–93.

[19] Smith, 'Puritanism and Neighbourhood', p. 81; V. Morgan, J. Key and B. Taylor (eds), *The Papers of Nathaniel Bacon of Stiffkey, iv: 1596–1602* (Norfolk Record Society, lxiv; Norwich, 2000) pp. 16–17.

[20] P. Collinson, 'Lectures by Combination: Structures and Characteristics of Church Life in Seventeenth-Century England' in *Godly People: Essays in English Protestantism and Puritanism* (1983) pp. 495–6.

[21] Collinson, 'Lectures by Combination...', p. 495.

[22] Collinson, 'Lectures by Combination...', p. 496.

[23] NRO, DS 625, Anonymous sermon notes, p. 299.

'settynge stooles' for the mayor.[24] In 1617 Edward Wright was paid again for 'keeping the door' at the green yard.[25] In 1626 the Chamberlain paid for the seats in the green yard to be mended and for the purchase of mats to cover the judges' seats.[26] After the sermon was delivered the mayor, aldermen and invited guests dined together, after which the proceedings were brought to a close.

The sermon, that 'immortal seed of regeneration', was a central concern of the Elizabethan and Jacobean church. Francis Bacon claimed that 'if the choice and best of these observations upon texts of scripture, which have been made dispersedly in sermons within your Majesty's island of Brittany by the space of these forty years and more...had been set down in a continuance, it had been the best work in divinity which had been written since the Apostle's time'.[27] To Richard Hooker, sermons were 'keys to the kingdom of heaven' and 'wings to the soul'.[28] For continental Calvinists, the sermon was the prime means of effectuating God's decree of election. As Calvin himself explained: 'the elect are gathered into Christ's flock by a call not immediately at birth, and not all at the same time, but according as it pleases God to dispense his grace to them. But before they are gathered unto the supreme Shepherd, they wander scattered in the wilderness common to all; and they do not differ at all from others except that they are protected by God's especial mercy from rushing headlong into the final ruin of death'.[29] For disciples of Calvin like the Norwich minister, Thomas Newhouse, preaching won, served and converted men's souls.[30] Francis Mason, archdeacon of Norfolk, thought that the word of God should 'abound like Euphrates, and as Jordan, in the time of harvest; that the doctrine of the Gospel might shine as the light and overflow as Geon in time of vintage'.[31]

The sermon also had a socio-political character. For Francis Bacon it was a barrier to anarchy: 'men are full of savage and unreclaimed desires, of profit, of lust, of revenge: which as long as they give ear to precepts, to laws, to religion, sweetly touched with eloquence and persuasion of books, of sermons, of harangues, so long is society and peace maintained; but if these instruments be silent, or that sedition and tumult make them not audible, all things dissolve into anarchy and confusion'. But there were hard-headed business considerations too. Sermons were wealth creating, a

---

[24] NRO, NCR, Chamberlain's Accounts, 1603–25, f. 126v.

[25] Chamberlain's Accounts, f. 282v.

[26] Chamberlain's Accounts, f. 48.

[27] Francis Bacon, *The Advancement of Learning* (ed) A. Johnston, (Oxford, 1974) p. 209.

[28] Richard Hooker, *Of the Laws of Ecclesiastical Polity*, ii (1907) p. 85.

[29] F.H. Kloster, *Calvin's Doctrine of Predestination* (Michigan, 1977) p. 46.

[30] Thomas Newhouse, *Certaine sermons* (1614) p.60.

[31] Francis Mason, *The Authoritie of the Church in Making Canons and Constitutions Concerning Things Indifferent* (1607) p. 18.

factor that was revealed quite unashamedly in a petition by 'divers of the citizens and inhabitants of Norwich' in 1624.[32] The petitioners claimed that bishop Samuel Harsnett's deprivation of five or six conformable preaching ministers and three weekly sermons had led to many gentlemen and others of good quality in the country no longer frequenting the city. Not only this, some citizens who 'set multitudes on work' had left the city with the result that trading was so decayed that there was a danger that the poor would not be maintained.

Thomas Kelly, in his classic study of the history of Norwich City Library, identified an interest in sermons as a characteristic of 'puritanism'.[33] In other words, the Library was a 'puritan' foundation. But an interest in sermons was all-encompassing in the Elizabethan and Jacobean Church. Matthew Parker, Queen Elizabeth's first archbishop of Canterbury, left money for the delivery of an annual sermon at Thetford, Wymondham, Norwich Cathedral and the parish church of St. Clement's. The first sermon was preached at Norwich Cathedral's green yard on Sunday 20 July 1567 by Thomas Goodwin, dean of Canterbury, later to be bishop of Bath and Wells. Among those present were not only the commissioners of the archbishop, then engaged in a visitation, the bishop of Norwich and the mayor, aldermen, sheriffs and common councillors but the leader of the religious conservatives in East Anglia, the duke of Norfolk.[34] In the Chichester diocese of bishop Richard Curteys in the late 1570s it was claimed that 'whereas it was a rare thing before his time to hear a learned sermon in Sussex, now the pulpits in most places sounds continuously with the voice of learned and godly preachers, he himself as *dux gregis* [35] giving a good example unto the rest'.[36] By the reign of James the preaching bishop was a common feature of diocesan life. Tobie Matthew, archbishop of York, kept a diary of his preaching activity between 1583 and 1622 in which he recorded the delivery of almost 2,000 sermons.[37]

Norwich City Assembly invested considerable sums of money in the provision of sermons. In 1609, for example, the City Chamberlain paid 6s. 8d. to William Wells, minister of St. Peter Mancroft, for a sermon at Mancroft during rogation week; 6s. 8d. to Thomas Newhouse, minister at St. Andrew's, for a sermon at St. Andrew's, again in rogation week; and 6s.

[32] Bodleian Library, Tanner MS 104, f. 204.

[33] T. Kelly, 'Norwich, Pioneer of Public Libraries', *Norfolk Archaeology*, xxxiv (1966–8) pp. 217–8.

[34] Blomefield, *History of Norfolk...*', pp. 312–3.

[35] Leader of the flock.

[36] P. Collinson, *The Religion of Protestants* (Oxford, 1982) p. 77.

[37] W.J. Shiels, 'An Archbishop in the Pulpit: Tobie Matthew's Preaching Diary, 1606–1622' in, D. Wood (ed), *Life and Thought in the Northern Church c1100–c1700* (Woodbridge, 1999) pp. 381–405.

8d. to Robert Kent, chaplain of St. Martin at Oak, for the Kett sermon.[38] In 1610 Thomas Newhouse was paid £13. 6s. 8d. for his 'yerely pension'.[39] The same amount was paid in 1611.[40] In 1612 the Assembly agreed to pay Paul Greaves, the 'common preacher' and author of *Grammatica Anglicana* (1594), £20 a year 'with the arrerage from the tyme of the death of Master Newhouse'.[41]

If sermons were so critically important and the provision of books to facilitate the composition of those sermons was so vital, why did it take so long for libraries to be established? One of the reasons may have been the effectiveness of the Books of Homilies of 1547 and 1563 in satisfying the preaching needs of most of the clergy. The first Book of Homilies passed through thirty-six editions by 1640, the second twenty editions.[42] Yet the efficacy of homilies was questioned. Richard Hooker thought homilies supplied 'the necessarie defect of sermons', but when it came to putting life into words by 'countenance, voice and gesture' sermons were superior.[43] John Donne thought homilies 'cold meat'.[44]

A far more compelling reason was the fact that the clergy were becoming better educated. In November 1561 there were only 57 licensed preachers in Norwich Diocese, out of a total of 1,200 benefices. In the Archdeaconry of Norwich less than one fifth of the beneficed clergy had university degrees. Almost half of the clergy were described as having 'little learning'. By 1605 there was a licensed preacher in almost every other parish. Of the 579 beneficed preachers within Norwich Diocese only seventy were licensed non-graduates, although there were a further 215 non-graduates.[45]

When the library was established considerable resources were invested in the refurbishment of the rooms at St. Andrew's Hall. Twenty-six square yards of 'wainscot ceiling' was taken out of the 'library chamber' as part of the alterations 'commanded' by the mayor, Sir John Pettus.[46] In 1608 William Lawes was paid twenty-one shillings 'for timber & work done by

---

[38] Chamberlain's Accounts, f. 127. In 1601 Kent had been summoned to face charges in the Consistory Court for a sermon in which he had complained that 'bribery and corruption were of prelates and church government'. To make matters worse he had made an 'ill conceived gesture' towards the bishop's palace (Reynolds, p.172).

[39] Chamberlain's Accounts, f. 151v.

[40] Chamberlain's Accounts, f. 169v.

[41] Assembly Book, f. 428v.

[42] I. Green, *Print and Protestantism in Early Modern England* (Oxford, 2000) p. 209.

[43] R.B. Bond (ed), *Certain Sermons or Homilies (1547) and A Homily against Disobedience and Wilful Rebellion* (1570) (Toronto, 1987) p. 11.

[44] Bond, *Certain Sermons*, p. 23.

[45] V. Morgan, *A History of the University of Cambridge, v2: 1546–1750* (Cambridge, 2004) pp. 235–7.

[46] Assembly Book, f. 258.

him at the Library'.[47] In 1609 the City Chamberlain was instructed to pay a mason 12? d. for work done at the library 'and for nails, lime and for other things there'.[48] At the same time a painter was paid for painting the 'chamber next the Library'.[49] However, there is no evidence that there was ever any intention on the part of the City Assembly to pay the librarians a salary. From 1657 the librarian was elected annually by the members of the library and served without payment. Once elected, the librarian appointed an under-librarian who was salaried in the sense that he was paid by the members.[50] One of the most important responsibilities of the under librarian was to look after the keys to the Library.

Except for one occasion in 1628 when the Assembly paid twenty shillings for a copy of John Minsheu's *Dictionary*[51] and another in 1641 when the Chamberlain paid 3s. 8d. for a map to be repaired,[52] there is no evidence that the Assembly donated money for the purchase of books, neither is there any evidence that there was ever a public appeal for money to buy books.[53] No catalogue appears to have been made during the first fifty years of the Library's existence and no large donation of books was received. The records are also silent on the question of whether any of the Assembly's preachers were involved in the promotion of the library. Although it is tempting to assume that Thomas Newhouse or William Batho, two of the most high-profile preachers amongst the Norwich clergy during the first decade of the seventeenth-century, promoted the establishment of the Library, evidence is lacking.[54] At King's Lynn the 'sedentary

[47] Chamberlain's Accounts, fol. 108v.

[48] NRO, NCR, Case 18a, Chamberlain's Accounts, 1603–25, f. 129.

[49] Chamberlain's Accounts, f. 129.

[50] This arrangement is reminiscent of Humphrey Prideaux's description of the library at Alexandria and of the career of Demetrius, its librarian. Apparently, Demetrius was 'above the mechanical employment and servile attendance of keeping and looking after a library, but not above that of having the superintendency and chief direction over it' (Humphrey Prideaux, *The Old and New Testament connected in the history of the Jews and neighbouring nations*, ii, 1719, p. 15).

[51] Chamberlain's Accounts, f. 88v.

[52] Chamberlain's Accounts, f. 368.

[53] Sir Thomas Bodley had been very much aware of the importance of endowments. He had 'by good observation found it apparent, that the principal occasion of the utter subversion and ruin of some of the famousest libraries in Christendom hath been the want of due provision of some certainty in revenue for their continual preservation' (I. Philip, *The Bodleian Library in the Seventeenth and Eighteenth Centuries*, Oxford, 1983, p. 6). The Bristol Assembly funded a librarian as early as 1615 (Tovey, *The Bristol City Library...*, p.5).

[54] Both Newhouse and Batho donated books to the library, but not until some years after its foundation. In 1616 Batho donated a copy of the works of St Gregory. On his death in 1624 he bequeathed all his books to his brother Toby 'except some 101 particulars which I have bownd and ingaged my selfe to leave to the library of this cittie of Norwich'. Unfortunately, these 'particulars' never materialised (NRO, NCC, 103 Gente, Will of William Batho, 1624). Newhouse, who died in 1611, bequeathed a copy of the works of John Chrysostom (NRO, NCC 135 Stywarde, Will of Thomas Newhouse, 1611).

scholar', John Arrowsmith (1602–59), vicar of St. Margaret's from 1631, made an important contribution to the establishment of St. Margaret's Library. Arrowsmith may even have listed the books purchased with the initial gifts. In 1641 there is a reference in the King's Lynn Chamberlain's Accounts to a donation book 'heretofore given by Mr. Arrowsmith'.[55]

The Reorganisation of 1657

After the initial refurbishment of the three rooms at St. Andrew's Hall there is no documentary evidence that the Assembly took any interest in the Library until 1628, twenty years after the foundation. In that year the Assembly, through the Town Clerk, paid twenty shillings for a copy of the second edition of John Minsheu's *Dictionary*.[56] There is no explanation for the purchase in the Assembly minutes, but it is reasonable to assume that it was the result of a petition on the part of the Library's users. There are at least three other recorded interventions before the dramatic reorganisation of the Library in 1657. In 1633 some unspecified work was done which cost the Chamberlain 2s.[57] In 1636 two loads of tile were purchased at a cost of 28s.[58] In 1641 the Chamberlain paid 3s. 8d. for a map to be repaired.[59] During the civil war and commonwealth the mayor, aldermen and common councillors had far more pressing priorities than concern with the Library. In 1648 the 'Great Blow', a royalist inspired riot, led to many deaths. In 1650 there was an unsuccessful royalist rising in Norwich. And there was frequent unrest over the payment of the hated excise tax. Religious life was similarly disrupted. In 1643 the city had regular services in all thirty-five parish churches. By 1646 regular services were held in less than a third.[60]

The neglect the Library suffered was not reversed until 1657. Perhaps the most crucial factor that inspired this change of policy lay in the provisions of the will of John Carter, vicar of St. Lawrence's, formerly minister of St. Peter Mancroft, and stern critic of the city magistrates. Carter, who died in 1655, had originally intended to bequeath a number of books to the Library. However, as he lamented in a codicil to his will, 'now seeing to my no small grief, that, that Library is locked up, ministers shut out of it, and that it is never like to be of public use again, but that the books are

---

[55] King's Lynn Borough Archives, KL/C7/11, Chamberlain's Accounts, f. 79v.

[56] NRO, NCR, Case 18a, Chamberlain's Accounts, 1625–48, f. 88v. The first edition of the *Dictionary* had been donated as early as 1617.

[57] Chamberlain's Accounts, f. 184v.

[58] Chamberlain's Accounts, f. 244.

[59] Chamberlain's Accounts, f. 368. This was probably the map of the Holy Land, donated by John Freeman in 1634.

[60] M.J.Crossly-Evans, 'The Anglican and Nonconformist clergy of Cheshire and Norfolk, 1630–1672' (Bristol Ph.D,, 1989) p. 632.

devoted to the worms, dust, and rottenness to the dishonour of God the
damage of the Ministry and the wrong of the Benefactors, the dead and
the living', he changed his mind: 'I have cancelled that clause of my will
with mine own hand and my will is that not one of those books be given to
the Library'. Might not the clergy who gathered at Carter's funeral have
felt themselves morally obliged to act on his wishes and re-open the
Library to 'public use'? It is also possible that the news of the establishment
of a library at Wisbech, just over the Norfolk border in Cambridgeshire,
sponsored by John Thurloe, Cromwell's secretary, may have helped to
galvanise the Norwich clergy into action.[61]

The refoundation occurred during the mayoralty of Samuel Puckle, a
Presbyterian-Independent sympathiser.[62] We can follow what happened in
some detail through the fortunate survival of a unique set of minutes. On 9
February 1657 eight clergymen met in the Library room at St. Andrew's
Hall to subscribe to a set of new rules drawn up by the City Assembly for
admission as members of the library. Contrary to the intention of the original foundation the clergy who appear in the minutes in 1657 were not
'visiting preachers' but mainly beneficed Norwich clergy. It was an
ecumenical gathering. The local leader of the Presbyterians, John
Collinges, rector of St. Stephen's and chaplain to the Hobart family of
Chapelfield House and Blickling Hall, was chosen as the first librarian. Of
the five other members whose confessional identities can be established,
three – Benjamin Snowden, Francis English and Joseph Morrant – were
Presbyterians and two – Theophilus Ellison and Isaac Clement – were
pastors of the 'stranger' churches. Each member pledged to pay twelve
pence quarterly to an 'underkeeper', chosen by the librarian. The following
week the original members were joined by another five ministers – John
Harwood, Joseph Harward, Edward Warnes, John Whitefoot and
Christopher Hartley – two of whom can be identified as 'of the prelatical
party', John Whitefoot, rector of Heigham and vicar of St. Gregory's and
Christopher Hartley, rector of St. John's Timberhill and vicar of
Morningthorpe. This ecumenical mix prevailed until several years after the
Restoration. In fact it was not until the summer of 1665 that noncon-
formists like Dr. John Collinges disappeared from the record. Benjamin
Snowden was made librarian as late as 1669.

Interestingly, the compilers of the minutes refer to their fellow library
members as 'brethren', a word 'full of sweetness, breathing forth more
than ordinary affection and love'.[63] John Brinsley, the leader of the
Presbyterians at Yarmouth, considered that Christians should look on one

---

[61] R. Banger, 'Some thoughts on the Town Library', *Wisbech Society Magazine* (1983) pp. 3–5.

[62] Puckle remained mayor until 1 May 1657, when his successor, the 'moderate conservative', Christopher Jay, a distant relation by marriage to Sir Thomas Browne, was elected.

[63] John Brinsley, *Arraignment of the present schism of new separation in Old England* (1646), p. 5.

another not as strangers, 'as the guise of these dividing times is: but as brethren. And that not onely calling one another so, but really acknowledging one another such'. The Church of God should be 'a true Philadelphia'.[64] Edward Reynolds, the first bishop of Norwich after the Restoration, echoed Brinsley's sentiments: 'Where there is agreement in fundamentals, there ought to be mutual and fraternall affections, notwithstanding differences in other things: no reproaches, no exasperations, no invidious consequences, no odious imputations, no uncharitable diglada-tions, but as owning of one another as brethren, and a discussing and ventilating of the points in difference with a spirit of love and meekness, saying to one another, as Abraham to Lot, let there be no strife between thee and me, for we be brethren'.[65] This may have been an idealisation but it was a concept the compilers of the minutes attempted to reflect by deliberately not recording any disagreements there may have been amongst the members.

Another word used by the members of the Library to describe themselves was 'society'. Two Latin sources gave a resonance to 'society', Cicero's *De Officiis* and, ironically, the Roman Catholic Mass ('And to us sinners, thy servants...deign to grant some part and society with thy holy apostles and martyrs'). In the Catholic tradition the idea of society had an intimate relationship with the process of salvation. It took on the order of the sacred. In other words, it was a saving fraternity.[66] And like the Norwich Florists' Society, which had flourished in a previous generation, the Library could clearly be described as one of the voluntary associations which so much characterised early modern England.[67]

The complexion of the library

The most prominent feature of the collection was the Bible, 'the most worthy writing that ever saw the light', as John Ward, the Norwich divine, explained.[68] The Bible remained the focus of intellectual life throughout the seventeenth century. As Richard Hooker expressed it in his *Laws of Ecclesiastical Polity*, there was 'no part of true philosophy, no art of account, no kind of science rightly so called, but the Scripture must contain it'.[69] It is not surprising therefore that the collection includes sixteen printed Bibles and five New Testaments. The great treasure of the collection is a Wycliffite

[64] Brinsley, *Arraignment*, p. 7.

[65] Edward Reynolds, *The substance of two sermons, one touching composing of controversies, another touching unity of judgement and love amongst brethren* (1659) p. 32.

[66] J. Bossy, 'Some Elementary Forms of Durkheim', *Past and Present*, xcv (1982) p. 11.

[67] P. Clark, *British clubs and societies, 1580–1800: the origins of an associational world* (Oxford, 2000).

[68] John Ward, *A Modell of Divinitie Catechistically Composed* (1623) p. 274.

[69] Quoted in C. Hill, *The English Bible and the Seventeenth-Century Revolution* (1993) p. 29.

Bible manuscript of the early fifteenth century, extending from Genesis to Proverbs. Although a King James Bible of 1611 went missing at an early date the collection includes copies of the Geneva Bible of 1560, dedicated to Queen Elisabeth and of course suppressed by Archbishop Laud, the Vulgate, the Great Bible of 1553 and a 1549 reprint of Matthew's Bible of 1537, popularly known as the 'Bug Bible'.

In their acquisition of the great Polyglot Bibles the members of the library and the donors showed their overriding preoccupation with textual interpretation. Two of the four great polyglots are present in the collection. The earliest, the *Biblia Polyglotta Industria Arnaldi Guillelmi de Brocario in Academia Complutensi*, popularly known as the Complutensian, the Spanish or Ximenes Polyglot, produced under the patronage of Cardinal Ximenes, archbishop of Toledo, is absent but the next Polyglot to be produced, the *Biblia Sacra Hebraica, Chaldaica, Graece, & Latine*, styled by some contemporaries *orbis miraculum*, has been in the collection since 1609. Known as the Antwerp, Plantin or Royal Polyglot, the languages included are Hebrew, Aramaic, Greek, Latin and Syriac. The third Polyglot, known as the Paris, or Le Jay's or Vitré's Polyglot, had Samaritan and Arabic as well. It was intended to be an enlarged and improved edition of the Antwerp Polyglot but was a comparative failure since it lacked the useful apparatus of the Antwerp Bible and was soon superseded by the London Polyglot. Perhaps this is the reason it is not present in the collection. The fourth, the *Biblia Sacra Polyglotta*, popularly known as the London or Walton Polyglot, which included the Ethiopian and Persian languages for the first time, is the most accurate and the best equipped with notes. In 1652 the publishers of the Walton Polyglot invited interested purchasers to subscribe. The Norwich Assembly's decision was recorded in the Assembly Book: 'A bible in several languages to be bought by the city – in five volumes – for the library'.[70]

Close study of the Biblical text was one of the main preoccupations of the ministers. As John Collinges expressed it:

'when we have consulted the Originall, weighed the Coherence of a Text, compared our thoughts with the thoughts of many other Divines, and chiefly compared a Scripture with other Scriptures, yet are we trembling, and see cause to cry out unto the Lord with St Austin...Grant Lord that we may neither be deceived our selves in the understanding of thy will, nor deceived others by a false interpretation; It is one of the greatest pieces of High Treason against the Almighty to adulterate the Coine of his Word, and wrest his meaning...'.[71]

[70] NRO, NCR, Case 16d, Assembly Folio Book, 1642–1668, f. 142v.
[71] John Collinges, *Vindiciae ministerii evangelici* (1651) sig. C2.

Other evidence of the ministers' preoccupation with textual exegesis is the presence of dictionaries and grammars. The importance of the study of languages was stressed by the early reformers, particularly Luther:

'When our faith...is held up to ridicule, where does the fault lie? It lies in our ignorance of the languages; and there is no other way out than to learn the languages...Even St Augustine himself is obliged to confess...that a Christian teacher who is to expound the Scriptures must know Greek and Hebrew in addition to Latin. Otherwise it is impossible to avoid constant stumbling...'.[72]

Hebrew dictionaries, translations and commentaries are particularly well represented in the library. Sanctes Pagninus, an Italian scholar and one of the most learned Hebraists of his time, made his own translation of the Bible from the Hebrew and Greek in 1528. He also produced a dictionary, the *Thesaurus linguae sanctae seu lexicon hebraicum*, based on the work of the Jewish exegete, David Kimchi, a copy of which is in the collection.[73] Sebastian Munster, the conversionist professor of Hebrew at Basle, composed a number of works specifically for the Jewish community. One was a translation of the Gospel of St Matthew into Hebrew, the *Evangelium secundum Matthaeum in lingua hebraica*, published in Basle in 1537.[74] Immanuel Tremellius, an Italian Hebraist and godfather to one of arch-bishop Matthew Parker's sons, produced a Latin translation of the Old Testament with annotations and an introduction to each book along with rabbinic explanations of difficult passages. The library has a copy of the 1617 edition, donated by Richard Ireland in 1692. Johann Forster, one of Luther's advisers on Hebrew, produced a Hebrew dictionary in 1543. The library has a copy of the 1564 edition.[75] One of the greatest classical scholars of the first half of the seventeenth-century was Edward Leigh. His *Critica sacra; or observations on all the radices or primitive Hebrew words of the Old Testament* is also present, donated by Francis Page in 1625. Other examples of dictionaries include John Baret's *An Aluearie or Quadruple Dictionarie, containing Foure Sundrie Tongues* (1580); Johannes Buxtorf's *Lexicon Hebraicarum et Chaldaicarum* (1631) and the same writer's *Lexicon Chaldaicum Talmudicum et Rabbinicum* (1640); Ambrosio Calepino's *Dictionarium Octolinguae* (1584), containing Latin, Hebrew, Greek, French, Italian, German, Spanish and English; Georg Pasor's *Lexicon Graeco Latinum in Novum Domini Nostri Jesu Christi testamentum* (1632), the standard Greek lexicon for use with the Greek New Testament; Johann Scapula's *Lexicon Graecolatinum* (1604), the most

---

[72] Quoted in G. Lloyd Jones, *The Discovery of Hebrew in Tudor England* (Manchester, 1983) pp. 65–6.
[73] Donated by Henry Bird in 1614.
[74] Donated by John Kirkpatrick in 1728.
[75] Donated by William Adamson, rector of St John Maddermarket, in 1700.

popular Greek-Latin lexicon of its day; Thomas Cooper's *Thesaurus Linguae Romane et Britannicae* (1565); and Valentine Schindler's *Lexicon Pentaglotton* (1612). Grammars include Eilhard Lubin's *Clavis Graecae Linguae* (1647); Petrus Martinius' *Grammatica Hebraea* (1621), possibly the best known and most widely used grammar; and Johannes Buxtorf's *Epitome Gramaticae Hebraeae* (1646). The library does not have a copy of Johannes Reuchlin's Hebrew grammar, *De Rudimentis Hebraicis*, however, the first significant gentile grammar and the basis of all subsequent grammars. Besides these Greek, Latin and Hebrew grammars there is also a copy of Thomas Erpinius' *Grammatica Arabica* (1636).

The number of works in Latin and Greek reflects the primacy of the classical languages in the educational curriculum in early modern England. In his *Re Ratione Studii* Erasmus had argued that Greek and Latin should be studied together 'not only because these two languages contain almost all that deserves to be known, but also because each is so closely related to the other that both can be more quickly grasped together than either without the other'.[76] Given the fact that Latin was the international language of learning it is not surprising that several important Latin translations of Greek works are present. John Christopherson, the Catholic Master of Trinity College, Cambridge during the reign of Queen Mary, produced a 'clear and eloquent' translation of the *Ecclesiastical History* of Eusebius, a copy of which is in the collection. In 1637 Patrick Young, biblical scholar and librarian to both James I and Charles I, translated Nicetas' *Catena Graecorum Patrum in Beatum Job* and dedicated it to Archbishop Laud. Nicetas, bishop of Serra and Heraclea in the eleventh century, gathered together more than twenty commentaries on Job by the Greek Fathers Athanasius, Basil, St John Chrysostom, Clement of Alexandria, Evagrius, Eusebius and Nilus. Christopher Angelos, a Greek refugee, published a Latin translation along with the original Greek text of his own *Enchiridion de Institutis Graecorum* (1619), an account of the rites of the Greek Church. There is no copy of his *De Apostasia Ecclesiae* (1624), however, a work which identified Mohammed with Antichrist.

Despite the fact that the users and many of the donors would have been steeped in Latin and Greek, the library provides little evidence of any interest in classical scholarship *per se*.[77] For example, the great French scholar, Claude de Saumaise, Scaliger's successor at the University of Leiden, is represented by just one work, the *Epistolarium* (1655).[78] Saumaise was invited by the exiled Charles II to compose a vindication of his father. The *Defensio Regia pro Carolo I* was published in 1649, provoking the

[76] Quoted in M.L. Clarke, *Classical Education in Britain, 1500–1900* (Cambridge, 1959) p. 18.

[77] For the following paragraphs I have used J.E. Sandys, *A History of Classical Scholarship* (New York, 1968).

[78] Donated by John Graile, rector of Blickling, in 1721.

inevitable rejoinder from Milton, the *Pro Populo Anglicana Defensio* (1651), but neither work is present in the collection. Charles Du Cange, another French classical scholar, is best known for his *Glossary of Medieval Latin* (1678) and *Glossary of Medieval Greek* (1688). The library has the six-volume edition of the Latin glossary dated 1733–6.[79] Pierre Daniel Huet, bishop of Soissons and tutor to the son of Louis XIV, is represented by his *Demonstratio Evangelica* (1679). There is nothing by Huet's learned contemporary, the Benedictine monk, Jean Mabillon, who produced an edition of the works of St Bernard, a history of the Benedictine order and a work on dating and verifying documents, the *De re Diplomatica*. Of the works of the great Bernard de Montfaucon the library has an English translation of the *Antiquité Expliquée*,[80] a work on classical antiquities, but that is all. Dutch classical scholars are poorly represented too. Justus Lipsius, who produced editions of Tacitus and Seneca, is represented by his *Opera Omnia*, donated by Sir Thomas Browne in 1666. Dominicus Baudius, who taught history at Leiden, is represented by his *Epistolae* (1662).[81] Gerard Vossius, professor of Greek at Leiden and Amsterdam, published a comprehensive work on rhetoric, the *Commentarium Rhetoricum*. He also wrote a work on Latin grammar, the *Etymologicon Linguae Latinae* and the *Aristarchus, sive de Arte Grammatica*. The library has editions of all three works. Jan de Meurs, professor of History and Greek at Leiden and once described as 'the true and legitimate mystagogue to the sanctuaries of Greece', is represented by his *Glossary of Medieval Greek*.[82]

Of the English classical scholars one of the most respected was Thomas Dempster, a Roman Catholic who was knighted by Pope Urban VIII. There is a copy of his *Antiquitates Romanae* in the collection, which is a reprint with many additions of a work by Johann Rossfeld or Rosinus.[83] Thomas Gataker published a Greek text of the meditations of Marcus Aurelius along with a Latin version and commentary. A copy was donated by Thomas Hill, Fellow of Trinity College, Cambridge, in 1708. There is also a copy of Gataker's *Certaine Sermons* (1637). As for Isaac Barrow, scholar, mathematician and divine, who resigned his position as Lucasian Professor of Mathematics at Cambridge in favour of Isaac Newton, the library has his sermons and commentaries. Thomas Gale, professor of Greek at Cambridge, produced editions of Herodotus and Cicero, but the library only has his *Sermons* (1704). John Selden is represented solely by the *Mare Clausum* (1635), which argued that Britain had a right to exclude Dutch fishermen from its seas and was a direct response to Grotius' *Mare*

---

[79] The copy of the 1678 glossary listed in the 1706 catalogue is missing.
[80] Donated by John Kirkpatrick in 1728.
[81] Donated by Thomas Nelson, rector of Morston.
[82] Donated by Bernard Church in 1678.
[83] Donated by Prudence Blosse in 1634.

Liberum (1633). James Duport, professor of Greek at Cambridge, an episcopalian royalist who produced verse glosses on the books of Job, Proverbs, Ecclesiastes and the Song of Solomon, is represented by his *Homeri Gnomologia* (1660), a collection of aphorisms from the Illiad and the Odyssey whose purpose was to illustrate the supposed similarities between Homer and the Bible. Sir William Temple's *Essay upon the Ancient and Modern Learning*, which championed the writers of the classical world against the moderns, is present in the second edition of 1690.[84] William Wotton's *Reflections upon Ancient and Modern Learning* (1690), the first effective critique of Temple's arguments, is also present. The other main protagonist on the side of the moderns, Richard Bentley, is represented by works unconnected with the so-called 'battle of the books'. Bentley's *Dissertation upon the Epistles of Phalaris*, which appeared as an appendix in the 1697 edition of Wotton's *Reflections*, is not present. There are no works by Richard Porson, the greatest classical scholar and philologist of the later eighteenth-century, despite the fact that he was born in East Ruston in Norfolk, or by any of that group of scholars dubbed 'the constellation of the Pleiades' by Burney, namely, Bentley,[85] Taylor, Markland, Dawes, Toup and Tyrwhitt.

The sixteenth and seventeenth centuries were the great ages of translation and the library has three examples by that 'translator general in his Age', Philemon Holland, namely *The Philosophy of Plutarch* (1603), Livy's *Roman History* (1600) and Pliny's *History of the World* (1635).[86] Also present are John Dryden's translations of the satires of Juvenal and Flaccus (1693) and his translation of the satires of Perseus (1693) However, there are no copies of Shelton's translations of Cervantes, Urquhart's translation of Rabelais or Chapman's translations of Homer.

Along with the Bibles, dictionaries and grammars, the collection includes numbers of Biblical commentaries and concordances. As might be expected, the most prominent commentaries are those of Calvin. Others are by Calvinists of various hues; for example, Gervase Babington on Moses; Joseph Caryl's twelve volumes on Job; Andrew Willet on Genesis, Daniel and the Epistle of Paul to the Romans; Mercer on Job, Proverbs, Ecclesiastes and the Song of Songs; Genebrard, Moller and Ainsworth on the Psalms; and the works of Musculus, Rivet and William Pemble. On the Roman Catholic side there is a copy of Benedict Pererius' *Commentaria in Genesim*, a work which was used by Sir Thomas Browne as a source for his views on the doctrine of original sin. Perhaps the most bibliographically significant concordance is the first to be published in English, John Marbeck's *A concordance* (1550), dedicated to Edward VI. There is also the

---

[84] Donated by Thomas Nelson, rector of Morston.

[85] There are two collections of sermons by Bentley in the library.

[86] There are no copies of Holland's translations of Suetonius (1606), Ammianus Marcellinus (1609), Camden's *Britannia* (1610) or Xenophon's *Cyropaedia* (1632).

Glossa compendiaria of the Lutheran theologian, Matthias Flacius, the 1671 edition of Henry Hammond's *A paraphrase and annotations upon all the books of the New Testament* (1653) and the 1693 edition of Sir Norton Knatchbull's *Animadversiones in libros novi testamenti* (1659).There is also a copy of that landmark in textual criticism, *The treatise of the corruptions of scripture* (1612) by Thomas James, Bodley's first librarian and one of the many collaborators of 'that miracle of learning', James Ussher, archbishop of Armagh.

As at Ipswich Library, there are very few devotional books. [87] There is a copy of Sir Thomas More's *Dialogue of Comfort* (1553),[88] a devotional work written in the Tower, but as for Protestant examples, there are no copies of Lewis Bayly's *The Practice of Pietie* (1613), Thomas Cooper's *The Sacred Mysterie of the Government of the Thoughts* (1619), Francis Quarles' *Divine Fancies*, Richard Rogers' *The Practice of Christianite* (1618), Nicholas Themylthorp's *The Posie of Godlie Prayers* (1636) or William Vaughan's *The Golden Grove* (1608). The sole representatives are Daniel Featley's *Ancilla Pietatis, or the Handmaid to Private Devotion* (1639),[89] which went through eight editions between 1626 and 1656, and Thomas Fuller's *Holy State* (1642).[90] Since such works were written for solitary study or family use they were perhaps considered unsuitable for a public collection.

Since the godly thought of themselves as the restorers of the pure doctrine of the early church and not theological innovators it is no surprise that the Church Fathers and scholastics are present in considerable numbers. The library has works by Athanasius, Hilary of Poitiers, Cyril of Jerusalem, St Basil, Ambrose of Milan, Jerome, John Chrysostom, Augustine, Cyril of Alexandria, Gregory the Great, Bede and Bernard of Clairvaux. Scholastic texts include works by Aquinas, Peter Lombard, Albertus Magnus and Boethius. There is nothing by Duns Scotus, Anselm, Abelard or William of Occam, however. Denis the Carthusian (Dionysius Carthusianus) or 'doctor ecstaticus', the most prolific scholastic theologian of the fifteenth century, is represented in an edition edited in Cologne by Dierick Loer between 1521 and 1538. William Durandus' *Rationale divinorum officiorum*, a complete exposition of medieval Roman Catholic worship, is present in a folio edition of 1563. The comprehensiveness of the *Rationale* was unrivalled. It dealt with ministers and their offices, vestments, the mass, Sundays, feasts, saints, time and the calendar – in other words, a complete textbook of Roman Catholic worship.

The great champions of the continental Reformation figure very promi-

---

[87] Dod and Cleaver's *Plaine and familiar exposition of the ten commandments*, the most popular work on personal ethics to be published in the first half of the seventeenth century, is not present in either Ipswich or Norwich Libraries.
[88] Donated by John Kirkpatrick in 1728.
[89] Donated by Richard Ireland in 1692.
[90] Donated by Thomas Nelson, rector of Morston.

nently in the Library. As far as donations are concerned, Calvin came first. His complete works in ten volumes were presented to the library as early as October 1609 by Sir Thomas Hyrne. The works of Calvin's successor in Geneva, Theodore Beza, are also present, but not in such numbers. Of the three Heidelberg theologians, Zanchius and Ursinus appear but not Olevianus. There is no copy of the Heidelberg Catechism, however, or of Ursinus' popular commentary on it, *The Summe of Christian Religion*, which went into eight editions between 1587 and 1633. Gualter, Lavater, Peter Martyr Vermigli and Musculus all appear, but not Bullinger.[91]

Of the great English exponents of Calvinist theology, William Perkins is represented, along with his most famous pupil, William Ames, but not Richard Rogers, John Dod, George Webbe or William Bradshaw. Arthur Hildersham's *Lectures upon the Fourth of John*,[92] which went through four editions between 1629 and 1656, and his *CLII Lectures upon Psalme LI*,[93] are both present. Robert Cleaver is represented by the *Plaine and Familiar Exposition of all the Chapters of the Proverbs of Salomon*. Richard Sibbes ('Of this blest man, let this just praise be given, Heaven was in him, before he was in heaven'[94]), who was ordained in Norwich in 1608, is represented by a sermon, *The Souls Conflict with itself*, of which there were five editions between 1633 and 1658, and the posthumous *A Learned Commentary or Exposition upon the First Chapter of the Second Epistle of S. Paul to the Corinthians*.[95] There is nothing by John Cotton or Thomas Hooker. John Preston, Laurence Chadderton's successor as Master of Emmanuel College, Cambridge and chaplain to Prince Charles, is represented by one of his sermons preached at Lincoln's Inn in London, *The Saints Daily Exercise*.[96]

While England never produced an organised Lutheran movement, it is impossible to understand the English Reformation without reference to Luther. Lutherans present in the collection are Luther himself, Melanchton, Brentius, Chemnitius, Chytraeus, Hunnius and Gerhard. Matthias Flacius is represented by two works, the *Clavis Scripturae Sacrae* and the *Historiae Ecclesiae Christi*, one of the first works to be donated to the library, the so-called *Centuries of Magdeburg*, a history of the church down to 1400, which attempted to show how the pure Christianity of the early church succumbed to the influence of the 'Papal Antichrist'.[97] The

[91] R.T. Kendall suggests that Bullinger's influence was only marginal in England after William Perkins began to publish (R.T. Kendall, *Calvin and English Calvinism*, Oxford, 1979, p. 38).

[92] Donated by Thomas Nelson, rector of Morston.

[93] Donated by Thomas Tanner.

[94] Quoted in Kendall, *Calvin and English Calvinism*, p. 102.

[95] Donated by Thomas Nelson, rector of Morston.

[96] Donated by Thomas Tanner.

[97] The *Centuries* was donated by Sir John Pettus in 1608. The library also has a copy of the *Annales Ecclesiastici* of Caesare Baronius, a Cardinal of the Roman Catholic Church and librarian of the Vatican Library. The *Annales* was a direct response to the *Centuries of Magdeburg*.

Plate 1. Detail from an engraving by Daniel King of St Andrew's Hall showing the swordbearer's lodgings that housed the Library, from *The Cathedrall and Conventual Churches of England and Wales, orthographically delineated*, [1656].

Plate 2. Title page of the Donation Book, memorialising the foundation of the Library by Sir John Pettus and praising the generosity of subsequent benefactors and donors.

Man's but a shadow, and a Picture is
That shadow's shadow, yet don't judge amiss.
Though here you onely on the shadow look
What followes read. The Substance is i'th'book.

Plate 3. Dr John Collinges (1623/4–1691), chaplain to the Hobart family of Blickling Hall and Chapelfield House, vicar of St Stephen's and librarian in 1657.

Plate 4. The antiquary, John Kirkpatrick (1687–1728), one of the members of the Society of Icenians, the discoverer of the text of the Norwich Grocers' play and one of the Library's most generous donors.

Lutheran philosopher and mystic, Jacob Boehme, is well represented too.

The collection is particularly strong on theological controversy.[98] In Elizabeth's reign the first great dispute between the Reformers and the Catholic Church featured on the one side John Jewel and on the other Thomas Harding. It began in 1559 with Jewel delivering his famous 'challenge sermon' at St Paul's Cross, which invited Catholics to justify their beliefs. The gauntlet was taken up by Thomas Harding, formerly Regius Professor of Hebrew at Oxford and a lapsed Protestant. Two items from the subsequent pamphlet war, Jewel's *A Replie unto M. Hardinges Answeare* (1565) and Harding's *A Rejoindre to M. Jewels Replie against the Sacrifice of the Masse* (1567) are in the collection. In 1562 Jewel brought out his *Apologie*, first in Latin, then in English, but the library does not have a copy, neither does it have a copy of Harding's answer, his *Confutation* of 1565. However, it does have Jewel's *A Defense of the Apologie of the Church of England* in an edition of 1571. It also has the *Dialogi sex contra summi Pontificatus, Monasticae Vitae, Sanctorum, Sacrarum Imaginum Oppugnatores, et Pseudomartyres* (1566).[99] This was a work written by Nicholas Harpsfield (alias Alan Cope), an archdeacon of Canterbury who was later imprisoned in the Tower. Harpsfield not only attacked Jewel's *Apologie* but also Foxe's *Book of Martyrs*.

The Oath of Supremacy was the next major political event which led to attitudes being struck. Robert Horne, bishop of Winchester, attacked an unpublished manuscript by John Feckenham, the imprisoned abbot of Westminster. Feckenham had scruples about taking the Oath of Supremacy and had recorded those scruples on paper. The library has a copy of *An Answeare Made by Rob. Bishoppe of Wynchester, to a Booke Entitled, The Declaration of Suche Scruples and Staies of Conscience, Touchinge the Othe of Supremacy* (1566) but not Thomas Stapleton's rejoinder, *A Counterblast to M. Hornes Vayne Blaste against M. Fekenham, touching, the Othe of Supremacy* (1567).

There is nothing on the Queen's controversial decision to retain a cross in her private chapel or on the Vestiarian Controversy but the Admonition Controversy of the 1570s is represented, albeit by a single work. The dispute came about as a result of John Field and Thomas Wilcox's anonymous *Admonition* of 1572 in which they criticised the bishops for their 'popish tyranny'. Although the collection does not include this work there is a copy of John Whitgift's *The Defense of the Aunswere to the Admonition against the Replie of Thomas Cartwright* (1574).[100]

A similar broken pattern is evident in the titles produced as a result of the appearance of the new Catholic translation of the New Testament at

[98] On theological controversies in the Elizabethan and Jacobean periods I have relied on P. Milward's *Religious Controversies of the Elizabethan Age* (1977) and the same author's *Religious Controversies of the Jacobean Age* (1978).

[99] Donated by Thomas Nelson, rector of Morston.

[100] Donated by Richard Ireland in 1692.

Rheims in 1582. Although there is no copy of the translation there is a copy of William Fulke's attack on it, *The Text of the New Testament of Jesus Christ, translated out of the Vulgar Latine by the Papists of the Traiterous Seminarie at Rhemes*, in an edition of 1633. There is also a copy of the Warden of Winchester, Thomas Bilson's *The True Difference betweene Christian Subjection and Unchristian Rebellion...with a Demonstration that the things reformed in the Church of England by the Lawes of this Realme are truly Catholike, Notwithstanding the Vaine Shew made to the Contrarie in their late Rhemish Testament* (1585). In fact, the major part of this work was a reply to William Allen's *Defence of English Catholiques* in which Allen argued that the priests who had been executed in England were martyrs for the Catholic faith.

Given the fact that several of the ministers who refounded the library in 1657 were Presbyterian it is not surprising that there is evidence of an interest in the role of bishops. There is, for example, a copy of Thomas Bilson's *The Perpetual Governement of Christes Church* (1593),[101] which argued for the traditional Catholic doctrine of the apostolic succession and the divine institution of episcopacy, an argument first hinted at by Bancroft. There is also a copy of Herbert Thorndike's *Primitive Government of the Church* (1650), which defended episcopacy, and of George Downame's *A Defence of the sermon Preached at the Consecration of the Bishop of Bath and Wells, against a Confutation thereof by a Nameless Author* (1611).[102] The *Defence* is divided into four books. The first argued that there was no Scriptural warrant for lay elders; the second that there were no parishes in the primitive church but rather dioceses; the third that the bishops had always been superior to other ministers; and the fourth that the Episcopal function was both apostolic and divinely instituted. There are no examples of the works of those who disputed with Downame, however; none by Paul Baynes or by the anonymous puritan 'answerer'. There is a copy of Beza's *Ad Tractionem de Ministrorum Evangelii Gradibus, ab Hadriano Saravia Belga Editam* (1592),[103] which is an attack on Hadrian Saravia's defence of the apostolic origin of bishops. Not only is there no early edition of the epistles of Ignatius, bishop of Antioch, which attempted to prove the existence of bishops in the early church but there is no copy of Vedelius's 1623 edition of Ignatius which rejected half of the epistles as forgeries. There is nothing on the Marprelate controversy. James Ussher joined in the controversy over the apostolic succession of Anglican bishops with his *De Christiarum Ecclesiarum*. The library has the 1658 edition. The only Catholic work present is Anthony Champney's *De Vocatione Ministrorum Tractatus* (1618).[104] It was against this work and others that Francis Mason produced his *Vindiciae Ecclesiae Anglicanae* (1625).[105]

[101] Donated by Richard Ireland in 1692.   [102] Donated by Richard Ireland in 1692.
[103] Donated by Richard Ireland in 1692.   [104] Donated by Richard Ireland in 1692.
[105] Donated by Brampton Gurdon in 1708.

In the general area of Protestant-Catholic controversy the representation is again eclectic. The controversy between Thomas Bell, once a Catholic priest, and Philip Woodward of the Douai Seminary enlivened the early years of James' reign. However, the collection only contains Bell's *The Pope's Funerall* (1606), the second edition with the altered title-page. There is a copy of the most popular anti-papist book of the time, Andrew Willet's *Synopsis Papismi* (1614), the main target of which was the *Controversies* of Robert Bellarmine, but no copy of Willet's *Tetrastylon Papisticum* (1593) or his *A Catholicon, that is, a Generall Preservative or Remedie against the Pseudocatholike Religion* (1602). There is nothing by Josias Nichols or Oliver Ormerod but there are two works by Matthew Sutcliffe, *The Subversion of Robert Parsons* (1606) and *The Examination and Confutation of a Certain Scurrilous Treatise Entitled, the Newe Religion, Published by Matthew Kellison* (1606). Kellison was a professor at the English college at Douai. Richard Field, dean of Gloucester, refuted Bellarmine and Stapleton in his *Of the Church*. The Library has the 1635 edition of this work, donated by Richard Ireland in 1692. The Huguenot scholar, Isaac Casaubon, who had settled in England in 1610, in his criticism of the *Annales* of Baronius, *De Rebus Sacris et Ecclesiasticis Exercitationes*, included a 'digression' against the Jesuit, Andreas Eudaemon-Joannes. There is a copy of the *De Rebus* in the collection, donated by Nathaniel Cock in 1695. The Library also has a copy of Launcelot Andrewes' *Tortura Torti*, a response to Bellarmine's attack on the Oath of Allegiance, which all English Catholics were legally obliged to swear. In the 1620s James Ussher was drawn into a dispute with the Irish Jesuit, William Malone, and published *An Answer to a Challenge made by a Jesuit in Ireland*. The library has the second edition of 1625 but, typically, it does not have anything by Malone. On the Catholic side there is a copy of the Jesuit theologian, Martin van der Beeck's *Opera Omnia* of 1630–1. Beeck carried on a pamphlet war with a number of English divines. The Spanish Jesuit, Francis Suarez's *Defensio Fidei Catholicae* is also in the collection, though there are no copies of the responses of any of his English opponents. Robert Bellarmine's *De Controversiis Christianae Fidei* (1608) is present, but there are none of the published responses by his most pertinacious opponent, Matthew Sutcliffe, dean of Exeter.[106] However, the Library does have the *Praelectiones Doctissimi Viri Guilielmi Whitakeri*, published after Whittaker's death by John Allenson.

John Brereley, a pseudonym used by a seminary priest, caused a sensation by publishing an attack on Protestants composed of testimonies by Protestants themselves, *The Apologie of the Roman Church* (1604).[107] Thomas

[106] Sutcliffe's controversy with the Jesuit, Robert Persons, rector of the English Church in Rome, is represented by his *The subversion of Robert Persons his confused and worthlesse worke, entitled, a treatise of three conversions of England from paganism to the Christian religion* (1606).

[107] Brereley's *The Lyturgie of the Masse* (1620) is also in the collection. It attempts to show that the Catholic Church's liturgy stemmed from the primitive church. It was donated by William Adamson, rector of St John Maddermarket, in 1700.

Morton responded to Briereley's first work with his *Apologia Catholica* (1606), a copy of which is in the collection. There is also a copy of Morton's response to Brereley's second work, *A Catholike Appeale for Protestants*, in the 1610 edition.[108] Another seminary priest, Edward Mayhew, published *A Treatise of the Groundes of the Old and Newe Religion* (1608) in which he attacked, among other works, Richard Crashaw's *Romish Forgeries and Falsifications* (1606). Neither of these works is present. However, the collection does include Thomas James' defence of Crashaw, *A Treatise of the Corruptions of Scripture* (1611).[109]

During James's reign the controversies over the ceremonies of kneeling at communion, the use of the sign of the cross in baptism and the wearing of the surplice continued. Strangely, however, the library contains none of the works by Thomas Morton, bishop of Chester, on the one side or by the Presbyterian, David Calderwood, on the other. Althought there is a copy of John Dove's *The Conversion of Salomon* (1613),[110] his *A Defence of Church Government* (1605), which argued against William Bradshaw's criticism of the making of the sign of the cross in baptism, is absent.

Early in the new reign there was a controversy over the use of the Book of Common Prayer. In 1604 subscription was required of all ministers on pain of ejection. Samuel Hieron, minister of Modbury in Devon, was one of the defenders of those who refused to subscribe. A folio copy of his collected works is in the collection.

Coincidentally, in the same year as the government fiat on subscription, Thomas Bilson published *The Survey of Christ's Sufferings* (1604),[111] a work that argued in favour of the Calvinist view that Christ had suffered the pains of Hell on the cross. Along with this work, donated by Richard Ireland in 1692, the library also has copies of Andrew Willet's *Synopsis Papismi* (1614)[112] and Hugh Sanford's *De Descens Domini nostri Jesu Christi ad Inferos* (1611). Although there is no copy of Richard Parkes on the episcopal side there is a copy of Bellarmine's *Controversies*.

As far as the Arminian controversy is concerned, there is a copy of the complete works of Jacob Arminius, printed at Frankfurt in 1635.[113] Francis Gomar, Arminius' chief opponent, is represented by the three-volume Amsterdam edition of his works, published in 1644.[114] There is a copy of the works of the systematiser of Arminianism, Simon Bischop who, with twelve other Remonstrants, was condemned at the Synod of Dort. The Synod of Dort, or Dordrecht, saw judgement being passed on the Arminians and the vindication of Calvinist orthodoxy. The conclusions of

[108] Both Morton's works were donated by Thomas Nelson, rector of Morston.
[109] Donated by Nathaniel Cock in 1675.   [110] Donated by Richard Ireland in 1692.
[111] Donated by Richard Ireland in 1692.   [112] Donated by Robert Gallard in c1625.
[113] Donated by Thomasin Brooke in 1659.
[114] Donated by Alderman John Mann in 1664.

the Synod were published and the library has a copy of the Latin version, *Dordrechtanae Synopsis Acta* (1620).[115] Because Arminians believed in universal redemption and free will they were accused of pelagianism. This is the reason that the Arminian, Gerhard Jan Voss, published his *Historia Pelagiana* just before the Synod of Dort, a copy of which is in the library, donated by Richard Ireland. There is also a copy of James Ussher's *Historia Gotteschalci* (1631), a celebration of the ninth-century Benedictine monk and anti-Pelagian predestinarian, Gottschalk or Gotteschalcus. There is nothing on the controversy surrounding the publication of Richard Mountague's *A Gagg for the New Gospell?* or his *Appello Caesarem*, however, despite the fact that Mountague became bishop of Norwich.

Although John Collinges, the first librarian after the refoundation in 1657, was a convinced Sabbatarian there is nothing in the library by the major writers on the subject, Humphrey Roberts, John Northbrooke, Philip Stubbes, John Field, Richard Greenham or Nicholas Bownd. The only relevant work is an orthodox statement by Francis White, *A Treatise of the Sabbath Day* (1635). [116]

There is surprisingly little evidence of any interest in the radical movements on the English religious scene. For example, there is nothing on the familists.[117] There are no works by Henry Niclaes,[118] the founder, and nothing by any of the opponents of familism such as Stephen Denison. There is evidence of an interest in the works of the Independents, however, particularly the Norfolk born Arminian Independent, John Goodwin, whose anti-Calvinist views ('I found [predestination] ever and anon gravellish in my mouth, and corroding and fretting in my bowels') were forcibly expressed in his *Imputatio Fidei; or a Treatise of Justification* (1642), his *Redemption Redeemed* (1651) and his *Paraphrase of the Ninth Chapter of the Epistle to the Romans* (1652). Noticeably absent are any of Goodwin's politically sensitive works such as *The Obstructors of Justice; or a Defence of the Honourable Sentence passed upon the late King* (1649), *The Butcher's Blessing; or The Bloody Intentions of Romish Cavaliers against the City of London* (1642) and *Anti-Cavalierism; or Truth pleading as well as Necessity as the Lawfulness of the Present War* (1642). On the other hand there is a copy of his *The Christian's Engagement for the Gospell* (1641), which is dedicated to John Pym. Besides Goodwin there are works by other Independents such as Henry Ainsworth's *Annotations upon the Five Books of Moses* (1627), Jeremiah

---

[115] Donated by Richard Ireland in 1692.

[116] Donated by Edmund Prideaux in 1730.

[117] John Kirkpatrick donated a copy of John Rodgers' *The displaying of an horrible secte of grosse and wicked heretiques…the Family of Love* (1579), which went missing or was deliberately disposed of at an early date.

[118] An unidentified work by Nicklaes is listed in Brett's catalogue of 1706 but had disappeared by 1732.

Burroughs' *Two Sermons Preached at Michael's, Cornhill* (1643), his *Irenicum to the Lovers of Truth and Peace* (1646) and William Bridge's *Works* (1649). As far as the Baptists are concerned, there is nothing by John Tombes or Henry Jessey, the two outstanding Baptist intellectuals. The Quakers are represented by William Penn's *Address to Protestants* (1676), but there is nothing by George Fox or Isaac Pennington.

There is little evidence of any interest in anti-Jewish polemics. There is a copy of the Spanish Dominican, Raymond Martini's *Pugio Fidei* (1651) but there is nothing by those ornaments of anti-semitism, Alfonso de Spina, Salvatus Portchetus or Antonius Margaritha. As far as other more miscellaneous controversies are concerned, the library contains the works of Smectymnius, *Smectymnius Redivivus* and *A Vindication of the Answer to the Humble Remonstrance*, both bound with one of Joseph Hall's replies, *A Short Answer to the Tedious Vindication of Smectymnius*. There is also a copy of John Milton's *Apology for Smectymnius*, bound with his *Reason of Church Government*.

The main apologist of the Church of England during the Commonwealth was Henry Hammond. Representative works by Hammond include *Of Schisme: a Defence of the Church of England against the Objections of the Romanist*, where the pope's claims to universal pastorship are dismissed as unhistorical and non-Biblical, and *Dissertationes Quatuor*, which was composed '*cum duo inter Reformatos magna nomina, Claudius Salmasius & David Blondellus, Episcoporum ordinem tam strenue & prolixe invaserint*'[119] and is a defence of the government of the church by bishops. Hammond corresponded with Joseph Hall on theological matters during the latter's enforced retirement at Heigham. He also clashed with John Collinges on the observation of Christmas Day. Collinges attacked Hammond's views in an appendix to his *Responsaria ad Erratica Piscatoris*. According to Collinges, the observance of Christmas Day in England before Augustine was assumed, not proven. The library does not have a copy of the *Responsaria* but there is a copy of Hammond's *Letter of Resolution to Six Quaeres in Present Use in the Church of England*, which contained a defence of the orthodox view.[120]

John Goodwin disputed with Vavasour Powell on the universality of redemption. His *Apolutrosis Apolutroseos* contained a vigorous statement of his views: 'When we teach, that Christ dyed for all Men, we mean, not onely that He put all Men without exception, into a capability of being saved...but also that He wholly dissolved, and took off from all Men by Adams Transgression'. There is nothing by Vavasour Powell in the library's collections, however. Goodwin's response to Thomas Edwards' 'ulcerous treatise' *Gangreana* is present but *Gangreana* itself is not. Also present is *De Usu Patrum*, the Latin translation of Jean Daillé's *Traicte de l'Employ des Saintes Peres*, which demonstrated that the Fathers contradicted

---

[119] Henry Hammond, *Dissertationes Quatuor* (London, 1651) sig. A3.
[120] Donated by John Jermy in 1731.

one another. Daillé's work was attacked later by John Pearson, bishop of Chester, William Beveridge, bishop of St Asaph and William Cave, the patristic scholar. All three figure in the Library's collections.

It has been pointed out that the Library at Ipswich does not include a single book by an archbishop, even though much of the work produced was uncontroversial.[121] By contrast Norwich Library has works by Thomas Cranmer, Edmund Grindal, George Abbot, William Laud, Edwin Sandys, John Spottiswoode, James Ussher and John Whitgift. Ussher is represented by no less than seven works but he was a special case in that he was widely respected as a scholar during the Commonwealth, so much so that he was given a state funeral by Cromwell. Laud is represented not only by Heylyn's hagiography, *Cyprianus Anglicus*,[122] in an edition of 1671, but by his own *Remains*.[123]

The Library contains a remarkable amount on Socinianism, a doctrine which questioned the divinity of Christ, rejected the immortality of the soul and defended the authority of the Scriptures on rational and historical grounds rather than on the testimony of the Holy Spirit. There are works by Socinus, Schlichting, Völkel, Crell, Wolzogen and Stegmann in the Library. There is also a copy of the *Bibilotheca Fratrum Polonorum*, the cele- brated statement of Socinianism in its mature form. Strangely enough, however, there is nothing by the most important English disciples of Socinus, Thomas Lushington, John Biddle and Paul Best. A copy of the *Racovian Catechism*, the first statement of Socinian principles, an English translation of which by John Biddle, published in Amsterdam in 1652, was ordered to be burned by Cromwell, was donated by Thomas Tanner in 1675. There are also works by anti-Socinians like John Hoornbeck and Samuel Maresius, both Dutch Calvinists. Ironically, the only work by Bishop Wren in the collection is his attack on the *Racovian Catechism*, the *Increpatio bar Jesu*, composed during his imprisonment in the Tower. The Library also contains George Ashwell's *De Socino et Socinianismo Dissertatio* (1680). Ashwell was a one time Fellow of Wadham and friend of Heylyn.

Anyone that was liberal in theology was likely to be accused of Socinianism. Such a man was Lucius Carey, Viscount Falkland, godson of Archbishop Laud. At Falkland's house at Great Tew near Oxford gathered the extraordinary band of like-minded individuals, described so graphically by Clarendon in his *Life*. Falkland's *Of the Infallibilitie of the Church of Rome*[124] is in the library along with Thomas White's reply. William Chillingworth was another member of the Great Tew circle and his *Religion of Protestants* is in the collection too. So is the French Huguenot and Platonist, Philippe du

[121] J. Blatchly, *The Town Library of Ipswich* (Woodbridge, 1989) p. 76n.
[122] Donated by William Adamson in 1700.
[123] Donated by Thomas Nelson, rector of Morston.
[124] Donated by William Adamson.

Plessis Mornay's *Trewness of Christ's Religion* (1587), translated by Sir Philip Sydney and Arthur Golding. Mornay's work was explicitly commended by Falkland, Chillingworth and Hammond. Other members of the Great Tew circle whose works are represented are George Sandys, Thomas Hobbes, Abraham Cowley, Robert Boyle and Henry Hammond.

Another prominent feature of the collection is the number of historical works. The notion of history being in Cicero's phrase a guide to life (*magistra vitae*) was the leitmotiv behind *The Method and Order of Reading Histories*, the work that made the academic reputation of Degory Wheare, the first Camden Professor of History at Oxford. There is a copy of the Latin edition published in 1662 in the Library. The *Method* is a guide to historical writing, the only widely-known English example of the Renaissance *ars historica*, with advice on the best exponents through the centuries. Although there is nothing by Herodotus, Thucydides, Caesar or Sallust in the Library, the works of other ancient historians including Polybius, Xenophon, Livy, Josephus, Tacitus, Plutarch, Suetonius, Eusebius and Amminianus are present. The great English chronicler historians – Camden, Holinshed, Stow, Ralegh and Edward Hall – are represented too, along with Polidore Virgil, whose *Anglica Historia*, the beginning of modern English historiography, is present in two copies. There is also a copy of George Buck's *History of King Richard the Third* (1646), one of the most original pieces of historical writing to be produced in the seventeenth century and the first full-scale reappraisal of a king's reign. There is a copy of William Martyn's *The Historie and Lives of the Kings of England* (1615). A lawyer by profession, Martyn began his history with the fall of the Saxon monarchy and the Norman Conquest. He is vitriolic on Edward II, describing him as cultivating 'an adulterous consortship of wanton curtizans, and shameless whores', and on the Stuart kings of Scotland, whom he accuses of being blatant liars. Richard Verstigan's *A Restitution of Decayed Intelligence* is present in two different editions, 1628 and 1634. Verstigan was a Catholic and the work begins with a commendatory verse from a fellow Catholic, Richard White of Basingstoke, who was well-known for his protests at Elizabeth's treatment of Jesuit priests. There are also copies of the works of lesser writers like Richard Grafton and Sir Richard Baker. The royalist apologist Robert Brady's *An Introduction to the Old English History* (1684) and his *A Compleat History of England* (1685) are both present. Brady is balanced by James Tyrrell's *Bibliotheca Politica* (1694), which argued for the antiquity both of the common law and Parliament and of the rights of the subject. There is also a copy of Tyrrell's *General History of England* (1697–1704). There is a particular focus on the reign of Elizabeth, still regarded as the heroine of the English Reformation, exemplified by the presence of Heywood Townshend's *Historical Collections; or an Exact Account of the Proceedings of the Last Four Parliaments of Queen Elizabeth of*

Famous Memory (1680) and Thomas Browne's *Historie of the Life and Reign of that Famous Princess Elizabeth* (1619).

Not surprisingly, there are a number of histories of the Reformation. As well as John Strype's *Annals of the Reformation* (1709) there is John Sleidan's *Commentarii de Statu Religionis et Rei Publicae Carolo V. Caesare* (1559), a folio volume of twenty-five books first published in 1555 covering the period from 1517, a 'model of balance and good manners', in the words of a modern commentator.[125] There is also a copy of the much more partisan *Ecclesia Restaurata, or the History of the Reformation of the Church of England* (1661) by Peter Heylyn. A later French viewpoint is provided by Louis Ellies Dupin's *A New Ecclesiastical History of the Sixteenth Century* (1703–6). Strangely, the collection does not include Thomas Fuller's *The Church History of Britain* (1650), one of Pepys' favourite books which he loved to dip into on Sundays. Other religious histories focus on conflict; for example, Fuller's history of the crusades, *The Historie of the Holy Warre*, in the second edition of 1640, Enrico Davila's *History of the Civil Wars of France* (1647) and Christopher Potter's *The History of the Quarrels of Pope Paul with the State of Venice* (1626).

Despite the presence of these wide-ranging religious histories, the collection can be described as parochial in the sense that there are no general works on other European countries with the exception of Edward Grimeston's *A General Historie of the Netherlands* (1627), Juan Mariana's *General History of Spain* (1609) and James Howell's *Survey of the Signorie of Venice* (1651). Unlike, for example, Griffin Higgs' library, which was donated to Merton College, Oxford, the collection does not include Guicciardini on Italy, Cassan on France or Heinsius, Meteren or Junius on the Low Countries. There is a copy of a work recommended by Sir Thomas Browne, Paul Rycaut's *History of the Turks* (1700), but not its predecessor, Richard Knolles' *General History of the Turks* (1603). Contemporary history is lacking too. There is very little on the events leading up to the civil war. Interestingly, there is a copy of George Bate's *Elenchus Motuum Nuperorum in Anglia* (1663), which is a defence of Charles I's conduct during the war. But there are no copies of Thomas May's *History of the Parliament* (1647) or of Arthur Wilson's *History of Great Britain* (1651) and nothing by Arthur Weldon or Godfrey Goodman. There are very few of the histories of the Puritan Revolution published during the Restoration period. There is nothing by Heath, Dugdale or Nelson. On the other hand there are copies of William Sanderson's *A Compleat History of the Life and Reign of King Charles I, from his Cradle to his Grave* (1658); Bulstrode Whitelocke's *Memorial of the English Affairs; or, an Historical Account of what passed from the Beginning of the*

---

[125] A.G. Dickens, 'Johannes Sleidan and reformation history' in, *Reformation Conformity and Dissent, Essays in honour of Geoffrey Nuttall*, ed. By R.B. Knox (London, 1977) p. 30.

Reign of King Charles the First to King Charles the Second, his Happy Restauration (1682); the *Cabala, or Mysteries of State in Letters of the Great Ministers of King James and Charles wherein much of the Publique Manage of Affaires is Related* (1654); Henry Guthry's *Wherein the Conspiracies and Rebellion against Charles I are Narrated* (1702); and that outstanding work of the Commonwealth, John Rushworth's *Historical Collections* (1659). A copy of Edmund Ludlow's *Memoirs*, published in Switzerland in 1698, is recorded in Joseph Brett's catalogue of 1706 but had disappeared by the time Benjamin Mackerell's catalogue was published in 1732. There are no copies of the memoirs of Sir John Berkeley, Denzil Holles or Thomas Lord Fairfax. There is a part set of Clarendon's *History of the Rebellion and Civil Wars* (1706), but there are no copies of the memoirs of Sir Philip Warwick or Sir Thomas Herbert, Clarendon's fellow Tories.

It was during the 1570s that local history first began to be written and the library has the first published example of the genre in English, William Lambarde's *A Perambulation of Kent*, in the edition of 1596. There are also copies of Sir William Dugdale's *Antiquities of Warwickshire* (1730), a second edition of Robert Plot's *Natural History of Oxfordshire* (1705), Sir Henry Chauncy's *Historical Antiquities of Hertfordshire* (1700), Samuel Isaac's *Remarkable Antiquities of the City of Exeter* (1724), Charles Leigh's *The Natural History of Lancashire, Cheshire and the Peak in Derbyshire* (1700), James Torr's *Antiquities of York City* (1719) and Samuel Dale's *History and Antiquities of Harwich and Dovercourt* (1730). Most interestingly of all, there is a copy of Alexander Neville's *De Furoribus Norfolciensium Ketto Duce* (1575),[126] a history of Kett's rebellion, an event which must have been very familiar to all the members of the library since it was commemorated every year in a sermon funded by the City Assembly. It is also worth recording that there are copies of both the first published history of a parish, White Kennett's *Parochial Antiquities Attempted in the History of Ambrosden, Burcester and other Adjacent Parts in the Counties of Oxford and Bucks* (1694), and of the first town history, William Somner's *The Antiquities of Canterbury*, in an edition of 1703.

Maps are another feature of the collection. Writing in the 1580s Thomas Blundeville, a Norfolk author and gentleman, claimed that 'I daylie see many that delight to looke on Mappes, and can point to England, France, Germanie, and to the East and West Indies, and to divers other places therin described'.[127] Blundeville thought that without a knowledge of geography 'the necessarie reading of Histories is half lame, and is neither so pleasant, nor so profitable as otherwise it would be'.[128] Most of the cartographers of Tudor and Stuart England had begun their careers as compilers

---

[126] Donated by John Kirkpatrick in 1728.
[127] V. Morgan, 'The Cartographic Image of the County in Early Modern England', *Transactions of the Royal Historical Society*, fifth series, xxix (1979) p. 147.
[128] Morgan, 'The Cartographic Image', p. 148.

of estate maps. Since many of the ministers had investments in land they would no doubt have developed an interest in maps for practical reasons. They would also have needed road maps if they had to deliver sermons in distant parishes. But the overriding reason was the inherent fascination that maps have always possessed. Although there are no copies of Christopher Saxton's map of Norfolk[129] and nothing by Norden or Mercator the collection does include John Speed's *The Theatre of the Empire of Great Britain* (1611), Braun and Hogenburg's *Civitates Orbis Terrarum* (1581–1617), Ortelius' *Theatrum Orbis Terrarum* (1570),[130] Lewis Roberts' *The Merchant's Map of Commerce, Necessarie for all such as shall be imployed in Publique Affaires of Princes in Foraine Parts* (1638)[131] and Richard Peers' *English Atlas* (1682).

Other subject areas are less well covered, though the number of titles is still significant. On law and jurisprudence the library has nothing like the collection owned by Bishop Lancelot Andrewes. Of 398 books in Andrewes' library 51 were on politics and the law.[132] There are no copies of the works of the great French legal writers, Bodin and Hotman, and nothing by Marsilius of Padua or Gerson. On civil law, there is a copy of Godefroy's' *Corpus Juris Civilis* (1650). Carranza's *Summa Omnium Conciliorum et Pontificum* is present in an edition of 1633. On English law there are copies of *The Law of Corporations* (1702), the *Statutes at Large from Magna Carta to James* (1618), William Noy's *Reports and Cases taken in the time of Queen Elizabeth, King James and King Charles* (1656), John Herne's *The Law of Charitable Uses* (1661), Dawson's *Origo Legum* (1694), Edmund Plowden's *Les Commentaries ou Reportes de Divers Cases Esteant Matters en Ley* (1599), Sir Richard Hulton's *Law Reports* (1652), Sir George Croke's *Law Reports*, Sir John Popham's *Reports and Cases* (1656), Sir John Davies' *Le Prime Report des Cases & Matters en Ley* (1615), John March's *Reports of New Cases taken in the Fifteenth, Sixteenth, Seventeenth and Eighteenth Years of King Charles I* (1675), Edward Coke's *The First Part of the Institutes of the Lawes of England* (1629) and the eleven volumes of his *Les Reports de L'Attorney Generall* (1619–) and John Selden's book on international law, the *Mare Clausum* (1635). Interestingly, there are several guides written specifically for the use of the Justices of the Peace including Michael Dalton's *The Countrey Justice* (1661) and Bond's *Guide for Justices of the Peace* (1696). There are also copies of John Cowell's *The Law Interpreter* (1684) and a third edition of Thomas Blount's *A Law Dictionary* (1712).

In philosophy there are works by Augustine, Aristotle, Plato, Boethius, Epictetus and Aquinas. There are copies of Bacon's *Advancement of Learning*

---

[129] From 1607 derivatives of Saxton's maps were included in Camden's *Britannia*. There is a copy of the 1695 edition of the *Britannia* in the collection..

[130] Donated by Thomas Nelson.

[131] Donated by Thomas Tanner.

[132] D.D.C. Chambers, 'A catalogue of the library of Bishop Lancelot Andrewes (1555–1626)', *Cambridge Bibliographical Society*, v (1970) p. 103.

(1603), Descartes' *Principia Philosophiae* (1672) and a Latin translation of his *Discourse on Method* (1672). It is strange that the only work by Hobbes in the collection is his *De Cive* (1657), strange in that the Malmesbury Hydra was the most infamous philosopher of the seventeenth-century, a man whom everyone loved to attack. Charles Robotham, rector of Reepham, described him as a kind of force of nature: 'Who is this Colossus lying stretched out in the sea in all his enormity, his dreadful jaws gaping fiercely, and with obscene regurgitations belching forth abominable dogma which befouls the British coastlines. It is the Malmesbury Hydra, the enormous Leviathan, the gigantic dragon, the hideous monstrosity and British beast, the Propagator of execrable doctrines, the Promulgator of mad wisdom, the Herald and Pugilist of impious death, the Insipid Venerator of a Material God, the Renowned Fabricator of a monocondyte Symbol, the Depraved Renewer of old heresies to the faith, the Nonsensical roguish vendor of falsifications, a strenuous hoer of weeds and producer of deceits'.[133] In 1683 the *Leviathan* and *De Cive* were both proscribed by Oxford University as 'false, seditious and impious...Heretical and Blasphemous, infamous to Christian Religion, and destructive to all Government in Church and State'.[134] Despite this fascination with Hobbes the only critique in the collection is Bishop John Bramhall's *The Catching of the Leviathan, or the Great Whale*, which is present as part of Bramhall's *Complete Works* (1676),[135] though he also appears in John Whitefoot's funeral sermon on bishop Joseph Hall, where he is taken to task for allowing men to deny Christ 'if the infidel magistrate commands it'.[136]

Other more conventional examples of philosophy in the collection are Kenelm Digby's *Two Treatises* (1658), Montaigne's *Essays* (1632) and 'L'Herbe de Montaigne', Pierre Charron's *Of Wisdom* (1658), translated by Samuel Lennard, with its famous attack on the gullibility of the masses, quarried by Sir Thomas Browne for his *Pseudodoxia Epidemica:* 'the Vulgar multitude is the mother of ignorance, injustice, inconstancie, idolatrie, vanitie, which never yet could be pleased: their motto is, Vox populi, vox Dei, The voice of the people is the voice of God: but we may say, Vox populi, vox stultorum; The voice of the people is the voyce of fooles'.[137] There is a copy of a remarkable work by Joseph Glanvill, *Scepsis Scientifica* (1665), which could be interpreted as an attack on civil war enthusiasm. As Glanvill expressed it, ''tis zeal for opinions that hath filled our Hemisphear with smoke and darkness, and by a dear experience we know the fury of

---

[133] S.I. Mintz, *The Hunting of the Leviathan* (Cambridge, 1962) p. 56.

[134] Mintz, *The Hunting of the Leviathan*, pp. 61–2.

[135] Bramhall wrote *The Catching of the Leviathan* in order to demonstrate that 'no man who is thoroughly a Hobbist can be a good Christian' (Mintz, *The Hunting of the Leviathan*, p. 55).

[136] John Whitefoot, *Deaths alarum* (1656) p. 3.

[137] Sir T. Browne, *Pseudodoxia Epidemica*, ii, p. 656.

those flames it hath kindled'.[138] There are a number of works by the Jesuit thinker, Francisco Suarez. But there is nothing in the collection by Cumberland, Leibnitz, Malebranche, Pascal or Spinoza, even though all the major works of these writers were available by 1675. There is nothing by John Locke either, athough there is a copy of Henry Lee's *Anti-Scepticism; or Notes upon Each Chapter of Locke's Essay concerning Human Understanding* (1702).[139] There is little evidence of any interest in philosophical utopias. Although the complete works of Sir Thomas More are present there is no copy of Harrington's *Oceania*. The only work by that other famous utopian, Tommaso Campanella, is his *Discourse concerning the Spanish Monarchy* (1654).[140]

In science the collection is even more eclectic. Although the Newtonians Samuel Clarke, William Whiston and Richard Laughton were members of the Library in the 1690s they left no trace on the collection. The Library never owned a copy of Newton's *Principia*, Samuel Clarke's Latin translation of Newton's *Optics* nor any of the early works of popularisation such as John Keill's *Introductio ad veram physicam* (1701) or David Gregory's *Astronomiae physicae, et geometricae elementa* (1702). The books on astronomy are very unrepresentative compared with the specialist libraries assembled by George Hartgill,[141] the Dorset clergyman, or by Sir Thomas Browne and his son, Edward.[142] There are no copies of Kepler's *Harmonices Mundi* (1619), Copernicus' *De Revolutionibus Orbium Coelestium* (1566) or Tycho Brahe's *Astronomiae Instauratae Mechanica* (1602). However, there are copies of Galileo's *System of the World* (1661),[143] translated by Thomas Salusbury, Gassendi's *Insitutio Astronomica* (1653), which dealt with both Galileo and Kepler, Robert Hues' *De Globis* (1651),[144] Johannes de

---

[138] J. Glanvill, *Scepsis Scientifica* (London, 1665) p. 169. The *Scepsis* has a passage which summarises some of the new cosmology: 'every fixt star is a Sun, and that they are as distinct from each other, as we from some of them: That the Sun, which lights us, is in the Centre of our World, and our Earth a Planet that wheels about it: that this Globe is a Star, only crusted over with the grosser Element, and that its Centre is of the same nature with the Sun: That it may recover its light again, and shine amongst the other Luminaries: That our Sun may be swallow'd up of another, and become a Planet' (Glanvill, *Scepsis scientifica*, pp. 144–5).

[139] Donated by Edmund Prideaux in 1730.

[140] Donated by Thomas Cory in 1609. Perhaps it is not surprising that Campanella's *Civitas solis* (1623) is absent since it advocated government on the style of Plato's *Republic* with philosopher priests under the supreme authority of the pope.

[141] P. Morgan, 'George Hartgill and his Library', *Annals of Science*, xxiv (1968) pp. 295–311.

[142] J. Finch, *A Catalogue of the Libraries of Sir Thomas Browne and Dr Edward Browne, his son* (Leiden, 1986).

[143] Donated by Archibald Adams in 1706.

[144] Donated by Francis Page in 1625. Hues was a friend of Sir Thomas Browne, who described him as 'a very good & playne dealing man, & had read Euclid & Ptolomie very accurately, and also Aristotle, whereof wee should often discourse, and I cannot butt remember him with some content' (Keynes, *Works of Sir Thomas Browne*, iv, p. 84).

Sacro Bosco's *Opus Sphericum* (1508) and the Jesuit Christopher Clavius' *In Sphaerum Joannis de Sacro Busto Commentarius* (1607).[145] There is also a copy of a more popular work, the globe-maker Joseph Moxon's *A Tutor to Astronomie and Geographie: or an Easie and Speedy Way to know the use of both the Globes, Coelestial and Terrestial* (1659), which includes the famous acrostic by John Booker advertising the superiority of Moxon's globes: 'Must we not also Praise in this our Age/ Our Authors skill, and Pains, who doth ingage/ X Thousand Thanks, not for this Book alone/ Of his, But for the Globes he makes there's none/ Now extant made so perfect'. Interestingly, there's also a copy of Joannes Baptista van Helmont's *Ortus Medicinae* (1652), which contains an account of the transmutation of the alchemist's stone.

In mathematics there are copies of Euclid's *Elements* (1516, 1659 and 1665), Peter Ramus' *Arithmeticae* (1599),[146] Thomas Salusbury's *Mathematical Collections* (1655), Thomas Masterson's *Booke of Arithmetic* (1634), Sebastian Munster's *Rudimenta Mathematica* (1551), Tacquet's *Opera Mathematica* (1668) and Ciruelo's *Tractatus Arithmetice* (1505). There are no copies of Napier's *Logarithms* or Newton's *Principia Mathematica*, however. Neither is there anything by Archimedes, Viète, Snell or Fermat.

In medicine there is a manuscript herbal, translated from the French, bound with Braunschweig's *The Vertuose Boke of Distylacyon of the Waters of all Maner of Herbes* (1527), Hippocrates' *Magni Opera* (1657), Andrew Boorde's *Breviary of Health* (1557), Guarnerius' *Medicine Preclarissimi Practica* (1497), Christopher a Costa's *Aromatum et Medicamentorum* (1593), Thomas Venner's *Vita Recta et Vita Longam* (1628), Daniel Voet's *Physiologia* (1661),[147] Thomas Willis' *Cerebro Anatome* (1664), two copies of Thomas Bartholinus' *Anatomia* (1635 and 1660),[148] John Johnston's *Idea Universae Medicinae Practicae* (1648),[149] Walter Bruel's *Praxis Medicinae* (1632)[150] and John Woodall's *The Surgeon's Mate* (1665).[151] Two conspicuous absentees are Harvey's *De Motu Cordis* (1628) and Vesalius' *De Humani Corporis Fabrica* (1543).[152] However, there is a copy of Kenelm Digby's *Two Treatises* (1658)[153] which, as well as introducing Gassendian and Cartesian atomism to the British reading public, contains the first important defence in English of Harvey's theory of the circulation of the blood. The only botanical work is Theophrastus' *De Historia et Causis Plantarum*,[154] which was written as a counterpart to Aristotle's work on animals. The *Historia* is concerned with the description, classification and

---

[145] Donated by Richard Ireland.   [146] Donated by John Kirkpatrick.

[147] Donated by Thomas Nelson.

[148] Donated by Thomas Nelson and William Adamson.

[149] Donated by William Adamson.   [150] Donated by John Kirkpatrick.

[151] Donated by Thomas Nelson.

[152] A manuscript note of a copy of Vesalius appears in the 1706 catalogue. The copy was missing by the time Mackerell published his catalogue in 1732.

[153] Donated by Thomas Nelson.   [154] Donated by John Kirkpatrick.

analysis of plants, the *De Causis* with generation and propagation. The Library's copy was translated from the Greek by Theodorus Gaza.

If the collections on science are eclectic the literary works are even more so. There are copies of Cowley's *Works* (1668),[155] Drayton's *Poly-Olbion* (1613),[156] 'a prettie booke...in smooth verse', according to Sir Thomas Browne, Gower's *Confessio Amantis* (1554),[157] Burton's *Anatomy of Melancholy* (1632), Chaucer's *Works* (1721), Herbert's *The Temple* (1633), Walton's *Lives* (1750)[158] and Browne's *Pseudodoxia Epidemica* (1672). Jeremy Taylor is represented, but not by his most well-known works, *The Rule and Exercises of Holy Living* (1650) and *The Rule and Exercises of Holy Dying* (1651). It is easy to account for the presence of Joseph Beaumont's *Psyche, or Love's Mystery* (1702)[159] since the poem is a universal allegory of the pilgrimage of the soul through earthly trials to heavenly felicity, but it is not so easy to account for the absence of Spenser, Bunyan, Shakespeare, Carew, Crashaw, Davenant, Jonson, Fletcher, Quarles, Marvell, Lovelace, Suckling, Vaughan and Waller. Milton is represented, but only by his polemical pamphlets, *An Apology for Smectymnuus* and *The Reason of Church Government*. Similarly, Donne is represented by his sermons, not his poetry. Interestingly, there is a copy of the rabidly royalist Owen Feltham's *Resolves*[160] ('Of all objects of sorrow a distressed king is the most pitiful'), a collection of two hundred essays. To Feltham, Charles I was 'Christ the Second'. There is a total lack of foreign literature, no Dante, Boccaccio, Tasso or Ariosto, no Cervantes, not even anything by the popular Huguenot poet Du Bartas, whose work was widely available in translation.[161]

George Stephen was misleading when he claimed that history and travel were next in importance to theology.[162] Travel is a subject that has only a modest representation, not surprisingly since the feelings of contemporaries about travel were ambiguous, even fearful. The anxiety was that visitors to Catholic countries would be subjected to determined proselytisation. Joseph Hall warned against 'travel of curiosity' for this reason and urged the potential traveller to travel through the world of books by their own fireside instead: 'those...that crosse the seas to fill their braine doe but travel Northward for heat, and seeke that candle which they carry in their hand'.[163] Certainly, the creators of Norwich Library failed to follow Hall's advice if the lack of books on travel is any evidence. There are copies of

[155] Donated by Thomas Tanner.
[156] Donated by Anthony Mingay.
[157] Donated by John Kirkpatrick.
[158] Donated by Thomas Nelson.
[159] Donated by Thomas Nelson.
[160] Donated by Thomas Nelson.
[161] Du Bartas' *Divine weekes and workes* was read by Pepys in Sylvester's translation (Latham and Matthews, *The Diary of Samuel Pepys*, iii, p. 247).
[162] G. Stephen, *Three centuries of a City Library* (Norwich, 1917) p. 34.
[163] J. Hall, *Quo vadis? A just censure of travel as it is commonly undertaken by the gentlemen of our nation* (1617) p. 25.

Hackluyt's *The Principal Navigations, Voyages, Traffics and Discoveries of the English Nation* (1598–9), John Harris' *Navigantium et Itinerantium Bibliotheca* (1705)[164] and George Sandys' *Travels* (1650).[165] Although there is a copy of Samuel Purchas' *Purchas his Pilgrimage, or Relations of the World and the Religions Observed in all Ages and Places* (1627)[166] there is no copy of Purchas' massive collection of voyages, *Hakluytus Posthumus*. On geography there are copies of Strabo, translated as *Rerum Geographicarum* (1587),[167] Ptolemy's *Geographiae* (1551) and Sebastian Munster's *Cosmographie Universalis* (1559).[168] Clearly, there was no danger of Sir Thomas Browne's fine collection on travel being overshadowed by the city's official collection.

It is difficult to draw any meaningful conclusions from a collection which was largely the result of donations. But its unstructured character may not derive solely from the fact that it was donated. The notion of a structured reading programme was an unfamiliar one in the early modern period. Students worked from commonplace books rather than from the classical texts they studied. Montaigne's education at the college of Guyenne was about the presentation of knowledge, not the search for knowledge, and all knowledge was presented in the form of commonplaces in books of commonplaces.[169] Commonplace books contained collections of quotations drawn from authors who were considered to be authoritative arranged under alphabeticised headings. Since every student composed a commonplace book as soon as he could read and write it is not surprising that the Library has several printed examples. Peter Martyr Vermigli's *Loci Communes* is present in the 1603 edition.[170] First published in 1576, the work is based on Calvin's *Institutes* and applied the commonplace method to Calvinist theology. Johann Gerhard's *Locorum Communes Theologici* (1657) applied commonplace methods to Lutheran theology, as did Martin Chemnitius' *Loci Theologici Quibus et Loci Communes D. Phil. Melancthones perspicum explicantur* (1615).[171] Other examples of commonplace books in the collection are Wolfgang Musculus' *Loci Communes Theologicae Sacrae* (1597), Benedictus Aretius' *Theologica Problemata Hoc est Loci Communes Christiannae Religiones* (1604), [172] Augustinus Marloratus' *Propheticae et Apostolicae in Locos Communes* (1600)[173] and the *Loci Communis ex Scriptis distribute a Theodosio Fabricio* (1651). But perhaps the most impressive is Theodore Zwinger's *Theatrum Vitae Humanae* (1604).[174] The *Theatrum* went through five progressively enlarged editions between 1565 and 1604. By 1604 it contained over

---

[164] Donated by Thomas Nelson.   [165] Donated by Thomas Nelson.
[166] Donated by Thomas Catlyn in 1617.   [167] Donated by Richard Ireland.
[168] Donated by William Adamson.
[169] Z.S. Schiffman, *On the Threshold of Modernity: Relativism in the French Renaissance* (Baltimore, 1991) p. 15.
[170] Donated by Samuel Doyly in 1708.   [171] Donated by Edward Nutting in 1616.
[172] Donated by John Kirkpatrick.   [173] Donated by Edmund Prideaux.
[174] Donated by Augustine Pettus, Sir John Pettus' son, in 1610.

5,000 double-column folio pages of small type drawn from 601 authors. Zwinger undertook to treat universal history in terms of good and evil. He treated good and bad things of the soul, of the body, good and bad chance events, good and bad practical philosophical habits, the good and bad aspects of religious and secular justice and a myriad of other subjects.

In their exhaustiveness commonplace books resembled encyclopaedias. Among the most important classical and medieval encyclopaedias were Pliny's *Historia naturalis*, Martianus Capella's *De Nuptiis Philologiae et Mercurii*, Cassiodorus' *Institutiones*, Isidore of Seville's *Etymologiae* and Vincent of Beauvais' *Speculum maius*. Of these the Library only has Pliny's *Historia naturalis*, donated by Richard Ireland in 1692. But encyclopaedias more than resembled commonplace books; they served the same function. The seventeenth-century gentleman bibliophile, William Drake, read his Pliny for proverbs, axioms and adages '*sententiae promiscue collectae*'.[175] One can imagine the ministers reading Pliny for exempla to illustrate their sermons or for material to add to their commonplace books.

Book purchases

Although the books were donated a considerable number were acquired by purchase. The first reference to book purchases in the minutes occurs on 13 April 1657 when it was agreed to sell the anti-papal writer Andrew Willet's *Commentary on Genesis* 'of an ill edition' in order to buy a new edition of the same work and also to sell a duplicate copy of the works of Epithanius. This was unexceptionable. In 1658 Alderman Joseph Payne gave the generous sum of £20 to four of the ministers, Whitefoot, Harmer, Collinges and George Cock, 'to buy such bookes with it as they shall judge most fit for the City Library'. The whole committee when it next met authorised Collinges to negotiate with the London bookseller, Robert Littlebury.[176] Littlebury was to send Collinges a 'certain account' of the cost of the Lutheran theologian, Johann Gerhard's *Loci Communes Theologici* 'of the last edition', his commentaries plus his *Harmoniae Evangelistarum* 'of Rotterdam print'. In his subsequent report to the committee Collinges advised that the commentaries should not be bought for the moment because they would soon be printed in folio. Eventually, the committee agreed to purchase Gerhard's commonplaced exposition of Lutheran

---

[175] K. Sharpe, R*eading Revolutions: the Politics of Reading in Early Modern England* (New Haven, 2000) p. 193.

[176] Littlebury also supplied books to Richard Johnson, John Tildsley and Richard Hollinworth, the three ministers who were responsible for selecting the stock of Chetham's Library in Manchester (H.S.A. Smith, 'Readers and Books in a Seventeenth-Century Library', *Library Association Record*, 65, 1963, p. 367).

doctrine, the *Loci Communes Theologici* (1657);[177] Theophilact, a Byzantine exegete; St Basil; Oecumenius, the tenth-century bishop of Tricca; and two Jewish writers, the historian Josephus and the philosopher, Philo Judaeius.

Another bout of purchasing was recorded in the minutes of 9 April and 9 July 1660. On those dates John Whitefoot brought in some new books paid for out of a bequest left by Thomasina Brooke. Amongst the authors and titles that can be identified are Calvin's *Lexicon Iuridicium* (1653), Arminius' *Opera Theologica* (1635), the Jesuit Cornelius a Lapide's *Commentaria in IV Evangelia* (1638), Suda's *Sudas, cuius integrum Latinam interpretationem & Graeci textus emendationem Aemilius Portus* (1619), Erasmus Schmidius' *Concordance on the Greek New Testament* (1538), Gaspar Sanctius' *In Canticum Canticorum Commentarii* (1616) and the same author's *Commentarii in Actus Apostolorum*, the Lutheran David Paraeus' *Operum theologicorum* (1647), Martin de Azpilcuete's *Manuale Confessariorum*, Josephus' *Opera* (1634), André Rivet's *Operum theologicorum* (1651–60), Bonacina's *Opera* (1632), Vincent Filliucius' *Moralium Questionum de Christianis Officiis* (1629), the Jesuit Francisco de Toledo's *Instructio Sacerdotum* (1619) and, perhaps most interesting of all, John Cameron's *Works* (1658). Cameron was 'the learnedst Divine that the Church of Scotland hath affourded in this last age'.[178] He founded a school of contemporary theology whose main ornaments were Samuel Bochart and John Daille. There are works by both Cameron's acolytes in the Library. Daille is represented by the *Apologia pro Ecclesiis Religiosi* (1677), the *Adversus Latinorum* (1664) and the *De Usu Patrum* (1656), Bochart by the *Geographia Sacra* (1647) and the *Hierozoicon sive Bipertitum* (1675). It is tempting to conclude that the presence of these titles is evidence of a systematic collections policy. However, Bochart's works were not acquired until 1681, Daille's as late as 1700.

Other purchases followed those made in April and July 1660. On 11 November 1661 Collinges brought into the Library Pagninus' *Thesaurus Linguae Sanctae* (1575), 'bought for the use of the library at 17s.' On 13 October 1662 John Whitefoot wrote to George Thomason, the London bookseller, inviting him to 'send down' Tostado's *Commentaries* and Stephanus' *Thesaurus Linguae Graecae* 'with the glossary'.

It is revealing if the purchases listed above are compared with the collection put together by that arch-Arminian conservative, Samuel Harsnett, bishop of Norwich from 1619 to 1628.[179] Harsnett had examples of the

---

[177] Edward Leigh acknowledged his indebtedness to both Chemnitz and Gerhard: 'I confess myself most beholding every way to Chemnitius, a German Divine, whose Harmony Whitaker calleth Caput Veneris; and Gerhardus, the glory of the Lutherans; who, in his History, and Supplement of the Harmony, lately put forth, hath done excellently' (E. Leigh, *Critica sacra: or philologicall and theological observations upon all the Greek words of the New Testament*, sig. A4–A4v).

[178] Joseph Hall, *The Peacemaker* (London 1645), p. 49

[179] See G. Goodwin, *A Catalogue of the Harsnett Library at Colchester* (London, 1888).

works of Pagninus, Tostado, Stephanus, Calvin, Willet, St Basil, Philo Judaeius, Zanchius and Pareus. To express it in another way, Harsnett had forty-five per cent of the authors bought by Collinges and Whitefoot in his own collection at least a generation earlier. What the Norwich ministers were doing in the 1650s and 1660s was what all collectors attempt to do, namely, to renew the old world.[180] In this sense their activities were almost an exercise in nostalgia. Francis Bacon put this another way when he wrote that libraries were 'the shrines where all the relics of the ancient saints…are preserved and reposed'.[181]

Another significant purchase of books was signalled on 3 October 1676 when John Whitefoot reported to the committee on the receipt of twenty pounds, the bequest of the late bishop of Norwich, Edward Reynolds, for the 'augmentation' of the Library. The nineteen books purchased with this money were listed in the donation book under the year 1676. The two most recently published works were a 1676 edition of Sir Walter Raleigh's *History of the World*, his 'great Minerva', and Father Paul's *History of the Council of Trent* (1676). Another recently published work was Sir Richard Baker's *Chronicle of the Kings of England* (1674). Then came Peter Heylyn's *Cosmographie* (1669) in four books, two on Europe, one on Asia and one on Africa and the Americas. (Heylyn's appendix dealt with *Terra Australis Incognita*, or the Southern Continent, Tierra del Fuego, the Solomons, New Guinea, the voyages of Quiros, Hawkins, Le Maire and others, More's *Utopia* and Joseph Hall's *Mundus Alter et Idem*). Another historical work was Joseph Scaliger's *Thesaurus Temporum*, which contained a partial reconstruction of Eusebius of Caesarea's *Chronicon*, a summary of universal history with a table of dates.

The ministers were clearly interested in the earliest critiques of Christianity since they purchased Origen's response to Celsius, the *Contra Celsum* (1676). They were interested in theological controversies, but only those which were safely in the past.[182] They bought William Laud's response to the Jesuit John Fisher, in which Laud claimed that the Church of England and the Roman Catholic Church were both parts of the same Church Catholic. They also bought the complete works of the Arminian theologian, Simon Biscop, as well as John Pearson's exhaustive and thoroughly orthodox *Exposition of the Creed* (1676).

There were three donations of money in 1678. Alderman Thomas Wisse gave £3, Alderman Bernard Church gave £3 and Alderman Augustine Briggs gave £5. In 1681 the City Assembly agreed, 'at the request of the

---

[180] W. Benjamin, *Illuminations* (London, 1992) p. 63.

[181] Francis Bacon, *The Advancement of Learning* (ed) A. Johnston (Oxford, 1974) pp. 61–2.

[182] That prodigy of reading, William Drake, had no taste for current polemical pamphlets either. What he appeared to be interested in was not the new but the familiar (Sharpe, *Reading Revolutions*, pp. 176, 189).

ministers of this city', to subscribe to Moses Pitts' Atlas '& pay the same when the books are delivered according to Mr Pitts his proposalles'.[183] The last recorded gift of money came in 1682 when Humphrey Prideaux, a prebend of Norwich Cathedral, gave 20s. After that date contributions were exclusively in the form of gifts of books.

The difficulty of assessing the significance of the acquisition of individual titles is illustrated by the case of Raleigh's *History of the World*. If the interest in the text was political, the *History* could validate both a radical and a conformist agenda.[184] Even when interpreted as a work of history Raleigh's text was multivalent. It might have been composed in order to illustrate Bacon's opinion that 'the true office of history [was] to represent the events themselves together with the counsels and to leave the observations and conclusions thereupon to the liberty and faculty of every man's judgement'.[185] Evidence of marginal annotations from the first edition to the 1628 edition shows that some readers' interests were in the work's providentialism. In a passage on the fates of the earls of Hastings and March the annotator of the first edition in the Bodleian Library wrote of the 'terryble judgements of god' and 'gods just judgement'.[186] In a 1628 edition the annotator glossed Raleigh's treatment of the kings of France with the admonitory 'observe then what will be the end of Lewes XIV, a more inhumane persecutor than any of the pagan Emp[erors]', and on his analysis of Spanish rule in the Netherlands, 'And now what is become so miserable as the Spanish Monarchy? O Just God!'[187]

Perhaps the truth was that the ministers were merely indulging what Walter Benjamin described as the thrill of acquisition, 'the most profound enchantment for the collector'.[188]

Bindings

There is little evidence in the minutes of much concern with binding. John Collinges and Robert Harmer were invited to advise on the binding of the Walton Polyglot Bible, bought by the City in 1658, but this was exceptional. The binder employed was Michael Crotch, who also worked on some of the books in St Peter Mancroft Parish Library. Collinges and Harmer instructed Crotch to bind the Walton Polyglot with gilt leaves '& something stiffer' pasteboard than he normally used. On 1 September

---

[183] NRO NCR Case 16d/8, Assembly folio book of proceedings, 1668–1707, f. 85.
[184] A.R. Beer, *Sir Walter Ralegh and his Readers in the Seventeenth Century* (Basingstoke, 1997) p. 154. Of course readers could totally ignore a text's ideological freight.
[185] Bacon, *Advancement of Learning*, p. 77.
[186] Beer, *Sir Walter Ralegh*, pp. 149–50.
[187] Beer, *Sir Walter Ralegh*, p. 150.
[188] Benjamin, *Illuminations*, p. 62.

1674 the brethren ordered the binding of Scaliger's *De emendatione temporum*, but no details are given.

Although the fire at Norwich Central Library in 1994 damaged many fine bindings beyond repair, some survived. George Stephen highlighted *Articella cum quam plurimis tractatibus superadditis* (Venice, 1507), which has on its front cover the arms of Henry VIII supported by two angels and is signed G.G. He also noticed *Cathena aurea super Psalmos ex dictis sanctorum* [B. e. 1], printed in Paris in 1520, a work of the London binder John Reynes,[189] and a 1518 edition of the works of Plato [B. g. 9]. Two manuscripts, Berengaudus' 'In Apocalypsin' and Richard of Wetheringsett's 'Qui bene presunt', are still in their medieval binding of bevelled wooden boards. Although the Wycliffite Bible manuscript was rebound in the nineteenth century, the sixteenth century covers were preserved and relaid. Neil Ker noticed the binders' initials 'CH' within the frame at the foot of the front cover.[190] The copy of Antonius Andreae's *Scriptum super logica*, printed at St Albans's in 1483, was in a binding crafted by the Unicorn binder but was comprehensively rebound by Riley, Dunn and Wilson after the 1994 fire, as was the *Mammotrectus super Bibliam* [B. c. 16], printed in Strassburg in 1494, and two printings by Richard Pynson, *Expositio Hymnorum secundam usum Sarum* and *Expositio sequentiarum secundum usum Sarum*, both dated 1497.

Some medieval manuscripts in use as pastedowns, flyleaves or wrappers were also destroyed as a result of the events of 1994. Two leaves from the Sentences of Peter Lombard dating from the thirteenth century have disappeared from the copy of Antonius Andreae's *Scriptum super logica*, though four leaves from a thirteenth-century Psalter that were present in a copy of Joannes Herolt's *Sermones de tempore et de sanctis* have survived. Other losses probably date from much earlier. Major repair work was commissioned by the City Libraries Committee, mainly in the decade 1870 to 1880. This work is characterised by the use of red leather title labels, marbled endpapers and the stamping of publication dates at the foot of the spine. Some of the cruder repair work may predate these interventions, but is undocumented.

Subsequent history of the library

After around 1680 the minutes become less full, often recording little else but the names of members and the payment of fees, a development that possibly reflected a growing anxiety over funding. But even the bare record of names is not without interest. William Whiston, Isaac Newton's successor as Lucasian professor of mathematics at Cambridge, was a

---

189 The title page has the note 'Emptus Londini 1528'.
190 N.Ker, *Medieval Manuscripts in British* Libraries, iii (Oxford, 1983), p. 558.

member between 1695 and 1697. His friend, the theologian Samuel Clarke, was a member from December 1697 to October 1698. Richard Laughton, one of the popularisers of Newtonian physics, was a member from August 1693 until June 1694. One of the greatest collectors of books and manuscripts that England has ever produced, Thomas Tanner, joined the library in January 1707 and remained a member for over twenty-four years, during which time he donated over a hundred volumes to the library. Dr Samuel Salter, a member of Dr Johnson's Rambler Club, joined the Library in 1709 and remained a member until 1729. One of the final names to be recorded in the minutes was the poet, John Whaley, who became tutor to Horace Walpole.

The reduction in the fullness of the entries coincided with a change in personnel. On 2 March 1675 a physician, Dr. John Ellsworth, was admitted to the library. He is recorded in the minutes seven times in 1675 and six times in 1676. In 1678 he was elected librarian. Ellsworth was the first of a number of physicians who joined the library in the 1670s.

Dr. Simon Blenkarne followed on 15 February 1678.[191] The most famous Norwich physician of them all, Sir Thomas Browne, donated copies of the works of Justus Lipsius to the Library as well as copies of his own works, but never joined.

Despite the changes in its composition, the library continued to be dominated by the clergy but gradually shed its nonconformists, becoming exclusively Anglican. The published sermons and tracts produced by members of the library in the period 1676 to 1688 were often openly partisan, a phenomenon that reflected the success of the Tory party in capturing and retaining political power in Norwich. For Robert Connold, for example, politics was a question of the unreasonableness of separating from a national church established by the law of a 'lawfull and Christian Prince'. To obey the government was a 'plain Christian Law, and therefore if men dissolve this Unity, and disobey them who are set over them, they had need be secure of such a weighty Reason as they may adventure to plead at the Day of Judgement'. Unsurprisingly, his conclusion was that there was no such 'weighty Reason'.[192]

The publication of a printed catalogue in 1706 provoked a flood of donations from academics at Cambridge University. The compiler of the catalogue, Joseph Brett, rector of St Clement's, who had been a Fellow of Caius College, must have had contacts at the university that he was able to influence but the fact that the members had been willing to spend money on advertising must also have helped. Another member of the Library,

---

[191] Blenkarne presented a skeleton 'done by himself: and a case'- presumably to mount the skeleton – to the library at St. Margaret's Church, King's Lynn (NHC KL 018.2 *A Catalogue of St. Margaret's Church Library, King's Lynn*, p. 32).

[192] Robert Connold, *A sermon preached before the mayor* (London 1675) p. 6.

John Reddington, Fellow of Trinity College and headmaster of Norwich School, would have been a useful contact too. However, by the 1720s another period of decline had set in. Several members left and there seems to have been a dispute over Benjamin Mackerell holding the post of librarian for longer than was normal. Forced to resign, Mackerell attacked the city administration for not providing a salary for the librarian in his unpublished history of Norwich.[193]

The minutes end abruptly in 1733. Entries in the donation book continued a little longer but they too stopped in 1737. Ironically, the final entry in the minute book came only a year after a committee appointed to 'examine into the state of the library' delivered its report to the City Assembly recommending annual inspections, a subscription fee of one shilling plus a quarterly shilling payment and a further print-run of Benjamin Mackerell's 1732 catalogue.[194] Despite the absence of any surviving official record of the main business of the Library, donations of money continued to be received. There is a note in the library's copy of the 1503 edition of James Voragine's *Golden Legend* recording Isaac Preston's[195] donation of money for the book to be bound 'that it might the better be preserved being an authentick & antient evidence of the extravagant foppery and superstition of the Church of Rome, & the necessity of the Reformation'. The date of Preston's gift was 1742. On 21 October 1754 the City's Tonnage Committee ordered the Chamberlain to arrange for the repair of the roof of the library. On 6 October 1755 the 'front' of the library was whitewashed. On 22 August 1757 a new 'good lock' was provided for the library. At the same time the wicker in the room over the library was repaired, a new shutter erected at the other window on the south side and the room was swept. Then in June 1772 the City Assembly ordered that the library be 'taken down so far as may be necessary and rebuilt in a convenient manner'.[196] The original building was replaced by a structure in the Gothic style. It must have been an expensive undertaking since a committee was appointed in June 1775 'to examine the workmen's bills for the rebuilding the City Library and the several alternatives at or near the New Hall'.[197] The heavy financial outlay was the signal for the Assembly to reassess the collection. In May 1775 the Reverend William Pinching was invited 'to regulate and make a catalogue of the City Library

[193] NHC N942.615, Mackerell's History of Norwich, ii, p. 217.

[194] NRO, NCR, Case 16d, Assembly Folio Book, 1707–1745, ff. 178–9.

[195] Isaac Preston of Beeston St Lawrence was one of the executors of the will of Reuben King, another donor (NRO NCC 30 Tetsall, Will of Reuben King, 1733). In his own will he bequeathed his library of books 'as in the catalogue' to his son, Jacob (TNA PROB 11/939, Will of Isaac Preston, 1768).

[196] Assembly Folio Book, 1745–1773, f. 348.

[197] Assembly Folio Book, 1774–1800, f. 23v.

& to report the state thereof'.[198] The Reverend Pinching was also to dispose of the 'useless books'. The catalogue duly appeared in 1776, compiled not by the Reverend Pinching but by John Simpson, minister of St Andrew's.[199] Simpson listed the books by format, beginning with folios, then quartos, then octavos and, finally, 'smaller' books. Within these formats the arrangement was alphabetical by author or title. Simpson included an alphabetical list of the benefactors of the library. One of these, Dr Samuel Salter, a grandson of John Jeffrey, bequeathed a collection of books in 1770.[200] This was the last recorded donation before the City Library was absorbed into the Subscription Library.

In the summer of 1784 the wealthy Norwich surgeon and pillar of the Octagon Chapel, Philip Meadows Martineau, conceived the plan of founding a subscription library.[201] On 23 August thirty-three people attended a meeting in the 'Library room' at St Andrew's Hall.[202] Of the twenty-four members of the first committee only five were clergymen. Five were physicians and no less that fourteen were businessmen. Of the original 140 subscribers nineteen, or 26 percent, were women.

The members of the Subscription Library were given permission for the catalogue of the City Library to 'remain on the library table'. They were also granted access to the stock 'under the same restrictions that they use any of their own'. John Tubby, the librarian, was given the keys to the presses in which the city's books were kept so, in effect, Tubby became librarian of the City Library too. Clearly, the members regarded the City Library as being still of use. The final page of their first published catalogue featured a list of twenty-two of the City Library's 'valuable books', as they are described.

In 1816 the anonymous compiler of a manuscript catalogue calculated that there were 1,311 works in 1,855 volumes in the collection.[203] It is clear that members of the corporation continued to take advantage of the privilege of being able to borrow books since the compiler of the manuscript catalogue added a note to the effect that the lawyer Henry Francis, a member of the common council since 1807, had in his custody twenty volumes, including the fifteenth-century Wycliffite Bible.

Another catalogue was published in 1825, when the corporation also printed a short history of the library.[204] Despite this investment of money,

[198] Assembly Folio Book, 1774–1800, f. 21.

[199] NRO, MS 4230, Catalogue of the City Library, 1776.

[200] The donation is not mentioned in Salter's will (TNA PROB 11/1042, Will of Samuel Salter, 1778).

[201] NRO SO 50/1/50, Founders of Norwich Subscription Library, unpaginated and unfoliated.

[202] NRO SO 50/1/1, Minutes of the Annual General Meeting of the Subscribers, 1784–1825, unpaginated and unfoliated.

[203] NRO, MS 4231, A Catalogue of the Library of the City of Norwich, 1816.

[204] *Account of the Library belonging to the Corporation of Norwich* (Norwich, 1825).

time and effort, opinion over the way the library was being looked after differed. The following note was written on the front pastedown of a manuscript copy of the 1825 catalogue:

'It is disgraceful to the City to see the neglected state of this Library and is a proof of the decay of intelligence in the present Corporation; their predecessors could provide them with a valuable collection of books, while they will neither use them nor preserve them for the use of others. *Stare super antiques vias*'.[205]

In 1835 the Library was transferred to the new premises of the Subscription Library on Guildhall Hill. When the antiquary, Beriah Botfield, visited in 1854 he found the City Library shelved on a gallery above 'the lighter literature below' and noted with satisfaction the 'sombre attire' of the 'tomes of former years'.[206]

On 22 August 1856, seven months before the new Free Public Library opened its doors to the public, the council suggested that the City Library be transferred to the care of the Subscription Library's rival, the Norfolk and Norwich Literary Institution, which rented rooms in the new Free Public Library building on Charing Cross. However, the committee of the Literary Institution 'would not entertain the question'.[207] Instead the council resolved that the City Library be transferred to the 'hall' of the Public Library and that the books be protected by a 'wire facing'.[208] This suggestion caused further controversy. An indignant commentator demanded:

'Will it be believed that the Corporation of Norwich are about to transfer this venerable collection from the safe custody of the shelves where they now repose, to the dust, the gas, the clogged atmosphere, and casualties of a crowded room; to the disregard, the neglect, the contempt of a promiscuous assemblage, who cannot reverence what they cannot appreciate, and who, however decorous and respectable, cannot appreciate Baronius, Eusebius, or Salisbury Missals. I appeal to the lovers of learning in England to protest against this desecration'.[209]

The controversy seems to have paralysed the Library Committee because, despite their resolution, the books were still in the Subscription Library three years later. However, on 22 December 1859 John Quinton,

[205] NRO, MS 4233, City Library Alphabetical and Press Catalogue, 1825. The Latin tag can be translated as 'preserve the old ways of doing things'.
[206] Beriah Botfield, *Notes on Libraries* (1854) p. 10.
[207] NRO MS 4300, Norwich Free Library Committee Minutes, 1854–1857, unfoliated and unpaginated.
[208] Free Library Committee Minutes, 1854–1857.
[209] 'Notes on Books,' *Notes and Queries*, 4 (1857) p. 279.

the librarian of the Norfolk and Norwich Literary Institution, was invited to advise on the best way of transferring the collection to the Public Library at Charing Cross.[210] Quinton suggested that the books should be placed on the shelves in 'as mainly the same order as they are marked as the shelves will admit'. He also thought that the collection should be kept together and not mixed in with the Public Library book-stock.[211] By 5 June 1862 the books had at last been removed, but it proved impossible to retain the old arrangement because the shelves that were to accommodate the books were not 'suitable'. Quinton suggested that the collection should be re-classified. He recommended that each case be labelled alphabetically, that each shelf be lettered in lower case and that the books be numbered consecutively from left to right.

It is clear that books continued to be loaned, and not just to members of the corporation. On 26 August 1872 the secretary of the Norfolk and Norwich Law Library requested the loan of over 30 volumes of law books, a request that was readily granted.[212] Money continued to be invested in the collection. On 14 July 1871 the library committee resolved to invite John Quinton to repair some of the books. On 6 October 1880 the committee received a bill for £61. 1s. 5d. for making and erecting book-cases for the City Library on the first floor of the Public Library.[213] In 1882 a new catalogue was commissioned from Frederic Kitton a respected Norwich naturalist.[214] Printing the catalogue cost £51. 7s. 6d. At the same time responsibility for the collection was conferred on the City Librarian, who was granted an extra £5. 5s. 0d. 'for his trouble'.[215]

In 1963, when the new Central Library designed by the city architect, David Percival, was opened to the public the books were transferred there and located in glass-fronted bookcases in the basement corridor that led to the Norfolk and Norwich Record Office. Here they remained until 1 August 1994, the day of the library fire. After a major salvage operation they were stored temporarily in the Ipswich branch of Suffolk Record Office. In 2001, just before the new Norfolk and Norwich Millennium Library was opened to the public, they were moved to the Norfolk Heritage Centre, an amalgamation of the former Norfolk Studies Library and elements of Norfolk Record Office.

[210] NRO MS 4274, Library Committee Minutes, 1857–1893, unpaginated and unfoliated.
[211] Library Committee Minutes, 1857–1893.
[212] Library Committee Minutes, 1857–1893.
[213] Library Committee Minutes, 1857–1893.
[214] Frederic Kitton, *Catalogus Librorum in Bibliotheca Norvicensi* (Norwich, 1883).
[215] NRO, NCR N/TC6/7, City Committee, 3 January 1878–17 February 1882, p. 418.

Norwich City Library Minute Book 1657–1733 (MS 4226)

The minute book begins with a list of the surnames of members of the library, with the dates they were admitted to membership, from November 1682. New members were obliged to sign their names upon admission to the library, a public acknowledgement that they agreed to abide by the rules drawn up by the City Assembly on 16 January 1657. Interestingly, when members resigned they were said to have 'taken their names out of the list'.

The significance of the letter 'x' before each name (and, occasionally, after the date of admission) is problematic. Since it appears in almost every case it may be simply a marker indicating where the new member should sign. The second 'x' might signify a resignation or a death. The record of members between 1657 and late 1682 (if it ever existed) has not survived.

The list contains the occasional mistake. For example, according to the entry in the minutes, Joseph Ellis was admitted to the Library on 2 March 1686, not 2 February.

Prosopographical details of the members appear in the footnotes attached to the transcript of the minutes below.

x Mr [*John*] Pitts, was admitted Nov: 7 1682.
x Mr [*Nathaniel*] Nobbs Aug: 7 1683.
x Mr [*Pierre*] Chauvin Aug: 7 1683. x
x Mr [*Peter*] Burgess Sept: 2 1684.
x Mr [*John*] Grail July 7 1685.
x Mr [*Joseph*] Ellis Febr: 2 1686.
x Mr [*John*] Robinson May 3 1687.
x Mr [*Bernard*] Skelton Dec: 6 1687.
x Mr [*Thomas*] Clayton Dec 6 1687.
x Mr [*John*] Richardson Dec: 4 1688.
x Mr [*William*] Adamson Feb: 5 1689.
x Mr [*Isaac*] Girling Feb: 16 1689.
x Mr [*William*] Hawes May 7 1689.
x Mr [*John*] Havett Oct: 1 1689.
x Mr [*Charles*] Lullman Oct 1 1689. x
x Mr [*John*] Brandon Jan: 7 1690.

x Mr [*Benjamin*] Nobbs May 6 1690. x

x Mr [*John*] Barker Aug: 4 1691.

x Mr [*William?*] Martin May 7 1695.

x Mr [*Edward*] Revely July 2 1695.

x Mr [*William*] Whiston Sept: 3 1695.

x Mr [*Charles*] Trimnel April 2 1695.

x Mr [*Theophilus*] Brown Oct: 1 1695.

x Mr [*Richard*] Agas Jun: 2 1696.

x Mr [*Samuel*] Clark Dec: 7 1697.

x Mr [*Joseph*] Brett May 26 1698.

x Mr [*John*] Layton July 1 1701.

x Mr [*John*] Herne June 2 1702.

< Mr [*Robert*] Dannye June 2 1702. >

< Mr [*Mark*] Purt April 6 1703. >

< Mr [*Samuel*] Jones April 3 1705. >

x Mr [*John*] Whitefoot admitted Feb 1 1676 was chosen library keeper
    March 6 1682.

< x Mr [*John*] Burton > Jan 15 1678.

< x Dr [*John*] Jeffery > died April 2 1720, Feb 4 1679 was chosen library
    keeper March 4 1684.

x Mr [*John*] Grail July 7 1685 chosen library keeper Jan: 3 1693.

< x Mr [*Joseph*] Ellis > March 2 1686 chosen library keeper Jan: 5 1697

< x Mr [*John*] Richardson dyed > Dec: 4 1688 chosen library keeper Jan:
    1 1695.

< x Mr [*William*] Adamson > Feb 5: 1689 chosen library keeper Aug: 8
    1690.

< x Mr [*Isaac*] Girling > Feb 16 1689 chosen library keeper Feb: 7 1699.

< x Mr [*John*] Barker died > Aug: 4 1691 chosen library keeper Feb: 4.
    1701.

< x Mr [*Edward*] Rively died > July 2 1695 chosen library keeper Jan: 5
    1703

< x Mr [*Joseph*] Brett > died Oct 1719 May 26 1698 chosen library
    keeper Jan 2 1705

Mr [*Thomas*] Clayton Dec 6 1687 chosen library keeper Feb 6 1700

< x Mr [*John*] Robinson died > May 3 1687

x Mr [*John*] Layton July 1 1701.

x Mr [*William*] Herne June 2 1702 chosen library keeper March 7 1709.

x Mr [*Robert*] Dannye June 2 1702.

< x Mr [*Mark*] Purt > April 6 1703.

< x Mr [*Samuel*] Jones died > April 3 1705 chosen library keeper Feb 5
    1711.

x Mr [*John*] Havett Oct 1 1689 chosen library keeper Jan: 7 1708.

< x Mr [*John*] Paul died >

x Mr [*Francis*] Fayrman Oct: 1 1706 chosen library keeper Jan: 5 1713.

< x Mr [*Isaac*] Sayer died > Dec: 3 1706.

x Mr [*Thomas*] Tanner, chancellor, Jan: 7 1708.

Mr [*John*] Clarke Dec: 1 1707 chosen library keeper Jan: 5 1713.

x Mr [*Mark*] Purt Oct: 3 1709.

x Mr [*Samuel*] Salter April 4 1709 chosen library keeper Feb: 1 1715.

x Mr [*Henry*] Fish Jan: 5 1713.

x Mr [*John*] Brand Sept: 6 1714 chosen library keeper Feb: 6 1716.

x Mr Benjamin Mackerell April 15 1715 chosen library keeper June 1 1724.

x John Mompesson

x Thomas Gamble Sept: 2 1717.

x Robert Camell Nov: 3 1718.

< x Pexall Forster Dec: 1 1716 > Died Oct 4 1719.

x Mr Peter Parham Jan: 5 1719.

< x Francis Greene April 6 1719. >

x John Fox Dec 7 1719 chosen library keeper May 7 1722.

Admitted x Mr [*John*] Jeffery March 7 1719.

x Mr [*Thomas*] Aylmer.

x Mr [*John*] Morrant October 13 1720 chosen library keeper June 4 1722.

Mr William Herne September 3 1722.

x Mr [*John*] Mingay November 5 1722.

x Mr [*Francis*] Johnson September 2 1723.

Mr [*John*] Francis October 7 1723.

John Jermy Esq June 1 1724.

2 Nov 1724

x William Massey	< x Jonathan Thornton >	
< 1 March 1725 >	< x Thomas Johnson >	
13 August 1725	John Gardner	
5 February 1728	x John Beale	Thomas Manlove

The Minutes

At a meeting in the library 9 February 1657. Present: Mr [*Thomas*] Watts,[1] Mr [*Benjamin*] Snowden,[2] Mr [*Samuel*] Cullyer,[3] Mr [*Theophilus*] Ellison,[4] Mr [*Joseph*] Morrant,[5] Mr [*John*] Collinges,[6] Mr [*Isaac*] Clemant,[7] Mr [*Francis*] English.[8]

[1] Born at East Ruston, Thomas Watts attended North Walsham grammar school. He was admitted as a pensioner at Caius College, Cambridge on 2 July 1623, graduated BA in 1627 and proceeded MA in 1630. Ordained in Norwich in 1628 and instituted rector of Rockland St. Andrew in September 1639 by Richard Berney, Watts was sequestered during the civil war for having accused 'Robert Allen and the troopers that took away the service books' of being 'sacrilegious thieves' and that 'those who stood against the service book stood more for a Rebellion than for any Religion'. In 1657 he had his lease of property in the parish of St. Martin at Oak extended by the City Assembly. He was restored as rector of Rockland St Andrew in 1661. When a codicil was added to his will in 1661 he was living in Bacton (NRO NCC 324 Tennant, Will of Thomas Watts, 1661).

[2] Born in the parish of St George Tombland in 1624, Benjamin Snowden was admitted sizar at Emmanuel College, Cambridge, in 1641, graduating BA in 1646. Rector of St. Clement's, Fyebridge, and a lifelong friend of John Collinges, he was entrusted with the distribution of forty shillings to the poor under the terms of Collinges' will. Like Collinges, he was a member of Lady Frances Hobart's circle of godly ministers. He was ejected or resigned from his living in 1662. In 1669 he presided over a conventicle in the parish of St. John Maddermarket, along with Collinges (S.W. Carruthers, 'Norfolk Presbyterianism in the seventeenth century', *Norfolk Archaeology*, xxx (1950) p. 10). He died in 1696 and was buried at St. George, Colegate (J. and E. Taylor, *History of the Octagon Chapel, Norwich*, London, 1848, p. 14).

[3] Samuel Cullyer attended Norwich School and Caius College Cambridge, graduating in 1626. He was rector of St. Simon and St. Jude from 1633 to 1640 and then rector of Thurlton, presented by Richard Harmon, mayor of Norwich. He was removed from the library for non-payment of arrears on 14 February 1659.

[4] Theophilus Ellison, 'the scholar', as he is referred to in his father's will (NRO NCC 194 Green, Will of John Ellison, 1639), was educated at Caius College, Cambridge and succeeded his father as minister of the Norwich Dutch Church in 1639. The Dutch had been granted the use of Blackfriars Hall as a church as early as 1565 and the Ellisons were part of an unbroken line of scholarly ministers there. Theophilus Ellison's will was proved in 1676 (TNA PROB 11/351, Will of Theophilus Ellison, 1676).

[5] Joseph Morrant was born in the parish of St. Michael Coslany, son of William Morrant, a clergyman. Educated at Caius College, Cambridge, he was ordained for the Presbyterian ministry in 1649 at St. Leonards's, Eastcheap, and was translated to Cromer in 1658. When he drew up his will in 1670 he was living in North Tuddenham (NRO ANF 228, Will of Joseph Morrant, 1670).

[6] John Collinges was born at Boxted, Essex, in 1623, the son of Edward Collinges, a clergyman. He was educated at Dedham Grammar School and Emmanuel College, Cambridge. In 1646 he became chaplain to the Hobarts of Chapelfield House. He was ejected or resigned from his living at St. Stephen's in 1662. A prolific writer and controversialist, he was prominent in Whig politics in Norwich after the Restoration (A.S. Hankinson, 'Dr John Collinges of Norwich, 1623–90', *Norfolk Archaeology*, xlii, 1997, pp.511–19)

[7] Isaac Clement was born at Middleburg in 1632 and studied at Utrecht under Gijsbert Voetius. He was appointed minister of the French Church in Norwich in 1650. He returned to

The orders appointed by the court of common councell [9] for regulation of the library being read all the ministers present subscribed them and were admitted to the use of the said library. They ordered two frames to bee provided at a common charge, the one for the orders agreed by the court for the regulation of the library, the other for the extract of those orders which concern every minister uppon his admission to subscribe. They made choice of Mr John Collinges for library keeper till January 1658. They ordered that Goodman[10] Lambert's first quarter should end 25 March 1658 and that then each minister admitted to the use of the library should pay him 12d. & so quarterly. They ordered a book should be bought for regestring the acts of the ministers at their severall meetings in the library and sheets of parchment fit for the engrossing of the orders and that the library keeper be desired to provide these against the next meeting. They ordered the next meeting to be at 2 of the clock [*on*] 16 February and the absent ministers to have notice of the said meeting.

Holland on 29 April 1657 on leave of absence and wrote on 27 June 1657 to the elders and deacons to inform them that his parents did not wish him to return to Norwich and that 'he left them free and wished to be the same'. He was removed from membership of the library for non-payment of arrears on 14 February 1658 and died at Flushing in December 1666 (W.J.C. Moens, *The Walloons and their Church at Norwich*, Lymington, 1887–8, p. 235).

[8] Francis English was admitted sizar at Corpus Christi College, Cambridge, in 1644 and graduated BA in 1649 and was admitted MA in 1655. He was granted a lease of the rectory and tithes of the parish of Cringleford by the Norwich City Assembly in 1653 and became rector of St. Lawrence's after the death of John Carter. He was ejected or resigned from his living in 1662. In 1667 he published *The Saints Ebenezer*, a meditation on God's sustaining power in times of 'saddening disappointment, sinking discouragement and shaking desolation'. In 1669 he presided over a meeting of between 400 and 500 dissenters at Yarmouth (Carruthers, 'Norfolk Presbyterianism', p. 10). He died intestate in the parish of St. Mary Coslany in 1671 (NRO ANW 74, Administration of Francis English, 1671).

[9] The Norwich administration was bicameral. There were 24 aldermen and 2 sheriffs, presided over by the mayor, and a common council of 60 elected by the freemen with a speaker president.

[10] Clearly, Lambert the under librarian or under keeper was of a lower social status than the librarian.

At a publike meeting of ministers in the library 16 February 1657.
Present: Mr [*John*] Whitefoot,[11] Mr [*John*] Harwood,[12] Mr [*Joseph*] Morrant, Mr [*Christopher*] Hartly,[13] Mr [*Joseph*] Harward,[14] Mr [*Benjamin*] Snowden, Mr [*Samuel*] Cullyer, Mr [*Edward*] Warnes,[15] Mr [*Isaac*] Clemant, Mr [*John*] Collinges.

All the ministers present at this meeting deposed sixpence apiece in Mr Collinges' hand towards the providing of frames & parchment for the orders for the regulation of the library, in all 5s., and ordered such as were not present if admitted already or such as hereafter should bee admitted should at their admission or next appearing at meeting lay down so much towards the frames & parchment aforesaid and the buying of a book to register the acts of the ministers in. Three pence of the aforesaid money

[11] A life-long friend of Sir Thomas Browne, John Whitefoot was vicar of St. Gregory's, Norwich, and rector of Heigham. In 1642 he was imprisoned for refusing to pay Parliamentary subscription money. In 1656 he preached bishop Joseph Hall's funeral sermon in which he declared unequivocally that the predecessors of the bishops were the apostles and that 'Prelacie and piety are not such inconsistent things as some would make them; and that the men which are of, or for that order, should not be excluded...from the number of saints (John Whitefoot, *Deaths alarum*, London, 1656, sig. A7). He remained a member of the library until his death in 1699 aged 89. His biography of Sir Thomas Browne appeared posthumously (John Whitefoot, 'Some minutes for the life of Sir Thomas Browne' in, *Posthumous works of the learned Sir Thomas Browne*, 1722).

[12] A graduate of Caius College, Cambridge, John Harwood was curate of St. Luke's Chapel in the Cathedral Close for 32 years, curate of St. Mary in the Marsh and parish chaplain of St. Martin at Palace. His wife, Alice, was daughter of Dr. Hassall, dean of Norwich, an active supporter of bishop Wren. Harwood died at his house in the Close on 21 June 1691 aged 65 (NHC Colman Collection, E. A. Tillett, *St. Simon and St. Jude*, 1904, f. 171). He had bequeathed all his books to his son Bartholomew ten years before (NRO, Dean and Chapter Peculiar, IV, 107, Will of John Harwood, 1691).

[13] Hartley matriculated sizar at Trinity College, Cambridge, in 1619 and graduated BA in 1623, proceeding MA in 1626. He was ordained in Norwich on 19 December 1624 and was instituted rector of All Saints Timberhill and of Morningthorpe near Long Stratton in 1637. It seems very likely that Hartley was the 'Mr Christopher' of All Saints named as one of the scandalous pro-Wrenite clergy who were 'least affected to Parliament' in the Norwich Remonstrance of 1643 (Bodleian Library, Tanner MS 220, ff. 131–5). He died in 1679.

[14] Virtually nothing is known about Joseph Harward except that he was instituted rector of St. Martin at Palace in 1662 (NRO DN/REG/30, Thomas Tanner's Abstract of the Norwich Diocese Registration Books, f. 29).

[15] Warnes was admitted to Corpus Christi College, Cambridge, in 1630 and graduated BA in 1635, proceeding MA in 1638. He was ordained deacon in Norwich on 22 September 1638 and priest on 20 December 1640. In the same year he was appointed master of Paston School, North Walsham (C. Forder, *A History of the Paston School North Walsham Norfolk*, North Walsham, 1975, pp. 48–9). He was rector of Lammas from 1645 to 1700 and of Great Hautbois from 1661 to 1700. He died in 1700 aged 87. His will is provocatively High Church. He used the church fathers to justify his request for the inscription on his tomb of prayers for his soul, claiming that such a practice was in accordance with the doctrines of the Church of England which 'acknowledges itself to be the follower of the original church in all things...(as bishop Jewell of Salisbury witnesses), whose custom became fixed in ancient times to pray for the souls which have departed thence' (NRO, NCC, 101 Edwards, Will of Edward Warnes, 1700).

was at that meeting paid for firing. Mr Whitefoot, Mr Hartly, Mr Harwood, Mr Harward and Mr Warnes this day subscribed the orders & were admitted to the use of the library. The ministers ordered that henceforth their meetings in the library bee monthly, viz the 2d Monday in each moneth between 2 & 3 of the clock *post prandium*.[16]

At a publike meeting of ministers in the library 9 March being the 2nd Monday in that month. Present: Mr [*John*] Harwood, Mr [*Christopher*] Hartly, Mr [*Thomas*] Watts, Mr [*Joseph*] Morrant, Mr [*Theophilus*] Ellison, Mr [*Isaac*] Clemant, Mr [*John*] Whitefoot, Mr [*Samuel*] Cullyer, Mr [*Benjamin*] Snowden, Mr [*John*] Collinges.

/2. 6
1. 4
2. 0
1. 4
7. 2 /

Received more of Mr Ellison and Mr English * and of Mr Watts * sixpence apiece. Mr Collinges gave the ministers an account that hee had laid out for a book for the use of the meeting 2s. 6d. for parchment, 1s. 4d. for 2 frames, two shillings for the colouring and for the backs for the frames, 1s. 4d. In all 7s. 2d. which was 8d. more than hee had received besides 3d. for firing in all 11d. [*word deleted*] more than hee had received.

At a meeting in the library 13 April 1657. Present at the meeting: Mr [*Christopher*] Hartly, Mr [*Samuel*] Cullyer, Mr [*Isaac*] Clemant, Mr [*John*] Collinges, Mr [*Benjamin*] Snowden, Mr [*Francis*] English.
This beeing the quarter day for payment of the under keeper the ministers present all paid him 12d. a piece & Mr. Watts excusing his coming to the meeting also paid him. The library keeper represented to the ministers that Epiphanius[17] is double[18] in the library, one of the best editions Greek-Latin. another of a Latine edition and that the Latine edition might bee sold for the advantage of the library. And that Dr. Willet on Genesis of an ill edition and the ministers thought fit that Epithanius & Willet should bee sold and that with the money a perfect Willet uppon Genesis & Exodus should bee bought and to that end the library keeper should informe himself of the price of Willet's *Hexapla in Genesis et Exodum*[19] against the next meeting.

[16] After dinner.
[17] St. Epiphanius: *Opera omnia in duos Tomos distributa* (Paris, 1622).
[18] The Epiphanius was a duplicate copy.
[19] Andrew Willet: *Hexapla in Genesin: that is, a sixfold commentarie upon Genesis, wherein sexe severall translations, that is, the Septuagint, and the Chalde, two Latin, of Hierome and Tremellius, two English, the great Bible, and the Geneva edition are compared, where they differ, with the original Hebrew, and Pagnine, and Montanus interlinearie interpretation* (Cambridge, 1605)

At a meeting in the library 11 May 1657. Present at the meeting Mr
[*Thomas*]Watts, Mr [*Joseph*] Morrant, Mr [*Samuel*] Culyer, Mr [*Benjamin*]
Snowden.

The underkeeper of the library informed the ministers mett that Mr
Ellison, Mr Harward, Mr Morrant had paid their 12d. a piece to him.

At a meeting in the library 8 June 1657. Present: Mr [*Thomas*] Watts,
Mr [*Benjamin*] Snowden, Mr [*Francis*] English,   Mr [*Joseph*] Harward,
Mr [*Joseph*] Morrant, Mr [*Theophilus*] Ellison.

The library keeper this day brought in catalogues of the bookes, which
were affixed. Sixpence was ordered to bee given to a boy for pasting up the
catalogues. Another meeting was appointed the 2d Munday in July & that
speciall notice bee given to all the ministers to bee here present that day.

The meeting appointed on the 2d Munday in July was adjourned to the 10
August. At a meeting in the library 10 August 1657. Present: Mr [*John*]
Harwood, Mr [*John*] Collinges,Mr [*Thomas*] Watts, Mr [*Joseph*] Morrant,
Mr [*Francis*] English.

There being no more brethren present the meeting was adjourned till the
2d Munday in September.

At a meeting in the library 14 September 1657. Present: Mr [*Joseph*]
Harward, Mr [*Francis*] English, Mr [*Joseph*] Morrant, Jacques le Franc.[20]
This meeting was again adjourned for want of company.

At a meeting in the library 12 October 1657. Present: Mr [*John*] Whitefoot,
Mr [*Thomas*] Watts, Mr [*Francis*] English, Mr [*Joseph*] Morrant, Mr [*John*]
Collinges.

Mr Whitefoot, Mr English & Mr Collinges paid their quarterly payment to
Goodman Lambert. Mr John Whitefoot gave to the * use of the * library
Bacon uppon the Sentences in 2 volumes edition Cremond 1620,[21] bound
up fairly in 2 volumes. Three pence was laid out for tobacco pipes which
added to 11d & 6d before makes up 1s. 8d. laid out by the library keeper
for the ministers' use. It was agreed that Mr Whitefoot should have the

---

[20] A protégé of John Evelyn, the diarist, who introduced him to Jeremy Taylor, with whom
he discussed original sin in Latin (E.S. De Beer, ed, *The Diary of John Evelyn*, 1959, pp.368–9),
Jacques le Franc was appointed minister of the French church in Norwich in succession to
Isaac Clement on 30 July 1657. He resigned on 4 December 1664 and in 1668 was inducted as
the Anglican rector of St. Clement's. While he was still minister of the French church he
published *The touch-stone of truth: wherein verity by Scripture and antiquity is plainly confirmed and errour
confuted* (Cambridge, 1662). He died in 1680 (W.J.C. Moens, *The Walloons and their Church at
Norwich*, Lymington, 1887–8, p. 235). One of the witnesses to his will was Peter de la Hay, a
minor canon of Norwich Cathedral, who joined the Library on 4 December 1683 (NRO ANW
W 12, Will of Jacques le Franc, 1680).

[21] John Baconthorpe: *Quaestiones in quatuor libros Sententiarum, & Quodlibetales* (Cremona, 1618).

latine Epithanius which is double in the library and that hee shall pay for it either 5d. in money to bee laid out for the use of the library or else give a book the ministers shall judge to bee of that value.

At a meeting in the library 4 January 1658. Present: Mr [*John*] Whitefoot, Mr [*Thomas*] Watts, Mr [*John*] Collinges, Mr [*Benjamin*] Snowden.
Mr Whitefoot paid in 1s. for his quarterly payment to the library keeper.
Mr Snowden paid in 2s. for 2 quarters. Mr Watts also paid in 1s. for the quarter. Mr Collinges gave an account of 1s. laid out for coales & wood for the drying of the books harmed by the raine. Mr [*Alexander*] Burnet [22] was admitted to the library. Another meeting appointed 11 January at 2 of the clock.

At a meeting of ministers in the library 11 January 1658. Present at the meeting: Mr [*John*] Collinges, Mr [*Christopher*] Hartly, Mr [*John*] Whitefoot, Mr [*Francis*] English, Mr [*Joseph*] Morrant, Mr [*Benjamin*] Snowden, Mr [*Theophilus*] Ellison, Mr [*Thomas*] Watts.
Mr. English paid in 1s. due to the library keeper for the last quarter. Mr Ellison paid in 2s. for the last quarters due to the under keeper. Mr Hartly paid in 2s. for the 2 last quarters due as aforesaid. Mr Morrant paid in 2s. for his arrears to the library keeper. All the ministers present paid in 12d. apiece and the like summe was ordered to bee paid by all the ministers admitted to the use of the library, 2s.2d. of which mony was ordered to reimburse the library keeper and such a proportion of the rest mony (as by the library keeper should bee thought fit) ordered to bee paid for a book consisting of 3 quires of thick, Venice paper to bee bound up to make a booke to containe catalogues of the books in the library. The remainder of the mony to remaine in the library keeper's hand for publike expences. Mr Collinges was desired to keep the office of library keeper untill the aforesaid book bee bought and the catalogues made. Mr. Whitefoot promising that (that work being done) uppon Mr. Collings desire hee would take it the remaining part of the yeare.

---

[22] Son of Dunkin Burnet, a Norwich physician, Alexander Burnet graduated M.B. from Emmanuel College, Cambridge, in 1639, proceeding M.D. in 1648. He was admitted as an Honorary Fellow of the Royal College of Physicians in 1664 and, according to Samuel Pepys, died of the plague in London in 1665 (W. Munk, *The Roll of the Royal College of Physicians of London*, I: 1518–1700, 1878, p. 334).

At a meeting of ministers 8 February 1658. Present: Mr [*Christopher*] Hartly, Mr [*Francis*] English, Mr [*John*] Collinges, Mr [*John*] Whitefoot, Mr [*Joseph*] Morrant, Mr [*Benjamin*] Snowden.

Mr [*Robert*] Harmar[23] this day subscribed the Engagement[24] & was admitted to the use of the library. It was agreed that the widow of Goodman Lambert (under keeper to the library & deceased) should keep the keyes untill the 25 March 1658. The choice of a person for under keeper to the library was deferred untill the next meeting of ministers.

At a meeting of ministers 29 March 1658. Present: Mr [*Christopher*] Hartly, Mr [*Francis*] English, Mr [*Robert*] Harmar, Mr [*Benjamin*] Snowden, Mr [*John*] Collinges, Mr [*John*] Whitefoot, Mr [*Alexander*] Burnet, Mr [*Joseph*] Morrant.

All the ministers present paid in their quarterage to the widow Lambert according to the order of the last meeting. Mr Burnet paid in 1s according to the order of 11 January. It beeing resolved that the choice of the under-keeper of the library was in the power of the minister chosen for the year Mr Collinges engaged to keep the office untill January 1659 and made choice of James Rush of St. Andrew's parish for under-keeper for that library for that time.

At the meeting of ministers 10 May 1658: Mr [*Robert*] Harmar, Mr [*Benjamin*] Snowden, Mr [*Alexander*] Burnet, Mr [*John*] Collinges.

At the meeting of ministers in the library 9 August 1658: Present at the meeting Mr [*John*]Whitefoot, Dr [*John*] Collinges, Mr [*Benjamin*] Snowden, Mr [*Joseph*] Morrant.

The ministers present paid their quarterly payment to the library keeper

At the meeting of ministers in the library 8 November 1658. Present at the meeting: Mr [*John*] Whitefoot, Mr [*Francis*] English, Mr [*Robert*] Harmar, Dr [*John*] Collinges, Mr [*Thomas*] Watts, Mr [*Theophilus*] Ellison, Mr [*Alexander*] Burnet.

[23] Robert Harmer was curate of St. Andrew's from 1657. A John Harmer, possibly a relation, signed the pro-Covenant *Attestation of the ministers of the county of Norfolk* (1648). Robert Harmer conformed at the Restoration, so is likely to have shared his friend Collinges' Presbyterianism (Blomefield, *History of Norfolk*, iv, p. 303). In 1658 Harmer and Collinges were invited by the City Assembly to advise on the binding of the Walton Polyglot Bible. In 1658–9 Harmer was paid by the City Chamberlain for delivering sermons on Kett's Day. When he drew up his will he was living in Norwich (in 1671 he was paying tax on 10 hearths in the parish of St Andrew's), though he owned property in Barton Turf, Antingham and Trunch (NML N929.3, J. Pound, 'Norwich Hearth Tax 1671', 2004, p. 3; NRO, NCC OW10, Will of Robert Harmer, 1678).

[24] An allusion to the Engagement Act of 2 January 1650 that required all adult males to take an oath of loyalty to the government.

The ministers agree that Alderman Man[25] bee desired to put the n[ew] Bible[26] <subscribed by the City> which is in hands for the use of the library to G[oodman] Crotch[27] to bee bound with gilt leaves & something stiffer parseboards then he ordinarily useth. Mr Harmar, Mr Whitefoot & all the rest not present paid to the under keeper of the library all which was due at Michaelmas[28] last.

At the meeting of ministers in the publike library 13 December 1658.
Present at the meeting: Mr [John] Whitefoot, Mr [Francis] English, Mr [Robert] Harmar, Mr [Benjamin] Snowden.
The library keeper brought in a * paper * book ruled containing a classical and an alphabeticall catalogue of all the books in the library.[29] He informed the ministers mett this day that having at the meeting 11 January and the meeting 29 March received 8s.of the brethren 2s. 2d. of which was due to him for former disbursements and 1s. ordered to bee returned to one of the brethren not conceived fit to bear an equall share of charges with the rest. There remained in his hands 4s. 10d. to buy the book mentioned in the order of 11 January. He further informed them that hee had laid out 3s. for paper & 4s. for the ruling & binding the said book, in all 7s. which is more then he received 2s. 10d. That hee had procured 2 catalogues to bee wrote in it fairly. That for the catalogue of commentators it was begun & should before the next meeting be perfected by his own hand. Mr Whitefoot, Mr Harmar & Dr Collinges made report to the rest of the brethren mett this day that Mr Joseph Paine,[30] alderman of the city of Norwich, uppon Munday preceding this meeting * sent for the 3 ministers aforesaid to his house * and there did give into the hands of Mr John

[25] John Mann, a mercer, the father-in-law of Samuel Chapman, one of the founders of the Bethel Hospital, was sheriff of Norwich in 1649 and mayor in 1653. He was one of the leaders of the Whig party in Norwich after the Restoration (Evans, p. 502). He died in 1695 and was buried in St. Andrew's (Cozens-Hardy, p. 87). In his will he left money to Benedict Rively and John Jeffery, both members of the Library, to buy mourning rings. He also left Benjamin Snowden 40s. (NRO NCC 123 Jones, Will of John Mann, 1695).

[26] Brian Walton: *Biblia Sacra Polyglotta* (London, 1657).

[27] Michael Crotch obtained his freedom as a bookbinder in 1632. In 1663–4 there are references in the St Peter Mancroft Churchwardens' Accounts to payments to Goodman Crotch for repairing books (D. Stoker, 'The Norwich Book Trades before 1700', *Cambridge Bibliographical Society*, viii, 1981, pp. 97–8). His sons, Adam and John, carried on the business after his death.

[28] 29 September.

[29] A classical catalogue was a subject catalogue. An alphabetical catalogue was, of course, an author/title catalogue.

[30] A wealthy hosier, Joseph Paine was sheriff in 1654 and mayor in 1660. During his mayoralty he was knighted by Charles II (Cozens-Hardy, p. 90). In his will he left money for the repair of the north window in the chancel of St Gregory's. His executors, Thomas Wisse and Augustine Briggs, both left money to the Library in 1678 (TNA PROB 11/328, Will of Sir Joseph Paine, 1668).

Whitefoot one of the aforesaid ministers twenty pounds declaring it his mind that it should bee laid out at the discretion of the 3 ministers afore-said together with Mr George Cock[31] to bee added to them to buy such books with it as they shall judge most fit for the City library. It was ordered that Dr Collinges should send to his stationer at London to send him a certaine account of the price of Gerard's Commonplaces[32] of the last edition & also his commentaryes together with Chemnitius & Lysergus and Gerard's Harmony,[33] the latter of Rotterdam print[ing], and report it to the brethren at their next meeting.

At the meeting of ministers 24 January 1659. Present: Mr [John] Whitefoot, Mr [Christopher] Hatley, Dr [John] Collinges, Mr [Robert] Harmar, Mr [John] Martin.[34]

Dr. Collinges reports to the brethren that hee had advised with a stationer concerning Gerard's works. That Gerard's Commonplaces new will cost £3. 4s. in 4 volumes new. His harmony with Chemnitius (Gerard being of Rotterdam print) will cost £2. That his other commentaryes in 4o will cost £1. 17s. (that uppon Deuteronomy being 12s.). That the stationer offers for 8s. to make that Chemnitius already in the library perfect by setting up the harm[ony] of the passion alone. And that he adviseth the other commen-taryes should not be yet bought because it is probable they will soone be printed in folio. He further let the brethren know that hee had viewed Oecumenius[35] in 2 volumes folio grand collation,[36] Theophilact[37] in 2

---

[31] Probably the son of George Cock, mayor in 1613, Cock was ordained by Bishop Harsnett in February 1627. Minister at St. Andrew's from September 1635 he was a supporter of Bishop Wren. On 8 November 1636 he was instituted rector of Barsham in Suffolk by Joseph Fleming of Woodton. He was John Boatman's successor as minister of St. Peter Mancroft, where he remained until his death. Under the terms of his will his books were left to his children, with the exception of the works of Suarez, which he bequeathed to the City Library. The books were sold for £338. 6s. 5d, which was 14 % of the value of his estate (K. Tremain, 'Stationers and the inception of the Enlightenment in Norwich, 1660–1720', MA thesis, UEA, 2007, p. 74). John Whitefoot and Benjamin Rively, both fellow members of the Library, were witnesses to the will (NRO NCC 57 Wiseman, Will of George Cock, 1675).

[32] John Gerhard: *Loci Theologici cum pro adstruenda veritate* (Frankfurt & Hamburg, 1657)

[33] John Gerhard: *Harmoniae Evangelistarum Chemnitio Lyserianae continuatio* (Rotterdam, 1646)

[34] John Martin was admitted sizar at Caius College, Cambridge, on 13 June 1613 and grad-uated BA in 1617, proceeding MA in 1620. He was ordained on 21 December 1617. He was rector of Edgefield from 1620 to 1659 and was one of the signatories of the pro-Covenant *Attestation of the ministers of the county of Norfolk* (1648). He was assistant to the Committee for the Ejection of Scandalous Ministers in 1654. On his death he bequeathed 'every my bookes within my studdy' to his son, James, except for some English books, to be selected by his wife, Ursula (NRO ANW 678/655, Will of John Martin, 1659).

[35] Oecumenius: *Commentaria in Hosce Novi Testamenti Tractatus* (Paris, 1631)

[36] Grand collation means, in effect, the collected works of an author.

[37] Theophilact: *Commentarii in Quatuor Evangelia* (Paris, 1635)

volumes folio grand collation, Basil[38] in 2 volumes folio grand collation in Mr Littlebury's[39] hands & judgeth them worth the money asked for them which is in all £4. Basil at £1. 14 s., Oecumenius at £1. 4s. Theophilact at £1. 2s. The brethren ordered that Dr. Collinges bee desired to send to Mr. Littlebury for so many books as shall amount to £12. 11s. to bee paid out of Mr. Alderman Paine's £20 in Mr. Whitefoot's hand. The other 20s. beeing given by Dr Collinges to buy a book for the library. They further ordered the books to be sent for to be

1	Gerard's commonplaces in 4 volumes folio the last print	03 – 14 – 00
2	Oecumenius in 2 volumes folio grand collation Latin	01 – 02 – 00
3	Basil: in 2 volumes folio grand collation	01 – 14 – 00
4	Theophilact: folio 2 volumes grand collation	01 – 04 – 00
5	The Supplement of the harmony begun by Chemnitius continued by Lysergius & Gerard	00 – 08 – 00
6	Gerards continuation Rotterdam print about	01 – 04 – 00
7	Josephus[40] grand collation	
8	Philo Judeus [41] grand collation	

The brethren ordered that Mr John Whitefoot bee library keeper for the ensuing yeare. Mr Harmar, Mr Whitefoot, Mr Snowden, Dr Collinges all paid what was due to the library keeper to this day. Mr Hatly paid 2s. supposing that all due, the question beeing onely uppon Midsummer quarter.

At the meeting of ministers in the publike library 14 February 1659. Present at the meeting: Mr [John] Whitefoot, Mr [Benjamin] Snowden, Dr [John] Collinges, Mr [Robert] Harmar, Mr [Francis] English, Mr [Thomas] Watts, Mr [Theophilus] Ellison, Mr [Joseph] Morrant].
Mr Ellison, Mr Morrant, Mr Watts, Mr English discharged all arrears due to the library keeper at the 25 December last. Mr Whitefoot reports to the brethren that hee had made choice of Tho[mas] Scot, clerke of Andrew's parish, for library keeper under him, with a reservation to the widow of James Rush to have all the profits which shall bee due at 25 March next. The ministers ordered a review of all admitted to the use of the library that it may appear who have equally contributed uppon the order for payment of 6d. apiece made 16 February 1657 & the order for 12d. apiece made 11

---

[38] St Basil: *Opera Omnia, quae repereri potueruit* (Paris, 1618)
[39] Robert Littlebury was a bookseller in London from 1652 to 1685. He was one of the overseers of the will of William Dugard, who printed the first edition of *Eikon Basilike* (H. Plomer, *A Dictionary of the Booksellers and Printers who were at work in England, Scotland and Ireland from 1641 to 1667* (London, 1907) p. 119.
[40] Josephus: *Judei historici pre clara opera non parva* (Paris, 1519)
[41] Philo Judaeus: *Omnia Quae Extant Opera* (Paris, 1640)

January 1658 towards the charges of the frames, parchment; & the booke conteining the catalogues of the books. Mr Harmar and Mr Cock (the latter of which was this day admitted to the use of the library) paid their 1s. 6d. a piece according to the orders aforesaid.

The names of the ministers who have paid according to both these orders.

Mr George Cock.	The names of such as are in arrears	
Mr Robert Harmar.	upon the orders aforesaid	
Dr Collinges.	Mr Cullyer removed	
Mr Whitefoot.	Mr Burnet for both orders	00 – 01 – 06
Mr Snowden.	Mr Warnes upon both orders	00 – 01 – 06
Mr English.	Mr Clemant removed	
Mr Watts.	Mr Harwood upon the 2d order	00 – 01 – 00
Mr Ellison.	Mr Harward upon the 2d order	00 – 01 – 00
Mr Hatly.	Mr Martin.	01 – 01 – 06
Mr Morrant.	In arreares uppon both the orders	00 – 06 – 06

There being 2s. 10d. in arreares to Dr Collinges three shillings beeing paid by Mr Cock & Mr Harmar uppon the orders aforesaid, it was ordered to the reimbursing of Dr. Collinges & to pay for 4 fires of which the last [was] made this day. Dr Collinges gave account to the brethren that Cyprians works[42] *& Schindler's *Lex Polyglotton*[43] * are found in the catalogue of bene-factours, but was missing in the library when hee took the charge of it.[44]

At the meeting of ministers in the public library 14 March 1659.

Present at the meeting: Mr [George] Cock, Mr [Thomas]Watts, Mr [Francis] English, Mr [Robert] Harmar, Mr [Benjamin] Snowden, Mr [John] Whitefoot, Dr [John] Collinges.

Mr Whitefoot gave the ministers an account that hee had brought into the library

Gerard's *commonplaces* in 4 volumes folio at	03 – 13 – 00
Basilii *opera* Graec. Lat 2 volumes folio at	01 – 14 – 00
Oecumenii *opera* Gr Lat 2 volumes folio at	01 – 04 – 00
Theophilacti *opera* in 2 volumes folio at	01 – 02 – 00
Philonis Judae *opera* Gr Lat 1 volumes folio	00 – 16 – 00
Gerard's *Harmony of the passion*[45]	00 – 07 – 06

---

[42] Saint Cyprian: *Opera, Nicolai Rigaltii observationibus ad veterum exemplarium fidem recognita et illustrata.* (Paris, 1649).

[43] Valentin Schindler: *Lexicon pentaglotton, Hebraicum, Chaldaicum, Syriacum, Talmudico-Rabbinicum, et Arabicum.* (Frankfurt, 1612). The library's copy of Schindler's *Lexicon* was returned by William Stinnet on 12 September 1659.

[44] This suggests that Collinges conducted a security audit of the stock of the library as part of the 1657 reorganisation.

[45] John Gerhard: *Harmoniam Historiae Evangelicae de passione crucifixione* (Frankfurt, 1622)

And he further acquainted them that hee had paid Dr Collinges £10 (part of the mony given by Mr. Alderman Paine) to bee returned to Mr R[obert] Littlebury at London in payment for the aforesaid books. The reecit of which £10 also Dr. Collinges acknowledged, and that hee had accordingly returned it.

11 April 1659. At a meeting of ministers in the library. Present: Mr [Robert] Harmar, Dr [John] Collinges, Mr [George] Cock, Mr [John] Martin.
Mr Martin paid1s. 6d. uppon the 2 orders of 16 February 1657 & 11 January 1658. Mr Harmar, * Mr Cock,* Dr Collinges, Mr Whitefoot, Mr Snowden, Mr Watts, Mr Martin all paid 1s. apiece for their quarterly payment to the library keeper. Mr Whitefoot paid the widow Rush for her time in keeping of the library and paid her oure 3s. for so much time as is passed of this quarter and the keyes were ordered to bee delivered to Thomas Scott chosen by Mr Whitefoot to bee library keeper. Mr Harmar reimbursed Mr Whitefoot his 3s so that Mr Harmar hath paid his share to the library keeper untill the 25 December next. It was agreed that those who are in arreares for the keeping of the library till the 25 March 1660 pay in the said arreares to the widow Rush. Mr [Francis] English paid his arrears 13 June 1659.

At a meeting of ministers 11 July 1659. Present: Mr [George] Cock, Mr [Benjamin] Snoding, Mr [John] Whitefoote, Mr [Robert] Harmar, Mr [Francis] English, Mr [Thomas] Watts.
The library keeper brought in a catalogue of the books & benefactors' names fairely written in a parchment booke, for the writing whereof hee paid to the cleark 7s. For the repayment of which monye it was agreed every minister should pay 8d. which monye was paid by as many as were then present. The ministers present paid their quarteridge[46] to the under library keeper.

At a meeting of ministers 8 August 1659. Present: Mr [George] Cock, Mr [John] Harrwood, Mr [John] Martin, Mr [John] Whitefoote.
Mr Martin, Mr Harrwood paid the underlibrary keeper his quarteridge, together with their parts for the catalogue.

At a meeting of ministers in the library 12 September 1659. Present: Mr [George] Cock, Mr [Theophilus] Ellison, Dr [John] Collinges, Mr [John] Martin, Mr [Robert] Harmar, Mr [John] Whitefoot, Mr [Joseph] Morrant.
Dr Collinges and Mr Morrant and Mr Ellison paid to the underkeeper of the library 12d. a piece for the quarter due 24 June 1659. Dr Collinges &

[46] The quarterage was the members' quarterly payment of 12d.

Mr Morrant & Mr Ellison paid also their 12d. a piece for the writing of the catalogue of the benefactors according to the order of the 11 July. Mr Stinet[47] sent in this day Schindler's * Lexicon * Pentaglotton [48] formerly belonging to the library and also sent in Forsteri Lexicon Hebraicum,[49] Ainsworth's workes,[50] Summa Sylvestrina,[51] Wecker's Antidotarium,[52] all which hee gave to the library.

At a meeting of ministers in the publike library 11 October 1659. Present: Mr [George] Cock, Dr [John] Collinges, Mr [John] Whitefoot, Mr [Robert] Harmer, Mr [Francis] English. All the ministers present paid in 12d. a piece due to the library keeper at the 29 September last.

At a meeting of ministers in the library 14 November 1659. Present: Mr [Robert] Harmar, Mr [John] Whitefoote, Mr [Theophilus] Ellison, Mr [Francis] Inglish, Mr [George] Cock, Mr [Joseph] Harward.
Mr Whitefoote took out of the library a Latin Epithanius for which hee is to pay to the library 5s. by order aggreed 12 October 1657. Mr Harmer tooke with him a Latin Theophilact for which hee is to pay 4s by consent of the company. Received of the gift of Mr Thomas Allen[53] minister his chaine of scripture chronologie.[54] Mr Harward, *Mr Watts* & Mr Ellison paid the underkeeper his quarteridge.

At a meeting of ministers in the library 12 December 1659. Present: Mr [Robert] Harmar, Mr [John] Whitefoot, Mr [Thomas] Watts, Dr [John] Collinges, Mr [Benjamin] Snowden, Mr [Theophilus] Ellison.

---

[47] A graduate and benefactor of Christ's College, Cambridge, William Stinnet obtained a licence to practise medicine and surgery. Suspended by Bishop Matthew Wren in 1636 (Reynolds, p. 191), he was rector of St John Maddermarket for 50 years and was buried there in 1664 (Blomefield, *History of Norfolk*, iv, p. 298; M. Pelling, 'Occupational diversity: barbersurgeons and the trade of Norwich, 1550–1640', *Bulletin of the History of Medicine*, 56, 1982, p. 509).

[48] Valentin Schindler: *Lexicon pentaglotton Hebraicum, Chaldaicum, Syriacum, Talmudico-Rabbinicum, et Arabicum* (Frankfurt, 1612)

[49] Johann Forster: *Dictionarium Hebraicum novum* (Basle, 1564)

[50] Henry Ainsworth: *Annotations upon the five bookes of Moses* (London, 1627).

[51] Silvestro Mazzolini: *Summae sylvestrinae* (Lyon, 1593)

[52] Johann Jacob Wecker: *Antidotarium speciale* (Basle, 1574)

[53] Thomas Allen was born in Norwich, the son of a dyer. He was admitted to Caius College, Cambridge, in 1624, graduating BA in 1628 and proceeding MA in 1631. He was deprived of his ministry at St. Edmund's in Norwich by bishop Wren for refusing to read the Book of Sports. By 1638 he was in New England. He returned to Norwich in 1651–2 where he became city preacher. Ejected in 1662, he received a license as an Independent in St Andrew's in 1672. He died in 1673 (ODNB).

[54] Thomas Allen: *A chain of scripture chronology; from the creation of the world to the death of Jesus Christ* (London, 1659).

Mr Whitefoot acknowledged himself to have received of Mistress Brooke,[55] widow, to the use of the library to bee laid out uppon bookes by the consent of the ministers the summe of twenty pounds. Mr Snowden paid the library keep[er] his quarterage due 29 September.

At a meeting of ministers in the library 9 January 1660. Present: Mr [Robert] Harmar, Dr [John] Collinges, Mr [Joseph] Morrant, Mr [George] Cock, Mr [Christopher] Hatly, Mr [Benjamin] Snowden, Mr [John] Whitefoot. Mr [Francis] English. Mr Nicholas Sheppard[56] & Mr Sam[uel] Snowden[57] were this day admitted to the use of the library. All present paid the library keeper for all due from them to this day to the library keeper. Mr Whitefoot was chosen keeper of the library for the ensuing yeare. The Biblia Polyglotta[58] in 6 volumes folio given by the City to the library were this day brought into the library.

At a meeting of ministers in the library 13 February 1660. Present: Mr [George] Cock, Mr [John] Whitefoot, Mr [Benjamin] Snowden, Mr [Joseph] Morrant, Mr [Robert] Harmar, Mr [Francis] English, Dr [John] Collinges, Mr [Thomas] Watts. Mr Whitefoot proposed to the brethren the disposall of ten pounds of the money in his hands (for the use of the library) in sending for *two* bookes which was accordingly assented to & it was left to Mr Whitefoot which bookes to send for. Mr Haward & Mr Watts paid the library keeper for the last quarter.

At the meeting of ministers in the Library 12 March 1660. Present: Mr [George] Cock, Mr [John] Whitefoot, Dr [John] Collinges, Mr [Robert] Harmar, Mr [Benjamin] Snowden. Dr Collinges this day brought in Hugo Cardinalis his works in 6 volumes folio,[59] which hee gave to the library.

[55] In her will Thomasine Brooke expected to receive the 'blessed inheritance of gods Elect Children' and left her daughter Rose 'a Greate Jewell sett with Dyamonds with the Gold Chayne thereunto belonging & in which Jewell is contained the Pictures of King Charles the first & of the Kings Majestie that now is & of henry late Prince of Wales' (NRO NCC, OW 74, Will of Thomasine Brook, 1676). As well as being extremely wealthy she was very well connected. Her friends in the city administration included Aldermen Wood, Briggs, Wisse, Thacker and Bendish. Alderman Watts was her brother-in-law.

[56] Nicholas Shepherd matriculated at King's College, Cambridge, in 1639, graduating BA in 1641. He was rector of Poringland between 1647 and 1672.

[57] Born in the parish of St George Tombland in 1636, Samuel Snowden graduated BA from Corpus Christi College Cambridge in 1657, proceeding MA in 1660. He was rector of Fritton from 1661 to 1668, rector of Framingham Pigot from 1669 to 1673, rector of Swainsthorpe in 1671 and rector of Newton Flotman in 1672. The author of *Alexipharmacon spirituale* (Norwich, 1689) and *A sermon preached upon the thirteenth of January 1694/5* (Norwich, 1695), both published by the Norwich bookseller, Edward Giles, it is very possible that he was Benjamin Snowden's nephew.

[58] *Biblia sacra polyglotta* (London, 1657). Presumably the copy ordered to be bound on 8 November 1658.

[59] *Repertorium apostillarum utriusque testamenti domini Hugonis Cardinalis* (Basle, 1504).

At the meeting of ministers in the library 9April 1660. Present: Mr [*Robert*] Harmar, Dr [*John*] Collinges, Mr [*Benjamin*] Snowden, Mr [*John*] Whitefoot, Mr [*Thomas*] Watts, Mr [*George*] Cock. These following bookes were brought into the library by Mr Whitefoot, beeing bought with part of Mistress Brooke's mony.

Calvini Lexicon Juridicium[60]	00 – 12 – 00
Bonacina[61]	00 – 14 – 00
Azorij Institut moral 3 vol[62]	01 – 01 – 00
Cameronii opera[63]	00 – 12 – 00
Arminij opera[64]	00 – 07 – 00
Tolleti Causus[65]	00 – 03 – 00
Navarri Enchyridion[66]	00 – 02 – 00
Cornel: a Lapide in Evangel[67]	01 – 00 – 00
Filiuecius[68]	01 – 00 – 00
Suidas[69] in 2 vol fol Gr Col	01 – 08 – 00
Smidij Concord[70]	00 – 18 – 00
Josephi opera[71] Gr Collat	00 – 18 – 00

/ 8.   12.   00. /

All ministers present paid 12d. a piece due to the library keeper for the last quarterage.

At the meeting of ministers in the publike library 7 May 1660.
Present at the meeting: Dr [*John*] Collinges, Mr [*Benjamin*] Snowden, Mr [*Robert*] Harmer, Mr [*Theophilus*] Ellison, Mr [*Joseph*] Morrant.
Mr Ellison gave account to the brethren that since the last meeting hee had paid 2s. (being arreares) to the keeper of the library. Uppon debates what bookes to send for to London to the value of £11 of Mistress Brooke's

[60] John Calvin: *Lexicon Juridicum: Juris Caesarei simul et canonici* (Hanover, 1619)

[61] Martinus Bonacina: *Opera omnia* (Paris, 1632).

[62] Johannes Azorius: *Institutiones morales: in quibus universae quaestiones ad conscientiam recte* (Cologne, 1613)

[63] John Cameron: *Ta sozomena, sive opera partim ab auctore ipso edita* (Geneva, 1658)

[64] Jacobus Arminius: *Iacobi Arminii Veteraquinatis Batavi, ss. Theologiae doctoris eximii, opera theological* (Frankfurt, 1635)

[65] Franciscus Toletus: *Instructio sacerdotum in libros octo distincta* (Rouen, 1619)

[66] Martin de Azpilcueta: *Enchiridion: siue, Manuale confessariorum et poenitentium.*

[67] Cornelius a Lapide: *Commentarii in iv Evangelia* (Lyon, 1638)

[68] Vincentus Filliucius: *Moralium Quaestionum de Christianis Officiis et casibus conscientiae* (Cologne, 1629)

[69] Suidas: *Cuius integram Latinam interpretationem* (Geneva, 1619)

[70] Erasmus Schmid: *Novi Testamenti Jesu Christi graeci, hoc est, originalis linguae tameion (aliis concordantiae)* (Wittenberg, 1638).

[71] Josephus: *Judei historici pre clara opera non parva* (Paris, 1519).

mony yet in Mr Whitefoot's hands it was agreed that Mr Harmer bee desired to write to Mr Whitefoot to lay it out for so many of the bookes under written, as hee can procure for the mony, or such of them as hee shall thinke fit.

Parei opera omnia[72] Tostati opera[73] Sanctij opera omnia[74]

Mr Morrant paid in his money to the library keeper for the last quarter.

At the meeting of ministers in the publike library 9 July 1660. Present at the meeting: Dr [*John*] Collinges, Mr [*Robert*] Harmar, Mr [*John*] Whitefoot, Mr [*Joseph*] Morrant, Mr [*George*] Cock, Mr [*Benjamin*] Snowden.

Mr Whitefoot gave an account to the brethren of his laying out twenty pounds given to the library by Mistress Brookes.

Imprimis as on the bill set downe at the meeting April 9 1660	08	12	00
Item for Sanctius his workes in 9 volumes of which 7 in folios 2 in quarto	04	08	00
Parei opera omnia in 2 volumes folio imp: Francof. 1647[75]	02	08	00
Rivett opera in 3 volumes folio Roterod 1652[76]	03	18	00
Paid for carriage, portage & boxes	00	14	00
Toto	20	00	00

All which were this day brought into the library. [*Line of text cancelled and illegible.*] All ministers present paid in their mony due for the last quarterage to the library keeper.

At a meeting of ministers in the library 13 August 1660. Present: Mr [*George*] Cock, Mr [*Thomas*] Watts, Mr [*John*] Whitefoot, Mr [*Robert*] Harmar, Mr [*Benjamin*] Snowden, Dr [*John*] Collinges.

Mr Watts paid in his quarterage to the library keeper.

At a meeting of ministers in the library 10 September 1660. Present: Mr [*George*] Cock, Mr [*Benjamin*] Snoden, Mr [*Robert*] Harmer, Mr [*Joseph*] Morrant.

At a meeting of ministers in the library 8 October 1660. Present: Mr [*George*] Cock, Dr [*John*] Collinges, Mr [*Robert*] Harmar, Mr [*Joseph*] Morrant, Mr [*John*] Whitefoot. All the ministers present paid their quarterly payment to the library keeper. Mr Snoding & Mr Ellison paid since & Mr Watts.

[72] David Pareius: *Operum theologicorum* (Frankfurt, 1647)
[73] Alphonus Tostatus: *Opera nuperrime vetustissimo* (Venice, 1615)
[74] Gaspar Sanctius: *Opera* (Lyons, 1615–28).
[75] David Pareus: *Operum theologicorum exegeticorum* (Frankfurt, 1647).
[76] André Rivet: *Operum theologicorum* (Rotterdam, 1650).

At a meeting of ministers in the library 12 November 1660. Present: Mr [*Robert*] Harmar, Mr [*John*] Whitefoot, Dr [*John*] Collinges, Mr [*Joseph*] Morrant. Nothing done at this meeting.

At a meeting of ministers in the library 10 December 1660. Present at the meeting: Mr [*George*] Cock, Dr [*John*] Collinges, Mr [*John*] Whitefoot, Mr [*Robert*] Harmar. Mr [*Samuel*] Snowden junior hath paid his quarterage to the library keeper.

At a meeting of ministers in the library 14 January 1661. Present: Mr [*John*] Whitefoot, Mr [*Theophilus*] Ellison, Mr [*George*] Cock, Mr [*Robert*] Harmar, Dr [*John*] Collinges. All present paid their monyes due to the library keeper for the last quarter ending 25 December 1660. The ministers present all agreed in the choice of Mr Harmar to bee library keeper for the next yeare.

11 February 1661. Present: Mr [*George*] Cock, Mr [*Robert*] Harmar, Mr [*Benjamin*] Snowden, Mr [*John*] Whitefoot, Dr [*John*] Collinges, Mr [*Joseph*] Morrant. Mr Snowden & Mr Morrant paid in their quarterage to the under library keeper.

11 March 1661. Present: Dr [*John*] Collings, Mr [*Joseph*] Morrant, Mr [*John*] Whitefoote, Mr [*George*] Cock.

8 April 1661. At the meeting of ministers in the library.
Mr [*George*] Cock, Mr [*John*] Whitefoot, Dr [*John*] Collinges, Mr [*Robert*] Harmar, Mr [*Benjamin*] Snowden, Mr [*Theophilus*] Ellison.
All present paid in their quarterages for the last quarter ending 25 March.

13 May 1661. At the meeting of ministers in the library. Present:
Dr [*John*] Collings, Mr [*George*] Cock, Mr [*Robert*] Harmer, Mr [*John*] Whitefoote, Mr [*Joseph*] Morrant. Mr Morrant & Mr Watts paid their quarteridge to the library keeper.

11 June 1661. Present   Mr [*George*] Cock, Mr [*John*] Whitefoot, Dr [*John*] Collinges, Mr [*Francis*] English, Mr [*Benjamin*] Snowden.

1 July 1661. Present: Mr [*George*] Cock, Mr [*John*] Whitefoot, Mr [*Robert*] Harmar, Dr [*John*] Collings, Mr [*Benjamin*] Snowden. All present paid in their quarterage due to the library keeper. Mr Whitefoot gave an account of £5 in his hands given by Mr Austine Scottow [77] for the use of the library.

---

[77] Augustine Scottow had been one of the Norwich feoffees for impropriation, patrons of the preaching activities of Bishop Matthew Wren's *bête noir*, William Bridge (Evans, pp. 87–8; Reynolds, pp. 162–3).

9 September 1661. Present: Mr [*John*] Whitefoot, Dr [*John*] Collinges, Mr [*Benjamin*] Snowden, Mr [*Robert*] Harmar, Mr [*George*] Cock, Mr [*Joseph*] Morrant. Mr Whitefoot brought in the Criticks of Mr [?Bee's] edition in 9 volumes bought for £14. 15s. of which ten pounds were the remainder of the £20 given by Sir Joseph Pain the other part of £5 given by Mr Augustine Scottow. Mr John Smith[78] was this day admitted to the use of the library.

14 October 1661. Present: Mr [*George*] Cock, Mr S[*amuel*] Snowden, Mr [*Robert*] Harmar, Dr [*John*] Collinges, Mr [*John*] Whitefoot, Mr [*Joseph*] Morrant. Mr Cock, Mr Harmar, Mr Whitefoot, Mr Sam[*uel*] Snowden, *Mr Morrant,* & Dr Collinges paid their quarterage to the library keep[*er*]. Mr [*John*] Hasbart,[79] Mr [*Philip*] Goodwyn[80] & Mr Hanson[81] were all admitted to the use of the library.

11 November 1661. Present: Mr [*George*] Cock, Dr [*John*] Collings, Mr [*Robert*] Harmar, Mr [*John*] Smith, Mr [*John*] Whitefoote, Mr [*John*] Hasbart.
Mr English paid 3 quarters to the library keeper & Mr Snowden and Mr Smith for the last quarter. Mr Smith sent in Fulk on the Rhemish Testament,[82] which hee gave to the library. Dr Collinges sent in Pagnines Thesaurus linguae Hebraicae[83] which he bought for the use of the library at 17s. Thomas Barret[84] Esquire, late alderman of the City, gave £5 to the use of the library, which Mr Cock acknowledged to have in his hand.

[78] Born at Strumpshaw the son of a lawyer, John Smith was admitted a pensioner at Caius College, Cambridge, in 1633. He graduated BA in 1637 and proceeded to MA in 1640. He was ordained in 1640. He was vicar of Rockland until 1676 and vicar of St. Michael Coslany from 1663 to 1676. A rich man, he bequeathed £500 to his wife and £150 to his son, Charles (NRO NCC, 219 Wiseman, Will of John Smith, 1676).

[79] John Hasbert graduated BA from Corpus Christi College, Cambridge, in 1659. Calamy claimed that Hasbert was a Norwich minister and that in 1662 he either resigned or was ejected, but there is no evidence that he was beneficed (Matthews, *Calamy Revised*, p. 252). According to Palmer, he was 'a very rousing, awakening preacher' (Samuel Palmer, *The Nonconformist's Memorial*, London, 1775, p. 202). In his will he is described as 'now of the city of Norwich, minister of the Gospel' (NRO, NCC, 65 Alexander, Will of John Hasbert, 1707). His nephew, Samuel Hasbert, the founder of the *Norwich Gazette*, is mentioned in the will as is Henry Crossgrove, who was at that time working for Samuel Hasbert as a journeyman printer (Stoker, 'The Norwich Book Trades before 1800', p. 96). Hasbert left 'unto my said executors all my books which shall remain at the time of my death to be sold for their advantages'.

[80] Philip Goodwin, rector of Great Moulton, 1661–73.

[81] Possibly Francis Hunston, vicar of Islington, Norfolk, who graduated BA from Queens' College, Cambridge, in 1639, proceeding MA in 1642. He only attended on this one occasion.

[82] William Fulke: *The text of the New Testament translated out of the vulgar Latine by the Papists of the traitorous Seminarie at Rhemes* (London, 1633).

[83] Sanctes Pagninus: *Thesaurus linguae sanctae, sive lexicon Hebraicum* (Lyon, 1575).

[84] A grocer, Barret was sheriff in 1644 and mayor in 1650. During the first civil war he was

At the meeting in December – nothing done.

13 January 1662. Present: Mr [*John*] Whitefoot, Mr [*John*] Hasbout, Mr [*Joseph*] Morrant, Dr [*John*] Collinges, Mr [*Philip*] Goodwin, Mr [*Robert*] Harmar. All the ministers present paid 12d. a piece to the library keeper. All the ministers present chose Mr Harmar for library keeper for the ensuing yeare.

10 February 1662. Present: Mr [*John*] Whitefoot, Mr [*Benjamin*] Snowden, Dr [*John*] Collinges, Mr [*Robert*] Harmar, Mr [*Joseph*] Morrant, Mr Sam[*uel*] Snowden, Mr [*George*] Cock. Mr Snowden senior et junior paid their quarterly payments to the library. Mr Cock also paid the library-keeper.

20 March 1662. Present: Mr [*George*] Cock, Mr [*John*] Whitefoot, Mr [*John*] Hasbout, Mr [*Robert*] Harmar, Mr [*Benjamin*] Snowden, Dr [*John*] Collinges.
Mr Harmar paid in 4s for Theophilact in Latin, which hee bought of the ministers. Mr Whitefoot paid in 5s, beeing the remainder of twenty-five pounds which hee had from Sir Jos[*eph*] Paine & Mr Aug[*ustine*] Scottow to lay out for the use of the library. The ministers present paid the aforesaid summes making 9s. in part of 17s. due to Dr Collinges, which he laid out for Pagnines' Thesaurus linguae sanctae[85] brought into the library.

At the meeting of ministers in the publike library 13 April 1662.
Present at the meeting   Mr [*George*] Cock, Mr [*Samuel*] Snowden junior, Mr [*John*] Whitefoot, Mr [*Robert*] Harmar, Dr [*John*] Collinges, Mr [*Benjamin*] Snowden. All present paid their 12d. apiece to the use of the library keeper. The ministers present agreed that Dr Collinges should have the old Latin Basil which was in the library to spare for the 8s. due to him, and they sold him Theophilact in Latin 2 little octavoes for 2s. which he accordingly paid.

12 May 1662. Present: Mr [*Robert*] Harmar, Mr [*John*] Whitefoote, Mr [*John*] Smith, Mr [*John*] Hasbart, Mr [*Benjamin* or *Samuel*] Snoding, Mr [*George*] Cock. Mr Francis Norris[86] alderman gave * to the use of the

a captain of a company of foot but in 1650 was promoted to the rank of lieutenant colonel. He was a member of the 1648 deputation to Parliament that complained of the royalism of mayor John Utting. In 1654 he was appointed one of the Norfolk commissioners for the ejection of scandalous ministers and the following year was put in command of the military defences of the city (Evans, p. 207). After the Restoration he was compelled to resign his aldermanship.

85 Sanctes Pagninus: *Thesaurus linguae sanctae, sive lexicon Hebraicum* (Lyon, 1575).

86 A successful maltster, Francis Norris was born in St. Andrew's parish in 1600. An opponent of the Long Parliament and of the Republic, he resigned his seat on the common council

library *Biblia Waltoniana in 6 volumes stitched in pastboards, & brought into the library which is to be exchanged for another booke.

9 June 1662. Present: Mr [*Robert*] Harmar, Mr [*John*] Hasbert, Mr [*John*] Whitefoote, Mr [*Benjamin*] Snoden elder, Mr [*George*] Cock, Dr [*John*] Collins, Mr [*John*] Smith.

14 July. Present: Mr [*Robert*] Harmer, Mr [*John*] Hasbert, Mr [*George*] Cock, Mr [*Samuel*] Snoden jun[*ior*], Mr [*John*] Smith. All present paid their 12d. to the use of the library keeper. And Mr Smith also for the quarter before this.

11 August. Present: Mr [*George*] Cock, Dr [*John*] Collings, Mr [*Robert*] Harmer, Mr [*Benjamin*] Snoding sen[*ior*], Mr [*John*] Whitefoote, Mr [*Samuel*] Snoding jun[*ior*]. Dr Collings & Mr Whitefoote paid the library keeper for the last quarter. So did Mr Snoding sen[*ior*]. Mr [*Theophilus*] Ellison also paid for the two last quarters.

13 October 1662. Present: Mr [*John*] Whitefoot, Mr [*Benjamin* or *Samuel*] Snowden, Mr [*Theophilus*] Ellison, Mr [*Robert*] Harmar, Dr [*John*] Collinges, Mr [*John*] Hasbout. All present paid the library keeper for the last quarter ending the 29 of September. Mr Thomasin,[87] bookseller in London, having agreed to allow fourteen pounds for the Biblia Polyglotta given to the library by Mr Alderman Norris <and sent up to Mr Thomasin> & Mr Alderman Barret having (as was before exprest) given £5 (which is yet in hand). The ministers agreed that Mr Harmar should this week send up the Biblia Polyglotta, and that Mr Whitefoot should write to Mr Thomasin to send down Tostatus his *Commentaryes*[88] & H. Stephani *thesaurus linguae Graecae* with the glossary. [89]

13 January 1663. Present: Mr [*George*] Cock, Mr [*John*] Whitefoot, Dr [*John*] Collinges, Mr [*Robert*] Harmar, Mr [*Benjamin* or *Samuel*] Snowden, Mr [*John*] Smith.

in 1642 and compounded out of the shrievalty in 1653. In 1660 he gave £65 as a free gift to Charles II. He died in August 1666. Two members of the library, Robert Harmer and John Whitefoot, were named beneficiaries in his will (TNA, PROB 11/323, f. 120v; Evans, pp. 48, 227n; Reynolds, pp. 175–6).

[87] George Thomason (c.1602–1666), the famous collector of civil war tracts, ran his London bookselling business at St Paul's Churchyard from the 1620s to his death in 1666, supplying the libraries of Oxford and Cambridge Universities. He had many Presbyterian friends including William Prynne and Edward Reynolds, bishop of Norwich after the Restoration.

[88] Alphonso Tostado: *Opera nuperrime vetustissimo originali configurata* (Venice, 1615).

[89] Henri Estienne: *Thesaurus Graecae linguae, ab Henrico Stephano constructus* ([Geneva], 1572).

All the ministers present paid their quarterly pay[ment] for the library keeper. Mr Snowden also paid for Mr Hasbout. This being the day for the choice of the library keeper the ministers present made choice of Mr George Cock to be library keeper for the yeare insuing. Mr Whitefoot reports, that according to the order at the last meeting the Biblia Polyglotta were sent up to Mr Thomasin, but in the sending were by wett something impaired, so that as yet hee could give us no account of what will bee allowed for it.

9 February 1663. Present: Mr [*John*] Whitefoot, Mr [*Benjamin or Samuel*] Snowden, Mr [*Robert*] Harmar, Mr [*George*] Cock, Dr [*John*] Collinges.
The brethren taking notice that no bookes were yet markd as the gift of Sir Jos[*eph*] Paine and Mr Whitefoot acquainting the brethren that he had procured printed pages to this purpose – *ex dono Domini Josephe Paine militis huius civitatis praetoris.* They ordered that some of those papers should be affixed to the 9 volumes of the Critiks,[90] which cost £15 & to the 4 volumes of Gerard's Common places which cost £3. 13s. & to the 2 volumes of Theophilact which cost £1. 2s in all £19. 17s. The other 3s. beeing accounted for the carriage. They also ordered that a like paper be affixed to < Newmans Concordance > Ravanella[91] before given to *the library* by the said Sir Jos[*eph*] Paine.

13 April 1663. Present: Mr [*Robert*] Harmar, Mr [*Benjamin or Samuel*] Snowden, Mr [*John*] Whitefoot, Mr [*John*] Smith, Dr [*John*] Collinges, Mr [*George*] Cock. All present paid their quarterages due 25 March 1663 to the under keeper of the library.

11 May 1663. Present: Mr [*George*] Cock, Mr [*Robert*] Harmar, Mr [*Benjamin or Samuel*] Snowden.

13 July 1663. Present: Mr [George] Cock, Mr [*Benjamin*] Snoding, Mr [*Robert*] Harmar, Dr [*John*] Collings, Mr [*John*] Whitefoote, Mr [*Samuel*] Snowden junior. Tostatus his workes in 14 volumes were received into the library, being the guift of Mr. Francis Norris, alderman. Henrici Stephanij *Thesaurus Linguae Graecae cum Glossario* in 5 volumes being the gift of Mr Thomas Barrett, sometimes mayor of this city, was brought into the library. Mr Whitefoote gave account to the brethren that while hee was at London hee procured Tostatus in 14 volumes for the Biblia Polyglotta formerly sent up to Mr Thomasin, he giving £2. 10s. more in exchange. The carriage of which *up & down with boxes* cost 14s., which summe of

---

[90] *Critici sacri: sive Doctissimorum virorum in ss. Biblia annotations, & tractatus* (London, 1660).
[91] Petrus Ravanellus: *Bibliotheca sacra, seu Thesaurus Scripturae Canonicae* (Geneva, 1650).

£3. 4s. paid in exchange for Tostatus & the mony laid out for carriage was paid to Mr Whitefoot by Fran[cis] Norris, gentleman, alderman of this city. Mr Cock paid to Mr Whitefoot £5 for Stephani Thesaurus &c. above mentioned. All present paid their quarterage to G[oodman] Scot [the under keeper].

12 October 1663. Present: Mr [John] Smith, Mr [John] Whitefoote, Mr [Benjamin] Snoding senior, Mr [George] Cock.
All present (with Dr Collings) paid the library keeper. Mr Thomas Morly,[92] minister of St John's at Timberhill, was admitted into the society of the library.

9 November 1663. Present: Dr [John] Collings, Mr [George] Cock, Mr [John] Smith, Mr [Robert] Harmer, Mr [John] Whitefoote, Mr [Benjamin or Samuel] Snoding.

14 December 1663. Present that day: Mr [George] Cock, Mr [John] Whitefoot, Mr [John] Smith, Dr [John] Collinges, Mr [Robert] Harmer.

11 January 1664. Mr [George] Cock, Mr [John] Smith, Mr [John] Whitefoot & Dr [John] Collinges beeing present all paid their quarterage to the keeper. Which Mr Snowden and Mr Hasbout had paid before.

18 February 1664. The ministers mett but did nothing materiall.

At the meeting of the ministers in the library 14 March 1664. Present: Mr [George] Cock, Mr [John] Whitefoot, Mr [Thomas] Morly, Mr Snowden, Mr [Robert] Harmer, Mr [John] Smith, Dr [John] Collinges.
Mr [Theophilus] Ellison paid his quarteridge to the keeper of the library.

11 April 1664. Present: Mr [George] Cock, Mr [John] Smith, Mr [Robert] Harmar, Mr [Benjamin] Snowden senior.
All present paid their quarterage to the keeper of the library.

9 May 1664. Present: Mr [Robert] Harmar, Mr [Francis] Morly junior,[93] Mr [Samuel] Snowden junior, Dr [John] Collinges, Mr [George] Cock, Mr [John]

[92] Thomas Morley graduated BA from Corpus Christi College Cambridge in 1662, proceeding MA in 1665. According to Venn, he was curate of St. Peter Hungate by 1673. He died in 1679.
[93] Possibly Thomas Morley's younger brother, Francis Morley graduated BA from Corpus Christi College, Cambridge, in 1656, proceeding MA in 1659. He is not referred to as being admitted to the Library so presumably did not become a member at this time. He joined on 1 April 1679, after Thomas Morley's death. His widow was recorded as paying his arrears to the library keeper on 2 June 1685.

Whitefoote. Dr Collings paid his quarterage to the library keeper. So also did Mr Morly & Mr Snowden junior had before done it, so also had Mr Whitefoot.

13 June 1664. Present: Mr [George] Cock, Mr [Benjamin or Samuel] Snowden, Mr [Robert] Harmar, Mr [John] Whitefoot, Dr [John] Collings, Mr [Thomas] Morly. Dr Collinges acquainting the ministers that Mr Alderman Man had an intention to give to the use of the library the new Bible ready bound with the volume of the lexicon already extant & his right to the other volume & the said Dr Collinges offering to exchange the < said booke > bible & lexicon for other bookes which hee had a desire to part with. The ministers present agreed uppon the following bookes to bee received of Dr Collinges and entred as the guift of Mr Alderman Mann[94] viz:

Vasquez in Thomam in 7 volumes folio[95]
Buxtorfij Lexicon: Rabbin[icum][96]
Chrysostom in 8 volumes ex editione Saviliana[97]
Gomarus in 3 volumes folio[98]
Silburgij Στυμολογικου μεγά [99]
Sigonij opera in 5 volumes[100]
Gualther in 12 volumes folio[101]
Funcij Chronologia [102]
In all 38 folios
Mr Morly brought in Ludolphus *de vita Christi*[103] to be added to the library.

11 July 1664. Present: Dr [John] Collings, Mr [George] Cock, Mr [Robert] Harmer, Mr [John] Whitefoot, Mr [Samuel] Snoden, Mr [Thomas] Morly, Mr [John] Smith. All present paid the librarie keeper. Mr Scamler,[104] Mr Toft,[105] Mr Beresford[106] were then admitted to the use of the librarie. Mr

---

[94] For John Mann see above n. 25.

[95] Gabriel Vasquez: *Opera omnia* (Antwerp, 1621)

[96] Johann Buxtorf: *Lexicon Hebraicum et Chaldaicum* (Basle, 1631)

[97] John Chrysostom: *Opera Graece. Cura Henry Savilii edita* (Eton, 1611)

[98] Franciscus Gomarus: *Opera theologica omnia* (Amsterdam, 1644)

[99] Fridericus Sylburgius: *Etymologicon magnum* (Heidelberg, 1594).

[100] Carolus Sigonius: *Opera* (Frankfurt and Basle, 1559–1604).

[101] Rudolph Gualther: *Opera* (Zurich and Leiden, 1568–85).

[102] Johann Funk: *Chronologia, hoc est omnium temporum* (Wittenberg, 1601)

[103] Ludolf von Sachsen: *Vita Jesu Christi e quatuor Evangeliis et scriptoribus orthodoxis* (Antwerp, 1618).

[104] John Scambler was admitted sizar at Clare in 1660 and graduated BA in 1664. By 1687 he was vicar of Eaton.

[105] Thomas Toft, son of Thomas Toft, rector of St. Michael at Plea, gained his BA at Pembroke College in 1664.

[106] Possibly Michael Beresford, who graduated from St John's College Cambridge in 1643, proceeding MA in 1646. He was vicar of Terrington and rector of Hopton, Suffolk, from 1660 to 1677.

Snoden junior paid the library keeper. All the ministers present agreed in a petition to the Mayor, Sheriffs, Aldermen &c at Court of Common Councell for the addition of a roome to the library and the better shelving of it. They further desired Mr George Cock and Mr Beresford to present the petition to the Common Councell at their next assembly. Mr Chamberlain[107] having first viewed the roome & computed the charge.

8 August 1664. Present: Dr [*John*] Collings, Mr [*George*] Cock, Mr [*Robert*] Harmar, Mr [*John*] Whitefoot, Mr [*Thomas*] Toft, Mr [*John*] Smith, Mr [*Thomas*] Morly, Mr [*Benjamin or Samuel*] Snowden. Admitted to the use of the library Mr [*Richard*] Ireland.[108]

12 September 1664. Present: Mr [*George*] Cock, Mr [*Robert*] Harmar, Mr [*Richard*] Ireland, Mr [*John*] Whitefoot, Mr [*John*] Smith, Mr [*Thomas*] Morly.

10 October 1664. Present: Mr [*John*] Whitefoote, Mr [*Richard*] Ireland, Mr [*Thomas*] Toft, Mr [*Michael*] Beresford, Mr T[*homas*] Morley, Mr [*Robert*] Harmar. All present paid the library keeper.

14 November 1664. Present: Mr [*George*] Cock, Dr [*John*] Collinges, Mr [*Thomas*] Morly, Mr [*John*] Whitefoot, Mr [*Benjamin or Samuel*] Snowden, Mr [*Robert*] Harmar, Mr [*John*] Smith. Dr Collings & Mr Snowden paid their quarterage due to the library keeper. Mr Reinulph Tench[109] was admitted to the use of the library. Mr Smith paid the library keeper & Mr Cock. Mr [*Richard*] Ferrar[110] was admitted to the use of the library, 12 December 1664.

---

[107] In 1664 the City Chamberlain was Thomas Cocke (T. Hawes, *An Index to Norwich City Officers*, Norfolk Record Society LII, 1989, p. xxxix).

[108] Born in Norwich in the parish of St Michael at Plea, Richard Ireland graduated BA from Clare College Cambridge in 1630. He was rector of St. Edmund's, Norwich, from 1638 to 1690 and died in September 1690 aged 80. He bequeathed all his books, except for two English Bibles, to the library. Several library members were mentioned in his will. John Toft, Benjamin Penning and John Shaw were to be pall bearers and John Connould, John Whitefoot and his son, also John, were left sums of money. John Jeffery's wife, formerly an Ireland, was also mentioned. John Burton and John Connould wre witnesses (TNA DEL 10/52, Will of Richard Ireland, 1690). Thanks are due to Jenifer Edmonds for tracing Ireland's will.

[109] Randolph Tench was admitted sizar aged 16 at St. John's College, Cambridge, on 14 June 1656, graduating BA in 1660 and proceeding MA in 1663. He was vicar of Scarning in 1662 and rector of Brampton, Suffolk, from 1662 to 1681.

[110] Richard Ferrer was ordained deacon in 1635. He was usher at Norwich School from 1655 to 1667. In 1661 he sent a petition to the Norwich Members of Parliament protesting that Dr John Collinges had established a rival school under Mark Lewis ('A Glimpse of Norwich Grammar School under Cromwell', *The Norvicensian*, Easter 1928, pp. 2–7).

9 January 1665. Present: Mr [*George*] Cock, Mr [*Richard*] Ferrar, Dr [*John*] Collinges, Mr [*John*] Smith, Mr [*Thomas*] Morly, Mr [*Michael*] Berisford, Mr [*John*] Scamler. Mr Snowden not present but had paid the library keeper. Mr John Whitefoot paid the library keeper. All present paid the library keeper and chose Mr Smith the library keeper for the insuing yeare.

13 February 1665. Present: Mr [*George*] Cock, Mr [*Robert*] Harmer, Mr [*John*] Whitefoot, Mr [*Richard*] Ireland, Mr [*Thomas*] Toft, Mr [*Randolph*] Tench. Mr [*Thomas*] Morly, Mr [*Benjamin*] Snowden senior.

10 Aprill 1665. Present: Dr [*John*] Collings, Mr [*Benjamin*] Snowden senior, Mr [*Randolph*] Tench, Mr [*Thomas*] Morley, Mr [*John*] Smyth, Mr [*Robert*] Harmor, Mr [*John*] Whitefoot, Mr [*Thomas*] Toft, Mr [*Richard*] Ireland. All present payd the library keeper. Mr [*Theophilus*] Ellison. Mr [*Richard*] Ferrer payd the under librarie keeper before. Mr [*George*] Cock payd the under library keeper.

10 July 1665. Present: Mr [*Robert*] Harmer, Mr [*Samuel*] Snowden junior, Dr [*John*] Collinges, Mr [*Benjamin*] Snowden senior, Mr [*Thomas*] Morley. All present with Mr [*Richard*] Ferrer paid the library keeper.

9 October 1665. Present: Mr [*Benjamin*] Snowden senior, Mr [*John*] Smyth. Mr [*Robert*] Harmar, Mr Snowden senior, Mr Snowden junior, Mr Smyth payd the under librarie keeper. Mr [*Randolph*] Tench payd. Mr Morley payd.This day was brought into the librarie an old concordance made in the reygne of Edward the Sixt which was given by Samuell Fromantell,[111] citizen.

8 January 1666. Present: Mr [*George*] Cock, Mr [*Thomas*] Morley. Mr Cock, Mr [*Robert*] Harmer, Mr [*John*] Whitefoot, Mr [*John*] Smith & Mr Morley paid the library keeper.

9 April 1666. Present: Mr [*John*] Whitefoote, Mr [*John*] Smith, Mr [*Thomas*] Morley. All present paid the library keeper. Mr [*Richard*] Ferrar. / At the same tyme brought in by Mr Whitefoote *Pugio fidei per Reymundum Martini*[112] and by Mr [*Joshua*] Meene[113] *Catena Graecorum Collectore Niceta* * in

---

[111] A freeman of Dutch descent, Samuel Fromantell had been apprenticed to Andrew Prime, a mercer, in 1630 (P. Millican, *The Register of the Freemen of Norwich*, Norwich, 1954, p. 224). He was buried at St Gregory's on 15 June 1670 (W.C.T. Moens, *The Walloons and their Church in Norwich*, Lymington, 1887–8, p. 125).

[112] Ramon Marti: *Pugio fidei Raymundi Marti Ordinis Praedicatorum Adversus Mauros, et Judaeos*, 1651.

[113] Joshua Meene was curate of St. Peter Permountergate. When he made his will in 1689 he was living in Yarmouth. He instructed his executor to sell his books 'for the best price' to

librum Jobi, * in one piece *[114] [and] Eusebius' *Ecclesiastical History*[115] to the use of the library. Mr Harmar paid the library keeper.

14 May 1666. Present: Mr [*George*] Cock, Mr [*Robert*] Harmer, Mr [*John*] Whitefoote. Brought into the library of the gift of Dr Thomas Browne,[116] doctor of physick, Justij Lipsij *opera* in 9 volumes, 4to.[117]

June 10 1666. Present: Mr [*George*] Cock, Mr [*Robert*] Harmer, Mr [*John*] Whitefoote, Mr [*Thomas*] Morly, Mr [*Benjamin or Samuel*] Snowden, Mr [*Richard*] Ferrer. Mr Thomas Bloome[118] was admitted to the use of the library. Mr Morly hath paid the library keep[*er*] till midsomer. Mr Cock and Mr Whitefoote paid the library keeper for 3 quarters. So did Mr Harmer and Mr Snoding sen[*ior*].

July 8 1666. Present: Mr [*George*] Cock, Mr [*Thomas*] Bloome, Mr [*Thomas*] Morley, which three paid the library keep[*er*]. Mr [*Thomas*] Toft paid the library keeper for halfe a yeare. Mr [*Benjamin*] Snowdon senior paid the library keep[*er*].

October 14 1666. Present: Mr [*George*] Cock, Mr [*John*] Whitefoote, Mr [*Benjamin or Samuel*] Snoding, Mr [*Thomas*] Morly, Mr [*Thomas*] Bloome. All present paid the library keeper with Mr [*Richard*] Ferrer. Mr Samuel Chapman[119] was admitted to the use of the library.

defray his debts. He wished his funeral to be 'modest' and 'sparing' since it contributed nothing to the advantage of the dead and was 'of no moment' to the living (NRO ANW 169/273, Will of Joshua Meene, 1689).

[114] *Catena Graecorum patrum in beatum Job collectore Niceta Heracleae Metropolita ex duobus MSS Bibliothecae Bodleianae codicibus* (London, 1637).

[115] Eusebius of Caesarea: *Eusebii Pamphili...Ecclesiastica Historia* (Basle, 1611).

[116] Dr Thomas Browne, author of *Religio medici* and a lifelong friend of John Whitefoot, had lived in Norwich since 1637.

[117] Justus Lipsius: *Opera omnia* (Antwerp, 1606–17).

[118] A Norwich man, Thomas Bloome was admitted sizar at Caius College in 1633, graduating BA in 1638 and proceeding MA in 1642. Ordained in Norwich in 1639 he was rector of Broome in 1643, Taverham in 1660, curate of St Giles in 1672 and rector of St Edmund's from 1673 to 1680. He left his 'library of bookes' to James Halman, Fellow of Caius College, Cambridge (NRO ANW 373, Will of Thomas Bloome, 1680).

[119] Samuel Chapman, rector of Thorpe St Andrew and co-founder with his wife, Mary, of the Bethel Hospital, had been ejected or had resigned from his living at Yoxford in Suffolk in 1662. However, as he grew older he appears to have become increasingly orthodox, that is if his choice of friends had any confessional significance. Two of the witnesses to his will were John Graile, rector of Blickling, and Alderman Peter Thacker. Graile was a Tory anti-exclusionist. According to Humphrey Prideaux, Thacker was a 'sturdy Tory' who played a major part in the attempted exclusion of a Whig candidate for the Norwich aldermanry in 1705 on the grounds that he was 'turbulent, malicious...and of uncivil behaviour in conversation'. The only certain thing about Chapman was his intellectual bent. He left money to found a scholarship in Hebrew

8 December 1666. Present: Present Mr [*George*] Cock, Mr [*Benjamin*] Snowdon sen[*ior*], Mr [*Samuel*] Chapman, Mr [*Richard*] Ferrer, Mr [*Thomas*] Morley, Mr [*Thomas*] Bloome, Mr [*Robert*] Harmer. Mr Benedict Rively[120] admitted to the use of the library.

January 13 1667. Present: Mr [*George*] Cock, Mr [*John*] Whitefoote, Mr [*Benedict*] Rively, Mr [*Thomas*] Morley, Mr [*Samuel*] Chapman, Mr [*Thomas*] Bloome, Mr [*Robert*] Harmer. Mr Cock, Mr Whitefoote, Mr Harmer, Mr Chapman, Mr Snowdon senior, Mr Morley paid the library keeper & soe did Mr Bloome. Mr Thomas Morley was chosen library keep[*er*] for the insuing yeare.

9 March 1667. Present: Mr [*George*] Cock, Mr [*Robert*] Harmer, Mr [*John*] Whitefoote, Mr [*Benjamin*] Snowden senior, Mr [*Samuel*] Chapman, Mr [*Benedict*] Rively, Mr [*Thomas*] Morley, by whom it was then ordered that the 2 shelves should be changed & set fast.

13 Aprill 1667. Present: Mr [*George*] Cock, Mr [*Samuel*] Chapman, Mr [*Richard*] Ferrer, Mr [*Benedict*] Rively, Mr [*Thomas*] Morley all present paid the library keep[*er*]. Mr Harmer & Mr Snowden senior paid the library keep[*er*]. Mr [*Nicholas*] Norgate[121] was admitted to the use of the library.

---

at Corpus Christi College, Cambridge, his former College. He also left money for the purchase of 'English protestant practical books' for the inmates of the Great Hospital. His own books he left to his wife (NRO, NCC, 33 Edwards, Will of Samuel Chapman, 1700).

[120] Benedict Riveley was admitted sizar at Emmanuel College Cambridge in 1644, graduating BA in 1649 and proceeding MA in 1652. He was curate of St Andrew's from 1679 to 1694. Chaplain to Edward Reynolds, bishop of Norwich, he preached Reynolds' funeral sermon at Norwich cathedral in 1676. The sermon echoed John Whitefoot's funeral sermon on bishop Joseph Hall with its call for another Elisha to follow 'this going Elijah'. Riveley emphasised Reynold's learning: 'What Melanchton was used to say – that himself was a logician, Pomeranus a grammarian, Justin Jonas an orator, but Luther was all; might be in a fuller way applied to this person we are speaking on'. He presented Reynolds as a civilising force after the ravages of the civil war. Reynolds came 'in our gore...This was he that entered our Augean Stable in its filth, and reduced it to that degree of cleanliness wherein you can find it'. He stigmatised nonconformists as 'absurd and unreasonable men' since they considered the words 'good' and 'bishop' incompatible. But Reynolds had succeeded in neutralising them. Riveley was a bookish man. In his will he gave to his son-in-law, Joseph Ellis, who had joined the library in 1685, 'all the books on the uppermost shelf in my study from one end to the other and what other sermon books my executor pleases to part with' (NRO, NCC, 40 Jones, Will of Benedict Riveley, 1694). Riveley bequeathed his portrait to his wife. A rich man, he owned significant amounts of property in Norwich and King's Lynn.

[121] Born at Aylsham, Nicholas Norgate was admitted sizar at Trinity College Cambridge in 1658, graduating BA in 1662 and proceeding MA in 1665. He was curate of St Simon and St Jude in 1668 and died in 1675.

8 June 1668. Present: Mr [*John*] Whitefoote, Mr [*Robert*] Harmer, Mr [*Richard*] Ferrer, Mr [*Benedict*] Rively, Mr [*Samuel*] Chapman, Mr [*Nicholas*] Norgate, Mr [*Thomas*] Morley, Mr [*George*] Cock, Mr [*Benjamin*] Snowden sen[*ior*]. Brought into the library of the gift of Mr [*William*] Oliver[122] bookseller Pererius in Genesin.[123]

July 13 1668 . Present: Mr [*Richard*] Farrer, Mr [*Nicholas*] Norgate, Mr [*Thomas*] Morley, Mr [*George*] Cock all present paid the library keep[*er*] with Mr [*Benedict*] Rively.

August 9 1668. Present: Mr [*John*] Whitefoote, Mr [*Samuel*] Chapman, who both paid the library keeper. Mr [*George*] Cock & Mr [*Thomas*] Bloome, who also hath paid the library keep[*er*].

September 14 1668. Present: Mr [*George*] Cock, Mr [*John*] Whitefoote, Mr [*Richard*] Ferrer.

12 October 1668. Present: Mr [*Benedict*] Rively, Mr [*Nicholas*] Norgate, Mr [*Thomas*] Morley, all present with Mr [*John*] Whitefoote paid the library keep[*er*]. Mr [*George*] Cock & Mr [*Robert*] Harmer paid also and Mr [*Benjamin*] Snowdon senior and Mr [*Richard*] Ferrer.

9 November 1668. Present: Mr [*George*] Cock, Mr [*Robert*] Harmer, Mr [*John*] Whitefoote, Mr [*Richard*] Ferrer, Mr [*Samuel*] Chapman, Mr [*Benedict*] Rively, Mr [*Benjamin*] Snowden sen[*ior*], Mr [*Nicholas*] Norgate, Mr [*Thomas*] Morley, Mr Chapman paid the library keeper for *a* quarter<age> due the 29 September.

11 January 1669. Present: Mr [*Richard*] Ferrer, Mr [*Nicholas*] Norgate, Mr [*Thomas*] Morley, Mr [*Benedict*] Rively, all present paid the library keep[*er*] & soe did Mr [*George*] Cock, Mr [*Samuel*] Chapman & Mr [*Benjamin or Samuel*] Snowdon. Mr [*John*] Whitefoote paid the library keep[*er*].

12 April 1669. Present: Mr [*George*] Cock, Mr [*Nicholas*] Norgate, Mr [*Thomas*] Morley, who paid the library keeper with Mr [*Samuel*] Chapman, Mr [*John*] Whitefoote, Mr [*Robert*] Harmer, Mr [*Richard*] Ferrer, Mr [*Benjamin or Samuel*] Snowdon.

---

[122] William Oliver was a Norwich bookseller active between 1662 and 1689. He published a number of works by royalist clergy, including three titles by John Winter, rector of Dereham, and established a close relationship with the city administration. He had the responsibility of entertaining visiting preachers and frequently supplied books for use in the Mayor's Court. He died in 1689 (D. Stoker, 'The Norwich Book Trades before 1700', *Cambridge Bibliographical Society*, 8 (1981) p. 113).

[123] Benedictus Pererius: *Commentariorum et disputationum in Genesim*. Coloniae Agrippinae, 1606. [Gk. 9]

10 May 1669. Present: Mr [*George*] Cock, Mr [*Richard*] Ferrer, Mr [*Nicholas*] Norgate, Mr [*Thomas*] Morley. Mr Henry Mazey,[124] Master Free Schoole admitted to the use of the library.

14 June 1669. Present: Mr [*John*] Whitefoote, Mr [*Samuel*] Chapman, Mr [*Thomas*] Morley. Mr Robert Connold[125] was admitted to the use of the library.

12 July 1669. Present: Mr [*George*] Cock, Mr [*Samuel*] Chapman, Mr [*Thomas*] Morley, who paid the library keep[*er*]. Soe did Mr [*Robert*] Harmer & Mr [*Nicholas*] Norgate & Mr [*Richard*] Ferrer.

August 9 1669. Present: Mr [*George*] Cock, Mr [*John*] Whitefoote, Mr [*Benedict*] Rively, Mr [*Richard*] Ferrer, Mr [*Nicholas*] Norgate, Mr [*Samuel*] Chapman. Mr Rively paid for 2 quarters past & Mr [*Benjamin*] Snowden sen[*ior*] paid the library keep[*er*] for the last quarter.

11 October 1669. Present: Mr [*George*] Cock, Mr [*Richard*] Ferrer, Mr [*Benjamin*] Snowden senior, Mr [*Robert*] Conold, Mr [*Thomas*] Morley, all present paid the library keep[*er*] with Mr [*Nicholas*] Norgate & soe did Mr [*Robert*] Harmer & Mr [*Benedict*] Rively.

10 January 1670. Present: Mr [*George*] Cock, Mr [*Robert*] Harmer, Mr [*Samuel*] Chapman, Mr [*Thomas*] Morley, who paid the library keeper, & so did Mr [*Benjamin or Samuel*] Snowden. / & Mr [*John*] Whitefoote, Mr [*Benedict*] Rively, & Mr [*Nicholas*] Norgate paid the Library keeper /
All present chose Mr Benjamin Snowdon library keeper for the ensuing yeare

[124] Henry Mazey was headmaster of Norwich School from 1665 to 1677 as well as holding the livings of Rockland and Egmere (Saunders, pp. 286–8). In his will he asked that his books 'be safely kept and preserved' for the use of his children 'if any of them shall be capable of the use of them' (NRO DCN III 174, Will of Henry Mazey, 1677).

[125] Robert Connold graduated BA from Corpus Christi College, Cambridge, in 1659–60, proceeding MA in 1663. He was rector of Bergh Apton from 1668 until his death in 1715 (G.I. Kelly, *The Book of Bergh Apton*, Tiverton, 2005, pp. 59–60). On 31 January 1676 he delivered the annual sermon on Charles I's execution on the text, 'And that we may be delivered from unreasonable and wicked men'. His religious affiliation is clear. In a letter to Sir William Cooke he claimed that he was 'as far from despondency as a Presbyterian is from modesty & loyalty, & that you will grant to be distance enough' (Bodleian Library, Tanner MS 37, f. 226). In the same letter he quoted a stanza from the *Cavaliers Litanie:* 'From the mass & the Directory bound in one volume/, from the Cabal of Trent & the Dort what do you call um/, From the worshippers of Saints & them that Peter and Paul um/, Libera Nos'. Connold found himself in trouble with his diocesan when he suggested that not one single soul in the great Turk's dominions should be damned or any of the Moors of Africa because they were Mohammedans, though he could not find anything in the Bible that gave these 'aliens' any entitlement to heavenly bliss (Bodleian Library, Tanner MS 27, f.1). Three of his children became ministers.

14 February 1670. Present: Mr [*Robert*] Harmer, Mr [*Benjamin or Samuel*] Snowdon, Mr [*Benedict*] Rively, Mr [*Nicholas*] Norgate, Mr [*Thomas*] Morley, Mr [*Samuel*] Chapman. Mr Peter Cushing[126] was admitted to the use of the library.

14 March 1670. Present at the meeting: Mr [*Richard*] Farrar, Mr [*Benedict*] Rively, Mr [*Thomas*] Morley, Mr [*Nicholas*] Norgate, Mr [*George*] Cock, Mr [*John*] Whitefoot, Mr [*Peter*] Cushing, Mr [*Benjamin or Samuel*] Snowden.

Aprill 11 1670. Present at the meeting: Mr [*George*] Cock, Mr [*Peter*] Cushing, Mr [*Thomas*] Morley, Mr [*Nicholas*] Norgate, Mr [*Benjamin or Samuel*] Snowden, who all paid the library keeper. So did Mr [*Benedict*] Riveley.

9 May 1670. Present Mr [*John*] Whitefoote, Mr [*Richard*] Ferrer (who all paid the library keep*er*), Mr [*Samuel*] Chapman, Mr [*Robert*] Connold, Mr [*Robert*] Harmer also have paid & Mr [*George*] Cock, Mr [*Peter*] Cushing, Mr [*Thomas*] Morley, Mr [*Benedict*] Riveley & Mr [*Benjamin or Samuel*] Snowden paid. Brought into the library the rest volumne of Mr Poole his Synopsis Criticorum[127] being the gift of Mr John Barnham.[128]

June 13 1670. Present at the meeting: Mr [*George*] Cock, Mr [*Richard*] Ferrer, Mr [*Thomas*] Morley, Mr [*Nicholas*] Norgate, Mr [*Benedict*] Riveley, Mr [*Benjamin or Samuel*] Snowden.

July 11 1670. Present: Mr [*Richard*] Ferrer, Mr [*Samuel*] Chapman, Mr [*Thomas*] Morley, Mr [*George*] Cock, who all payd the library keeper, so did Mr [*Peter*] Cushing, & Mr [*Benjamin or Samuel*] Snowden, Mr [*John*] Whitefoot & Mr [*Nicholas*] Norgate.

August 8 1670. Present at the meeting: Mr [*George*] Cock, Mr [*Robert*] Harmar, Mr [*John*] Whitefoot, Mr [*Richard*] Ferrer, Mr [*Samuel*] Chapman, Mr [*Peter*] Cushing, Mr [*Thomas*] Morley, Mr [*Nicholas*] Norgate, Mr [*Benjamin or Samuel*] Snowden.

---

[126] Peter Cushing graduated BA from Corpus Christi College Cambridge in 1644, proceeding to MA in 1647. He was rector of Lessingham from 1662 to 1672 and also rector of Eccles. He bequeathed to his son, Jedidiah, £5 worth of his books 'for him to take the same when he will' (NRO NCC 419 Alden, Will of Peter Cushing, 1671).

[127] Mathew Poole: *Synopsis criticorum aliorumque S. Scripturae interpretum.*

[128] John Barnham, a hosier, held dissenting meetings at his house in St John Maddermarket in 1669. The ministers involved were Dr John Collinges and Benjamin Snowden (C.B. Jewson, 'Return of Coventicles in Norwich Diocese 1669', *Norfolk Archaeology*, 33, 1965, p. 15).

7 October 10 1670. Present at the meeting: Mr [*George*] Cock, Mr [*Robert*] Harmer, /Mr [*Samuel*] Chapman & Mr [*Peter*] Cushing, / Mr [*Thomas*] Morley, Mr [*Nicholas*] Norgate, Mr [*Richard*] Ferrer, Mr [*Robert*] Conold, who all payd the library keeper, with Mr [*Benjamin or Samuel*] Snowden. Mr [*John*] Watson[129] admitted to the use of the library.

November 14 1670. Present: Mr [*George*] Cock, Mr [*John*] Whitefoote, Mr [*Peter*] Cushing, Mr [*John*] Watson, Mr [*Thomas*] Morley. Mr [*John*] Whitefoote then paid the library keeper.

December 12 1670. Present: Mr [*George*] Cock, Mr [*John*] Whitefoot, Mr [*Richard*] Ferrer, Mr [*Thomas*] Morley, Mr [*Nicholas*] Norgate, Mr [*Benedict*] Rively who payd the library keeper, Mr [*Robert*] Conold, Mr [*Benjamin or Samuel*] Snowden.

January 9 1671. Present: Mr [*Robert*] Harmer, Mr [*Samuel*] Chapman, Mr [*John*] Watson, Mr [*Benjamin or Samuel*] Snowden, who all payd the library keeper < & agreed that the next meeting day a new library keeper should be chosen > with Mr [*George*] Cock & Mr [*Benedict*] Riveley.

February 13 1671. Present at the meeting: Mr [*George*] Cock, Mr [*Peter*] Cushing, /Mr [*Benedict*] Riveley,/ Mr [*Samuel*] Chapman, Mr [*John*] Watson, Mr [*Benjamin or Samuel*] Snowden. Mr [*Peter*] Cushing payd the library keeper with Mr [*John*] Whitefoot & Mr [*Richard*] Ferrer.

March 13 1671. Present: Mr [*Richard*] Ferrer, Mr [*Nicholas*] Norgate, Mr [*John*] Watson, Mr [*Benjamin or Samuel*] Snowden, Mr [*George*] Cocke. Mr [*John*] Connould [130] was admitted to the use of the library. Mr [*Thomas*] Morley payd the library keeper.

---

[129] Born at Salle and educated at Norwich School, John Watson graduated BA at St John's College, Cambridge, in 1664 and proceeded MA at Corpus Christi in 1667. He was vicar of Wroxham from 1665 to 1692 and rector of Hingham from 1683 to 1727. He died in 1727.

[130] John Connold graduated BA from Trinity College, Cambridge, in 1667–8 and proceeded MA in 1671. He was rector of Catfield from 1680 to 1708, Vicar of St Simon and St Jude from 1683 to 1708 and vicar of St Stephen's from 1683 to 1708. A minor canon at the Cathedral, he also held the positions of gospeller, precentor and sacrist. He refused to take the oath of allegiance to King William and, after a third warning, was expelled from the Cathedral choir. A subscriber to Thomas Mace's *Musick's Monument,* published in 1676, he composed anthems and chants for performance at the Cathedral (T. Roast, 'Composers of Norwich Cathedral, 1620–1819', PhD UEA, 1998, p.77). In 1702 the mayor and aldermen invited him to produce a report on Norwich School (Saunders, p. 366). In his will he asked to be buried 'with as little charge, pomp or ceremony as is consistent with decency'. He left £190 to his wife and £100 to his daughter (NRO NCC 122 Alexander, Will of John Connold, 1708). One of the witnesses to the will was John Francis, another library member.

Aprill 10 1671. Present: Mr [*John*] Whitefoot, Mr [*Richard*] Ferrer, Mr [*Thomas*] Morley, Mr [*Robert*] Harmer, Mr [*Benedict*] Riveley, Mr [*Robert or John*] Connould, Mr [*Benjamin or Samuel*] Snowden, who al payd the library keeper, so did Mr [*George*] Cock & Mr [*Nicholas*] Norgate.

May 8 1671. Present: Mr [*Benedict*] Riveley, Mr [*Samuel*] Chapman, Mr [*Nicholas*] Norgate, Mr [*Thomas*] Morley, Mr [*Robert or John*] Conold, Mr Chapman payd the library keep[*er*] for the last quarter.

July 10 1671. Present: Mr [*George*] Cock, Mr [*Nicholas*] Norgate, Mr [*Robert or John*] Conold, Mr [*Benjamin or Samuel*] Snowden, Mr [*Thomas*] Morley, who all payd the library keeper & Mr [*John*] Watson who payd for two quarters. And Mr [*Benedict*] Riveley.

August 14 1671. Present at the meeting: Mr [*George*] Cock, Mr [*John*] Whitefoot, Mr [*Richard*] Ferrer, Mr [*Thomas*] Morley, Mr [*Nicholas*] Norgate, Mr [*John*] Watson, Mr [*Robert or John*] Conold, Mr [*Benjamin or Samuel*] Snowden, Mr [*John*] Whitefoot. Mr Ferrer, Mr [*Peter*] Cushing payd the library keeper for the quarter preceeding.

September 11 1671. At the meeting: Mr [*George*] Cock, Mr [*Robert*] Harmar, Mr [*Richard*] Ferrer, Mr [*Benedict*] Riveley, Mr [*Thomas*] Morley, Mr [*Benjamin or Samuel*] Snowden.

October 9 1671. Present at the meeting: Mr [*George*] Cock, Mr [*John*] Whitefoot, Mr [*Richard*] Ferrer, Mr [*Benedict*] Riveley, Mr [*Thomas*] Morley, Mr [*Nicholas*] Norgate, Mr [*Robert or John*] Conold, Mr [*Benedict or Samuel*] Snowden, who all payd the library keeper. So did Mr [*John*] Watson. Mr Ottenfeld[131] was the same day admitted to the use of the library.

November 13 1671. Present: Mr [*Richard*] Ferrer, Mr [*Thomas*] Morley, Mr [*Nicholas*] Norgate, Mr [*Robert or John*] Conold, Mr Ottenfeild. Mr [*Robert*] Harmar payd the library keeper & Mr [*Samuel*] Chapman for two quarters.

December 11 1671. Present at the meeting: Mr [*John*] Whitefoot, Mr [*Robert*] Harmar, Mr [*Thomas*] Morley, Mr [*Nicholas*] Norgate, Mr [*Robert*] Conold senior, Mr [*Benjamin or Samuel*] Snowden.

8 January 1672. Present at the meeting Mr [*Robert*] Harmar, Mr [*Nicholas*] Norgate, Mr [*John*] Watson, *Mr [*Benjamin or Samuel*] Snowden,* who all

---

[131] Possibly a visitor attached to the Dutch Church. He disappears from the record after 13 November 1671.

payd the library keeper. So did Mr [*George*] Cock & Mr [*Benedict*] Riveley & Mr [*Richard*] Ferrer & Mr [*Thomas*] Morley, * Mr [*John*] Whitefoot & Mr [*John*] Connould junior, Mr [*Samuel*] Chapman. * Mr [*John*] Barnham[132] sent in the 2d volume of Pool's Synopsis.[133] The ministers present chose Mr Norgate library keeper for the year following.

February 12 1672. Present at the meeting: Mr [*George*] Cock, Mr [*John*] Whitefoot, Mr [*Richard*] Ferrer, Mr [*Benjamin or Samuel*] Snowden, Mr [*Thomas*] Morly, Mr [*John*] Watson, Mr [*John*] Connould junior, Mr [*Nicholas*] Norgate.

March 11 1672. Present at the meeting: Mr [*George*] Cock, Mr [*Samuel*] Chapman, Mr [*Thomas*] Morly, Mr [*John*] Watson, Mr [*John*] Connould junior, Mr [*Nicholas*] Norgate. Mr Robert Bayfield [134] was admitted to the use of the library.

Aprill 15 1672. Present at the meeting: Mr [*Thomas*] Morley, Mr [*John*] Watson, Mr [*Robert or John*] Connould & Mr [*Nicholas*] Norgate all then paid the library keeper, so did Mr [*Robert*] Harmer, Mr [*Benjamin or Samuel*] Snowden & Mr [*George*] Cock. Mr [*Benedict*] Riveley also payd the library keeper for the quarter. Mr Thomas Nelson[135] was admitted to the use of the library.

June 10 1672. Present at the meeting: Mr [*George*] Cock, Mr [*John*] Whitefoot, Mr [*Thomas*] Morley, Mr [*John*] Watson, Mr [*John*] Connould junior, Mr [*Thomas*] Nelson, Mr [*Benjamin or Samuel*] Snowden, Mr [*Benedict*] Rively.

July 7 1672. Present at the meeting: Mr [*George*] Cock, Mr [*Robert*] Harmar, Mr [*Thomas*] Morly, Mr [*Thomas*] Nelson, & Mr [*Nicholas*] Norgate all paid the library keeper. So did Mr [*Benjamin or Samuel*] Snowden & so did Mr [*John*] Watson & Mr [*John*] Whitefoote.

August 12 1672. Present at the meeting: Mr [*Robert*] Connould senior, Mr [*John*] Watson, Mr [*Thomas*] Nelson & Mr [*Nicholas*] Norgate & Mr [*John*]

---

[132] For John Barnham see above n. 128.

[133] Matthew Poole: *Synopsis criticorum aliorumque S. Scripturae interpretum* (London, 1669–76)

[134] Robert Bayfield was admitted sizar at Trinity College Cambridge in 1668, graduating BA in 1672 and proceeding MA in 1675. He was ordained in Norwich in November 1673.

[135] It is clear from his will that Thomas Nelson owned a house in the parish of St Andrew's, conveniently near the library. He bequeathed all his books to the library, to be delivered 'at the charge' of his executrix. He also asked for his sermon notes 'whether in single papers or books' to be burned 'as soon as they shall come to [his executrix's] hands' (NRO NCC, 106 Melchior, Will of Thomas Nelson, 1714).

Whitefoote & Mr [*Robert*] Harmar. Mr [*Benedict*] Rivily & Mr [*Thomas*] Morly. Mr Thomas Studd [136] was admitted to the use of the library.

October 14 1672. Present at the meeting: Mr [*George*] Cock, Mr [*Robert*] Harmar, Mr [*Thomas*] Morley, Mr [*Thomas*] Nelson & Mr [*Nicholas*] Norgate all paid the library keep[*er*] & Mr [*Benedict*] Rivily, Mr [*Benjamin* or *Samuel*] Snowden & Mr [*John*] Watson & Mr [*Thomas*] Studd. Mr [*Robert* or *John*] Connould also paid him for two quarters.

November 11 1672. Present at the meeting: Mr [*Robert*] Harmar, Mr [*Benedict*] Rivily, Mr [*Thomas*] Morly, Mr Connold, Mr [*Thomas*] Nelson, Mr [*Robert*] Bayfield & Mr [*Nicholas*] Norgate & Mr [*Thomas*] Studd.

December 9 1672. Present: Mr [*John*] Whitefoote, Mr [*John*] Watson, Mr [*John* or *Robert*] Connold, Mr [*Thomas*] Nelson, Mr [*Robert*] Bayfield. Mr [*John*] Whitefoote paid the library keeper for last quarter. Mr [*Thomas*] Morley was also present & Mr Bayfield paid the librarie keeper for the last quarter.

January 13 1673. Present: Mr [*John*] Whitefoot, Mr [*Robert*] Harmar, Mr [*Benedict*] Rively, who all payd the library keeper. Mr [*Benjamin* or *Samuel*] Snowdon paid the library keeper for last quarter & so did Mr [*Thomas*] Morly & Mr [*Thomas*] Nelson & Mr [*George*] Cock.

February 10 1673. Present: Mr [*George*] Cock, Mr [*Benedict*] Rively, Mr [*Thomas*] Morley, Mr [*John* or *Robert*] Connould, Mr [*Thomas*] Nelson.

March 10 1673. Present: Mr [*George*] Cock, Mr [*John*] Whitefoot, Mr [*Benedict*] Rively, Mr [*Thomas*] Morly, Mr [*Robert* or *John*] Conold, Mr [*Thomas*] Nelson, Mr [*John*] Watson, who then paid the librarie keeper for the last quarter. Mr [*Robert*] Harmar was also present.

April 14 1673. Present: Mr [*George*] Cock, Mr [*Thomas*] Studd, Mr [*Thomas*] Nelson, who paid the library keeper for the last quarter; Mr Stud paid also for the former quarter. Mr [*Nicholas*] Norgate was also present, & payd the library keeper 2 quarters. Mr Benjamin Penning[137] was admitted to the

[136] Thomas Studd graduated BA from Caius College, Cambridge, in 1665. He was curate of Earl Stonham in 1665, rector of Great Waldingfield, also Suffolk, in 1670 and curate of St Mary Coslany, Norwich, in 1673. He tutored the Norwich-born philosopher and theologian, Samuel Clarke (Branford, p. 228).

[137] A pupil of Norwich School, Benjamin Penning was admitted sizar at Magdalen College, Cambridge, in 1663, graduating BA in 1667 and proceeding to MA in 1670. He was chaplain of St Paul and St James in 1673 and rector of St Clement's from 1680 to 1696. He left prints of the universities of Oxford and Cambridge to the library. He also gave £25 to the widows and orphans of clergymen charity to be administered by John Jeffery and John Whitefoot

use of the library. So was Mr William Ostlir[138] then admitted to the use of
the library.

11 May 1673. Present: Mr [*John*] Whitefoote, Mr [*Benedict*] Rively, Mr
[*Thomas*] Morley, Mr [*Thomas*] Nelson all have paid the library keep[*er*]. Dr
Jackson's workes in 3 volumes folio[139] were brought into the library, of the
gift of Mr Anthony Norris[140] citizen. Seneca's works in folio Latin[141] was
likewise brought into the library of the gift of *Mr* W[*illia*]m Oliver,[142]
bookseller.

July 14 1673. Present at the meeting: Mr [*John*] Watson, Mr [*Thomas*]
Studd, Mr [*Benjamin*] Penning, Mr [*Thomas*] Nelson & Mr [*Nicholas*]
Norgate; all paid the library keeper & so did Mr [*William*] Ostler. Mr
[*Benjamin* or *Samuel*] Snowden paid two quarters. Mr Joshua Balliston[143]
was then admitted to the use of the library. Mr [*Robert* or *John*] Connould
paid the library keeper for 3 quarters last past & Mr [*George*] Cock and Mr
[*John*] Whitefoot for one quarter. Mr [*Thomas*] Morly. Mr [*Robert*] Harmer
paid the library keeper for two quarters.

11 August 1673. Present at the meeting: Mr [*George*] Cock, Mr [*John*]
Whitefoote, Mr [*Thomas*] Morly, Mr [*Joshua*] Balliston, Mr [*Robert* or *John*]
Connould, Mr [*Thomas*] Stud, Mr [*Thomas*] Nelson & Mr [*Richard*] Norgate
& Mr [*William*] Ostler.

8 September 1673. Present at the meeting: Mr [*John*] Whitefoot, Mr
[*Joshua*] Balliston, Mr [*Benjamin*] Penning & Mr [*Thomas*] Nelson & Mr
[*Benedict*] Riveley.

---

junior. He was close to the Cathedral clergy. He left mourning rings to the Dean, Dr Fairfax,
Humphrey Prideaux, Nathaniel Hodges and Charles Trimnell (NRO, NCC, 171 Jones, Will of
Benjamin Penning, 1696).

[138] William Ostler was admitted sizar at Peterhouse in 1666 and graduated BA in 1670. He
was probably rector of Rackheath from 1671 to 1686 and rector of Crostwick from 1672.

[139] Thomas Jackson, *The works of the reverend and learned divine, Thomas Jackson* (London, 1673)

[140] The son of Francis Norris, Anthony Norris, a maltster, served as churchwarden at St
Andrew's in 1675. He restored the communion rails to their pre-civil war position 'to prevent
dogs pissing against [them] and other prophanations and abuses' and when the vestry refused
to reimburse his costs took the case to the archdeacon's court (Reynolds, p.176).

[141] Lucius Annaeus Seneca: *The workes of Lucius Annaeus Seneca, both morrall and naturall*
(London, 1614)

[142] For William Oliver see above n. 122.

[143] Joshua Balliston matriculated as a pensioner from Corpus Christi College, Cambridge,
in 1650, graduating BA in 1653 and proceeding MA in 1659. He was rector of Catfield.

13 October [*1673*]. Present: Mr [*Thomas*] Morley, Mr [*Joshua*] Ballestone, Mr [*Benjamin*] Penning, Mr [*Thomas*] Nelson, who all paid the library keeper for last quarter. Mr [*Nicholas*] Norgate was also present & paid the library keeper. So did Mr [*Robert*] Harmar, Mr [*John*] Whitefoot, Mr [*Benjamin* or *Samuel*] Snowdon, Mr [*Thomas*] Studd.

/ 10 November / [*1673*] Present: Mr [*John*] Whitefoot, Mr [*Thomas*] Morley, Mr [*Joshua*] Balleston, Mr [*Nicholas*] Norgate, Mr [*Benjamin*] Penning, Mr [*Thomas*] Studd, Mr [*Thomas*] Nelson, Mr W[*illiam*] Ostler. Mr Ostler paid last quarter to the library keeper.

December 8 1673. Present: Mr [*Thomas*] Morley, Mr [*Nicholas*] Norgate, Mr [*Benjamin*] Penning, Mr [*Thomas*] Nelson, Mr [*Robert* or *John*] Connould. Mr James Symonds[144] then admitted to the use of the library.

12 January 1674. Present at the meeting: Mr [*Benedict*] Rivily, Mr [*Henry*] Mazey, Mr [*Thomas*] Morly, Mr [*John*] Watson, Mr [*Robert* or *John*] Connould, Mr [*Thomas*] Nelson, Mr [*James*] Symonds. All paid the library keeper the year's arrears & so did Mr [*Benjamin* or *Samuel*] Snowden & Mr [*Robert*] Harmer & Mr [*William*] Ostler. Received into the library 18 volumes of Suarez,[145] which was bequiathed by the Reverend Mr George Cock, minister lately of St. Peter's.[146] Received from Mr Whitefoot Sir Thomas Brown's *Vulgar Errors*[147] etc. & 2 sermons of his.[148] The former was Sir Thomas Brown's gift. The ministers then present did elect Mr Rively library keeper for the following year and they did appoynt that Mr [*Nicholas*] Norgate should against their next meeting bring in a catalogue of the bookes to be delivered to the court and that he shall see that the bookes given to the library in his time be fayrely written in the vellam booke appointed to that purpose. It was then also consented that Mr Riveley and Mr Morley should attend uppon the court to crave their order for appoynting the time for the ministers meeting at the library for future to be upon the first Tuesday in every moneth.[149] And also for the taking downe of the waynscott doores.[150]

---

[144] Born in Norwich, James Symonds was admitted pensioner at St John's College Cambridge in 1667, graduating BA in 1672 and proceeding MA in 1675. In 1675 he was appointed curate of Havering in Essex.

[145] Francisco Suarez: *Opera omnia* (1614–29).

[146] St Peter Mancroft, Norwich.

[147] Sir Thomas Browne: *Pseudodoxia epidemica* (London, 1672).

[148] John Whitefoot: *Israea agchithanes, Deaths alarum, or, the presage of approaching death* (London, 1656). Another edition was published in 1657.

[149] The ministers had formerly met on the second Monday every month.

[150] Presumably wooden doors fitted to the shelving to provide additional security for the books. Both requests were granted by the City Assembly on 24 February 1674. On the orders of the City Chamberlain the doors were converted into shelves (NRO NCR Case 16d/8, Assembly folio book of proceedings, 1668–1707, f. 39).

February 9 1674. Present: Mr [*John*] Whitefoot, Mr [*John*] Watson, Mr [*Benjamin*] Penning, Mr [*Thomas*] Nelson, Mr [*James*] Symonds, Mr [*Benedict*] Riveley, Mr [*Joshua*] Ballistone, Mr [*Nicholas*] Norgate. Mr Penning and Mr Whitefoot then paid the library keeper for the quarter past. Mr [*Robert*] Harmar was here present also. Mr [*Thomas*] Tenison[151] was then admitted to the use of the library. Mr [*John*] Barnham sent in the third volume of Pool's Synopsis.[152]

9 March 1674. Present: Mr [*John*] Whitefoot, Mr [*Thomas*] Tennison, Mr [*John*] Watson, Mr [*Thomas*] Morley, Mr [*Robert* or *John*] Connold, Mr [*James*] Simonds, Mr [*Joshua*] Ballistone, Mr [*Benedict*] Riveley, Mr [*Thomas*] Nelson. Memorandum. By order of the court and Assembly of this city we agree that for time to come our meeteng at the library shall be on the first Tuesday in every moneth, & by the same authority we have also leave to take downe the waynscott doores which now conceale the bookes.

April 7 1674. Present: Mr [*Nicholas*] Norgate, Mr [*Thomas*] Nelson, Mr [*Joshua*] Balleston, Mr [*Benjamin*] Penning, Mr [*Benedict*] Rively, Mr [*William*] Ostler, Mr [*John*] Whitefoot, Mr [*Thomas*] Tennison, Mr [*Thomas*] Morley &c. This being the quarter day the persons aforesayd all payd the library keeper, and so did Mr [*Thomas*] Studd, Mr [*Benjamin* or *Samuel*] Snowden though not present, so did Mr [*James*] Simonds. I doe acknowledge that I have receivd the legacy of Mr Nath[*aniel*] Cock, Merchant of London to the library of Norwich from the hands of Mr Edmund Cock[153] of Norwich his executor which was twenty pounds. Ben[*jamin*] Riveley, Library Keeper.

May 5 1674. Present: Mr [*Thomas*] Morley, Mr [*Nicholas*] Norgate, Mr [*Robert* or *John*] Connould, Mr [*Benjamin*] Penning, Mr [*Thomas*] Nelson, Mr [*Benjamin*] Riveley. Mr [*John*] Watson who then payd the library keeper, as did also Mr Connould. Mr [*Henry*] Macey also paid the library keeper.

[151] Thomas Tenison was a pupil at Norwich School. He graduated from Corpus Christi College, Cambridge, in 1657. He was very well connected. His uncle married Ann Mileham, Sir Thomas Browne's sister-in-law. It has been suggested that he owed his appointment as minister of St Peter Mancroft to his connection with Sir Thomas, the most prominent member of the Mancroft congregation. Tenison remained a member of the library until 2 March 1675. On 6 April 1675 he donated George Codinus' *De officiis et officialibus magnae ecclesiae et aulae* (1625), Edward Herbert's *Religio gentilium* (1643), Peter Heylyn's *Historia quinquarticularis* (1660) and the *Racovian catechism*.

[152] Matthew Poole: *Synopsis criticorum aliorumque S. Scripturae interpretum* (London, 1669–76)

[153] Edmund Cock was a common councillor for Wymer Ward in Norwich in 1648 and again from 1660 to 1685 (Hawes, p. 39).

June 2 1674. Present: Mr [*John*] Whitefoot, Mr [*Thomas*] Tenison, Mr [*John*] Watson, Mr [*Benjamin*] Penning, Mr [*Thomas*] Nelson, Mr [*Joshua*] Balliston, Mr [*Benedict*] Riveley.

July 7 [*1674*]. Present att this meeting: Mr Nich[*olas*] Norgate, Mr [*John*] Watson both paid the librarie keeper. Mr [*Robert*] Harmer also paid the librarie for 2 quarters. Present also Mr [*Henry*] Mazey, Mr [*Robert or John*] Connold who also paid the librarie keeper. Mr Joshua Balleston was present allsoe & payd the librarie keeper. So did Mr [*Thomas*] Morley & Mr [*Thomas*] Nelson.

August 4 1674. Present at the meeting: Mr [*Joshua*] Balliston, Mr [*Thomas*] Morley, Mr [*John*] Watson. Mr [*Benjamin*] Penning was also present & paid the library keeper for the last quarter.

1 September 1674. Present: Mr [*Robert*] Harmer, Mr [*John*] Whitefoot, Mr [*Thomas*] Tennison, Mr [*Thomas*] Morley, Mr [*Benjamin*] Penning. Mr [*John*] Whitefoot & Mr [*Thomas*] Tenison paid the library keeper. Present also Mr [*Benjamin*] Riveley who also then payd the library keeper. Memorandum. We then ordered the binding of Scaliger de emendatione temporum.[154]

October 6 1674. Present: Mr [*John*] Whitefoot, Mr [*Thomas*] Tennison, Mr [*Benedict*] Riveley, Mr [*Joshua*] Balliston, Mr [*Nicholas*] Norgate, Mr [*Thomas*] Studd, all which payd the library keeper for the quarter ending at Michaelmas last past. Mr William Harmer,[155] Mr Anthony Buxton [156] were this day admitted to the use of the library. Mr [*Thomas*] Morley was also present and payd the library keeper. Mr John Ellisworth,[157] physician, put in to the Library two books viz Francis Georgij Veneti Problemata in SS Script:[158] & ejusdem Harmonia Mundi.[159]

November 3 1674. Present: Mr [*John*] Whitefoot, Mr [*Thomas*] Tennison, Mr [*Benedict*] Rively, Mr [*James*] Balliston, Mr [*Benjamin*] Penning, who then payd the library keeper for the quarter past. Present also Mr [*Thomas*]

---

[154] Joseph Scaliger, *De emendatione temporum* (Geneva, 1629).

[155] The son of Robert Harmer, William Harmer was admitted pensioner at Clare College in 1667, graduating BA in 1671 and proceeding MA in 1674. He was ordained in Norwich in 1674 and became rector of Stiffkey in 1679. He died in 1702.

[156] Born in Norwich, Anthony Buxton was admitted sizar at Caius College in 1665, graduating BA in 1669. He was rector of Sisland and Swardeston from 1674 to 1713 and rector of Thwaite from 1690 to 1713. He died in 1713.

[157] For John Ellsworth see below n. 164.

[158] Francesco Giorgio: *Francisci Georgii Veneti in scripturam sacram problemata*.

[159] Francesco Giorgio: *Francisci Georgii Veneti Minoritanae familiae, De harmonia mundi totius cantica tria* (Paris, 1546).

Morley, Mr [*William*] Harmer jun[*ior*], Mr [*William*] Kelynge,[160] who was this day admitted to the use of the library. Then Mr [*Benjamin* or *Samuel*] Snowden paid the library keeper. This day Mr [*John*] Whitefoot gave to the library another booke viz Grigorij Sayrj Casus Conscientii in folio.[161] We bound a new Scaliger de emendatione temporum.[162]

December 1 1674. Present: Mr [*John*] Whitefoot, Mr [*Thomas*] Morley, Mr [*Robert* or *John*] Connold, Mr [*Nicholas*] Norgate, Mr [*James*] Balliston, Mr [*Benedict*] Riveley. Mr Connold now payd the library keeper for the quarter last past.

January 5 1675. Present: Mr [*Robert* or *William*] Harmer, Mr [*John*] Whitefoot, Mr [*Benedict*] Riveley, Mr [*Thomas*] Morley, Mr [*James*] Ballistone, who all paid the library keeper.

February 2 1675. Present: Mr [*Nicholas*] Norgate, Mr [*John*] Watson, who then payd the library keeper for the quarter past. Present also Mr [*Thomas*] Morley, Mr [*Benedict*] Riveley, Mr [*William*] Harmar junior, Mr [*Robert* or *John*] Connold.

March 2 1675. Present: Mr [*John*] Whitefoot, Mr [*Thomas*] Tennison, Mr [*Thomas*] Morley. Mr Tennison paid the library keeper for the last quarter. Mr Thomas Tenison brought into the library Bishop Ussher's *Chronologia sacra*.[163] Dr John Ellsworth[164] was then admitted to the use of the library.

April 6 1675. Present: Dr [*John*] Ellsworth, Mr [*John*] Watson, Mr [*Nicholas*] Norgate, Mr [*Benedict*] Rively, who all paid the library keeper. Mr [*Thomas*] Tenison sent in as his gift to the library Codinus *de officiis &c. Ecclesiae & Aulae Constantinopolitanae*, folio, graecum latinum,[165] Herbert *de religio gentilium* in 4to,[166] Heylinij *Historia Quinqua articularis*,[167]

---

[160] William Kelling was admitted pensioner at Trinity College, Cambridge, in 1637. He was vicar of St Peter Southgate, Norwich, in 1673 and rector of All Saints from 1680 to 1685. He died in 1685.

[161] Gregory Sayer: *Cauis regia sacerdotum, casuum conscientiae siue theologiae moralis thesauri locos omnes aperiens* (Münster, 1628).

[162] Ordered to be bound on 1 September 1674.

[163] James Ussher: *Chronologia sacra sive chronologia annorum regum Israelis et Judae, ad calculum redacta et illustrata* (Oxford, 1660).

[164] John Ellsworth, a medical doctor, was never ordained. In 1678 he was chosen library keeper. On 6 August 1678 he was referred to as 'lately deceased'.

[165] George Codinus: *Georgius Codinus Cupropalata De officiis et officialibus magnae ecclesiae et aulae Constantinopolitanae*. (Paris, 1625).

[166] Edward Herbert: *De religione gentilium* (Amsterdam, 1663)

[167] Peter Heylyn: *Historia quinqua articularis: or, a declaration of the judgement of the western churches and more particularly of the Church of England* (London, 1660)

4to, the *Racovian catechism*, 12o.[168] Mr [*William*] Harmar junior was also present.

May 4 1675. Present: Dr [*John*] Ellsworth, Mr [*John*] Whitefoot, Mr [*Benedict*] Riveley, Mr [*Benjamin*] Penning who now payd the library keeper for halfe a yeare. Mr Whitefoot paid Scott [*the under keeper*] his quarteridge last past.

June 1 1675. Present: Mr [*John*] Whitefoot, Mr [*Benjamin*] Penning, Dr [*John*] Ellsworth, Mr [*William*] Harmar junior, Mr [*Benedict*] Riveley.

July 6 1675. Present: Mr [*John*] Watson, Mr [*William*] Harmar junior, Mr [*Benedict*] Riveley, who all payd the library keeper. Mr [*Benjamin*] Penning was also present and paid the library keeper. Mr [*John*] Toft jun[*ior*][169] was also admitted to the use of the library.

August 3 1675. Mr [*Thomas*] Stud, who paid the library keeper for 2 quarters. Dr [*John*] Ellsworth paid the library keeper for the last quarter & Mr [*Benedict*] Riveley.

September 7 1675. Present: Mr [*John*] Whitefoot, Dr [*John*] Ellsworth, Mr [*Benedict*] Riveley.

October 5 1675. Mr [*John*] Watson, Mr [*Thomas*] Toft & Mr [*Robert* or *John*] Connould paid the library keeper. So did Mr [*Thomas*] Morley, Dr [*John*] Ellsworth, Mr [*William*] Harmar junior.

November 2 1675. Present: Mr [*Thomas*] Stud & Mr [*Benedict*] Riveley, who both payd the library keeper. Mr [*Steven*] Paynter[170] also was then admitted to the use of the library. Mr [*Thomas*] Morley present. Mr [*Benjamin*] Penning also payd the library keeper.

January 4 1676. Present: Dr [*John*] Ellsworth, Mr [*Thomas*] Morley, Mr [*Benedict*] Riveley, who then payd Goodman Scott his quartridge. Mr [*John*] Watson was this day chosen library keeper for the yeare following.

---

[168] Matthias Flacius: *Ecclesiastica Historia, integrum Ecclesiae Christi ideam quantum ad locum* (Basle, 1562–74)

[169] John Toft was admitted pensioner at St Catherine's College, Cambridge, in 1665, graduating BA in 1669 and proceeding MA in 1673. He was ordained in Norwich in 1673.

[170] Steven Painter was admitted sizar at Trinity College, Cambridge, in 1667 and graduated BA in 1672, proceeding MA in 1675. He was rector of St Michael at Plea and died in 1689.

1 February 1676. Present: Mr [*John*] Whitefoote, Mr [*Benedict*] Riveley, Mr [*Thomas*] Morley, Mr [*John*] Watson, Mr [*William*] Harmer jun[*ior*], Mr [*Steven*] Painter, Mr Whitefoote paid the librarie for 3 quarters. Mr Watson, Mr Harmer *jun[*ior*],* Mr Painter for the last quarter. Mr [*John*] Whitefoot jun[*ior*][171] was admitted. Mr Whitefoot sen[*ior*], Mr Morley, Mr Watson & Mr Harmer jun[*ior*] paid Mr Riveley 6d. a piece towards 5s. 9d. he laid out in binding books.

7 March 1676. Present: Mr [*William*] Harmer ju[*nior*], Mr [*Steven*] Painter & Mr [*Thomas*] Morley. Memorandum: Mr [*Benedict*] Riveley, library keeper for the two years last past, having within that his time received twenty pounds of Mr Edmund Cock mercer in Norwich of the legacy of Mr Nathaniel Cock[172] merchant in London to the library of the city of Norwich, & having layd out the said summe of twenty pounds according to the intent of the donor in such books as the ministers of the city & members of the library thought usefull & needfull for the same (whose names are all fayrely written in the Vellam Book) is hereby discharged of the said money.

April 4 1676. Present: Dr [*John*] Ellsworth, Mr [*Benedict*] Riveley, Mr [*Thomas*] Studd, Mr [*Benjamin*] Penning, who all payd the library keeper for the last quarter & Mr Studd for one quarter before also, and so did Mr Penning.

May 2 1676. Present: Mr [*Thomas*] Morley and Mr [*Steven*] Painter, who both paid the library keeper for the last quarter. Mr Thomas Bradford[173] was then admitted to the use of the library. Mr [*Benedict*] Rivelry present also.

June 6 1676. Present: Mr [*Benedict*] Rively, Mr [*Thomas*] Bradford, Dr [*John*] Elsworth, Mr [*John*] Watson, who paid the librarie keeper for the last quarter.

[171] John Whitefoot, the son of John Whitefoot, rector of Heigham, was admitted pensioner at Caius College, Cambridge, in 1663, graduating BA in 1668 and proceeding MA in 1671. He was a Fellow of the College between 1671 and 1677. In 1676 he became rector of Hellesdon and succeeded his father as rector of Heigham in 1682. He died in 1731 and was buried at St Gregory's.

[172] Nathaniel Cock, Edmund Cock's brother, was a wealthy merchant living in the London parish of St Mary Woolnoth, so wealthy that he was able to leave his wife, Joanne, besides his best wrought-iron bed, £1200 in money and, for every year she lived after his decease, another £400. His brother, Edmund, was left £1000. Money was also left to the parish of St John de Sepulchre in Norwich where he had been born and £50 was to be distributed to 'such Godly ministers as need' (TNA PROB 11/342, Will of Nathaniel Cock, 1672).

[173] Born in Norwich, Thomas Bradford was admitted sizar at Caius College in 1643, graduating BA in 1647 and proceeding MA in 1651. He was rector of Winterton and Somerton from 1656 to 1662, master of Yarmouth Grammar School in 1667, chaplain of Norwich City Gaol and curate of St Augustine's, Norwich, and of St Margaret and St Swithin. At his death he was resident in St Lawrence's parish (NRO ANW A 26, Administration of Thomas Bradford, 1683).

July 4 1676. Present: Mr [*Thomas*] Bradford, Mr [*Steven*] Paynter, Mr [*Benjamin*] Penning, Mr [*Benedict*] Riveley who all payd the library keeper for the quarter ending at Midsummer last past.

August 4 1676. Present: Mr [*Thomas*] Bradford, Mr [*Thomas*] Morley & Mr [*John*] Watson, of which the 2 last paid the librarie keeper for the last quarter.

September 5 1676. Present: Mr [*Benedict*] Riveley, Mr [*Thomas*] Morley & Mr [*Steven*] Painter.

3 October 1676. Present: Mr [*John*] Whitefoot *sen[*io*]r,* Mr [*Benedict*] Riveley, Mr [*John*] Whitefoot jun[*ior*], Mr [*John*] Watson. Mr [*William*] Cecil,[174] who was then admitted to the use of the library. Memorandum. Mr Whitefoot *sen[*io*]r* paid the library keeper for 3 quarters last past. Mr Riveley payd him for the past quarter ending at Michaelmas, so did Mr Penning. Mr Whitefoot jun[*io*]r paid him for the two last quarters ending at Michaelmas. Mr Whitefoot sen[*io*]r reported to the company the receipt of twenty pounds of the gift of the Lord Bishop[175] late deceased to the augmentation of this library. Mr Watson paid the library keeper. Mr [*Thomas*] Morley who also paid the library keeper. Dr [*John*] Elsworth was present & did likewise pay the library for the 2 last quarters.

November 7 1676. Present att this meeting: Mr [*Benedict*] Riveley, Mr [*Thomas*] Bradford, Mr [*Thomas*] Morley, Dr [*John*] Ellsworth, Mr [*Steven*] Painter, Mr [*John*] Watson. Mr Bradford & Mr Painter paid the librarie keep[*er*].

December 5 1676. Present at this meeting: Mr [*John*] Whitefoote sen[*io*]r, Mr [*Thomas*] Morley, Mr [*William*] Cecill, Dr [*John*] Elsworth, Mr [*Thomas*] Bradford.

2 January 1677. Present: Mr [*John*] Whitefoot sen[*ior*], Mr [*Thomas*] Morley, Mr [*Robert* or *John*] Connould, Mr [*John*] Whitefoot ju[*nio*]r, Mr [*Steven*] Painter, Mr [*William*] Cecill, who all paid the library keeper for the last quarter. Dr Hawkins[176] was then admitted to the use of the library.

---

[174] William Cecil was one of the very few members of the Library who does not appear to have attended university. (NRO NCC, 225 Melchior, Will of William Cecil, 1715).

[175] Edward Reynolds, bishop of Norwich from 1661 to 1676.

[176] William Hawkins graduated BA from Magdalen College, Oxford, in 1653. He was a Fellow of his College from 1653 to 1659 and became a Doctor of Divinity in 1676. Vicar of Drayton in 1662 and rector of Hellesdon in 1663, he was a Cathedral Prebend from 1667 to 1691 (J. Foster, *Alumni Oxoniensis*, ii, Oxford, 1891, p. 677).

February 6 1677. Present at this meeting: Mr [*Benedict*] Riveley, Mr [*Thomas*] Bradford, Mr [*Thomas*] Morley, Mr [*Steven*] Painter, Mr [*John*] Watson. Mr Bradford, Mr Riveley & Mr Watson paid the librarie keeper.

March 6 1677. Present at this meeting: Mr [*John*] Whitefoote, Mr [*Benedict*] Riveley, Mr [*Thomas*] Bradford, Dr [*John*] Elsworth, who paid the librarie keep[*er*], Mr [*Robert or John*] Conold, Mr [*Steven*] Painter, Mr [*John*] Watson & Mr [*Thomas*] Morley.

April 3 1677. Present at this meeting: Mr [*John*] Whitefoot sen[*ior*], Mr [*Thomas*] Bradford, Mr [*Thomas*] Morley, Mr [*Steven*] Painter, Mr [*Benedict*] Rively, who all paid the library keeper.

July 3 1677. Present at this meeting: Mr [*Benjamin*] Penning, who paid the librarie keeper for three quarters, Mr [*John*] Watson who paid the librarie keeper for halfe a year.

August 7 1677. Present at this meeting: Mr [*Benjamin*] Penning, Mr [*Thomas*] Morly, Mr [*Steven*] Painter, Mr [*John*] Whitefoote sen[*io*]r, Mr [*John*] Whitefoote jun[*io*]r, all present paid the library keeper. Mr Whitefoote *sen[*io*]r* reported to the company the payment of twenty pound to Mr Will[*iam*] Oliver in full for bookes bought of him, with the money given by the late byshop of Norwich.[177] Thomas Studd paid then.

October 2 1677. Present: Mr [*John*] Whitefoot sen[*ior*], Mr [*Thomas*] Bradford, Mr [*Thomas*] Morley, Mr [*Benedict*] Riveley, who all payd the library keeper for this quarter. So did also Mr [*John*] Watson though absent.
November 6 1677. Present at this meeting: Mr [*Steven*] Painter & Mr [*John*] Watson. Mr Painter paid the librarie keeper.

December 4 1677. Present then: Mr [*John*] Whitefoot sen[*io*]r, Mr [*Thomas*] Bradford, Mr [*Benedict*] Rively, Mr [*Thomas*] Morley, Mr [*Robert and John*] Connold, Mr [*Thomas*] Studd, Mr [*William*] Cecil, who payed the library keeper to this day.

15 January 1678. Present att this meeting: Mr [*John*] Whitefoote sen[*ior*], Mr [*Thomas*] Bradford, Mr [*Benedict*] Riveley, Mr [*Robert or John*] Conold, Mr [*Thomas*] Studd, Mr [*Steven*] Painter, Mr [*John*] Whitefoote jun[*io*]r, Mr [*Thomas*] Morley, Mr [*John*] Watson, all which paid the library keeper

---

[177] Bishop Edward Reynolds (1599–1676). Reynolds left £20 to the library, a gift that was minuted on 3 October 1676.

to this day. And Mr [*John*] Burton[178] was admitted. Dr John Elsworth was also chosen librarie keeper for the ensuing year. / *pointing hand* / All that were then present did also order that all persons that will continue the use & benefitte of the librarie shall pay for every omission of meeting upon the day appointed the forfeiture of two pence, no exception to be admitted for absence. And the said forfeitures are to be dispos'd of every halfe year according *as* the major part of persons at the meeting shall determine.

February 5 1678. Present: Mr [*Thomas*] Bradford, Mr [*Benedict*] Riveley, Mr [*Thomas*] Morly, Mr [*John*] Watson, Mr [*John*] Burton and John Ellsworth, who paid the library keeper to this day. Dr Simon Blenkerne[179] and Mr John Horne [180] was [*sic*] then admitted to the use of the library.

March 5 1678. Present: Mr [*Thomas*] Bradford, Mr [*John*] Burton, Mr [*Thomas*] Morley, Mr [*Benedict*] Rively, Mr [*John*] Watson, Mr [*John*] Horne John Ellsworth.

2 April 1678. Present: Mr [*John*] Whitefoote sen[*io*]r, Mr [*Benedict*] Rively, Mr [*Steven*] Painter, Mr [*John*] Watson, who all paid the library keeper. Mr James Verdon[181] admitted to the use of the library.
[signed] John Ellsworth.

May 7 1678. Present: Dr [*Simon*] Blenkarne, Mr [*Thomas*] Bradford, Mr [*Thomas*] Morly, who all paid the library keeper. Mr [*Steven*] Painter.
[signed] John Ellsworth.

June 4 1678. Present: Mr [*Thomas*] Bradford, Mr [*Thomas*] Morly, Mr [*John*] Burton, Mr [*John*] Watson, Mr [*John*] Horne, Mr [*Steven*] Painter. Mr Burton

---

[178] John Burton (1629–99) was headmaster of Norwich School from 1677 to 1699. He was author of a history of Norwich Cathedral Carnary, published posthumously in 1712 (Saunders, pp. 290–3).

[179] Simon Blenkarne was born in York and graduated BA from Merton College Oxford in 1669. He is recorded as having donated a skeleton 'done by himself' to St Margaret's library, King's Lynn (NHC, KL 018.2, St Margaret's Library Catalogue). On 22 September 1674 he was made a freeman of Lynn (KL/C7/11, King's Lynn Hall Book, 532r). He was living in King's Lynn when he drew up his will (NRO ANW 13 23, Will of Simon Blenkarne, 1689). His sister-in-law was married to John Connold (NRO ANW 26, Will of Jane Blenkarne, 1689).

[180] John Horne was admitted pensioner at Caius College in 1659, graduating BA in 1663 and proceeding MA in 1666. He was Usher of Lynn Grammar School in 1668 and headmaster from 1678 to 1728. He was never ordained. He died in 1732.

[181] Born in Mutford, Suffolk, James Verdon graduated BA in 1674 and proceeded MA in 1677. He was ordained in Norwich in 1675 and was rector of East Dereham from 1677 to 1741. He died in 1741.

paid the library keeper. And Mr Horne. Mr Will[iam] Newton[182] admitted to the use of the library.

John Ellsworth.

July 2 1678. Present: Dr [Simon] Blenkarne, Mr [Benedict] Rively, Mr [John] Burton, Mr [Thomas] Bradford, Mr [Thomas] Morly, Mr [Robert or John] Connold, Mr [William] Cecil, Mr [Thomas] Studd, Mr [John] Horne, Mr [John] Whitefoot jun[io]r, who all paid the under library keeper to this day.

Received of the forfeitures	5	2
Expended by order	4	2
Rests	1	0

Mr [John] Watson sent by his guift Barrhadij *Commentaria* 2 vol. folio[183]

[signed] John Ellsworth

August 6 1678. Present: Mr [John] Whitefoot sen[ior], Mr [John] Watson, Mr [Robert or John] Connould, Mr [Benedict] Rively, Mr [Thomas] Morley, Mr W[illia]m Cecill. Mr John Connould then chosen library keeper in the place of Dr John Elsworth lately deceased. Mr Whitefoot sen[ior] & Mr Watson paid the library keeper to the last quarter. Present also Mr [John] Burton, Mr [John] Horn, Dr [Simon] Blenkarne.

3 September 1678. Present: Mr [John] Whitefoote sen[io]r, Mr [Benedict] Rively, Dr [Simon] Blenkarne, Mr [Thomas] Bradford, Mr [Robert or John] Connould, Mr [John] Horne. Mr [John] Whitefoote sen[io]r reported to the company that he hath received five pounds of Mr Alderman Briggs[184] towards the purchase of some bookes for the use of the library.

1 October 1678. Present: Mr [John] Whitefoot sen[ior], Mr [Benedict] Riveley, Mr [Thomas] Stud, Mr [William] Newton, Mr [John] Burton, Mr [Steven] Painter, who all payd the under library keep[er] to this day. Mr [John] Whitefoot sen[ior] does further acknowledge to have received to the use of the library the summe of three pounds given by Mr Alderman Wisse.[185] Memorandum. That by the persons here present John Scott,

---

[182] Born at Maidstone in Kent, William Newton graduated BA at Magdalen College Cambridge in 1673 and proceeded MA in 1676. He was ordained in Norwich in 1676 and became a petty canon at Norwich Cathedral. By 1719 he was vicar of West Hythe, Kent.

[183] Sebastiao Barradas: *Commentaria in concordiam et historiam Evangelicam* (Mainz, 1601–12).

[184] Augustine Briggs was sheriff in 1660 and mayor in 1670. He was MP for Norwich in 1677–9 and 1681. In 1681–2 he was described as being 'of the moderate party' and 'an honest old cavalier'. He died in 1684 and was buried in St Peter Mancroft. One of the supervisors of his will was Thomas Wisse, a fellow donor (Cozens-Hardy, pp. 93–4; TNA, PROB/11/378, Will of Augustine Briggs, 1684).

[185] Thomas Wisse, a grocer, was sheriff in 1659 and mayor in 1667. He died in 1702 and was buried in St Andrew's.

eldest son to our late under library keeper, deceased, was chosen into the place *durante beneplacito societatis*.[186]

5 November 1678. Present: Dr [*Simon*] Blenkarne, Mr [*John*] Whitefoote sen[*io*]r. Dr Blinkarne paid the library keeper. Mr Whitefoote sen[*io*]r doth acknowledge that he hath received three pounds of Mr Alderman [*Bernard*] Church[187] for the use of the library.

December 3 1678. Present: Mr [*John*] Whitefoot sen[*io*]r, Mr < [*Benedict*] Rively, > Mr [*John*] Burton, Mr [*John*] Watson, who then payd the library keeper. Mr [*Robert*] Connould also present payd the library keeper. Dr [*Simon*] Blenkarn, Mr [*Steven*] Painter. Then was then brought into the library a booke called *Liber chronicorum cum figuris et imaginibus ab initio mundi*, printed at Nurenberg by Anthon[*y*] Koberger, anno domini 1493[188] the gift of Mr Samuel Clerk,[189] rector of East Rainham in the county of Norffolk.

January 7 1679. Present: Mr [*John*] Whitefoote sen[*io*]r, Mr [*Thomas*] Stud, Mr [*William*] Newton, who all paid the library keeper. Also Mr [*Benedict*] Riveley, Mr [*John*] Burton, Mr [*Steven*] Painter then present paid the library keeper unto this day. Present also Mr [*Benjamin*] Penning.

February 4 1679. Present: Dr [*Simon*] Blenkarn, Mr [*Benedict*] Rively, Mr [*John*] Burton, Mr [*Benjamin*] Penning, Mr [*Steven*] Painter, Mr [*John*] Connould. Dr [*Simon*] Blenkarn & Mr Connould paid the library keeper for the last quarter. Mr [*John*] Jeffery[190] was then admitted to the use of the library.

---

[186] During the society's pleasure.

[187] Bernard Church was sheriff in 1644, mayor in 1651 and MP for Norwich in 1654 and 1656. He died in 1686 (Cozens-Hardy, pp. 86–7).

[188] Hartmann Schedel: *Liber chronicarum* (Nuremberg, 1493)

[189] Samuel Clarke left a record of the weather at East Raynham (NRO MS 9374, 8 A. 1, Observations of the weather from the year 1657 to 1686, communicated to the Royal Society by Dr Hans Sloane, 14 February 1700). I owe this reference to Paul Rutledge.

[190] John Jeffery (1647–1720) was minister of St Peter Mancroft and, from 1694, archdeacon of Norwich. He edited Sir Thomas Browne's *Christian Morals* for publication in 1716. He had a lifetime's interest in the work of that man of 'rare temper', Benjamin Whichcote, the Cambridge Platonist who 'formed his notions of religion'. Whichcote was Jeffery's 'oracle'. As he himself expressed it, 'after the great design of doing service to the interest of religion, and the souls of men, my care has been to do right to the Doctor's memory'. Jeffery published a thousand of Whichcote's moral and religious aphorisms, which, in his anonymous introduction, he compared to the meditations of Marcus Aurelius (*Moral and religious aphorisms*, Norwich, 1703).

March 4 1679. Present: Mr [*Benedict*] Rively, Mr [*John*] Burton, Mr [*Thomas*] Stud, Mr [*William*] Cecill, who payd the library keeper for two quarters. Dr [*Simon*] Blenkarne.

April 1 1679. Present: Dr [*Simon*] Blinkarne, Mr [*John*] Whitefoote sen[*io*]r, Mr [*Benedict*] Rively, Mr [*William*] Cecill, Mr [*John*] Whitefoot, Mr [*John*] Jeffery, Mr [*William*] Newton, Mr [*Thomas*] Bradford, Mr [*Benjamin*] Penning, Mr [*John*] Burton, Mr [*Steven*] Painter, who all payd the library keeper for last quarter. John Connould. Mr [*Thomas*] Bloome[191] & Mr Francis Morley[192] were this day admitted to the use of the library.

May 6 1679. Present: Dr [*Simon*] Blenckarne, Mr [*Thomas*] Blome, Mr [*Benedict*] Riveley.

June 3 1679. Present: Dr [*Simon*] Blenkarne, Mr [*John*] Whitefoote sen[*ior*], Mr [*John*] Whitefoote jun[*ior*], Mr [*Francis*] Morley, Mr [*Benedict*] Rively, Mr [*Thomas*] Bradford, Mr [*Thomas*] Bloome, Mr [*William*] Cecil, Mr [*John*] Jeffery, Mr [*Robert* or *John*] Conould, Mr [*John*] Burton. Mr Whitefoote sen[*io*]r brought into the library Matthew Paris his works,[193] which cost thirty shillings, being part of the money by him received for the use of the library. Mr [*John*] Watson was also present and payd the library keeper all his arrears.

July 1 1679. Present at the meeting and paid the library keeper, viz Mr [*Thomas*] Bradford, Mr [*Thomas*] Blome, Mr [*Francis*] Morley, Mr [*John*] Burton, Mr [*Thomas*] Stud, Mr [*William*] Newton, Mr [*Robert* or *John*] Connould, Mr [*Steven*] Painter.

August 5 1679. Mr [*Benjamin*] Penning sent his quartrage to the library keeper. Present: Mr [*Thomas*] Bradford, Mr [*Benedict*] Rively, Mr [*Francis*] Morley, Mr [*Thomas*] Blome, Mr [*William*] Cecil, Mr [*Robert* or *John*] Connould. Mr Rively & Mr Cecil payd the library keeper.

September 2 1679. Present: Mr [*John*] Whitefoot sen[*io*]r, Mr [*Thomas*] Bradford, Mr [*Francis*] Morley, Mr [*John*] Jeffry, Mr [*Robert* or *John*] Connould, Mr [*Thomas*] Blome, Mr [*John*] Burton, Mr [*Steven*] Painter. Memorandum that Mr [*John*] Whitefoot sen[*io*]r brought into the library

---

[191] Thomas Bloome, rector of St Edmund's, Norwich, had joined the Library on 1 April 1679 but had allowed his membership to lapse, possibly through illness. By the winter of 1680 he was dead.

[192] For Francis Morley see above n. 92. Thomas Morley had died in 1679. His last recorded attendance at the Library was on 6 August 1678.

[193] Matthew Paris: *Matthaei Paris monachi Albanensis Angli Historia major* (London, 1640)

these following bookes viz Aristotelis *opera* graece latine in 2 folios edit Lutet. Paris. AD 1629,[194] Plutarchi *opera* in 2 folios edit Francofurt AD 1629,[195] Platonis *opera* 1 folio edit Francforti 1602 graece latine.[196] Mr Whitefoot *sen[ior]* & Mr Jeoffry paid the library keeper for the last quarter.

October 7 1679. Present: Mr [*Benedict*] Rively, Mr [*Francis*] Morley, Mr [*John*] Jeoffry, Mr [*William*] Cecil, Mr [*John*] Whitefoot sen[io]r, Mr [*Thomas*] Bradford, Mr [*Thomas*] Blome, Mr [*Steven*] Painter, Mr [*John*] Burton, Mr [*Robert* or *John*] Connould, Mr [*John*] Watson, Mr [*Thomas*] Studd. All present (except Mr Cecil) paid the library keeper.

November 4 1679. Present at the meeting: Mr [*Benedict*] Rively, Mr [*Francis*] Morley, Mr [*Thomas*] Studd, Mr [*Robert* or *John*] Connould, Mr [*John*] Burton, Mr [*Thomas*] Blome, Mr [*Stephen*] Painter.

December 2 1679. Present: Mr [*Thomas*] Brome, Mr [*Francis*] Morley, Mr [*John*] Whitefoot sen[io]r, Mr [*Thomas*] Bradford, Mr [*John*] Jeoffery, Mr [*William*] Newton, Mr [*John*] Burton, Mr [*John*] Whitefoot jun[io]r, Mr [*Steven*] Painter, Mr [*Robert* or *John*] Connould. Mr Whitefoot payd all his arrears to the library keeper and so did Mr [*John*] Watson, who was not present. Mr Newton also paid for the last quarter.

January 6 *Festo Epiphanio* 1680.[197] Present: Mr [*Benedict*] Riveley, Mr [*Francis*] Morley, Mr [*William*] Newton, Mr [*Robert*] Connould, who payd the library keeper. Mr [*Thomas*] Studde was then chosen for library keeper the ensuing yeare, if it be approoved of at the next meeting.

February 3 1680. Present: Mr [*Benedict*] Riveley, Mr [*John*] Burton, Mr [*John*] Jeoffery, Mr [*Steven*] Paynter. Mr John Burton & Mr Paynter paid the library keeper for the last quarter.

March 2 1680. Present: Mr [*John*] Whitefoote sen[ior], Mr [*Benedict*] Rively, Mr [*John*] Burton, Mr [*John*] Jeofferys, Mr [*Thomas*] Bradford though not present paid the library keeper for 1 last quarter. Mr Whitefoote sen[io]r paid the library keeper for last quarter. Mr Whitefoot sen[io]r sent into the library Aretij *Demonstratio Evangelia* pretium £1. 2s.[198]

[194] Aristotle: *Opera omnia quae extant, Graece et Latine* (Paris, 1629).
[195] Plutarch: *Plutarchi Chaeronensis quae exstant omnia* (Frankfurt, 1620).
[196] Plato: *Opera omnia quae exstant* (Frankfurt, 1602).
[197] 6 January is the Feast of Epiphany.
[198] Benedictus Aretius: *In Novum Testamentum Domini Nostri Iesu Christi commentarii* (Geneva, 1618).

April 6 1680. Present: Mr [*John*] Whitefoot *sen[*ior*],* Mr [*William*] Cecil, Mr [*Francis*] Morley, Mr [*Benedict*] Riveley, Mr [*John*] Burton, Mr [*Steven*] Paynter, all which except Mr Cecil did then pay the under library for the last quarter. This day Mr Penning paid the under library keeper all his dues [*remainder of the sentence cancelled and illegible*]

May 4 1680. Present: Mr [*Thomas*] Bloome, Mr [*John*] Watson, Mr [*Benedict*] Rively, Mr [*Steven*] Painter, Mr [*William*] Cecil, Mr [*William*] Newton, Mr [*Thomas*] Studd, who paid the librarie keeper their arrears. Present also Mr [*Francis*] Morley.

June 1 1680. Present: Mr [*Thomas*] Bloome, Mr [*Benjamin*] Rively, Mr [*Francis*] Morley, Mr [*Robert or John*] Connold, Mr [*John*] Jeofferie, Mr [*William*] Cecil, present also Mr [*John*] Whitefoot sen[*ior*], Mr [*John*] Whitefoot junior. Mr Whitefoot junior paid the library keeper for two quarters. Mr Connould for the last.

July 6 1680. Present: Mr [*Benedict*] Rively, Mr [*Francis*] Morley, Mr [*Thomas*] Bloome, Mr [*John*] Watson, Mr [*John*] Burton, Mr [*John*] Jeofferie, Mr [*Steven*] Painter, Mr [*Thomas*] Studd, who all paid the library keeper for the last quarter their forfitures for the year past. Alderman [*Francis*] Gardiner[199] sent into the librarie Bocartus'[200] works in two volumes.

August 3 1680. Present: Mr [*Thomas*] Bloome, Mr [*Benjamin*] Rively, Mr [*John*] Burton, Mr [*Francis*] Morley, Mr [*William*] Cecil, Mr [*Steven*] Painter, Mr [*Thomas*] Studd.

7 September 1680. Present: Mr [*Thomas*] Bloome, Mr [*Francis*] Morley, Mr [*John*] Burton, Mr [*John*] Watson, Mr [*Robert or John*] Connould, Mr [*John*] Jeofferie. Mr Connould paid the librarie keeper for the last quarter. Present also Mr [*Steven*] Painter, Mr [*Thomas*] Studd. Mr [*John*] Whitefoot sen[*ior*] [*sic*] into the librarie five books viz. Photij *Epist*,[201] Philostorgij *Historiae Ecclesiae*,[202] Joannes Bona *de rebus Liturgicis*,[203] Joannis Meursi *Glossarium Graeco barbarum*,[204] *Institutiones Linguae Turcicae*.[205]

[199] A linen draper living in the wealthy parish of St Peter Mancroft, Francis Gardiner was sheriff in 1680, mayor in 1685 and an MP in 1695 (Cozens-Hardy, p. 101).

[200] Samuel Bochart: *Hierozoicon, sive bipertitum opus de animalibus sacrae Scripturae* (Frankfurt,1675); *Geographiae sacrae par prior: Phaleg seu de dispersione gentium et terrarium divisione facta in aedificatione turris Babel.*

[201] Photius: *Epistolae per reverendum virum Richardum Montacutium* (London, 1651).

[202] Philostorgius Cappadocis: *Ecclesiasticae Historiae a Constantino M. Arii initiis ad sua tempora* (Geneva, 1642).

[203] Giovanni Bona: *Rerum liturgicarum* (Cologne, 1674)

[204] Jan van Meurs: *Glossarium graeco-barbarum* (Lyon, 1614)

[205] Possibly Franciszek Meninski: *Thesaurus linguarum Orientalium Turcicae, Arabicae, Persicae* (Vienna, 1680).

October 5 1680. Present: Mr [*Francis*] Morley, Mr [*John*] Burton, Mr [*Steven*] Painter, Mr [*Thomas*] Studd, who all paid the library keeper for the last quarter.

November 2 1680. Present: Mr [*Benjamin*] Rively, Mr [*Francis*] Morley, Mr [*John*] Burton, Mr [*John*] Watson, *Mr [*Thomas*] Studd,* Mr [*John*] Jeofferie, Mr [*William*] Cecil, Mr [*William*] Newton, Mr [*Steven*] Painter. Mr Watson, Mr Cecil, Mr Jeofferie, Mr Rively, Mr Newton paid the library keeper their arrears. Mr [*Thomas*] Bradford paid for two quarters, but was not present.

December 7 1680. Present: Mr [*John*] Whitefoote sen[*io*]r, Mr [*Benjamin*] Rively, Mr [*John*] Burton, Mr [*Thomas*] Studd. Mr Whitefoot sen[*io*]r paid the library keeper for 2 quarters last past & testified that the books by him sent into the library do come to more than the money he received for the use of the library therefore he takes himself to be fully discharged of that money.

January 4 1681. Present: Mr [*Benjamin*] Rively, Mr [*John*] Jeofferrie, Mr [*Steven*] Painter, who all paid the library keeper.

February 1 1681. Present: Mr [*Francis*] Morley, Mr [*John*] Burton, Mr [*John*] Watson, Mr [*John*] Whitefoote jun[*ior*], Mr [*John*] Jeofferrie, Mr [*William*] Newton, [*Thomas*] Mr Studd. Mr Watson, Mr Morley, Mr Newton, Mr Burton, Mr Studd paid the library keeper for the last quarter. Mr Whitefoot jun[*ior*] paid for three quarters. Mr John Shaw[206] & Mr William Bedingfield[207] were then admitted to the use of the librarie.

1 March 1681. Present: Mr [*John*] Whitefoot sen[*io*]r, Mr [*Francis*] Morley, Mr [*John*] Shaw, Mr [*Robert* or *John*] Connould, Mr [*Benedict*] Riveley, Mr [*John*] Burton, Mr [*John*] Jifferey. Mr [*Steven*] Painter, Mr Whitefoot senior & Mr Connould did then pay the library keeper. Mr [*William*] Cecil payed the library keeper.
<Memorandum. That Newman's English Concordance [208] is missing and upon report said to be caryed out of the library by Mr Studd. The under library keeper is required to sommon the said Mr Studd to appear here at the library the next meeting day, and then and there to restore the said

---

[206] A John Shaw, who had been educated at St John's College, Cambridge, was ordained in Norwich in 1679.

[207] William Bedingfield graduated BA from Queen's College Cambridge in 1669 and proceeded MA in 1672. Rector of Ashwellthorpe and Wreningham in 1679 and rector of Braconash from 1684 to 1694, he died in 1694 and was buried at Braconash.

[208] Samuel Newman: *A large and complete concordance to the Bible in English, according to the last translation* (London, 1643)

book & pay such forfeiture or penalty as is required in the orders of the common council for regulating of the library. >

5 April 1681. Present: Mr [*Francis*] Morley, Mr [*John*] Shaw, who then paid the library keeper for the last quarter. Mr [*Benedict*] Riveley present & paid the library keeper for our Lady quarter.

May 3 1681. Present: Mr [*Benedict*] Riveley, Mr [*Francis*] Morley, Mr [*John*] Burton, Mr [*John*] Watson, Mr [*Steven*] Painter, Mr [*John*] Jefferies, Mr [*John*] Shaw. Mr Burton, Mr Watson, Mr Painter, Mr Jefferies & Mr [*William*] Cecill who also < paid > was present & all paid the librarie keeper for our Lady quarter[209] & Mr Painter paid also for Mr [*William*] Newton. They then chose Mr Cecil librarie keep[er] for the ensuing year.

June 7 1681. Present: Mr [*Benedict*] Rively, Mr [*Francis*] Morley, Mr [*John*] Burton, Mr [*John*] Jeffery, Mr [*John*] Shaw.

July 5 1681. Present: Mr [*John*] Burton, Mr [*Francis*] Morley, Mr [*John*] Jeffery & Mr [*John*] Watson all of them paid the library keeper for Midsummer quarter. Present also Mr [*Steven*] Paynter, who paid the library keeper.

August 2 1681. Present: Mr [*John*] Whitefoote sen[io]r, Mr [*Benjamin*] Rively, who both paid the library being for the last quarter. Mr [*William*] Bedingfield also paid the library keep[er]. Mr F[*rancis*] Morly & Mr [*John*] Burton were also present. Present also Mr [*Steven*] Paynter.

September 6 1681. Present: Mr [*Benjamin*] Rively, Mr [*John*] Burton, Mr [*Francis*] Morley, Mr [*John*] Jefferyes.

October 4 1681: Present: Mr [*John*] Whitefoot sen[io]r, Mr [*John*] Burton, Mr [*John*] Jeffreys, Mr [*Benjamin*] Riveley, who all paid the library keeper for the quarter ending at Michaelmas last past. Mr [*Steven*] Paynter also present paid the library keeper to this day.

November 1 1681: Present: Mr [*Steven*] Paynter, who received of Mr [*William*] Nurce[210] clerk all Tullies works in 2 volumes,[211] given by him for the use of the library. When also the under library keeper acknowledged that he had received of Mr [*Thomas*] Bradford (absent) 2s. for 2 quarters the latter ending at Christmas 1680.

[209] Lady Day, or the feast of the Annunciation, fell on 25 March.

[210] William Nurse has successfully evaded all attempts at identification. He was admitted as a member of the Library on 3 July 1683 but never attended again.

[211] Cicero, Marcus Tullius: *Opera omnia, quae exstant a Dionysio Lambino*. (Paris, 1566)

December 6 1681. Present: Mr [*John*] Burton, Mr [*John*] Shaw, who paid the library keeper for every quarter due to him till Michaelmas last. Mr [*Steven*] Paynter was also present.

January 3 1682: Present: Mr [*Benjamin*] Riveley onely – who paid the library keeper for the quarter last ended at Christmas.

February 7 1682: Present: Mr [*Francis*] Morley, Mr [*John*] Watson, Mr [*John*] Jeoffery, Mr [*Robert* or John] Connould, who all paid the library keeper. Mr [*Benjamin*] Rively, Mr [*John*] Burton also paid the library keeper.

March 7 1682. Present Mr [*Francis*] Morly, Mr [*John*] Whitefoote sen[*io*]r (who then paid the library keeper), Mr [*Benedict*] Riveley, Mr [*Steven*] Painter, Mr [*John*] Shaw, Mr [*John*] Burton. Of these Mr Shaw and Mr Painter paid the library keeper for [*the*] Christmas quarter. Mr Whitefoote brought in a booke given by Mr [*Humphrey*] Prideaux,[212] & reported 20s. more given by the same person, to be left in his hands for the purchase of another booke for the library. Mr [*John*] Whitefoote jun[*io*]r, present, & paid the library keeper till Our Lady next. Mr [*William*] Cecil then paid the library keeper till Our Lady next. Mr [*Robert* or *John*] Connold also present. Mr. Whitefoot sen[*io*]r brought in this day Prebend Prideaux his translation of a peice of Maimonides[213] in 4to, & acknowledges himselfe to have received of him more for the use of the library 20s. Moreover at this meeting an account was taken of the forfeitures to this day. And Mr. Cecill was by agreement continued library keeper to the end of this yeare viz. till January next.

April 4 1682. Present: Mr [*Francis*] Morley, Mr [*John*] Burton, Mr [*Steven*] Painter, Mr [*John*] Shaw, Mr [*Benedict*] Riveley, who all payd the library keeper for the quarter ending at Our Lady last past. Mr [*John*] Jeoffrey, Mr [*John*] Watson both which paid the library keeper.

May 2 1682. Present: Mr [*Francis*] Morley, Mr [*John*] Jeoffreys, Mr [*John*] Burton, Mr [*Robert* or *John*] Connold, Mr [*John*] Shaw, Mr [*Benjamin*] Riveley, Mr [*Gawin*] Nash,[214] who was then admitted to the use of the

[212] Humphrey Prideaux (1648–1724), prebend of Norwich Cathedral from 1681 and dean from 1702 to 1724, was the author of a *Life of Mahomet* (1697) and *The Old and New Testaments Connected*, a history of the Jews. The most charitable comment on Prideaux was by William Massey who considered that 'in his private capacity [he] was esteem'd somewhat too positive (NRO Rye MS 18, William Massey's 'Acta Norvicensia, 1720–1729).

[213] Moses Maimonides: *De jure pauperis et peregrine apud Judaeos. Latine vertit & notis illustravit Humphridus Prideaux.* (Oxford, 1679).

[214] Gawin Nash graduated BA in 1672 at Trinity College, Cambridge, and proceeded MA in 1675. He was a minor canon of Norwich Cathedral and vicar of Little Melton. He was deprived for not taking the oath to William III and died in 1706.

library. Mr [*William*] Cecill was also present. Mr Connould payed the library keeper for the last quarter and Mr Cecil.

June 6 1682. Present: Mr [*John*] Shaw, Mr [*Gawin*] Nash, Mr [*John*] Jeffery.

July 4 1682. Present: Mr [*John*] Burton, Mr [*Benjamin*] Rively, Mr [*John*] Jeffery, all which payd the library keeper for the last quarter. Mr [*Steven*] Painter also present paid the library keeper.

August 1 1682. Present: Mr [*Thomas*] Morley (who paid the library keeper for the last quarter), Mr [*John*] Whitefoot sen[*io*]r present paid the library keeper for 2 quarters past. Mr [*John*] Jeoffries, Mr [*John*] Burton, Mr [*Gawin*] Nash paid the library keeper.

September 5 1682. Present: Mr [*Francis*] Morley, Mr [*Gawin*] Nash, Mr [*John*] Jeffery, Mr [*Benedict*] Riveley, Mr [*John*] Watson, who paid the librarie keeper.

October 3 1682. Present: Mr [*Benedict*] Riveley, Mr [*John*] Burton, Mr [*John*] Watson, Mr [*Francis*] Morley, who all paid the library keeper. Mr [*John*] Jeffery, who also paid the library keeper.

7 November 1682. Present: Mr [*John*] Shaw, who paid the library keeper for the last quarter. Mr [*Francis*] Morley, Mr [*Benedict*] Rively, Mr [*John*] Jeffery, Mr [*John*] Burton. Mr [*John*] Pitts,[215] who was then admitted to the use of the library.

December 5 1682. Mr [*Robert* or *John*] Connould payd the library keeper his arrears.

January 2 1683. Present; Mr [*Benedict*] Riveley, Mr [*John*] Shaw, Mr [*John*] Pitts, who paid the library keeper for the quarter ending December 25 last past. Mr [*Gawin*] Nash and Mr [*John*] Whitefoot sen[*io*]r were also here present who both paid the library keeper the 2 last quarters past.

February 6 1683. Present: Mr [*Benedict*] Rively, Mr [*John*] Shaw, Mr [*John*] Pitts, Mr [*William*] Cecil, Mr [*Joseph*] Allison,[216] who was then admitted. Mr [*Steven*] Paynter was then chosen library keeper. Mr Cecil paid the

[215] Born at Walsingham, the son of a clergyman, John Pitts graduated BA from Pembroke College, Cambridge, in 1678. He was rector of St Lawrence's, Norwich, from 1683 to 1693, rector of Hackford from 1684 to 1689 and vicar of Moulton St Mary from 1711 to 1723.

[216] Joseph Alinson (or Alanson) graduated BA at St John's College, Cambridge, in 1680, proceeding MA in 1683. He was ordained in Norwich in December 1682.

library keeper 3 quarters last past. Present also Mr [*John*] Burton, Mr Paynter, who both paid the library keeper all dues to Christmas.

6 March 1683 Present: Mr [*Francis*] Morley, Mr [*John*] Burton, Mr [*John*] Jeoffrye, Mr [*William*] Cecil, Mr [*Steven*] Painter, Mr [*John*] Shaw, Mr [*Joseph*] Alanson, Mr [*John*] Pitts, Mr [*Robert* or *John*] Connould. Mr Morley, Mr Jeoffry & Mr Connould did then pay the library keeper due at Christmas last. Mr Painter being chosen library keeper for this yeare desired upon the payment of 20 sh[*illings*] to the use of the library according to the order in that case made *to be excused and* he was dismissed from his office and Mr John Whitefoot the yonger was chosen library keeper for the same yeare in his stead.[217]

April 3 1683. Present: Mr [*Benjamin*] Rively, Mr [*Francis*] Morley, Mr [*John*] Jeffries, Mr [*John*] Whitefoot, Mr [*Robert* or *John*] Conold, Mr [*John*] Shaw, Mr [*John*] Pitts, who did all pay the under library keeper his arrears, due at our Lady last past. Present also Mr [*John*] Burton, who paid the library keeper. Present also Mr [*Steven*] Painter, who paid the library keeper.

1 May 1683. Present: Mr [*Benjamin*] Rively, Mr [*Francis*] Morley, Mr [*John*] Shaw, Mr [*John*] Pitts.

5 June 1683. Present: Mr [*John*] Shaw, Mr [*John*] Pitts, Mr [*Francis*] Morley, Mr [*John*] Whitefoote sen[*io*]r, Mr [*Benjamin*] Rively, Mr [*John*] Jefferies. Mr Whitefoote sen[*ior*], paid the library keep[*er*]. Mr [*John*] Burton, Mr [*Steven*] Painter.

3 July 1683. Present: Mr [*Francis*] Morley, Mr [*John*] Shaw, Mr [*John*] Pitts, Mr [*John*] Jeffery, who did all pay the under library keeper for Midsummer last past. Mr [*William*] Nurse who was then admitted to the use of the library. Mr [*Steven*] Paynter also present paid the library keeper.

7 August 1683. Present: Mr [*Francis*] Morley, Mr [*John*] Jeffery, Mr [*Gawin*] Nash, Mr [*Nathaniel*] Nobbes,[218] who was then admitted to the use of the library, Mr [*Pierre*] Chauvin[219] who was then admitted to the use of the

---

[217] Painter continued to attend as a rank and file member.

[218] Nathaniel Nobbs was instituted rector of Felthorpe on 26 July 1689 by bishop Nathaniel Lloyd. He remained rector until 1703 (NRO DN/REG/30, Thomas Tanner's abstracts of the Norwich Diocese Registration Books, f.569).

[219] Pierre Chauvin was minister of Vieillevigne near Nantes from 1670 until the Revocation of the Edict of Nantes, when he fled to Holland. He was appointed pastor of the Norwich French Church on 21 January 1684. He had been ordained by bishop William Lloyd and frequently attended Anglican services. He was accused of preaching 'natural religion' after

library. Mr Nash paid the library keeper for the two last quarters. Present also Mr [*Benedict*] Riveley and Mr [*John*] Burton who paid the library keeper.

September 4 1683. Present: Mr [*Benedict*] Rively, Mr [*Robert* or *John*] Conold, Mr [*Francis*] Morley, Mr [*Gawin*] Nash, Mr [*John*] Jeffery, Mr [*John*] Pitts, Mr [*Nathaniel*] Nobbes. Mr Conold then paid the library keeper for Midsummer quarter. Mr [*John*] Watson paid the library keeper till Midsummer.

October 2 1683. Present: Mr [*Benedict*] Rively, Mr [*Robert* or *John*] Conold, Mr [*John*] Jeffery, Mr [*William*] Nurse, Mr [*John*] Shaw, Mr [*Francis*] Morley, < Mr [*Joseph*] Alanson >, who all paid the under library keeper for the last quarter. Mr Alanson, who paid the library keeper for the three last quarters. Mr [*Nathaniel*] Nobbs, who paid the library keeper. Mr [*John*] Burton, who also paid the library keeper.

November 5 1683. Present: Mr [*Benedict*] Riveley, Mr [*Francis*] Morley, Mr [*John*] Burton, Mr [*John*] Shaw, Mr [*Gawin*] Nash, who paid John Scott for last quarter. Mr [*Nathaniel*] Nobbs – memorandum, Mr [*Pierre*] Chauvin, the French minister, paid John Scott for the last quarter. Mr [*Steven*] Paynter also present paid the under library keeper for the last quarter.

December 4 1683. Present: Mr [*John*] Burton, Mr [*Francis*] Morley, Mr [*Steven*] Paynter, Mr [*John*] Pitts, Mr [*Benedict*] Riveley, Mr [*Nathaniel*] Nobbs. And at this our meeting Mr [*Peter*] De La Hay[220] was admitted to the use of the library.

January 1 1684. Present: Mr [*John*] Burton, Mr [*John*] Jefferie, Mr [*Francis*] Morley, Mr [*John*] Shaw, Mr [*Peter*] De La Hay, who all paid the under library keeper for the last quarter. Mr [*Steven*] Painter, who also paid the library keeper. Mr [*Benedict*] Rively was also present & paid the library keeper.

February 5 1684. Present: Mr [*Benedict*] Riveley, Mr [*Robert* or *John*] Conold & Mr [*Nathaniel*] Nobbs, who *both* paid the library keeper, & Mr

having published *De religione naturali liber* (Rotterdam, 1693) and defended himself in a pamphlet entitled *Éclairissements sur un livre de la religion naturelle* (1693) (W.J.C. Moens, *The Walloons and their Church at Norwich*, Lymington, 1888, p. 236).

[220] Born at Caen in Normandy, Peter de la Hay was admitted to St John's College, Cambridge, in 1671. He was awarded an MA in 1674. He was a minor canon of Norwich Cathedral and died in 1687.

[*John*] Pitts who likewise paid the library keeper. Mr [*John*] Burton was also present.

4 March 1684. Present: Mr [*Francis*] Morley, Mr [*John*] Burton, Mr [*Steven*] Paynter, Mr [*John*] Jeoffreys, Mr [*Benjamin*] Riveley, Mr [*John*] Pitts, Mr [*Robert* or *John*] Conold, Mr [*John*] Shaw, Mr [*Nathaniel*] Nobbs. Memorandum. An account was taken of the forfeitures to this day. The sum *received* was £0. 11s. 2d. out of which the under library keeper's expences were paid, viz. £0. 5s. 0d. The remainder of the money received, viz. 6s. 2d. <which retained > in the hands of Mr Jefferey, who was this day chosen library keeper for this year current.

April 1 1684. Present: Mr [*John*] Shaw, Mr [*Benjamin*] Nobbs, Mr [*John*] Jeffery (Mr [*William*] Cecil *not present* paid the under library keeper for 5 quarters, Mr [*John*] Whitefoot jun[*ior*] *not present* for 4), < Mr Nobbs for one >, Mr [*Peter*] De La Hay, all which paid the library keeper (Mr Connold *not present* paid for one quarter & Mr [*Pierre*] Chauvin for 2 quarters) Mr [*Francis*] Morley also present, & paid the library keeper. Mr [*Benedict*] Riveley present at that time.

May 6 1684. Present: Mr [*John*] Whitefoot sen[*ior*] (who paid the under library keeper for one whole year), Mr [*Gawin*] Nash (who paid for two quarters), Mr [*John*] Pitts, Mr [*John*] Burton, & Mr [*Steven*] Painter, which 3 paid for one quarter. Mr [*John*] Jeffery, Mr [*John*] Shaw, Mr [*Benedict*] Rively, who also paid the library keeper. Mr [*William*] Cecil, Mr [*Nathaniel*] Nobbs, Mr [*Francis*] Morley.

June 3 1684. Present: Mr [*Francis*] Morley, Mr [*Robert* or *John*] Connould, Mr [*John*] Shaw, Mr [*Peter*] de La Hay, Mr [*Nathaniel*] Nobbs. Present also Mr [*John*] Burton & Mr [*Steven*] Paynter.

July 1 1684. Present: Mr [*John*] Burton, Mr [*John*] Pitts, Mr [*Peter*] De La Hay, Mr [*John*] Shaw, Mr [*Nathaniel*] Nobbs, Mr [*Steven*] Paynter, who all paid the under library keeper for the last quarter. Mr [*Pierre*] Chauvin (absent) paid also the under library keeper.

August 5 1684. Present: Mr [*Francis*] Morley, Mr [*Gawin*] Nash, Mr [*John*] Jeffery, all who paid the library keeper for the last quarter. Present also Mr [*Nathaniel*] Nobbes.

2 September 1684. Present: Mr [*Francis*] Morley, Mr [*Nathaniel*] Nobs, Mr [*John*] Pitts, Mr [*Benedict*] Rively, Mr [*Robert* or *John*] Conold, who paid the library keeper Midsummer quarters and at this our meeting Mr [*Peter*]

Burgess[221] was admitted into this society. Mr Rively also paid the library keeper. Present also Mr [Gawin] Nash, Mr [John] Burton, Mr [John] Whitefoot sen[io]r, who also paid the library keep[er] Midsummer quarter & Mr [Steven] Painter.

October 7 1684. Present: Mr [Benedict] Rively, Mr [John] Shaw, Mr [John] Jeffery, Mr [Nathaniel] Nobbs, Mr [John] Pitts, Mr [Francis] Morley, all of them paid the under library keeper for Michaelmas quarter. Mr [John] Burton who paid the library keeper. Present also Mr [Peter] Burgesse.

November 4 1684. Present: Mr [Peter] Burgess, who paid the under library keeper for Michaelmas quarter. Mr [Gawin] Nash, *who also paid the library keeper for the last quarter.* Mr [Stephen] Griggs,[222] who was admitted to the use of the library. Mr [Francis] Morley, Mr [John] Jeffries, Mr [Benedict] Rively, Mr [Robert or John] Connould, who paid the library keeper for Michaelmas quarter. Mr [Nathaniel] Nobbes, Mr [John] Burton, Mr [Steven] Painter, who paid the library keeper.

2 December 1684. Present: Mr [Benedict] Riveley, Mr [John] Jeffreys, Mr [Francis] Morley, *Mr [John] Burton,* Mr [Robert or John] Connould, Mr [Gawin] Nash, Mr [Peter] Delahay, Mr [John] Shaw, Mr [Stephen] Griggs, Mr [Nathaniel] Nobbes, and at this our meeting were brought in unto the library by consent Suicerus's *Thesaurus Ecclesiasticus*[223] in two volumes and Hofman's *Lexicon*[224] in two volumes also, which together cost £3. 0s. 10d. whereof one pound was given by Mr [Humphrey] Prideaux[225] to the use of the library, one pound [of] which was Mr [Steven] Painter's *composition* mony,[226] the rest forfeitures. Memorandum: that Bishop Ussher's treatise *De Macedonum et Asianorum anno solari* [227] was missing this meeting. It was by the under keeper's attestation here the last meeting and has bin missing

[221] Son of Samuel Burgess, a Norwich weaver, Peter Burgess was admitted sizar at Pembroke College Cambridge in 1679, graduating BA in 1683 and proceeding MA in 1686. He was parish chaplain of St Martin Coslany, rector of Scarning and rector of Whinburgh until his death in 1723.

[222] Stephen Griggs was born in Norwich and was admitted to Corpus Christi College Cambridge in 1680. He graduated BA in 1684 and was ordained in Norwich in December 1680. He was rector of St Edward, St Julian and All Saints from 1688 to 1691, when he was deprived. Latterly, he appears to have been living in Saham Toney (NRO ANW 122, Administration of Stephen Griggs, 1706).

[223] Johann Kaspar Suicer: *Thesaurus ecclesiasticus* (Amsterdam, 1682).

[224] Johann Jakob Hofmann: *Lexicon universale historico-geographico-chronologico-poetico-philologicum* (Basle, 1677).

[225] For Prideaux see above n. 212.

[226] Painter's 'composition money' was the 20s. he paid on 6 March 1683 when he resigned his position as librarian.

[227] James Ussher: *De Macedonum et Asianorum anno solari dissertatio* (Lyon, 1683).

this three weeks. 'Tis desired that he that has it would be pleased to restore it. and not to do any such thing as is contrary to what he hath subscribed. At this meeting also Mr [Peter] Delahay paid the under library keeper for Michaelmas quarter. Present also Mr [John] Burton and Mr [Steven] Painter.

January 6 1685. Present: Mr [Francis] Morley, who paid the library keeper for Christmas quarter. Also Mr [John] Shaw & Mr [Peter] Burgess who likewise paid the library keeper for the last quarter. Mr Shavvin paid the library keeper. Mr [Benedict] Rively paid too.

February 2 1685. Present: Mr John WhitefootE sen[io]r, Mr [John] Whitefoote jun[io]r, Mr [Francis] Morlye, Mr [John] Jeoffery, Mr [Benedict] Riveley, Mr [John] Shaw, Mr [Joseph] Alanson, Mr [John] Pitts, Mr [Stephen] Griggs. Of these Mr Whitefoot sen[io]r paid the library keeper for the 2 last quarters past. Mr Alanson paid him also all arrears to this day. Mr Whitefoot jun[io]r paid him also his arrears till Christmas. Mr Pitts now also paid him the last quarter. Mr [Nathaniel] Nobbs present & paid the library keeper. Mr [John] Burton present & paid the library keeper. Mr [Steven] Paynter also (present) paid the library keeper. Present also Mr [Pierre] Chauvin.

3 March 1685. Present: Mr [Benedict] Rively, Mr [John] Jeffrey, Mr [John] Burton, Mr [Steven] Paynter, Mr [John] Shaw, Mr [John] Brown[228] (who was then admitted to the use of the library). Present also Mr [Joseph] Alanson, Mr [Nathaniel] Nobbs. This day the account of the last year was stated. The library keeper had received £4. 3s. 4d. & had expended £4. 11s. 10d. Due to him 8s. 6d. The choise of a library keeper for the ensuing year was deferred till the next month.

April 7 1685. Present: Mr [Benedict] Rively, Mr [Stephen] Griggs, who *both* paid the library keeper for the last quarter. Mr [William] Cecil not present paid the library keeper his arrears to this day. And Mr [Pierre] Chauvin for the last quarter. Present also Mr [John] Brown, Mr [John] Shaw, who both paid the library keeper for the last quarter. Mr [John] Whitefoot sen[ior], Mr [John] Pitts, who both paid the library keeper for the last quarter. Mr [John] Burton and Mr [Nathaniel] Nobbes, who both paid the library keeper.

---

[228] Born in Norwich, John Browne, son of Nicholas Browne, gentleman, was educated at Norwich Grammar School and Caius College, Cambridge, graduating BA in 1674 and proceeding MA in 1677. Venn suggests that he was licensed to practise surgery in 1675. Ordained priest in Norwich in 1679, he was instituted rector of Bedingham in 1679.

May 5 1685. Present: Mr [*Peter*] Burgesse, who paid the library keeper for the last quarter. Mr [*Joseph*] Alanson, Mr [*John*] Shaw, Mr Alanson paid the library keeper for the last quarter, present also Mr [*Robert* or *John*] Connould who paid the library keeper for the last two quarters present also Mr [*John*] Burton, Mr [*Nathaniel*] Nobbes.

June 2 1685. Present: Mr [*John*] Jeffryes, Mr [*Gawin*] Nash, Mr [*John*] Pitts, whereof Mr Jeffryes paid the library keeper for the last quarter & Mr Nash for the two last quarters. Present also Mr [*John*] Burton, Mr [*Benedict*] Rively and Mr [*Nathaniel*] Nobbes. This day also Mr Morley's [229] widow paid her husband's arrears due to the library keeper for the last quarter.

July 7 1685. Present: Mr [*Robert* or *John*] Conold, Mr [*John*] Pitts, Mr [*Peter*] Burgess, who all paid the under library keeper for the last quarter. Present also Mr [*John*] Graile,[230] who was then admitted to the use of the library. Mr [*Benedict*] Rively, Mr [*John*] Burton, Mr [*Benjamin*] Nobbes, who *all* paid the library keeper for the last quarter. Present also Mr [*Steven*] Paynter, who paid the under library keeper all arrears viz. 2s. unto Midsummer last.

August 4 1685. Present: Mr [*Robert* or *John*] Connould, Mr [*John*] Burton, Mr [*Benedict*] Riveley.

September 1 1685. Present: Mr [*Nathaniel*] Nobbs, Mr [*John*] Whitefoot sen[*ior*], Mr [*John*] Pitts, Mr [*Charles*] Chapman,[231] Mr [*John*] Jeffery, Mr [*John*] Graile. Mr Jeffery paid the under library keeper for the last quarter. This day Mr Charles Chapman was admitted to the use of the library. Mr Whitefoot sen[*ior*] paid the under library keeper for the last quarter.

---

[229] Francis Morley died in 1685 (Blomefield, iv, p. 362).

[230] The son of a Wiltshire clergyman, John Graile graduated BA from Exeter College, Oxford, in 1668, proceeding MA in 1670. He was instituted rector of Blickling in 1674. He was a Tory and an anti-Exclusionist. In a series of sermons dedicated to the Anglican convert, Henry, duke of Norfolk, he made a whole series of strongly expressed political statements which could not have been more explicitly partisan. For Graile the king was 'the Minster of God, and his Power ... the Ordnance of God'. The king's power was virtually unfettered. To take up arms against the king was to fight against God, whom the king represented and with whose authority he was invested. Graile viewed the Exclusion crisis as evidence of anti-monarchical sentiment on the part of a small group of 'horrid phanaticks'. If the 'phanaticks' were to prove successful and the fundamental hereditary right of lineal succession was violated then enslavement and ruin would be the inevitable outcome (John Graile, *Three Sermons preached at the Cathedral in Norwich*, London, 1685, pp. 56, 96, 118–9).

[231] Born at Great Snoring, Charles Chapman was admitted sizar at St John's College Cambridge in 1681, migrating to Jesus College in 1682. He graduated BA in 1685. He was ordained in Norwich in 1686 and was instituted vicar of Freethorpe by Richard Berney in 1692 (Blomefield, vii, p. 232).

October 5 [*1685*]. Present: Mr [*Peter*] Burgesse, Mr [*John*] Jefferies, Mr [*John*] Pitts, Mr [*Nathaniel*] Nobbes, Mr [*Steven*] Painter, Mr [*Charles*] Chapman, Mr [*John*] Shaw. Mr Burgesse paid the under library keeper for the last quarter and Mr Nobbes, Mr Charles Chapman, Mr Pitts for the last quarter. So also did Mr [*Pierre*] Chauvin and Mr [*John*] Jefferies. Mr [*Peter*] Delahay for a whole year. Mr Painter paid the under library keeper for the last quarter.

November 3 [*1685*]. Present: Mr [*Peter*] Burgesse, Mr [*Charles*] Chapman, Mr [*Joseph*] Alanson, Mr [*Nathaniel*] Nobbs, Mr [*Benedict*] Rively, Mr [*John*] Grayle, Mr [*John*] Shaw, Mr [*Gawin*] Nash, Mr [*Steven*] Painter, Mr [*John*] Burton, Mr [*John*] Pitts. Mr Rively paid the library for the last quarter and Mr Alanson for Midsummer last and Michaelmas. Mr Nash paid the two last quarters. Mr Grayl paid the library keeper for the last quarter. Mr Burton paid the library keeper for the last quarter.

December 1 [*1685*]. Present: Mr [*Peter*] Burgesse, Mr [*John*] Pitts, Mr [*Charles*] Chapman, Mr [*John*] Shaw, Mr [*Nathaniel*] Nobbs, Mr [*John*] Jeffery, Mr [*John*] Graile, Mr [*Benedict*] Rively, Mr [*Joseph*] Alanson, Mr [*John*] Burton.

January 5 1686. Present: Mr [*Peter*] Burgesse and Mr [*Charles*] Chapman both paid the under library keeper. Mr [*John*] Shaw paid the under library keeper. Mr [*Nathaniel*] Nobbs, so did Mr Nobbs. Mr [*Pierre*] Chauvin absent paid.

2 February 1686. Present: Mr [*John*] Burton, Mr [*John*] Pitts, Mr [*Benedict*] Riveley, Mr [*John*] Grayle, all which paid the under library keeper for the last quarter. Mr [*John*] Jeffery, who paid. Present also Mr [*Nathaniel*] Nobbes. Mr [*John*] Shaw is this day chosen library keeper for the two next ensuing years. Samuel Scot is also this day chosen under library keeper in the rome of his brother lately deceased.

March 2 1686. Mr [*Joseph*] Ellis,[232] who was this day admitted to the use of the library. Present: Mr [*Pierre*] Chauvin, Mr [*John*] Pitts, Mr [*Peter*] Burgesse, Mr [*Benedict*] Rively, Mr [*Nathaniel*] Nobbs, Mr [*Steven*] Paynter, Mr [*Charles*] Chapman, Mr [*John*] Burton. Mr Paynter paid the under library keeper the quarter ending at Christmas last.

---

[232] Joseph Ellis graduated BA from Corpus Christi College, Cambridge, in 1679, proceeding MA in 1682. He was vicar of Earlham from 1683 to 1712 and minister of St Andrew's from 1694 to 1712. He died in 1712.

April 6 1686. Present: Mr [*Joseph*] Ellis, who paid the under library keeper for the last quarter ending att our Lady last past. Present: Mr [*John*] Pitts, Mr [*Nathaniel*] Nobbs, Mr [*John*] Jefferies, Mr [*Charles*] Chapman, Mr [*John*] Burton, Mr [*John*] Grayle, Mr [*Robert* or *John*] Connold, Mr [*John*] Shaw, Mr [*Pierre*] Chauvin, Mr [*Peter*] Burgess.

May 4 1686. Present: Mr [*Peter*] Burgess, Mr [*Charles*] Chapman, Mr [*Nathaniel*] Nobbs, Mr [*Pierre*] Chauvin, Mr [*Steven*] Painter, Mr [*John*] Burton, who paid the under library keeper for the last quarter.

June 1 1686. Present: Mr [*Benedict*] Rively, Mr [*Nathaniel*] Nobbs, Mr [*John*] Pitts, Mr [*Charles*] Chapman, Mr [*John*] Shaw, Mr [*John*] Jeffery, Mr [*Peter*] Burgess, paid for 2 quarters.

July 6 1686. Present: Mr [*Pierre*] Chauvin, Mr [*John*] Shaw, Mr [*John*] Graile, Mr [*John*] Jeffery, Mr [*Benedict*] Rively, all of which paid the under library keeper for the last quarter.

August 3 1686. Present: Mr [*John*] Graile.

September 7 1686. Present: Mr [*John*] Whitefoot sen[*ior*], who paid the under library keeper for the two last quarters. Mr [*John*] Graile, Mr [*Peter*] Burgess, Mr [*John*] Jeffery (Mr Whitefoot *sen[*io*]r* paid all arrears to this day). Mr [*John*] Burton, who paid the library keeper for the last quarter.

October 5 1686. Present: Mr [*Benjamin*] Ellis, who paid the under library keeper for the last two quarters. Mr [*John*] Jeffery, who paid the under library keeper. Mr [*Benedict*] Rively, who paid &c. Mr [*Robert* or *John*] Connould & Mr [*Steven*] Paynter, who both paid all arrears. Mr [*John*] Pitts, who paid the library keeper. Mr [*John*] Burton (present) paid also the under library keeper.

November 2 1686. Present: Mr [*John*] Shaw, Mr [*Steven*] Painter, Mr [*Benjamin*] Ellis, Mr [*John*] Graile, Mr [*John*] Jeffery, Mr [*John*] Burton, who paid the under library keeper.

December 7 1686. Present: Mr [*Benedict*] Rively, Mr [*John*] Pitts, Mr [*Steven*] Painter, Mr [*Peter*] Burgess, Mr [*John*] Shaw, Mr [*John*] Graile, Mr [*Joseph*] Ellis.

January 4 1687. Present: Mr [*John*] Burton, Mr [*Pierre*] Chauvin, Mr [*Joseph*] Ellis, Mr [*Benedict*] Riveley, Mr [*John*] Graile, who all paid the library keeper for [*the*] Christmas quarter. Mr [*Pierre*] Chauvin paid for two quarters.

February 1 1687. Mr [*John*] Whitefoot sen[ior], Mr [*John*] Shaw, Mr [*Steven*] Paynter (present) all 3 paid the library keeper all arrears. Present also Mr [*John*] Pitts, Mr [*John*] Burton, Mr [*John*] Jeffery.

March 1 1687. Present: Mr [*Benedict*] Rively, Mr [*John*] Shaw, Mr [*John*] Pitts, Mr [*John*] Burton, Mr [*John*] Jeffery, Mr [*John*] Graile, Mr [*Steven*] Painter, who paid the under library keeper.

April 5 1687. Present: Mr [*John*] Jeffery, who paid the under library keeper, Mr [*John*] Shaw, Mr [*Benedict*] Rively, Mr [*John*] Burton, Mr [*John*] Pitts, Mr [*John*] Grayle, who all paid the under library keeper for the last quarter ended at our Lady Day last past. Present also Mr [*Nathaniel*] Nobbes.

May 3 1687. Present: Mr [*Nathaniel*] Nobbes, Mr [*Pierre*] Chauvin, who paid his quarter for the library keeper. Present: Mr [*Benedict*] Rively, Mr [*John*] Burton, Mr [*Steven*] Paynter, the last of whom paid the under library keeper. This day Mr [*John*] Robinson [233] was admitted to the use of the library.

June 7 1687. Present: Mr [*John*] Jefferies, Mr [*John*] Burton, Mr [*John*] Shaw, Mr [*Nathaniel*] Nobbes, Mr [*Steven*] Painter, Mr [*Benjamin*] Riveley, Mr [*Joseph*] Ellis.

July 5 1687. Present: Mr [*John*] Whitefoot sen[ior], who paid the library keeper, likewise Mr [*Benedict*] Rively. Mr [*John*] Shaw, Mr [*John*] Pitts & Mr [*John*] Burton & Mr [*Steven*] Painter, Mr [*John*] Robinson, who all paid the library keeper & Mr [*John*] Graile, who paid the library keeper.

August 2 1687. Present: Mr [*Joseph*] Ellis, who paid the under library keeper for two quarters. Mr [*John*] Jeffery, who paid the library keeper for the last quarter. Mr [*Nathaniel*] Nobbes, who paid the library keeper for the last quarter. Present also Mr [*John*] Burton and Mr [*John*] Pitts, Mr [*Steven*] Painter and Mr [*John*] Robinson.

September 6 1687. Present: Mr [*Joseph*] Ellis, Mr [*Benjamin*] Rively, Mr [*John*] Shaw, Mr [*John*] Robinson, Mr [*Nathaniel*] Nobbes.

October 4 1687. Present: Mr [*John*] Jeffery, who paid the library keeper. Mr [*Joseph*] Ellis, who paid the library keeper. Mr [*Pierre*] Chauvin, who

[233] Born at Elsing in Norfolk, John Robinson graduated BA from Caius College, Cambridge, in 1677, proceeding MA in 1680. He was usher of Norwich School from 1686 to 1700, rector of St Augustine's from 1688 to 1700 and rector of Reepham from 1700 to 1723.

paid these two last quarters to the library keeper. Mr [*John*] Robinson, who also paid the library keeper. Present the same day Mr [*John*] Burton who also paid the library keeper.

November 1 1687. Present: Mr [*Benedict*] Rively, Mr [*John*] Jeffery, who paid [*the*] library keeper, Mr [*John*] Graile, Mr [*John*] Robinson, who paid the library keeper, Mr [*Steven*] Paynter, Mr [*Joseph*] Ellis, who paid the library keeper. Mr [*Robert* or *John*] Connould paid the library keeper for 3 quarters but not present.

December 6 [*1687*]. Present: Mr [*Bernard*] Skelton,[234] who was this day admitted to the use of the library. Mr [*John*] Jeffery, Mr [*Nathaniel*] Nobbs, Mr [*Thomas*] Clayton, [235] who was this day admitted to the use of the library. Mr [*Joseph*] Ellis, Mr [*John*] Burton, Mr [*John*] Robinson, Mr [*Robert* or *John*] Connould, who paid his arrears.

January 3 1688. Present: Mr [*Bernard*] Skelton, Mr [*John*] Burton, Mr [*Benedict*] Rively, Mr [*John*] Jeffery, Mr [*John*] Shaw, Mr [*Robert* or *John*] Connold, which four last paid the under library keeper. Mr [*John*] Shaw paid for the two last quarters. Mr John Pitts was then chosen library keeper for the ensuing year.

February 7 1688. Present: Mr [*John*] Jeffery, Mr [*Joseph*] Ellis, Mr [*John*] Shaw who paid the under library keeper for the last quarter, Mr [*Thomas*] Clayton, who paid the under library keeper for the last quarter, Mr [*John*]

---

[234] Bernard Skelton was educated at St Paul's School, where he was a contemporary of Samuel Pepys (R. Latham and W. Matthews, *The Diary of Samuel Pepys*, iii, London, 1970, p. 218). He graduated BA from Peterhouse College, Cambridge, in 1655, proceeding MA in 1658. He was a Fellow of his College from 1659 to 1664. He was rector of Cantley in Norfolk from 1663 to 1690.

[235] Thomas Clayton, who was admitted pensioner at Corpus Christi College Cambridge in 1680, graduating BA in 1685 and proceeding MA in 1690, was rector of Colney and St Michael at Plea and was one of the longest -serving members of the library. He joined on 6 December 1687, was made library keeper on 6 February 1699 and last appeared in the minutes on 6 February 1732, a period of over forty years. In his sermon delivered at Norwich Cathedral on 9 January 1704 Clayton, like Joseph Brett, did not hesitate to criticise occasional conformists, those who 'upon some state preferment, or profitable place, have communicated with us'. By their actions they seem to be 'rather members of the state than of the church'. He invited dissenters to consider 'what dreadful calamities' issued from their separation from the church in the 'late unhappy times'. He made it clear that those who had showed a disposition to undermine the church should not be allowed to achieve power a second time. Like Joseph Brett, Clayton seems to have been a Tory. He voted for Robert Bene and Richard Berney in the Norwich election of 1715. However, he voted Whig in the election of 1734–5, perhaps because the Whig candidate was a Tory defector. He was close to members of the diocesan hierarchy. The Archdeacon of Norwich, Christopher Clark, was mentioned in his will (NRO NCC 2 Bloom, Will of Thomas Clayton, 1744).

Grayle, Mr [*Benedict*] Rively, Mr [*Bernard*] Skelton, Mr [*Nathaniel*] Nobbes, who also paid.

March 6 1688. Present: Mr [*Benedict*] Rively, Mr [*John*] Shaw, Mr [*John*] Graile, Mr [*John*] Jeffery, Mr [*Thomas*] Clayton, Mr [*Steven*] Paynter, which last paid the under library keeper.

April 3 1688. Present: Mr [*Benedict*] Rively, Mr [*Nathaniel*] Nobbes, Mr [*Bernard*] Skelton, Mr [*John*] Burton, Mr [*Pierre*] Chauvin, Mr [*John*] Robinson, Mr [*John*] Shaw, Mr [*Thomas*] Clayton, Mr [*John*] Grayle. Mr Chauvin paid the under library keeper for the *two* last quarters, and likewise Mr Skelton. Mr Burton paid the library keeper for the two last quarters. Mr Clayton paid for the last quarter. So did Mr Grayle and Mr Rively. Memorandum. Mr Shaw was this day discharged the office of library keeper and paid the under library keeper for the last quarter and discharged *all* the arrears due to him for the two years last past. Mr Robinson for the two last quarters.

May 1 1688. Present: Mr [*Pierre*] Chauvin, Mr [*John*] Pitts, who paid the library keeper for 3 quarters *past,* Mr [*Benedict*] Riveley, Mr [*Bernard*] Skelton, Mr [*John*] Shaw, Mr [*John*] Graile.

June 5 1688. Present: Mr [*John*] Jeffery, Mr [*Benedict*] Rively, Mr [*Pierre*] Chauvin, Mr [*John*] Graile, Mr [*Bernard*] Skelton, Archbishop Ussher's *Britannicarum ecclesiarum antiquitates*[236] was given to the library by Alderman Briggs.[237]

July 3 1688. Present: Mr [*Pierre*] Chauvin, who paid his quarter, Mr [*Benedict*] Rively paid the last quarter, Mr [*John*] Shaw paid the last quarter, Mr [*John*] Jeffery paid the last quarter, Mr [*Joseph*] Elis paid for the 2 last quarters, Mr [*Steven*] Paynter, who paid the under library keeper all arrears.

August 7 1688. Present: Mr [*John*] Burton, Mr [*Bernard*] Skelton, Mr [*John*] Jeffery, Mr [*Benedict*] Rively, Mr [*Joseph*] Alanson, Mr [*John*] Graile, Mr [*John*] Robinson. / Mr Burton paid the Under Keeper for the last Quarter. < Mr Robinson > also paid the library keeper / This day Mr Alanson paid the under library keeper 3s. in part of what was due to him. < But Mr Alanson was not present at the meeting. > Mr Graile also paid him for the last quarter.

---

[236] James Ussher: *Britannicarum ecclesiarum antiquitates* (London, 1687)

[237] Augustine Briggs, the eldest son of the Augustine Briggs who gave £5 to the Library in 1678, had been removed from his aldermanship in 1687 but was restored in 1688 and became mayor in 1693. His wife, Lydia, was the daughter of Edmund Cock (Cozens-Hardy, p. 104).

September 4 1688. Present: Mr [*Benedict*] Rively, Mr [*John*] Graile, Mr [*John*] Pitts, who paid the library keep[*er*] for the last quarter, Mr [*Pierre*] Chauvin, Mr [*John*] Burton.

October 2 1688. Present: Mr [*Pierre*] Chauvin, who paid the library keeper, Mr [*John*] Shaw, Mr [*Joseph*] Ellis, Mr [*John*] Robinson, who paid the library keeper, Mr [*John*] Burton, who allso paid the library keeper. Mr [*Bernard*] Skelton paid the library keeper for 2 quarters.

November 6 1688. Present: Mr [*John*] Grayle, Mr [*John*] Shaw, Mr [*Joseph*] Ellis, who all paid the library keeper. Mr [*Bernard*] Skelton, Mr [*Benedict*] Riveley, Mr [*John*] Jeffery, who also paid the library keeper. Mr [*John*] Burton, Mr [*Robert or John*] Connold, who payd the library keeper all his arrears.

December 4 1688. Present: Mr [*Pierre*] Chauvin, Mr [*John*] Richardson,[238] this day admitted to the use of the library, Mr [*John*] Jeffery, Mr [*Benedict*] Rively, Mr [*Joseph*] Ellis, Mr [*John*] Grayle, Mr [*John*] Burton.

January 1 1689. Present: Mr [*Benedict*] Riveley, Mr [*John*] Jeffery, who paid the under library keeper, Mr [*John*] Burton, Mr [*John*] Richardson, Mr [*Steven*] Paynter, who paid the under library keeper all *arrears.*

February 5 1689. Present: Mr John Richardon, Mr Bernard Skelton, who paid the library keeper, Mr [*Benedict*] Rively, who paid the library keeper, Mr [*John*] Burton, who paid the library keeper, Mr [*John*] Shaw, who paid the library keeper, Mr [*John*] Grayle, who paid the library keeper, Mr [*John*] Jeffery. This day Mr [*William*] Adamson[239] was admitted to the use of the library. Mr [*Steven*] Paynter present. Tis desired by the persons present that the library keeper take care that those books which are wanting of the Atlas be brought into the library.[240] Mr [*Gawin*] Nash paid the library keeper all his arrears.

[238] Possibly the John Richardson who graduated BA from Pembroke College, Cambridge, in 1681 and proceeded MA in 1684. He was rector of Little Melton in 1689. In his will all his books, sermons and manuscripts were bequeathed to the 'first of his grandchildren who shall study divinity when he enters into Holy Orders'. Until then they should be in the care of his wife, though if his daughter Sarah were to marry a clergyman he should look after them until the grandchild came of age (NRO DCN IV 364, Will of John Richardson, 1720).

[239] William Adamson graduated BA from Caius College, Cambridge, in 1648 and proceeded MA in 1651. He was a Fellow of Caius from 1651 to 1669. Rector of St John Maddermarket, he was buried there in 1707. He left his nephew and godson, John Heigham of Gislingham, gentleman, books to the value of £5. He also left to several unnamed friends 'some other parcels of books', the details of which he left 'in a written paper' (NRO ANW 92, Will of William Adamson, 1707).

[240] A reference to the fact that a volume of Moses Pitt's *English Atlas* was missing.

February 16 1689. Present: Our brethren the ministers of the city mett here this day about an extraordinary occasion, & then admitted Mr [*Isaac*] Gurling[241] to the use of the library.

February 18. Received of Mr [*William*] Cecil al arrears due to mee as under library keeper. [*signed*] Sam[*uel*] Scott.

March 5 1689. Present: Mr [*Isaac*] Gurling, Mr [*Benedict*] Rively, Mr [*John*] Shaw, Mr [*John*] Jeffery, Mr [*John*] Pitts, who paid the under library keeper his arrears, Mr [*William*] Adamson, Mr [*John*] Robinson, Mr [*John*] Burton.

April 2 1689. Present: Mr [*John*] Shaw, Mr [*John*] Jeffery, Mr [*Benedict*] Rively, Mr [*Robert* or *John*] Connold, Mr [*John*] Graile.

May 7 1689. Present: Mr [*William*] Adamson, Mr [*Isaac*] Gurling. This day Mr [*William*] Hawys[242] was admitted to the library.

June 4 1689. Present: Mr [*Benjamin*] Skelton, Mr [*John*] Pitts, Mr [*William*] Hawys, Mr [*John*] Richardson paid this *lady* quarter. Mr [*William*] Adamson who paid lady quarter. Mr [*John*] Robinson. Mr [*Benedict*] Rively who paid [*Samuel*] Scott. Mr [*John*] Burton paid Lady Day quarter.

/ Quarter day / July 2 1689. Present: Mr [*John*] Richardson, who paid the last quarter, Mr [*John*] Jeffery, who also paid the *two* last quarters, Mr [*Joseph*] Ellis not present paid the three last quarters, Mr [*Isaac*] Gurling paid the last quarter, Mr [*John*] Graile paid the two last quarters, Mr [*John*] Burton paid the last quarter, Mr [*William*] Adamson paid the last quarter, Mr [*John*] Robinson paid the three last quarters, Mr [*Benedict*] Riveley paid the last quarter.

August 6 1689. Present: Mr [*John*] Jeffery, Mr [*William*] Hawys who paid the last quarter, Mr [*John*] Richardson, Mr [*John*] Burton, Mr [*William*] Adamson, Mr [*Benedict*] Rively.

[241] Isaac Girling was born in Norwich and was admitted sizar at Caius College Cambridge in 1664, graduating BA in 1668 and proceeding MA in 1671. He was vicar of West Barsham in 1672 and chaplain of St Giles in 1690. He was living in lodgings when he drew up his will, but where is not specified (NRO ANW 5, Will of Isaac Girling, 1705).

[242] William Hawys graduated BA from Corpus Christi College, Cambridge, in 1685, proceeding MA in 1693. He was instituted vicar of Wymondham in 1691. While at Wymondham he collected a considerable library (see Wymondham Abbey, Parish Records, Tithe Book, 1691–2, class 4). His will was proved in 1700 (NRO NCC, 154 Edwards, Will of William Hawys, 1700).

September 3 1689. Present: Mr [*William*] Adamson, Mr [*Joseph*] Ellis, Mr [*William*] Hawys, Mr [*John*] Grayle, Mr [*John*] Richardson, Mr [*Isaac*] Gurling, Mr [*John*] Jeffery, Mr [*Benedict*] Rively, Mr [*John*] Burton.

October 1 1689. Present: Mr [*John*] Richardson paid the last quarter, Mr [*William*] Hawys paid the last quarter, Mr [*John*] Shaw paid the last quarter, Mr [*John*] Jeffery paid the last quarter. This day Mr [*John*] Havett[243] was admitted into the library. This day Mr [*Charles*] Lullman[244] was admitted to the use of the library. Mr [*Isaac*] Girling paid the last quarter. Mr [*John*] Graile, who paid the last quarter. Mr [*John*] Burton, who paid the last quarter.

November 5 1689. Present: Mr [*John*] Burton, Mr [*William*] Hawys, Mr [*William*] Adamson, Mr [*John*] Richardson, Mr [*John*] Graile.

December 3 1689. Present: Mr [*William*] Hawys, Mr [*William*] Adamson, who paid the last quarter, Mr [*Thomas*] Clayton, Mr [*Charles*] Lulman, Mr [*John*] Graile, Mr [*John*] Robinson, < Mr [*John*] Havett, > Mr [*John*] Jeffery, Mr [*John*] Richardson.

January 7 1690. Quarter day: Mr [*John*] Shaw, Mr [*Charles*] Lulman, Mr [*John*] Jeffery who paid the library keeper, Mr [*John*] Brandon [245] was this day admitted to the use of the library. Mr [*John*] Havett, who paid the library keeper, Mr [*William*] Hawys, who paid the library keeper, Mr [*William*] Adamson, who paid his quarterage, Mr [*Benedict*] Reveley, who paid his quarterage, Mr [*John*] Richardson, who paid this quarter.

February 4 1690. Present: Mr [*Joseph*] Ellis, who paid the two last quarters, Mr [*John*] Havett, Mr [*John*] Brandon, Mr [*John*] Graile, who paid the last quarter, Mr [*Charles*] Lulman, Mr [*Benedict*] Reveley, Mr [*John*] Burton, who paid the last quarter, Mr [*John*] Richardson, Mr [*John*] Jeffery, Mr [*William*] Adamson, Mr [*Bernard*] Skelton, who paid the library keeper all arrears.

---

[243] A Norwich man, John Havett was admitted to Corpus Christi College, Cambridge, in 1682. He graduated BA in 1686 and proceeded MA in 1689. He was chaplain of St Giles from 1709 to 1714 and was buried at St Andrew's in 1714.

[244] The son of Robert Lulman, a Norwich merchant, Charles Lulman was admitted pensioner at Caius College, Cambridge, in 1682, graduating BA in 1686 and proceeding MA in 1689. He was vicar of Postwick from 1688 to 1697 and was buried in St Julian's in Norwich.

[245] John Brandon graduated BA from Emmanuel College, Cambridge, in 1688. He was rector of Little Melton and Wramplingham from 1691. When he drew up his will he was living in Little Melton (NRO NCC 43 Withers, Will of John Brandon, 1743).

March 4 1690. Present: Mr [*John*] Havett, Mr [*Charles*] Lulman, Mr [*John*] Richardson, Mr [*Benedict*] Rively, Mr [*John*] Burton, Mr [*John*] Graile.

April the first quarter day 1690. /Memorandum./ That this day we present cast up the forfeitures of the last two years, viz. 1688, 1689. And the several persons are indebted in all two pounds, ten shillings, & four pence, as appears by the particulars in the books of forfeitures. /Memorandum./ That Mr [*John*] Pitts is this day discharged from the office of library keeper & is endebted to the under library keeper for his two years for fire, candle, pipes, pens, ink & paper, nine shillings. /Memorandum./ That Mr [*Peter*] Burges was chosen library keeper for the present year.
Present: Mr [*Benedict*] Rively, Mr [*John*] Jeffery, Mr [*John*] Richardson, who all paid the under library keeper for the last quarter.

May 6 1690. Present: Mr [*John*] Jeffery, Mr [*John*] Richardson, Mr [*Benedict*] Rively, Mr [*John*] Burton, who paid the last quarter, Mr [*Benjamin*] Nobbs junior,[246] who was this day admitted to the use of the library.

June 3 1690. Present: Mr [*John*] Richardson, Mr [*William*] Adamson, who paid for last quarter, Mr [*Charles*] Chapman, Mr [*Bernard*] Skelton, Mr [*Joseph*] Ellis, who paid the last quarter, Mr [*Benedict*] Rively, Mr [*John*] Burton, Mr [*John*] Graile, who paid the last quarter.

---

[246] Benjamin Nobbs was the first antiquarian to join the Library. There is evidence that he kept a school and that he taught the theologian Samuel Clarke as well as Clarke's brother, John, who became dean of Salisbury (NRO MS 453, T. Johnson, Letter concerning Nobbs' History of Norwich, 25 January 1755). Another of his pupils was Thomas Seaman, the son of Sir Peter Seaman, mayor of Norwich (Branford, p. 229). He was for many years parish clerk of St Gregory's. Nobbs' antiquarian work was used by John Kirkpatrick. A section of one of Kirkpatrick's manuscripts is headed 'Remarkable Things out of a MS written by Mr Nobbs (NRO COL/8/91, Kirkpatrick Manuscripts). Again, in an account of Stump Cross, Magdalen Street, Kirkpatrick recorded that it was 're-edified' in 1640 and gave as his source the 'Nobbs Manuscript' (John Kirkpatrick, *The Streets and Lanes of Norwich*, Norwich, 1889, p. 83). The only work attributed to Nobbs to have survived is a short manuscript history of Norwich (NRO MS 453, Benjamin Nobbs' Description of the City of Norwich). A reading of the manuscript provides a few more clues about its author. It is clear, for example, that he was an eyewitness of the events of the Glorious Revolution: 'This year Dec 1 [1688] the Duke of Norfolk rode into the market place at the head of about 300 knights and gentlemen, & declared for a free Parliament where the Mayor from the Guild-Hall met him & joined him'. He deplored the lack of religious and political unity amongst the inhabitants of Norwich. The city 'hath been stored with learned preachers for many years, by reason whereof the inhabitants are reasonably well instructed in the principles of religion, though of late, through too much liberty, they run into sects and parties'.

July 1 [*1690*]. Quarter day. Present: Mr [*John*] Graile, Mr [*Joseph*] Ellis, Mr [*John*] Richardson, who paid the last quarter, Mr [*Benedict*] Rively, who paid the last quarter, Mr [*Bernard*] Skelton, who paid the 2 last quarters. Mr [*John*] Burton, who paid the last quarter.

August 5 [*1690*]. Present: Mr [*John*] Richardson, Mr [*John*] Jeffery, who paid the last quarter, Mr [*John*] Graile, who paid the last quarter, Mr [*Bernard*] Skelton, Mr [*Thomas*] Clayton, who paid the last quarter, Mr [*John*] Burton, Mr [*Benedict*] Rively < paid the last quarter >, Mr [*William*] Adamson, who was this day chosen library keeper for this present year upon Mr [*Peter*] Burgess his refusal – paid the library keeper for the last quarter.

September 2 1690. Present: Mr [*Joseph*] Elis, Mr [*Bernard*] Skelton, Mr [*John*] Shaw, Mr [*John*] Burton, Mr [*John*] Richardson.

October 7 1690. Quarter day. Present: Mr [*John*] Jeffery, who paid the under library keeper, Mr [*Charles*] Chapman, who paid the last quarter, Mr [*John*] Richardson, who paid last quarter, Mr [*Thomas*] Clayton, who paid the library keeper, Mr [*William*] Adamson, who paid the library keeper, Mr [*John*] Brandon, who paid the 3 last quarters, Mr [*John*] Burton, who paid Michaelmas quarter, Mr [*Benedict*] Rively, who paid Michaelmas quarter.

November 4 [*1690*]. Mr [*John*] Richardson, Mr [*John*] Jeffery, Mr [*John*] Brandon, Mr [*William*] Adamson, Mr [*Joseph*] Ellys, who paid the 2 last quarters, Mr [*Bernard*] Skelton, Mr [*John*] Burton, Mr [*John*] Graile, who paid the last quarter, Mr [*Benedict*] Riveley.

December 2 [*1690*]. Present: Mr [*Joseph*] Ellis, Mr [*John*] Richardson, Mr [*John*] Brandon, Mr [*William*] Adamson, Mr [*Bernard*] Skelton, who paid the last quarter, Mr [*John*] Jeffery, Mr [*John*] Graile, Mr [*John*] Burton, Mr [*Benedict*] Riveley.

January 6 1691. Quarter day. Present: Mr [*Benedict*] Rively, Mr [*John*] Burton, who both paid Christmas quarter, Mr [*Bernard*] Skelton, Mr [*William*] Adamson, Mr [*John*] Graile.

February 3 1691. Mr [*John*] Richardson, who paid Christmas quarter, Mr [*William*] Adamson, who paid Christmas quarter, Mr [*Benedict*] Rivily, Mr [*Robert*] Lulman, who paid all the arrears, Mr John Jeffery, who paid Christmas quarter, Mr [*John*] Burton.

March 3 1691. Present: Mr [*John*] Richardson, Mr Connould paid all arrears to the under library keeper, Mr [*Bernard*] Skelton, Mr [*John*] Jeffryes, Mr [*Thomas*] Clayton, who paid Christmas quarter, Mr [*William*] Adamson, Mr [*John*] Burton, Mr [*Joseph*] Ellis.

April 7 1691. Quarter day. Present: Mr [*John*] Richardson, who paid the last quarter, Mr [*Joseph*] Ellis, Mr [*Thomas*] Clayton, Mr [*John*] Jeffery, who paid the last quarter, Mr [*Charles*] Lulman, Mr [*William*] Adamson, who paid this last quarter, Mr [*Bernard*] Skelton, who paid these 2 last quarters. Mr [*Benedict*] Reveley, who paid the library keeper, Mr [*John*] Burton, who paid the last quarter.

May 5 1691. Present: Mr [*John*] Jeffery, Mr [*John*] Richardson, Mr [*Benedict*] Revely, Mr [*Bernard*] Skelton, Mr [*John*] Brandon, Mr [*John*] Burton.

June 2 1691. Present: Mr [*John*] Jeffery, Mr [*Joseph*] Ellis, Mr [*William*] Adamson, Mr [*Charles*] Lullman, Mr [*John*] Richardson, Mr [*Benedict*] Revely, Mr [*John*] Graile, who paid the two last quarters.

July 7 1691. Quarter day. Present: Mr [*John*] Richardson, who paid this quarter, Mr [*Benedict*] Reveley, who paid also for this quarter, Mr [*Charles*] Lulman, who paid this quarter, Mr [*John*] Burton, who paid this quarter.

August 4 1691. Present: Mr [*William*] Adamson, who paid last quarter, Mr [*Benedict*] Reveley, Mr [*John*] Richardson, Mr [*John*] Grayle, who paid last quarter, Mr [*John*] Barker,[247] who is this day admitted to the use of the library, Mr [*Robert* or *John*] Conold who paid all to this day, Mr [*Bernard*] Skelton, who paid last quarter, Mr [*John*] Burton.

September 1 1691. Present: Mr [*Bernard*] Skelton, Mr [*Robert* or *John*] Conould, Mr [*John*] Richardson, Mr [*John*] Barker. Memorandum. About this time Mr [*William*] Adamson sent in *Corpus Juris Civilis* with Gothofredi[248] notes in 2 volumes, being his own gift.

Quarter day October 6 1691. Present: Mr [*William*] Adamson, who paid the last quarter, Mr [*Benedict*] Rively, who paid the last quarter, Mr [*John*]

[247] John Barker was admitted pensioner at Caius College, Cambridge, in 1683, graduating BA in 1687 snd proceeding MA in 1690. He was elected Fellow of his College in 1691. Curate of St Martin at Palace from 1692 to 1730, he was buried there in September 1730, though he appears to have lived in the parish of St Michael Coslany (NRO ANW 28, Administration of John Barker, 1730).

[248] Denis Godefroy, *Corpus civilis quo ius universum justinianeum comprehenditur* (Lyon, 1650)

Jeffery, who paid the two last quarters, Mr [*John*] Barker, who paid the library keeper, Mr [*John*] Burton, who paid the library keeper.

November 3 1691. Present: Mr [*Benedict*] Rively, Mr [*Joseph*] Ellis, Mr [*John*] Jeffery, Mr [*John*] Burton, Mr [*John*] Barker.

December 1 1691. Present: Mr [*John*] Richardson, who paid the last quarter, Mr [*William*] Adamson, Mr [*John*] Graile who paid the last quarter, Mr [*John*] Jeffery, Mr [*Thomas*] Clayton, who paid all arrears to the under library keeper.

January 5 1692. Quarter day. Present: Mr [*John*] Richardson, who paid the last quarter, Mr [*John*] Burton, who payd the library keeper, Mr [*Benedict*] Riveley, who payd the quarter, Mr [*William*] Adamson, who paid the quarter, Mr [*John*] Jefferies, who paid the library keeper last quarter, Mr [*John*] Graile, who paid the quarter.

February 2 1691. Present: Mr [*John*] Graile, Mr [*Charles*] Lulman, who paid one quarter, Mr [*John*] Richardson, Mr [*Benedict*] Reveley.

March 1 1691. Present: Mr [*John*] Richardson, Mr [*John*] Graile, Mr [*Benedict*] Rively, Mr [*William*] Adamson, Mr [*John*] Jeffery, Mr [*John*] Burton. Agreed that Mr Adamson be continued library keeper for the year ensuing.

April 5 1692. Quarter day. These persons following were present viz. Mr [*Benedict*] Reveley, Mr [*William*] Adamson, Mr [*John*] Barker paid 2 last quarters, Mr [*John*] Burton who paid last quarter.

May 3 1692. Present: Mr [*John*] Richardson, who paid the last quarter, Mr [*William*] Adamson, Mr [*John*] Jeffery, who paid the last quarter, Mr [*John*] Graile, who paid the last quarter. Mr [*Benedict*] Rively, Mr [*John*] Burton.

June 7 [*1692*]. Present: Mr [*Benedict*] Rively, Mr [*John*] Graile, Mr [*John*] Barker, Mr [*John*] Richardson, Mr [*William*] Adamson, Mr [*John*] Jeffery, Mr [*John*] Burton.

July 5 1692. Quarter day. Present: John Richardson, who paid this quarter, Mr [*John*] Barker, who paid this quarter, Mr Ber[*nard*] Skelton, who paid all arrears to this day, Mr [*William*] Adamson, who paid this last quarter, Mr [*John*] Jeffery, who paid the last quarter, Mr [*John*] Burton, who paid the last quarter, Mr [*Benedict*] Reveley.

August 2 [*1692*]. Present: Mr [*John*] Richardson, Mr [*John*] Jeffery, Mr [*Benedict*] Rively, who paid the under library keeper, Mr [*John*] Graile, who paid the under library keeper, Mr [*John*] Barker, Mr [*John*] Burton.

September 6 1692. Present: Mr [*Benedict*] Reveley, Mr [*John*] Barker, Mr [*John*] Burton, Mr [*John*] Richardson, Mr [*William*] Adamson.

October 4 1692. Quarter day. Present: Mr [*John*] Barker, who payd this quarter, Mr [*William*] Adamson, who paid this quarter, Mr [*John*] Richardson, Mr [*John*] Graile paid this quarter, Mr [*John*] Whitefoot paid this quarter, Mr [*John*] Burton who paid this quarter.

November 1 1692. Present: Mr [*William*] Adamson, Mr [*Bernard*] Skelton, who paid this quarter, Mr [*John*] Richardson, who paid this quarter, Mr [*Thomas*] Clayton, who paid all arrears to the under library keeper, Mr [*John*] Burton.

December 6 1692. Present: Mr [*Benedict*] Reveley, who paid Michaelmas quarter, Mr [*John*] Graile, Mr [*John*] Barker, Mr [*John*] Richardson, Mr [*John*] Burton.

January 3 [*1693*]. Quarter day. Present: Mr [*John*] Richardson, who paid Christmas quarter, Mr [*Benedict*] Reveley, who paid Christmas quarter, Mr [*William*] Adamson, who paid Christmas quarter, Mr [*John*] Jeffery, who paid the two last quarters, Mr [*John*] Graile, who paid Christmas quarter. Memorandum. That Mr Graile was chosen library keeper for the ensuing year & that Mr [*William*] Adamson paid the under library keeper his dues for the 2 preceding years.

February 7 [*1693*]. Present: Mr [*John*] Richardson, Mr [*William*] Adamson, Mr [*John*] Jeffery, Mr [*Benedict*] Reveley, Mr [*John*] Burton, who payd Christmas quarter, Mr [*John*] Graile, Mr [*Joseph*] Ellis, who paid all arrears which were due. Memorandum. That February 8 1692 Mr Adamson payd all his arrears to the library keeper. February 12 Memorandum. Mr [*Robert or John*] Conold payed then all arrears to the under library keeper. Sam[*uel*] Scott.

March 7 1693. Present: Mr [*John*] Richardson, Mr [*William*] Adamson, Mr [*John*] Whitefoot, who paid the last quarter, Mr [*John*] Burton, Mr [*Benedict*] Rively, Mr [*Bernard*] Skelton, who paid the last quarter, Mr [*John*] Jefferyes.

April 4 1693. Present: Mr [*William*] Adamson, who paid this quarter, Mr [*John*] Grayle, who paid this quarter, Mr [*John*] Jefferyes, who paid this quarter, Mr [*Benedict*] Rively, who paid this quarter.

May 2 1693. Present: Mr [*John*] Jeffery, Mr [*John*] Richardson paid this quarter, Mr [*John*] Barker paid Christmas & Lady quarters, Mr [*Benedict*] Rively, Mr [*John*] Burton payd Lady quarter, Mr [*John*] Graile, Mr [*William*] Adamson.

June 6 1693. Mr [*John*] Grayle, Mr [*John*] Richardson, Mr [*William*] Adamson.

July 4 Quarter day. 1693. Present: Mr [*John*] Whitefoot paid this quarter, Mr [*John*] Richardson paid this quarter, Mr [*John*] Barker paid this quarter, Mr [*Benedict*] Revely paid this quarter, Mr [*John*] Burton payd this quarter.

August 1 1693. Present: Mr [*William*] Adamson paid last quarter, Mr [*John*] Graile paid the library keeper, Mr [*John*] Burton, Mr [*John*] Richardson, Mr [*John*] Barker, Mr [*John*] Jeffery, Mr [*Richard*] Laughton,[249] who was this day admitted to the use of the library.

September 5 1693. Present: Mr [*John*] Jefferyes, Mr [*William*] Adamson, Mr [*John*] Richardson, Mr [*Benedict*] Rively, Mr [*John*] Burton.

October 3 Quarter day. 1693. Present: Mr [*Benedict*] Rively, Mr [*John*] Burton, who both paid the library keeper, Mr [*John*] Jeffery, who paid the library keeper, Mr [*John*] Graile, who paid the library keeper, Mr [*Richard*] Laughton, who paid the library keeper.

November 7 1693. Present: Mr [*Benedict*] Reveley, Mr [*John*] Burton.

December 5 1693. Present: Mr [*John*] Richardson, who paid the library keeper, Mr [*Benedict*] Rively, Mr [*John*] Barker, who paid the library keeper, Mr [*William*] Adamson, who paid the library keeper, Mr [*John*] Burton, Mr [*Benjamin*] Nobbes junior, Mr [*John*] Jeffery.

[249] A Londoner by birth, Richard Laughton graduated BA from Clare College, Cambridge, in 1685, proceeding MA in 1691. He was a Fellow of his College from 1686. In 1693 he became chaplain to bishop John Moore and, at the same time, joined the library. He was a great populariser of Newtonian physics and a vigorous partisan of the Whigs. His papers, which are deposited in Clare College, Cambridge, include an annotated copy of Newton's *Principia* (J. Gascoigne, 'Politics, patronage and Newtonianism: the Cambridge example', *Historical Journal*, xxvii, 1984, p. 15n).

January 2 Quarter day. 1694. Present: Mr [*Benedict*] Rively, Mr [*John*] Burton, who both payd the library keeper, Mr [*William*] Adamson, who hath paid the library keeper, Mr [*Benjamin*] Nobbes, who payd the library keeper.

February 6 1694. Present: Mr [*John*] Jeffery, who payd the library keeper, Mr [*Benedict*] Reveley, Mr [*William*] Adamson, Mr [*Benjamin*] Nobbes, Mr [*John*] Burton, Mr [*Thomas*] Clayton, who paid all arrears to the library keeper.

March 6 [*1694*]. Present: Mr [*William*] Adamson, Mr [*Benedict*] Revely, Mr [*Isaac*] Gurling, Mr [*John*] Barker, who paid the last quarter, Mr [*Benjamin*] Nobbs jun[*io*]r, Mr Girling paid all arrears to this day, Mr [*John*] Jeffery.

Aprill 3 1694. Quarter day. Present: Mr [*John*] Richardson paid the library keeper for 2 quarters, Mr [*William*] Adamson paid the library keeper, Mr [*John*] Barker payd the library keeper this quarter, Mr [*Benjamin*] Nobbes who paid the library keeper, Mr [*Benedict*] Revely, who paid the library keeper, Mr [*John*] Burton, who paid the library keeper.

May 1 1694. Present: Mr [*John*] Richardson, Mr [*John*] Burton, Mr [*Benedict*] Revely.

June 4 1694. Present: Mr [*John*] Jeffery, who paid the library keeper, Mr [*John*] Richardson, Mr [*Benjamin*] Nobbes, Mr [*William*] Adamson, Mr [*John*] Barker, Mr [*Richard*] Laughton paid the last 2 quarters, Mr [*Thomas*] Clayton, Mr [*John*] Burton.

July 3 1694. Quarter day. Present: Mr [*John*] Barker, who paid the library keeper, Mr [*Benjamin*] Nobbes, who paid the library keeper, Mr [*Thomas*] Clayton, who paid the library keeper all arrears, Mr [*Richard*] Laughton not present but paid the library keeper.

August 7 1694. Present: Mr [*William*] Adamson, who paid the last quarter, Mr [*John*] Richardson, who paid the last quarter, Mr [*John*] Burton, who payd the last quarter.

September 2 [*1694*]. Mr [*John*] Richardson, Mr [*John*] Burton, Mr [*John*] Jeffery, Mr [*John*] Graile, Mr [*Benedict*] Rively, Mr [*John*] Barker, Mr [*William*] Adamson.

October 2 1694. Quarter day. Present: Mr [*Benedict*] Rively, who paid this & the last quarter, Mr [*William*] Adamson, who paid the library keeper,

Jo[*hn*] Barker paid the library keeper, Mr [*Thomas*] Clayton, who paid the library keeper, Mr [*John*] Burton paid the library keeper.

November 6 1694. Present: Mr [*John*] Jeffery, who paid the two last quarters, Mr [*William*] Adamson, Mr [*Benedict*] Rively, Mr [*John*] Barker, Mr [*John*] Burton.

December 4 1694. Present: Mr Arch[*deacon*] Jeffery, Mr [*John*] Barker, Mr [*William*] Adamson, Mr [*Benedict*] Rively, Mr [*John*] Burton.

January 1 1695. Quarter day. Present: Mr [*John*] Burton, who paid the library keepers.

February 5 1695. Present: Mr [*John*] Burton, Mr [*William*] Adamson, who paid the library keeper, Mr [*John*] Barker, who paid the library keeper, Mr [*John*] Graile, who paid the charges of library keeper & all the arrears of this quarter.

March 5 1695. Present: Mr [*John*] Richardson, who paid the library keeper 2 quarters. Mr [*William*] Adamson, Mr [*John*] Burton, Mr [*John*] Barker, Mr [*John*] Whitefoot who paid this quarter & all arrears.

Quarter day. April 2 1695. Present: Mr [*John*] Barker, who paid the library keeper, Mr [*John*] Richardson, who paid the library keeper, Mr [*William*] Adamson, who paid the library keeper, Mr [*John*] Grayle, who paid the library keeper. Mr [*Charles*] Trimnell[250] was this day admitted to the use of the library. Mr [*John*] Burton paid the library keeper. Mr [*Benedict*] Rieveley's arrears were all paid. Memorandum. Mr Richardson chosen library keeper for the next year from Christmas last 1694.

May 7 1695. Present: Mr [*John*] Richardson, Mr [*William*] Adamson, Mr [*John*] Barker, Mr [*Benjamin*] Nobbs paid the under library keeper all

[250] Benjamin Mackerell, who knew Trimnell well, painted a flattering portrait of a man with a gift for friendship: 'He was Remarkable for his Great Affability, Humility and Sweetness of Disposition, wherever he came, he was a Great Benefactor. He was a man of Great Worth integrity & Probity of Great Hospitality and Charity. Beloved by all that knew him' (NRO, MS 79, Benjamin Mackerell, History of Norwich, p. 120). Trimnell's politics were clearly Whiggish. In a sermon on Charles I's execution ('base, black and monstrous') he vigorously criticised the king's advisers, suggesting that their mistakes had been responsible for the civil war (Charles Trimnell, *A sermon preached before the Lords Spiritual and Temporal, in Parliament Assembled*, London, 1712, p. 10). He was consecrated bishop of Norwich in 1708, in succession to John Moore. In 1714, 'being willing to encourage soe good a design', he granted a faculty to St Margaret's church, King's Lynn, to convert a corner of the south-west end of the nave for a library on condition that 'a true and perfect catalogue of all the books in the said library,' signed by the minister, be delivered to the diocesan authorities (NHC, KL018.2, St Margaret's Church Library Catalogue, 1631, pp. 37–8).

arrears, Mr [*John*] Graile, Mr [*John*] Burton. Mr [*William*] Martin[251] was this day admitted to the use of the library. Mr [*Joseph*] Ellis paid all arrears to Lady [*day*].

June 4 1695. Present: Mr [*John*] Barker, Mr [*William*] Adamson, Mr [*Thomas*] Clayton paid all arrears to the library keeper, Mr Arch[*deacon*] Jeffery, who paid the two last quarters, Mr [*John*] Burton.

July 2 1695. Quarter day. Present: Mr [*John*] Richardson, who paid the library keeper, Mr [*John*] Barker, who paid this quarter, Mr [*William*] Adamson payd this quarter, Mr [*Benjamin*] Nobbes, who paid this quarter. Mr Edward Revely[252] was this day admitted to the use of the library. Mr [*John*] Burton, who payd this quarter, Mr [*John*] Graile, who paid this quarter.

August 6 1695. Present: Mr [*John*] Barker, Mr [*Benjamin*] Nobbes, Mr [*John*] Richardson, Mr [*William*] Martin, who payd the last quarter, Mr [*John*] Burton.

September 3 1695. Present: Mr [*William*] Adamson, Mr [*Edward*] Revely, Mr [*John*] Barker, Mr [*John*] Burton, Mr [*William*] Whiston[253] this day admitted to the use of the library.

October 1 Quarter day. Present: Mr [*John*] Richardson paid the library keeper this quarter, Mr [*William*] Adamson paid the library keeper this quarter, Mr [*William*] Whiston paid the library keeper this quarter, Mr [*Benjamin*] Nobbs paid the library keeper this quarter, Mr [*John*] Burton paid the library keeper this quarter, Mr [*John*] Graile paid the library keeper this quarter, Mr [*Theophilus*] Browne[254] this day admitted to the use of the library.

[251] Possibly William Martin, the father of the antiquary, 'Honest' Tom Martin, of Thetford. Educated at Bury St Edmunds, William Martin graduated BA from Jesus College, Cambridge, in 1676, proceeding MA in 1679. Ordained in Norwich, he was rector of St Mary's, Thetford.

[252] The son of Benedict Riveley, Edward Riveley graduated BA from Corpus Christi College Cambridge in 1685 and proceeded MA in 1688. He was ordained in Norwich in December 1686. He was vicar of St Benedict's, St Swithin and St Margaret's, Norwich, and died in 1729.

[253] William Whiston, philosopher, theologian and friend of Isaac Newton, was chaplain to Bishop John Moore, vicar of Drayton and vicar of Lowestoft. He succeeded Newton as Lucasian Professor of Mathematics at Cambridge in May 1702. It was while he was living in Norwich that Whiston published his first book, *A new theory of the earth* (1696), in which he attempted to prove the Genesis story to his own satisfaction 'on Newtonian grounds', explaining the Flood by the collision of a comet with the Earth.

[254] Theophilus Browne graduated BA from Corpus Christi College, Cambridge, in 1693 and proceeded MA in 1696. He was rector of Swanton Abbots in 1698, rector of Thwaite in

November 5 1695. Present: Mr [*William*] Whiston, Mr [*Theophilus*] Brown, Mr [*John*] Barker, who payd the last quarter.

December 3 1695. Present: Mr [*Edward*] Rively payd the last quarter, Mr [*John*] Barker, Mr [*John*] Burton.

January 7 1696. Quarter day. Present; Mr [*John*] Burton, who paid this last quarter, Mr [*John*] Whitefoot, who paid this last quarter & arrears, Mr [*John*] Richardson, who paid this last quarter, Mr [*William*] Adamson, who payed this quarter, Mr Arch[*deacon*] Jeffery, who paid all arrears to this day, Mr [*John*] Graile, who paid this last quarter, Mr [*Joseph*] Ellis paid all arrears, Mr [*Benjamin*] Nobbes paid this last quarter, Mr [*William*] Martin paid all arrears to this day.

February 4 1696. Present: Mr [*John*] Whitefoot, Mr [*John*] Barker, who paid the last quarter, Mr [*Edward*] Rively, who paid the last quarter, Mr [*John*] Burton, Mr [*John*] Grayle, T[*heophilus*] Browne, who paid the last quarter, Mr [*Benjamin*] Nobbes.

March 3 1696. Present: Mr [*John*] Richardson, Mr [*William*] Adamson, Mr [*John*] Barker, Mr [*Theophilus*] Brown, Mr [*Edward*] Riveley, Mr [*John*] Burton.

April 7 [*1696*] Quarter day. Present: Mr [*William*] Adamson, who paid the last quarter, Mr [*Edward*] Reveley, who paid the last quarter, Mr [*John*] Burton also paid the last quarter.

May 5 1696. Present: Mr [*John*] Richardson paid the last quarter, Mr [*Charles*] Trimnell paid the last quarter, Mr [*John*] Burton, Mr [*John*] Barker paid the last quarter, Mr [*Benjamin*] Nobbes paid the last quarter, Mr [*John*] Graile, who paid the last quarter.

June 2 1696. Present: Mr A[*rchdeacon*] Jeffery paid the last quarter, Mr [*Joseph*] Ellis, Mr [*John*] Whitefoot paid the last quarter, Mr [*Thomas*] Clayton, Mr [*William*] Adamson, Mr [*Benjamin*] Nobbes, Mr [*John*] Graile. Mr [*William*] Agas[255] was this day admitted to the use of the library.

1700 and vicar of Calthorpe until 1700. He owned property in Framingham Earl, Framingham Pigot, Brooke, Howe, Thwaite, Alby, Brundall, Bradeston, Great and Little Plumstead, Witton and Poringland (NRO ANW 308, Will of Theophilus Browne, 1733).

[255] William Agas graduated BA from St Catherine's College, Cambridge, in 1695 and proceeded MA in 1702. Ordained deacon in Norwich in June 1696, he was instituted vicar of Hempnall in 1697.

July 7 1696. Quarter day. Mr [*John*] Burton paid the last quarter, Mr [*John*] Grail paid the last quarter.

August 4 1696. Present: Mr [*John*] Barker, who paid the last quarter, Dr [*John*] Jefferyes,[256] Mr [*John*] Burton.

September 1 1696. Present: Mr [*John*] Barker, Mr [*Thomas*] Clayton paid all arrears, Mr [*John*] Burton, Mr [*John*] Graile, Mr [*Joseph*] Ellis, who paid all arrears, Mr [*Isaac*] Girling, who paid all arrears.

October 6 1696. Quarter day. Present: Mr [*Joseph*] Ellis, Mr [*Edward*] Reveley paid all arrears, Mr [*Benjamin*] Nobbs paid all arrears, Mr [*John*] Barker, who paid the last quarter, Mr [*John*] Burton, who paid the library keeper, Mr [*Theophilus*] Brown, who paid the library keeper.

November 3 1696. Present: Mr [*Edward*] Reveley, Mr [*John*] Burton.

December 1 1696. Present: Mr [*Edward*] Reveley, Mr [*John*] Barker, Mr [*John*] Richardson paid all arrears to the library keeper, Mr [*John*] Burton. Mr Richardson was this day dismissed from being library keeper, having first paid to Sam[*uel*] Scott nine shillings for 2 years charges. Mr [*William*] Cecil take himself out of the library this day and owe the under library keeper for three years and three quarters £0. 15s. 00.

January 5 1697. Quarter day. Present: Mr [*John*] Graile, who paid all arrears, Mr [*Edward*] Reveley, who paid the last quarter, Mr [*John*] Whitefoot paid all arrears, Mr [*John*] Richardson paid the last quarter. /Memorandum/ Mr [*Joseph*] Ellis chosen library keeper for the two ensuing years.

February 2 1697. Present: Mr [*John*] Barker, who paid the last quarter, Mr [*John*] Burton, who paid the last quarter.

March 2 1697. Present: Mr [*Edward*] Reveley, Mr [*John*] Barker, Mr [*John*] Graile, Mr [*John*] Burton.

Aprill 6 1697. Quarter day. Mr [*John*] Barker, who paid the last quarter, Mr [*John*] Richardson paid the last quarter, Mr [*Edward*] Reveley paid the last quarter, Mr [*John*] Graile paid the last quarter, Mr A[*rch*]d[*eacon*] Jefferies paid all arrears to this time, Mr [*William*] Adamson paid all arrears to this time.

---

[256] John Jeffery was awarded a Doctorate in Divinity in 1696 (ODNB).

May 4 1697. Present: Mr [*John*] Barker, Mr [*John*] Richardson, Mr [*John*] Burton paid the last quarter, Mr [*Theophilus*] Browne paid the two last quarters, Dr [*John*] Jeffery.

June 1 1697. Present: Mr [*William*] Whiston, Mr [*John*] Richardson, Mr [*Edward*] Reveley, Mr [*John*] Burton, Dr [*John*] Jeffery.

July 6 1697. Quarter day. Present: Mr [*John*] Barker, who paid the last quarter, Mr [*John*] Burton, who paid the last quarter, Mr [*John*] Richardson, who paid the last quarter.

August 3 1697. Present: Mr [*William*] Adamson, who paid the last quarter, Mr [*John*] Barker.

September 7 1697. Present: Mr [*John*] Barker, Mr [*Thomas*] Clayton paid all arrears to this day, Mr [*John*] Graile, Mr [*John*] Burton.

October 5 [*1697*]. Quarter day. Present: Mr [*Theophilus*] Brown, who paid the 2 last quarters, Mr [*John*] Barker, who paid the last quarter, Mr [*William*] Adamson, who paid this quarter, Mr [*John*] Burton, who paid the library keeper.

November 2 1697. Present: Mr [*John*] Barker, Mr [*Edward*] Reveley, Mr [*William*] Adamson, Mr [*John*] Burton.

December 7 1697. Present: Mr [*Joseph*] Ellis paid all arrears to this day, Mr [*Edward*] Revely, who paid the 2 last quarters, Mr [*Theophilus*] Browne, Mr [*John*] Whitefoot paid all arrears to this day. Mr Samuel Clerk[257] was this day admitted. Mr [*John*] Barker.

January 4 1698. Quarter day. Present: Mr [*Edward*] Reveley, who paid the last quarter, Mr [*John*] Burton, who payd the last quarter.

February 1 1698. Present: Mr [*John*] Whitefoot, who paid the last quarter, Mr [*Samuel*] Clerk, Mr [*John*] Barker, who paid the last quarter, Mr [*William*] Adamson, who paid the last quarter, Mr [*John*] Graile, who paid all arrears, Mr [*John*] Burton.

[257] Samuel Clarke, the son of the Norwich Member of Parliament, Edward Clarke, had been educated at Norwich School and Caius College, Cambridge. He was elected a Fellow at Caius in 1696. William Whiston recorded meeting Clarke in a Norwich coffee-house in 1697 where they discussed the 'sublime discoveries' of Isaac Newton. Whiston introduced Clarke to bishop John Moore. When Whiston was given the living of Lowesoft Clarke succeeded him as chaplain to Bishop Moore (William Whiston, *Historical Memoirs of the Life of Dr Samuel Clarke*, London, 1730, pp. 5–9).

March 1 1698. Present: Mr [*John*] Whitefoot, Mr [*John*] Barker, Mr [*William*] Adamson, Mr [*Edward*] Reveley, Mr [*Samuel*] Clerk, Dr [*John*] Jeffery, who paid 3 quarters all due.

April 5 1698. Quarter day. Present: Mr [*John*] Barker, who paid the last quarter, Mr [*John*] Burton, who paid the last quarter, Mr [*Samuel*] Clarke, who paid the last quarter, Mr [*William*] Adamson, who paid the last quarter, Mr [*Edward*] Reveley, who paid the last quarter.

May 3 1698. Present: Mr [*John*] Richardson, who paid all arrears, Mr [*John*] Burton, Mr [*Theophilus*] Brown, who paid all arrears. Mr Joseph Brett[258] was admitted to the use of the library, May 26.

June 7 1698. Present: Mr [*John*] Richardson, Mr [*Samuel*] Clerke, Mr [*Edward*] Reveley, Mr [*Joseph*] Brett, Mr [*John*] Barker, Mr [*John*] Whitefoot, who paid the last quarter, Mr [*John*] Burton.

July 5 1698. Quarter day. Present: Mr [*Joseph*] Brett, who paid the last quarter, Mr [*John*] Barker, who paid the last quarter, Mr [*William*] Adamson, who paid the last quarter, Mr [*John*] Burton, who paid the last quarter, Mr [*Samuel*] Clark, who paid the last quarter, Mr [*Theophilus*] Browne, who paid the last quarter.

August 2 1698. Present: Mr [*William*] Adamson, Mr [*Samuel*] Clerke, Mr [*John*] Burton, Mr [*John*] Barker.

September 6 1698. Present: Mr [*Edward*] Reveley, who paid the last quarter, Mr [*John*] Barker, Mr [*William*] Adamson, Mr [*John*] Burton, Mr [*John*] Richardson, who paid the last quarter.

October 4 1698. Quarter day. Present: Mr [*John*] Barker, who paid the last quarter, Mr [*William*] Adamson, who paid the last quarter, Mr [*Benedict*] Reveley, who paid the last quarter, Mr [*Joseph*] Brett, who paid the last

[258] Born in Norwich the son of a mercer, Joseph Brett was educated at Caius College, Cambridge, where he was a Fellow. He was rector of St Clement's, Norwich, from 1696 to 1719 and of St Augustine's from 1700. In a sermon delivered at the Cathedral he attacked occasional conformists, branding them as odious as church papists, in fact more so since they had succeeded in effecting the ruin of both the monarchy and the Church of England during the civil war, whereas the papists had only attempted it (Joseph Brett, *A Sermon Preach'd in the Cathedral Church of Norwich upon 8 March 1703–4*, Norwich, 1704, pp. 23–4). Not surprisingly, Brett voted for the Tory candidates, Robert Bene and Richard Berney, in the Norwich election of 1715 (*An alphabetical draught of the poll in the city of Norwich of Robert Bene and Richard Berney*, Norwich, 1714, p. 6). His will was proved in 1719 (NRO NCC 275 Butter, Will of Joseph Brett, 1719).

quarter, Mr [*Samuel*] Clark, who paid the last quarter, Mr [*John*] Burton, who paid the last quarter.

November 1 1698. Present: Mr [*Edward*] Reveley, Mr [*John*] Burton, Mr [*John*] Barker.

December 6 1698. Present: Mr [*Edward*] Reveley, Mr [*John*] Graile, who paid all arrears, Mr [*John*] Richardson, who paid the last quarter, Mr [*John*] Barker, Mr [*Joseph*] Brett, Mr [*John*] Burton.

January 3 [*1699*]. Quarter day. Present: Mr [*Joseph*] Brett, who paid the last quarter, Mr [*John*] Burton, who paid the last quarter, Mr [*William*] Adamson, who paid the last quarter, Dr [*John*] Jeffery, who paid all arrears.

February 7 1699. Present: Mr [*John*] Richardson, Mr [*John*] Barker, who paid the last quarter, Mr [*Joseph*] Brett, Mr [*Joseph*] Ellis, who paid 9s. for 2 yeares charge of library keeper, & 5s. in arrears for quarterage & was discharged from the office of library keeper. Mr [*John*] Burton. Memorandum. That Mr [*Isaac*] Girling was this day chosen library keeper for the two years ensuing.

March 7 1699. Present: Mr [*John*] Burton, Mr [*Edward*] Reveley, who paid the last quarter, Mr [*John*] Barker, Mr [*William*] Adamson, Mr [*John*] Richardson paid the last quarter, Mr [*Joseph*] Brett, Mr [*Theophilus*] Browne, who paid the two last quarters then exchanged with Mr [*William*] Adamson Aretius in 2 volumes being a duplicate for Lonicer *de rebus Turcicis*,[259] Camerarius his *observations*[260] & Pemble's *works*.[261]

April 4 1699. Quarter day. Present: Mr [*John*] Richardson, who paid this quarter, Mr [*Edward*] Reveley, who paid the last quarter, Mr [*Joseph*] Brett, who paid the last quarter, Mr [*John*] Burton, who paid the last quarter, Mr [*John*] Barker, who paid the last quarter.

May 2 1699. Present: Mr [*Joseph*] Brett, Mr [*John*] Barker, Mr [*John*] Richardson, Mr [*William*] Adamson, who paid the last quarter.

May 15 1699. Mr [*Thomas*] Clayton paid all arrears.

[259] Philipp Lonicer: *Chronicorum Turcicorum, in quibus Turcorum origo* (Frankfurt, 1578).

[260] Philipp Camerarius: *The living librarie, or Meditations and observations historical, natural, moral, political and poetical.*

[261] William Pemble: *The workes of that learned Minister of Gods holy Word, Mr William Pemble* (London, 1635)

June 6 1699. Present: Mr [*Joseph*] Brett, Mr [*John*] Barker, Mr [*John*] Burton.

July 4 1699. Quarter day. Present: Mr [*John*] Barker, who paid the last quarter, Mr [*Joseph*] Brett, who paid the last quarter, Dr [*John*] Jeffery, who paid all arrears, Mr [*John*] Burton, who paid the last quarter, Mr [*John*] Graile, who paid all arrears to this day, Mr [*Theophilus*] Browne takes himself out of library this day.

August 1 1699. Present: Mr [*Joseph*] Brett, Mr [*William*] Adamson, who paid the last quarter, Mr [*John*] Richardson, who paid this quarter.

September 5 1699. Present: Mr [*William*] Adamson, Mr [*John*] Richardson.

October 3 1699. Quarter day. Present: Mr [*William*] Adamson, who paid this quarter, Mr [*Thomas*] Clayton, who paid all arrears, Mr [*Joseph*] Brett, who paid the last quarter, Mr [*John*] Barker, who paid the last quarter.

November 7 1699. Present: Mr [*John*] Richardson, who paid the last quarter, Mr [*Edward*] Reveley, who paid all arrears, Mr [*Joseph*] Brett.

December 5 1699. Present: Dr [*John*] Jeffery, Mr [*John*] Richardson, Mr [*Joseph*] Brett, Mr [*John*] Whitefoot, who paid all arrears, Mr [*Edward*] Reveley, Mr [*John*] Barker, Mr [*William*] Adamson.

January 2 1700. Quarter day. Present: Archdeacon [*John*] Jeffery, who paid all arrears & this quarter, Mr [*John*] Whitefoot, who paid this quarter, Mr [*William*] Adamson, who paid this quarter, Mr [*Thomas*] Clayton, who paid this quarter, Mr [*Joseph*] Brett, who paid this quarter.

February 6 1700. Present: Mr [*John*] Richardson, who paid this quarter, Mr [*Edward*] Reveley, who paid the last quarter, Mr [*William*] Adamson, Mr [*Joseph*] Brett, Mr [*John*] Robinson. Memorandum. That Mr [*Thomas*] Clayton was this day chosen library keeper for the two years next ensuing by reason of Mr [*Isaac*] Girling's refusing to hold it any longer. Mr Girling owe to the under library keeper for three years and a half fourteen shillings, £0. 14s. 0d.

March 5 1700. Present: Mr [*John*] Whitefoot, Mr [*John*] Richardson, Mr [*John*] Barker, who paid the last quarter, Mr [*Thomas*] Clayton, Mr [*Joseph*] Brett.

April 2 1700. Quarter day. Present: Mr [*John*] Richardson paid the last quarter, Mr [*Joseph*] Brett paid the last quarter, Mr [*John*] Whitefoot paid the last quarter, Mr [*William*] Adamson paid the last quarter, Mr A[*rch*]d[*eacon*] [*John*] Jeffery paid the last quarter, Mr [*John*] Barker paid the last quarter, Mr [*John*] Robinson paid the last quarter.

May 7 1700. Present: Dr [*John*] Jeffery, Mr [*John*] Whitefoot, Mr [*William*] Adamson, Mr [*John*] Robinson, Mr [*Joseph*] Ellys, Mr [*John*] Grayle.

June 4 1700. Present: Mr [*Joseph*] Brett, Mr [*William*] Adamson, Mr [*Edward*] Reveley, who payd the last quarter, Mr [*John*] Barker.

July 2 1700. Quarter day. Present: Mr [*Joseph*] Brett, who paid the last quarter.

August 6 1700. Present: Mr [*John*] Richardson paid this quarter, Mr [*Joseph*] Brett, Mr [*John*] Graile, who paid all arrears, Mr [*Edward*] Reveley paid this quarter, Dr [*John*] Jeffery paid this quarter.

September 3 1700. Present: Mr [*John*] Richardson, Mr [*John*] Barker who paid the last quarter, Mr [*Thomas*] Clayton, who paid all arrears, Mr [*Edward*] Reveley, Mr [*John*] Robinson, who paid the last quarter.

October 1 1700. Quarter day. Present: Mr [*William*] Adamson, who paid this quarter & last, Dr [*John*] Jeffery, who paid this quarter, Mr [*Joseph*] Brett, who paid this quarter. Memorandum. That Mr [*Joseph*] Ellys (though absent) paid all arrears to this day.

November 5 1700. Present: Mr [*John*] Barker, who paid the last quarter, Mr [*Joseph*] Brett, Mr [*Edward*] Reveley, who paid the last quarter, Mr [*William*] Adamson.

December 2 1700. Present: Mr [*John*] Richardson, who paid this quarter, Mr [*John*] Graile, who paid this quarter, Mr [*Edward*] Reveley, Mr [*John*] Barker, Mr [*William*] Adamson.

January 7 1701. Quarter day. Present: Mr [*Joseph*] Brett, who paid this quarter, Mr [*John*] Graile, who paid this quarter, Mr [*Thomas*] Clayton, who paid all arrears and at the same time nine shillings for being library keeper.

February 4 1701. Present: Mr [*John*] Richardson, who paid this quarter, Mr [*Joseph*] Ellis, Mr [*John*] Barker, who paid this quarter, Mr [*John*]

Graile, Mr [*Edward*] Rively, who paid the last quarter, Mr [*William*] Adamson, who paid the last quarter, Dr [*John*] Jeffery, who paid the last quarter. This day Mr [*John*] Barker is chosen library keeper. Present besides the forementioned, Mr [*Thomas*] Clayton, Mr [*Joseph*] Brett.

March 4 1701. Present: Mr [*William*] Adamson, Mr [*Joseph*] Brett, Mr [*John*] Grail, Mr [*John*] Barker.

April the first quarter day 1701. Present: Mr [*William*] Adamson who paid the quarter, Dr [*John*] Jefferey, who paid the last quarter, Mr [*Edward*] Reveley, who paid the last quarter, Mr [*John*] Graile, who paid this quarter, Mr [*John*] Barker, who paid the quarter, Mr [*John*] Robinson paid the two last quarters. Memorandum. It was then agreed by the company that Hierom's workes [262] which came among Mr Irelands & had a note of his handwriting that the booke was Mistress Esther Bayfeild's & he ordered it to be restored forthwith to her, dated 30 May 1664 may be restored to her or her heir & accordingly do approve Mr Adamson's delivering it to her onely son George Bayfield[263] 22 March 1701.

May 6 1701. Present: Mr [*Joseph*] Brett, who paid the last quarter, Mr [*Joseph*] Ellys, Mr [*Edward*] Riveley.

June 3 1701. Present: Mr [*William*] Adamson, Mr [*John*] Richardson, who paid the last quarter, Mr [*Edward*] Reveley, Mr [*John*] Barker, Mr [*Joseph*] Brett.

July 1 1701. Quarter day. Present: Mr [*Edward*] Reveley, who paid this quarter, Mr [*Joseph*] Brett, who paid this quarter, Mr [*John*] Barker, who paid this quarter, Dr [*John*] Jeffery, who paid this quarter, Mr [*John*] Richardson, who paid this quarter. Mr [*John*] Layton[264] was this day admitted to the use of the library.

August 5 1701. Present: Mr [*William*] Adamson, who paid the last quarter, Mr [*Joseph*] Brett, Mr [*Edward*] Reveley, Mr [*John*] Graile, who paid the last quarter, Mr [*John*] Barker.

September 2 1701. Present: Mr [*William*] Adamson, Mr [*John*] Graile, Mr [*Thomas*] Clayton, who paid all arrears, Mr [*Edward*] Reveley.

---

[262] *Sancti Hieronymi opera omnia quae reperiri potuerunt* (Paris, 1609) [Gh. 10–12]

[263] George Bayfield was a councillor for Wymer Ward from 1688 to 1701 and again in 1703 (Hawes, p. 14).

[264] John Layton graduated BA from King's College Cambridge in 1680, proceeding MA in 1683. He was ordained in London in 1686 and was rector of Horstead and Coltishall from 1700 to 1728. He was buried at Horstead in 1728.

1701 October 7. Quarter day. Present: Mr [*John*] Richardson, who paid this quarter, Mr [*William*] Adamson, who paid this quarter, Mr [*John*] Barker, who paid this quarter, Mr [*Joseph*] Brett, who paid this quarter, Mr [*Joseph*] Ellys paid this quarter & all arrears.

November 4 1701. Present: Mr [*John*] Whitefoot, who paid all arrears, Mr [*William*] Adamson, Dr [*John*] Jeffery, who paid the last quarter, Mr [*John*] Richardson, Mr [*Joseph*] Brett, Mr [*Benedict*] Reveley, who paid the last quarter.

December 2 1701. Present: Mr [*Joseph*] Brett, Mr [*William*] Adamson, Mr [*John*] Barker, Mr Archdeacon Jeffery. Mr [*Thomas*] Clayton paid last quarter.

January 6 1702. Quarter day. Present: Mr [*William*] Adamson, who paid this quarter, Mr [*Joseph*] Brett, who paid the last quarter.

February 3 1702. Present: Mr [*John*] Richardson, who paid this quarter, Mr [*William*] Adamson, Mr [*Edward*] Reveley, who paid the last quarter, Mr [*John*] Barker, who paid the last quarter, Mr [*Joseph*] Brett.

March 3 1702. Present: Mr [*William*] Adamson, Mr [*Edward*] Reveley, Mr [*Joseph*] Brett, Mr [*John*] Barker.

April 7 1702. Present: Mr [*William*] Adamson, Dr [*John*] Jeffery, who paid the under library keeper for two quarters, Mr [*Thomas*] Clayton, who paid all arrears, Mr [*John*] Barker, who paid the last quarter, Mr Adamson, who paid the last quarter, Mr [*Edward*] Rively, who paid the last quarter, Mr [*John*] Richardson, who paid the last quarter, Dr Jeffery.

5 May 1702. Memorandum. Paid to Mr [*John*] Barker for the purchase of Ainsworth on the Pentateuch[265] four shillings & for Fulk on the N[*ew*] T[*estament*][266] five shillings & for Archbishop Laud against Fisher[267] foure shillings, in all £0. 13s. 0d.

June 2 1702. Present: Dr [*John*] Jeffrey, Mr [*Edward*] Reveley, Mr [*William*] Herne[268] was this day admitted to the use of the library. Mr Robert

[265] Henry Ainsworth: *Annotations vpon the Five Bookes of Moses, the Booke of Psalmes, and the Song of Songs or Canticles* (London, 1627).

[266] William Fulke: *The text of the New Testament of Iesus Christ, translated out of the vulgar Latine by the Papists of the traitorous Seminarie at Rhemes* (London, 1633).

[267] William Laud: *A Relation of the Conference between William Laud and Mr Fisher, the Iesuite.*

[268] Born in Norwich, William Herne graduated BA from Caius College, Cambridge, in 1692, proceeding MA in 1695. He became a Doctor of Divinity in 1709. He was rector of St George Colegate from 1715 to 1745.

Dannye[269] was this day admitted to the use of the library. Mr [*John*] Barker, Mr [*John*] Richardson.

July 7 1702. Quarter day. Present: Mr [*William*] Adamson, who paid this quarter, Mr [*John*] Richardson, who paid the last quarter, Dr [*John*] Jeffery, who paid the last quarter, Mr [*Joseph*] Brett, who paid the two last quarters, Mr [*John*] Barker, who paid the last quarter, Mr [*William*] Herne.

August 4 [*1702*]. Present: Mr [*William*] Adamson, Mr [*William*] Herne.

September 7 1702. Present: Mr [*Edward*] Reveley, who paid the last quarter, Mr [*Joseph*] Brett, Mr [*John*] Barker, Mr [*William*] Herne.

October 6 1702. Quarter day. Present: Mr [*John*] Richardson, who paid the last quarter, Mr [*Joseph*] Brett, who paid the last quarter. Mr A[*rch*]d[*eacon*] Jeffery, who paid the last quarter, Mr [*William*] Adamson, who paid the last quarter, Mr [*John*] Barker, who paid the last quarter, Mr [*Robert*] Dannye, who paid the last quarter, Mr [*William*] Herne, who paid the last quarter.

November 3 1702. Present: Mr [*John*] Richardson, Mr [*Edward*] Reveley, who paid the last quarter, Mr [*Thomas*] Clayton, who paid the two last quarters, Mr [*William*] Herne.

December 1 1702. Present: Mr [*William*] Adamson, Mr [*John*] Barker, Mr [*John*] Whitefoot, who paid all arrears, Mr [*John*] Jeffery, Mr [*Joseph*] Brett, Mr [*William*] Herne.

January 5 1703. Quarter day. Present: Mr [*John*] Barker, who paid 9s. for 2 years being library keeper, & this quarter, Mr [*John*] Richardson, who paid this quarter, Mr [*Edward*] Reveley, who paid the last quarter & was this day chosen library keeper, Mr [*William*] Adamson paid this quarterage.

February 2 1703. Present: Mr [*Joseph*] Brett, who paid the last quarter, Mr [*William*] Adamson, Dr [*John*] Jefferies, who paid the last quarter, Mr [*John*] Barker, Mr [*John*] Richardson, Mr [*Edward*] Reveley.

March 2 1703. Present: Mr [*Joseph*] Ellys paid all arrears to this day (tho absent), Mr [*John*] Barker, Mr [*William*] Adamson, Mr [*John*] Whitefoot

---

[269] Robert Danny graduated BA from Corpus Christi College, Cambridge, in 1700, proceeding MA in 1703. He was elected a Fellow in 1702 and eventually became Chancellor of Cambridge University. He died in 1729.

paid the last quarter, Mr [*Edward*] Reveley, Mr [*Thomas*] Clayton paid the last quarter, Mr [*William*] Herne, who paid the last quarter, Mr [*Joseph*] Brett.

1703. April 6. Quarter day. Present: Mr [*Joseph*] Brett, who paid the last quarter, Mr [*Mark*] Purt [270] was this day admitted to the use of the library. Mr [*Edward*] Reveley, who paid the last quarter, Mr [*John*] Whitefoot, who paid the last quarter, Mr [*William*] Adamson, who paid the last quarter, Mr [*John*] Richardson, who paid the last quarter, Mr [*William*] Herne, who paid the last quarter.

May 4 [1703]. Present: Mr [*William*] Adamson, Mr [*Edward*] Reveley, Mr [*Mark*] Purt, Mr [*William*] Herne.

June 1 [*1703*]. Present: Mr [*William*] Adamson, Mr [*John*] Richardson, Mr [*Joseph*] Brett, Mr [*Edward*] Reveley, Mr [*William*] Herne, Dr [*John*] Jeffery, who paid the last quarter, Mr [*Mark*] Purt.

July 6 Quarter day. 1703. Present: Mr [*William*] Adamson, who paid this quarter, Mr [*William*] Herne, who paid this quarter, Mr [*Mark*] Purt, who paid this quarter, Mr [*John*] Whitefoot paid this quarter.

August 3 1703. Present: Mr [*William*] Herne, Mr [*William*] Adamson, Mr [*John*] Whitefoot.

September 7 1703. Present: Mr [*William*] Adamson, Mr [*William*] Herne, Mr [*Mark*] Purt.

5 October 1703. Quarter Day. Present: Mr [*Joseph*] Brett, who paid the last two quarters, Mr [*William*] Adamson, who paid the last quarter, Mr [*John*] Whitefoot, who paid the last quarter, Dr [*John*] Jeffery who paid the two last quarters, Mr [*Mark*] Purt who paid the last quarter. This day it was agreed to exchange Mr [*Richard*] Ireland's polyglot Bible[271] in 6 volumes unbound with Mr [*John*] Whitefoot's Ortelius[272] & Ptolemy,[273] Herodotus[274] & Cave's first volume *de Scriptoribus Ecclesiasticis.*[275] Mr [*Thomas*] Clayton paid all arrears.

[270] Mark Purt, a graduate of Edinburgh University and St Catherine's College, Cambridge, tutored the son of Peter Thacker, a leading city lawyer. Clerk to St John Maddermarket, he taught Latin and Greek to between 10 and 15 students, either for university entrance or for employment as attorneys' clerks or apothecaries (Branford, p. 229).

[271] Brian Walton: *Biblia sacra polyglotta* (London, 1657).

[272] Abraham Ortelius: *Theatrum orbis terrarum* (Antwerp, 1570).

[273] Ptolemy: *Geographiae* (Frankfurt, 1605).

[274] Herodotus: *Historiarum libri ix* (Frankfurt, 1608).

[275] William Cave: *Scriptorum ecclesiasticorum historia literaria a Christo nato usque ad saeculum XIV facili methodo digesta.*(London, 1688–98).

November 2 1703. Present: Mr [*John*] Richardson, who paid the two last quarters, Mr [*William*] Herne, who paid the last quarter, Mr [*William*] Adamson, Dr [*John*] Jeffrey, Mr Connould paid all arrears, Mr [*Mark*] Purtt.

December 7 [*1703*]. Present: Mr [*John*] Whitefoot, Mr [*William*] Adamson, Mr [*Joseph*] Brett, Mr [*William*] Herne, Mr [*Thomas*] Morly who paid all arrears, Mr Connould, Mr [*Mark*] Purtt.

January 4 1704. Quarter day. Present: Mr [*William*] Herne, who paid the last quarter, Dr [*John*] Jeffrey, who paid the last quarter, Mr [*William*] Adamson, who paid the last quarter, Mr [*Joseph*] Brett, who paid last quarter, Mr [*John*] Whitefoot, who paid the last quarter, Mr [*John*] Barker, who paid all arrears to this day.

February 1 1704. Present: Mr [*John*] Richardson, who paid this quarter, Mr [*Edward*] Reveley, who paid the last quarter, Mr [*John*] Barker, Mr [*William*] Adamson, Mr [*Mark*] Purt, who paid this quarter, Mr [*Joseph*] Brett, Mr [*John*] Whitefoot, Dr [*John*] Jeffrey, Mr [*Robert* or *John*] Connould, who paid the library keeper, Mr [*William*] Herne.

March 7 1704. Present: Mr [*William*] Adamson, Mr [*Mark*] Purt, Mr [*Edward*] Reveley, Mr [*Joseph*] Brett, Mr [*William*] Herne.

April 4 [*1704*] Quarter day. Present: Mr [*John*] Barker paid this quarter, Mr [*Joseph*] Brett, who paid the last quarter, Mr [*Mark*] Purt, who paid the last quarter, Mr [*William*] Adamson, who paid the last quarter, Mr [*Edward*] Reveley, who paid the last quarter, Mr [*William*] Herne, who paid the last quarter, Mr [*Robert* or *John*] Connould, who paid the last quarter.

May 2 1704. Present: Mr [*John*] Richardson, who paid the last quarter, Mr [*John*] Barker, Mr [*Joseph*] Brett, Mr [*Mark*] Purt, Mr [*William*] Herne.

June 6 1704. Present: Mr [*Robert* or *John*] Connould, Mr [*John*] Richardson, Mr [*Joseph*] Brett, Mr [*Thomas*] Clayton, who paid all arrears, Mr [*Joseph*] Ellys, Mr [*Edward*] Reveley, Dr [*John*] Jeffrey, who paid the last quarter.

June 6 1704. Present: Mr [*William*] Adamson, Mr [*John*] Barker, Mr [*William*] Herne.

July 4 1704. Quarter day.

July 9 1704. Present: Mr [*William*] Adamson, who paid the last quarter, Mr [*Robert* or *John*] Conold, who paid the last quarter, Mr [*John*] Barker, who paid his last quarter, Mr [*Joseph*] Brett, who paid the last quarter, Mr [*John*] Richardson, who paid quarter day, Mr [*Edward*] Reveley, who paid the last quarter, Dr [*John*] Jeffrey, who paid the last quarter, Mr [*William*] Herne, who paid the last quarter, Mr [*Joseph*] Ellis, Mr [*Thomas*] Clayton, who paid the last quarter, Mr [*John*] Whitefoot, who paid the last quarter, Dr [*Charles*] Trimnel, Mr [*Mark*] Purtt, who paid the last quarter.

August 1 1704. Present: Mr [*William*] Herne, Dr [*John*] Jeffery, Mr [*Edward*] Revely, Mr [*Joseph*] Brett, Mr [*William*] Adamson, Mr [*Thomas*] Clayton, Mr [*Mark*] Purtt, Mr [*Robert* or *John*] Conold, Mr [*John*] Richardson.

September 3 1704. Present: Mr [*John*] Barker, Mr [*Joseph*] Brett, Mr [*William*] Adamson, Mr [*Edward*] Revely, Mr [*William*] Herne, Mr [*Mark*] Purtt.

October 3 Quarter day. 1704. Present: Dr [*Charles*] Trimnel, who paid the last quarter, Mr [*Joseph*] Brett, who paid the last quarter, Mr [*Thomas*] Clayton, who paid the last quarter, Mr [*William*] Adamson, who paid the last quarter, Dr [*John*] Jeffrey, who paid the last quarter, Mr [*William*] Herne, who paid the last quarter, Mr [*Robert* or *John*] Connould, who paid the last quarter, Mr [*Mark*] Purtt, who paid the last quarter, Mr [*John*] Barker, who paid the last quarter. Mr [*Joseph*] Ellis paid all arrears (tho absent).

November 7 1704. Present: Mr [*John*] Richardson, who paid the last quarter, Mr [*Edward*] Reveley, who paid the last quarter, Mr [*William*] Herne, Mr [*Mark*] Purt.

December 5 1704. Present: Dr [*John*] Jeffery, Mr [*Robert* or *John*] Connould, Mr [*John*] Barker, Mr [*Joseph*] Brett, Mr [*William*] Adamson, Mr [*William*] Herne.

January 2 Quarter day. 1705. Present: Mr [*Edward*] Reveley, who paid the last quarter & 9s. for 2 years being library keeper, Mr [*William*] Herne, who paid the last quarter, Mr [*John*] Whitefoot, who paid the 2 last quarters, Mr [*Joseph*] Brett, who paid the last quarter & was this day chosen library keeper, Mr [*Thomas*] Clayton, who paid the last quarter.

February 6 1705. Present: Mr [*William*] Adamson, who paid the last quarter, Mr [*John*] Richardson, who paid the last quarter, Mr [*Robert* or

John] Conold, who paid the last quarter, Mr [*John*] Whitefoot, Mr [*Joseph*] Brett, Mr [*William*] Herne.

March 6 1705. Present: Dr [*John*] Jeffery paid the last quarter, Mr [*John*] Richardson, Mr [*William*] Herne, Mr [*William*] Adamson, Mr [*Robert* or *John*] Connold, Mr [*Joseph*] Brett, Mr [*John*] Whitefoot, Mr [*John*] Barker paid the last quarter, Tho[*mas*] Clayton.

April 3 1705. Quarter day. Present: Mr [*John*] Richardson paid the last quarter, Mr [*William*] Adamson paid the last quarter, Mr [*Edward*] Reveley, who paid the last quarter, Mr [*Joseph*] Brett, who paid the last quarter, Thomas Clayton paid the last quarter. Mr [*Samuel*] Jones[276] was then admitted to the library. Mr [*William*] Herne, who paid the last quarter, Mr [*John*] Barker, who paid the last quarter, Mr [*Mark*] Purt paid the two last quarters.

May 1 1705. Present: Mr [*William*] Herne, Mr [*Samuel*] Jones.

June [*1705*]. Present: Mr [*Joseph*] Brett, Mr [*William*] Herne, Mr [*Mark*] Purt, Mr [*William*] Adamson, Mr [*John*] Barker, Mr [*Edward*] Revely, Mr [*Robert* or *John*] Conold, who paid the last quarter, Mr [*John*] Richardson, Dr [*John*] Jeffery, who paid the last quarter, Mr [*John*] Havett.

July 3 1705. Quarter day. Present: Mr [*Joseph*] Brett, who paid the last quarter, Mr [*John*] Havett, Mr [*John*] Whitefoot, who paid the last two quarters, Mr [*Samuel*] Jones, who paid the last quarter, Mr Jo[*hn*] Connould, who paid the last quarter, Mr [*Thomas*] Clayton, who paid the last quarter, Mr [*William*] Adamson, who paid the last quarter, Dr [*John*] Jeffery, who paid the last quarter, Dr [*Charles*] Trimnell, who paid the last quarter.

---

[276] Samuel Jones, rector of St John Maddermarket, first appeared in the Chamberlain's Accounts in 1706 when he delivered the Gunpowder Plot sermon (NRO, NCR Case 18b, Chamberlain's Accounts, 1706–7, unpaginated and unfoliated). He also delivered the Gunpowder Plot sermon in 1708. In 1712 and 1713 he preached the annual sermon on King Charles' martyrdom. He defended the benefits of learning in a sermon delivered at St Michael at Plea. If God framed men's minds to be naturally inquisitive and also endowed them with 'faculties fitted for the pursuit of knowledge', how can it not be lawful for them to pursue this knowledge. Philosophy was not just for ornament, it was also useful, particularly in politics. Moreover, the further men penetrated into the nature of things, the more was discovered of the 'Beauty of Providence' and of the 'Divine Government'. Some philosophers attempted to persuade people that there was no God, endeavouring to seduce men into atheism. But this was an abuse of philosophy and was merely sophistry, or 'vain deceit' (Samuel Jones, *A Sermon Preached on the Archdeacon's Visitation* (Norwich, 1708).

August 7 1705. Present: Mr [*William*] Adamson, Mr [*Edward*] Rively, who paid the last quarter, Mr [*John*] Richardson, who paid the last quarter, Mr [*John*] Barker, who paid the last quarter, Mr [*Robert* or *John*] Conold. August 7 1705. Mr [*William*] Herne, who paid the last quarter.

September 4 1705. Present: Mr [*William*] Herne, Mr [*Joseph*] Brett, Dr [*Charles*] Trimnell.

October 2 1705. Quarter day. Present: Mr [*Joseph*] Brett, who paid the last quarter, Mr [*Edward*] Reveley, who paid the last quarter, Mr [*William*] Adamson, who paid the last quarter, Mr [*John*] Havett, who paid the last quarter, Mr [*John*] Herne.

October 10 1705. Mr [*Mark*] Purt, who paid the two last quarters.

November 6 1705. Present: Mr [*John*] Havet, Mr [*Robert* or *John*] Connould & paid the last quarter, Mr [*William*] Herne, who paid the last quarter, Mr [*Edward*] Reveley.

December 4 1705. Present: Mr [*John*] Richardson paid the last quarter, Mr [*Edward*] Reveley, Mr [*Robert* or *John*] Connould, Mr [*Joseph*] Brett, Mr [*John*] Havett, Mr [*William*] Adamson, Mr [*John*] Barker, who paid the last quarter, Mr [*William*] Herne.

January 1 1706. Quarter day. Present: Mr [*Joseph*] Brett, who paid the last quarter, Mr [*Samuel*] Jones, who paid the two last quarters, Mr [*John*] Richardson paid this quarter.

February 5 1706. Present: Dr [*John*] Jeffery, who paid the last two quarters, Mr [*William*] Adamson, who paid the last quarter, Mr [*John*] Whitefoot, who paid the two last quarters, Mr [*Samuel*] Jones, Mr [*Joseph*] Brett, Mr [*William*] Herne, who paid the last quarter.

March 5 1706. Present: Dr [*John*] Jeffery, Mr [*William*] Adamson, Mr [*John*] Whitefoot, Mr [*Edward*] Reveley, who paid the last quarter, Mr [*John*] Havett, Mr [*Samuel*] Jones. Mr Thomas Clayton, who paid all arrears, Mr [*William*] Herne.

April 2 1706. Quarter day. Present: Mr [*Edward*] Reveley, who paid the last quarter, Mr [*John*] Havett, who paid the last quarter, Mr [*William*] Adamson, who paid the last quarter, Mr [*Robert* or *John*] Conold paid the 2 last quarters, Mr [*William*] Herne, who paid the last quarter.

May 7 1706. Present: Mr [*John*] Richardson, Mr [*William*] Havett, Dr [*John*] Jeffery, who paid this quarter, Mr [*Robert* or *John*] Conold, Mr [*Edward*] Reveley, Mr [*William*] Adamson, Mr [*Joseph*] Brett, who paid the last quarter, Mr [*Samuel*] Jones, who paid the last quarter, Mr [*Thomas*] Clayton, who paid the last quarter, Mr [*William*] Herne.

June 4 1706. Present: Mr [*Joseph*] Brett, Mr [*William*] Adamson, Mr [*John*] Barker, who paid the Christmas & Lady quarters, Mr [*William*] Herne, Mr [*Samuel*] Jones, Mr [*John*] Havett.

July 2 1706. Present: Dr [*John*] Jeffery, who paid the last quarter, Mr [*Edward*] Reveley, who paid the last quarter, Mr [*John*] Havett, who paid the last quarter, Mr [*Samuel*] Jones, who paid the last quarter, Mr [*John*] Richardson paid all arrears, Mr [*John*] Whitefoot paid all arrears, Mr [*Robert* or *John*] Conold paid the last quarter.

August 6 1706. Present: Mr [*William*] Adamson, who paid the last quarter, Mr [*Edward*] Reveley, Mr [*John*] Havett, Dr [*Charles*] Trimnel, who paid 4 quarters to Midsummer last, Mr [*Thomas*] Clayton, who paid the last quarter, Mr [*William*] Herne, who paid the last quarter.

September 3 1706. Present: Dr [*Charles*] Trimnell, Mr [*William*] Adamson, Mr [*John*] Whitefoot, Mr [*William*] Herne.

October 1 [*1706*] Quarter day. Present: Mr [*Robert* or *John*] Connold paid the last quarter, Mr [*Joseph*] Brett, who paid the 2 last quarters, Mr [*William*] Adamson, who paid the last quarter, Mr [*William*] Herne, who paid the last quarter. Mr [*John*] Paul[277] and Mr [*Francis*] Fayerman[278] were this day admitted to the use of the library, Mr [*Edward*] Reveley, who paid the last quarter, Mr [*John*] Havet, who paid the last quarter, Mr [*John*] Whitefoot paid this quarter.

[277] Born in Norwich, John Paul graduated BA from Caius College, Cambridge, in 1702, proceeding MA in 1705. He was ordained in 1704 and was appointed master of Great Yarmouth Grammar School in 1705. He was chaplain of St Giles and St Gregory in 1714 and rector of Little Moulton from 1720 to 1725. However, when he drew up his will he was living in Norwich Cathedral Close. His 'library of books' he left to his nephew 'if my said nephew shall be educated in the University of Cambridge' (NRO NCC 60 Palmer, Will of John Paul, 1726).

[278] Born in Norwich, Francis Fayerman graduated BA from Pembroke College Cambridge in 1702, proceeding MA in 1705. He was ordained in Norwich in June 1704. He was rector of Thurlton from 1713 to 1756 and rector of Geldeston from 1732 to 1754. He was the author of *Zarah: that is, Christianity before Judaism* (Norwich, 1756). When he drew up his will he was living in Chedgrave. Books and manuscripts are mentioned but their fate is unclear (NRO ANF 82 215, Will of Francis Fayerman, 1756–7).

November 5 1706. Present: Mr [*William*] Adamson, Mr [*Joseph*] Brett, who this day brought into the library Lord Bacon's *Natural History*[279] given by Thornagh Gurdon Esquire & Ammiani Marcellani *Historia*[280] given by Mr [*Benjamin*] Resbury,[281] rector of Cranworth cum Letton & Galileus Galileus his *Systeme of the World* [282] given by Mr Archibald Adams.[283] Mr [*Edward*] Reveley, Mr [*John*] Paul.

December 3 1706. Present: Dr [*John*] Jeffery, who paid the last quarter, Mr [*John*] Whitefoot, < Mr [*William*] Adamson, > Mr [*Edward*] Reveley, Mr [*Samuel*] Jones, who paid the last quarter, Mr Firmin,[284] Mr [*John*] Paull, Mr [*William*] Adamson, who brought into the library Eusebius with Valesius[285] & the other historians greek & latin in 3 volumes given by the Lord Bishop Moore.[286] Mr [*Joseph*] Brett, Mr [*William*] Herne. Ordered then that the *Alphabeticall Catalogue of the City Library* be printed by the Widow Burgies.[287] Mr Isaac Sayer[288] was this day admitted to the use of the library.

7 January 1707 Quarter Day. Present: Mr [*John*] Richardson, who paid all arrears, Mr [*William*] Herne, who paid the last quarter, Mr [*John*] Paul, who paid the last quarter, Dr [*John*] Jeffery, who paid the last quarter, Mr [*John*] Whitefoot, who paid the last quarter, Mr [*Joseph*] Brett, who paid the last quarter. January 7 1707. Present: Mr [*John*] Barker, who paid Midsummer, Michaelmas & Christmas quarters. Mr [*Thomas*] Tanner,[289]

---

[279] Francis Bacon: *Historia naturalis & experimentalis de ventis* (Lyon, 1648)

[280] Ammianus Marcellinus: *Ammiani Marcellini rerum gestarum* (Paris, 1681).

[281] Benjamin Resbury was admitted sizar at Emmanuel College in 1662, graduated BA in 1665 and proceeded MA in 1669. He was instituted rector of Cranworth by Brampton Gurdon in 1680. In his will he bequeathed the whole of his estate to his brother, Dr Nathaniel Resbury, rector of St Paul's, Shadwell, in Middlesex (NRO NCC 321 Melchior, Will of Benjamin Resbury, 1715).

[282] Galileo Galilei: *The systeme of the world: in four dialogues wherein the two grand systems of Ptolomy and Copernicus are largely discussed* (London, 1661)

[283] Archibald Adams succeeded in evading all attempts at indentification.

[284] Almost certainly Francis Fayerman.

[285] Eusebius: *Ecclesiasticae historiae libri decem. De vita Imp. Constantini. Libri IV* (Paris, 1678)

[286] The famous bibliophile, John Moore, was bishop of Norwich from 1691 to 1707.

[287] Elizabeth Burgess, the widow of Francis Burgess, the man who re-introduced printing to Norwich, continued her husband's business near the Red Well in Norwich until her own death in November 1708. The business continued under different proprietors until 1718.

[288] Born in Norwich, Isaac Sayer graduated BA from Caius College in 1706 and proceeded MA in 1711. He was ordained in Norwich in March 1709 and was appointed Master of Saham Toney School in 1708. From 1712 to 1721 he was Master of Wymondham School. He was rector of Crownthorpe in 1714 and of East Bradenham from 1716 to 1721. He died in 1722.

[289] Tanner began his career in Norwich diocese as chaplain to bishop John Moore. In March 1701 he was promoted to the chancellorship. His main donation to the library was made in 1726 when he presented 'more than a hundred books'. It was a chronologically varied

Chancellour of the Diocese of Norwich, was this day admitted to the use of the library. Mr [*Isaac*] Sayer. This day Mr [*John*] Havett was chosen library keeper for the two years next ensuing & Mr [*Joseph*] Brett the last library keeper paid the under keeper 9s. & Mr *Brett* brought into the library Binij *Bibliotheca patrum*[290] in 5 volumes & Onuphrij *Fasti* [291] given by the Chancellour Mr. Tanner.

4 February 1707. Present: Dr [*John*] Jeffery Mr [*William*] Adamson, who paid the last quarter, Mr [*John*] Whitefoot, Mr [*John*] Richardson, Mr [*Joseph*] Brett, Mr [*William*] Herne, Mr [*John*] Havett, who paid the last quarter, Mr [*Francis*] Feyerman, who paid the last quarter. Mr [*Henry*] Sheppey[292] was this day admitted to the use of the library. This day Mr Havett brought into the library Dr Beveridge his *Cannons*.[293] And this day Mr Brett brought in the catalogue of books printed [294] which cost two pounds sixteen shillings and three pence and *he was* allowed also a shilling for printing an advertisement. Mr [*John*] Connold, who paid the last quarter, Mr [*Thomas*] Clayton who paid all arrears, Mr [*Edward*] Riveley, who paid the last quarter.

March 4 1707. Present: Dr [*John*] Jeffery, Mr [*John*] Richardson, Mr [*William*] Herne, Mr [*John*] Paul, Mr [*John*] Havett, Mr [*Samuel*] Jones, Mr [*Edward*] Rively, Mr [*John*] Barker, Mr Connold, Mr [*Henry*] Sheppey. This day Mr Richardson brought into the library the following books given by Justice [*Michael*] Beverly[295] of the Citty of Norwich; Caelius Rhodiginus,[296]

collection, ranging in date from Pancirolli's *De rerum memorabilium* (1447) to Thomas Pyle's *Paraphrase with useful notes* (1725). Most of the titles – over 50 percent – were London imprints. Only one, a work by Erasmus Warren, was printed in Norwich. The number of works by Norfolk and Norwich writers was striking. There were titles by John Caius, John Jeffery, John More, Thomas Pyle, Edward Reynolds, Erasmus Warren and Henry Wharton. Tanner presented not duplicates but superseded editions (M.J. Sommerlad, 'The Historical and Antiquarian Interests of Thomas Tanner 1674–1735, Bishop of St Asaph', Oxford PhD, 1962, p. 347n). For example, in the case of Van Marnix van Sant Aldegonde's *Beehive of the Romish Church* (1598), Fabricius' *Sacrae conciones* (1623) and St Amour's *Journals* (1660) Tanner retained the later editions of 1636, 1641 and 1664 respectively.

[290] Marguerin de la Bigne: *Sacrae bibliothecae Sanctorum Patrum* (Paris, 1589).

[291] Onofrio Panvinio: *Onuphrii Panuinii Veronensis fratris. eremitae Augustiniani Fastorum libri V a Romulo rege vsque ad imp. Caesarem Carolum V Austrium Augustum* (Heidelberg, 1588).

[292] Henry Sheppy was admitted pensioner at Jesus College Cambridge in 1690 and migrated to Trinity in 1692. He graduated BA in 1694, possibly proceeding to MA in 1728. He was rector of St. Edmund's and St. Julian in 1704 and rector of All Saints from 1704 to 1737.

[293] William Beveridge: *Synodikon, sive, Pandectae canonum ss. Apostolorum, et conciliorum ab ecclesia Graeca receptorum* (Oxford, 1672).

[294] *A catalogue of the Books in the Library of the City of Norwich in the Year 1706* (Norwich, 1706)

[295] Michael Beverley had been a councillor, auditor, alderman, sheriff, coroner and mayor. 'Justice' Beverley alludes to his status as a magistrate sitting in the Mayor's Court.

[296] Ludovicus Caelius Rhodiginus: *Lectionum antiquarum libri triginta* (1599)

Athenaeus *Deipnosophicta*,[297] Lloyd's *Memoirs*, Suetonius with Casaubon's *commentaries*,[298] Jacob Behme's *works* in four quartos.[299]

April 1 1707. Quarter day. This day Mr [*Joseph*] Brett brought into the library Tacquet *Opera Mathematica*[300] & Henricus Stephani *Concordantiae*, N.T. Graeco Latin[301] the former given by Algernon Potts Esquire,[302] the latter by Thornagh Gurdon Esquire. Present: Mr [*John*] Havett, who paid the last quarter, Mr [*John*] Paul, who paid the last quarter, Mr [*Joseph*] Brett, who paid the last quarter, Mr Connold, who paid the last quarter, Mr [*Edward*] Riveley, who paid the last quarter, Mr [*William*] Adamson, who paid the last quarter, Mr [*William*] Herne, who paid the last quarter, Mr [*Francis*] Fayarman, who paid the last quarter, Mr [*Thomas*] Clayton, who paid the last quarter, Mr [*John*] Whitefoot, who paid the last quarter, Mr [*Joseph*] Ellis, who paid all arrears.

May 6 1707. Present: Mr [*William*] Herne, Mr [*John*] Paul, Mr [*Joseph*] Brett, Mr [*Samuel*] Jones, who paid the last quarter, Mr [*William*] Adamson, Mr [*Edward*] Revely, Mr [*John*] Barker, who paid the last quarter, Mr Chancellour paid the last quarter, Mr [*John*] Havett.

June 3 [*1707*]. Present: Mr [*William*] Herne, Mr [*Edward*] Rively, Mr [*John*] Paul, Mr [*Joseph*] Brett, Mr [*Henry*] Shippey, who paid the last quarter, Mr [*Francis*] Fayerman.

July 1 1707. Quarter day. Present: Mr [*William*] Havett, who paid the last quarter, Mr [*Francis*] Fayerman, who paid the last quarter, Mr [*Edward*]

---

[297] Athenaeus: *Athenaiou deipnosophiston biblia pentekaide ka...Isaacus Casaubonus recensit, & ex antiques membranis supplevit*

[298] Suetonius: *Caius Suetonius Tranquillus cum Isaaci Casauboni animadversionibus et dissertationibus politicis* (Strasbourg, 1647)

[299] Jakob Boehme: *Signatura rerum, or, the signature of all things: shewing the sign and signification of the severall forms and shapes in the creation, and what the beginning, ruin, and cure of everything is* (London, 1651); *Concerning the election of grace, or, O God's will towards man, commonly called predestination* (London, 1655); *Aurora, that is the day-spring...that is the root or matter of philosophie, astrologie & theologie from the true ground* (London, 1656); *Several treatises of Jacob Behme: not printed in English before* (London, 1610).

[300] André Tacquet: *Opera mathematica demonstrata et propugnata a Simone Laurentio Veterani ex comitibus Montis Calvi* (Louvain, 1668).

[301] *Concordantiae Testamenti Novi Graecolatine.* [Geneva],1594.

[302] Born at Great Ellingham, Algernon Potts was educated at Bury Grammar School, Magdalen College, Cambridge, and Lincoln's Inn. He inherited the baronetcy in 1711 on the death of his father, Sir Roger Potts. The Potts family library at Mannington Hall was sold by the Norwich bookseller, William Chase, in 1737 (*Catalogue of a Valuable Collection of Books in most Faculties; Most of which were brought out of the Study of the late Sir Charles Potts at Mannington, near Aylsham*, Norwich, 1737).

Reveley, who paid the last 2 quarters, Mr [*John*] Barker, who paid the last quarter, Dr [*John*] Jeffery, who paid the two last quarters, Mr [*William*] Herne, who paid the last quarter. The day following Mr [*Joseph*] Ellis sent into the library (being the gift of Mr Thomas Nelson,[303] rector of Morston in Norfolk), Vossij (Gerardi Johannis) *Aristarchus sive de arte grammatica*. Amstelodami 1695,[304] Erasmi *Adagia*. 1629,[305] Woodall (John) *Surgeon's mate* London . 1655.[306]

July 3 1707. Sir William Cook,[307] baronett this day sent into the library by the hands of Mr [*Joseph*] Brett these following books, as his gift viz. Cardinall Du Perron's Works in 3 volumes. French. Paris, 1620,[308] Aquinatis (Tho:) *Summa Contra Gentiles*. Paris, 1587,[309] Sigonij (Caroli) *De Antiquo jure civium Romanorum* &c. Francofurt 1593,[310] Maffeij (Petri) *Historia Iudicarum cum Ignatij Loyolae Vita*. Coloniae Agrippinae. 1589.[311] Masoni (Franc.) *De Ministeris Ecclesiae Anglicanae*. London. 1638.[312] Morton (Dr Tho:) Catholike Appeal for Protestants. London 1610.[313] *Commentarius de Bestia Apocalyptica*. Delphis. 1621.[314]

August 5 1707. Present: Mr [*Joseph*] Brett, who paid the last quarter, Mr [*William*] Adamson, who paid the last quarter, Mr [*Edward*] Reveley, Mr Connould, who paid the last quarter, Mr [*Thomas*] Clayton, who paid the last quarter, Mr [*William*] Herne, Mr [*John*] Paul, who paid the last quarter, Mr [*Henry*] Shippey, who paid the last quarter, Mr [*Francis*] Fayerman. Sold to Mr Brett Sigonius *de Jure Civium Romanorum* [315]&c for 3s. This day was

---

[303] For Thomas Nelson see n. 135 above.

[304] Gerardus Vossius: *Gerardi Joannis Vossii Aristarchus, sive De arte grammatica libri septem* (Amsterdam, 1695).

[305] Desiderius Erasmus: *Adagia, id est, Prouerbiorum, paroemiarum et parabolarum omnium, quae apud Graecos, Latinos, Hebraeos, Arabas, &c. in vsu fuerunt, collectio absolutissima in locos communes digesta* (Rotterdam, 1629).

[306] John Woodall: *The surgeons mate, or, Military & domestique surgery* (London, 1655).

[307] Sir William Cooke of Brome Hall, who died in 1708.

[308] Jacques Davy du Perron: *Les ambassades et negotiations de l'illustrissime & reverendissime cardinal Du Perron* (Paris, 1623); *Replique a la response du serenissime roy de la Grand Bretagne* (Paris, 1620); *Les diverses oeuvres de l'illustrissime Cardinal Du Perron* (Paris, 1622)

[309] Thomas Aquinas: *Summa contra gentiles*

[310] Carolus Sigonius: *De antiquo jure civium Romanorum* (Frankfurt, 1593)

[311] Giovanni Pietro Maffei: *Historiarum Indicarum libri XVI. Selectarum, item, ex India epistolarum, eodem interprete, libri IV. Accessit Ignati Loiolae vita* (Cologne, 1589)

[312] Francis Mason: *Vindiciae Ecclesiae Anglicanae; sive De legitimo eiusdem ministerio* (London, 1638).

[313] Thomas Morton: *A catholike appeale for Protestants; out of the confessions of the Romane doctors; particularly answering the mis-named Catholike apologie for the Romane faith, out of the Protestants* (London, 1610)

[314] William Alabaster: *Commentarius de bestia Apocalyptica* (Delft, 1622)

[315] See n. 100 above

brought into *the* library by Mr [*John*] Reddington,[316] Fellow of Trinity College in Cambridge, these following books, being the gift of several persons of the said College, as here follows, Josephus his works translated by Sir Roger Lestrange. London, 1702.[317] Grotius (Hugo) *De Jure Belli & Pacis* per Gronovium Amstelodami, 1689.[318] Mr Young's *Sermons.* Dean of Sarum 2 volumes. London, 1703. [319] These the gift of Mr Henry Eden,[320] Fellow of Trinity College, Cambridge. Hodius (Humfredi) *de Textibus Originalibus Bibliorum.* Oxon. 1705.[321] Simon (Father) *Critical History of the Old Testament.* London. 1682.[322] Critical enquiries. London. 1684.[323] Nectarius *contra Imperium Papae.* Latin, translated by Dr Alix. London 1712.[324] These *four last* the gift of Mr John Laughton, [325] conduct [326] of the said College & library keeper of the University. Hyde (Tho:) *Catalogus librorum Bibliothecae Bodleianae.* Oxon. 1674.[327] Plot (Dr Robert) *Natural History of Oxford-shire.* Oxford, 1705.[328] Hooker (Richard) *Of Ecclesiastical Polity.* 5 Books. London.[329] These three the gift of Mr Edward Rudd,[330] Fellow of the said College. Aeschyli *Tragediae Graecae* per Henricum Stephanus. 1557.[331] The gift of Sam[*uel*] Bradshaw, A.B. of the said College. Lycophron. Oxon. 1702.[332] The gift of Gilbert Granger[333] A.B. of the said College. Another

[316] Born in Cambridge, John Reddington graduated BA from Trinity College, in 1702, proceeding MA in 1705. He became a Fellow of Trinity in 1704 and was ordained in 1708. He was headmaster of Norwich School from 1712 to 1737 and died in 1739 (H.W. Saunders, *A History of Norwich Grammar School*, Norwich, 1932, pp. 303–4).

[317] *A compleat collection of the genuine works of Flavius Josephus, translated by Sir Roger L'Estrange* (London, 1732).

[318] Hugo Grotius: *De jure belli ac pacis libri tres* (Amsterdam, 1689)

[319] Edward Young: *Sermons on several occasions* (London, 1703–6)

[320] Born at Durham, Henry Eden graduated BA from Trinity College, Cambridge, in 1697, proceeding MA in 1700. He was elected a Fellow of his College in 1699 and died in 1711.

[321] Humphrey Hody: *De Bibliorum textibus originalibus, versionibus Graecis, et Latina vulgata: libri IV* (Oxford, 1705)

[322] Richard Simon: *Critical History of the Old Testament* (London, 1682)

[323] Richard Simon: *Critical enquiries into the various editions of the Bible* (London, 1684)

[324] Nectarius: *Confutatio imperii papae in Ecclesiam* (London, 1702)

[325] John Laughton was librarian of Trinity College from 1686 to 1712. He was known to have had an outstanding library.

[326] Chaplain.

[327] Thomas Hyde: *Catalogus impressorum librorum bibliothecae Bodleianae in academia Oxoniensi* (Oxford, 1674)

[328] Robert Plot: *The Natural History of Oxfordshire, being an essay towards the natural history of England* (Oxford, 1705)

[329] Richard Hooker: *Of the lawes of ecclesiastical politie* (London, 1622)

[330] Edward Rudd was elected Fellow in 1710. He was rector of North Runcton from 1719 to 1727.

[331] Aeschylus: *Aeschyli Tragoediae VII* (Geneva, 1557).

[332] Lycophron: *Lycophronis Chalcidensis Alexandra: obscurum poema. Cum graeco Isacii, seu potius Joannis, Tzetzae commentario* (Oxford, 1702).

[333] Born in Shillington, Bedfordshire, Gilbert Granger graduated BA from Trinity College, Cambridge, in 1707. He was ordained in 1709.

the gift of Mr Mathew Snow[334] of the said College. Chillingworth (William) *Protestants safe way*. Oxford. 1638.[335] The gift of Mr William Chamberlain[336] Fellow of the said College. Pearsonij (Episcopus) *Opera Posthuma*. London, 1688.[337] The gift of Mr Ralph Bourchier[338] of the said College. Bennet (Tho) *Abridgement of the London cases to the Dissenters*. Cambridge. 1700.[339] The gift of Mr Roger Cotes,[340] *Fellow* of the said College. Idem, *Confutation of Popery*. Cambridge, 1701.[341] Idem, *Discourse of Schism*. Cambridge, 1702.[342] These two likewise the gift of Mr [*Roger*] Cotes. Virgilij *Opera*. In usum Delphini. London, 1695.[343] Flori (Annaei) Historia in usum Delphini. London, 1692.[344] Salustij (Crisp) Historia in usum Delphini. London, 1697.[345] Lucani *Pharsaliae*.[346] *The Fathers Counsel to his Children*. London, 1678.[347] These 5 the gift of Mr Laurence Eusden[348] of the said College. Thysij (Anton.) *Roma Illustrata*. Amstelodami, 1657.[349]

Cicero (M. Tullius) *de Officijs* per Graevium. Amstelodami, 1691.[350]

Grotius (Hugo) *de Veritate Religionis Christianae*. Paris, 1640.[351]

These three the gift of Mr Edward Smith[352] of the said College.

Juvenalis & Persius in usum Delphini. Paris, 1684. The gift of David Fleming[353] A.B. of the said College.

---

[334] Born in Clipsham, Rutland, Mathew Snow was admitted pensioner at Trinity College, Cambridge, in April 1704, graduating BA in 1708 and proceeding MA in 1711. He was a Fellow of his College in 1710.

[335] William Chillingworth: *The religion of Protestants a safe way to salvation* (London, 1674)

[336] William Chamberlain was elected Fellow of Trinity College in 1703.

[337] John Pearson: *Opera posthuma chronological* (London, 1688)

[338] Son of Sir Barrington Bourchier of Beningbrough, Yorkshire, Ralph Bourchier was admitted pensioner at Trinity in 1706, graduating MB in 1711 and MD in 1717.

[339] Thomas Bennet: *An answer to the dissenters pleas for separation, or, An abridgement of the London cases* (Cambridge, 1700)

[340] Born at Burbage, Leicestershire, Roger Coates graduated BA from Trinity College, Cambridge, in 1702, proceeding MA in 1706. He was nominated professor of Astronomy and Experimental Philosophy in the same year. He helped Isaac Newton prepare the second edition of the *Principia* (*ODNB*).

[341] Thomas Bennet: *A confutation of popery* (Cambridge, 1701)

[342] Thomas Bennet: *A discourse of schism* (Cambridge, 1702) [Cambridge, 1702]

[343] Virgil: *P. Virgilii Maronis Opera* (London, 1695).

[344] Lucius Annaeus Florus: *Rerum romanorum epitome* (London, 1692).

[345] Sallust: *C. Sallusti Crispi Quae extant: in usum Delphini* (London, 1697).

[346] Lucan: *Pharsaliae*

[347] *The fathers legacy: or, Counsels to his children* (London, 1678).

[348] A Yorkshireman, Laurence Eusden was elected Fellow in 1711. He was Poet Laureate from 1718 to 1730 and had the distinction of being one of those writers satirised in Pope's *Dunciad*.

[349] Justus Lipsius: *Roma illustrata: sive, Antiquitatum Romanorum breviarium...ex nova recensione Antonii Thysii postrema editio* (Amsterdam, 1657)

[350] Marcus Tullius Cicero: *De officiis: ex recensione Joannis Georgii Graevii* (Amsterdam, 1691).

[351] Hugo Grotius: *De veritate religionis Christianae* (Paris, 1640)

[352] Edward Smith was elected Fellow in 1710.

[353] David Fleming graduated BA from Trinity College in 1707, proceeding MA in 1710.

September 2 1707. Present: Dr [*Charles*] Trimnell, who paid 4 quarters to Midsummer last, Mr [*Edward*] Reveley, Mr [*John*] Havett, Mr [*John*] Barker, Mr [William] Herne. Dr [Charles] Trimnel bought Arminius' *works*,[354] Toleti *instructio sacerdotis*,[355] with seven pamphlets, & paid four shillings for them to Mr Havett library keeper. Mr [*Francis*] Fayerman, Mr [*William*] Adamson.

October 7 Quarter day 1707. Present: Mr Connould paid, Mr [*John*] Paul paid the last quarter, Mr [*John*] Havett paid the last quarter, Mr [*Edward*] Rively paid the last quarter, Mr [*William*] Herne paid the last quarter, Mr [*John*] Richardson paid all arrears, Mr [*Francis*] Fayerman paid the last quarter, Mr [*John*] Barker paid the last quarter.

November 3 1707. Present: Mr [*John*] Whitefoot, who paid the last two quarters, Mr [*Samuel*] Jones, who paid the two last quarters, Mr [*John*] Barker, Mr [*John*] Havett, Mr [*Edward*] Reveley, Mr Chancellor, who paid the two last quarters, Mr [*John*] Paul, Mr [*Joseph*] Brett.

November 3 1707. Mr [*Francis*] Fayerman, Mr [*William*] Herne, Mr [*Thomas*] Clayton paid the last quarter.

December 1 1707. Present: Dr [*John*] Jeffery, Mr [*William*] Herne, Mr [*John*] Clarke[356] was this day admitted to the use of the library, Mr [*Samuel*] Jones, Mr [*John*] Paul, Mr Chancellor, Mr [*John*] Whitefoot, Mr [*John*] Havett, Mr [*John*] Richardson.

January 5 1708. Quarter day. Present: Mr Chancellour, who paid the last quarter, Mr [*John*] Havett, who paid the last quarter, Mr [*Joseph*] Brett, who paid the last quarter, Mr [*John*] Clark, Mr [*John*] Paul, who paid the last quarter, Mr [*William*] Herne, who paid the last quarter, Mr [*Francis*] Fayerman, who paid the last quarter, Mr [*John*] Barker, who paid the last quarter, Dr [*John*] Jeffery, who paid the last quarter, Mr [*John*] Whitefoot paid the last quarter.

He was elected Fellow of his College in 1709. Rector of Bixley, Framingham Earl and Marlingford from 1723 to 1738, he left instructions in his will for his wife to burn all his papers and sermons (NRO NCC 63 Peppen, Will of David Fleming, 1747).

[354] Jacobus Arminius: *Iacobi Armini Veteraquinatis Bataui, ss. Theologiae doctoris eximij, opera theologica, nunc denuo conjunctim recusa* (Frankfurt, 1635).

[355] Francisco de Toledo: *Instructio sacerdotum in libros octo distincta. Quae nunc sexto cum authographo accurate collata.......*

[356] The younger brother of the theologian, Samuel Clarke, John Clarke graduated BA from Caius College, Cambridge, in 1704, proceeding MA in 1707. He became a Doctor of Divinity in 1717. He was curate of St George Tombland, a prebend of Norwich Cathedral and a canon of Canterbury Cathedral. In 1728 he was instituted to the deanery of Salisbury and died there in 1757 (ODNB).

February 2 1708. Present: Mr Chancelour, Mr [*John*] Richardson paid the last quarter, Mr [*Francis*] Fayerman, Mr [*Joseph*] Ellys, Mr [*Joseph*] Brett paid the last quarter, Mr [*Thomas*] Clayton, Mr [*John*] Paul, Mr [*William*] Herne.

March 1 1708. Present: Mr [*William*] Herne, Dr [*John*] Jeffery, Mr [*John*] Richardson, Mr Chancellor, Mr [*John*] Barker, Mr [*John*] Clarke, Mr [*Francis*] Fayerman, Mr [*Joseph*] Brett, Mr [*Edward*] Rively paid the last quarter, Mr [*John*] Whitefoot, Mr [*John*] Paul, Mr [*Henry*] Sheppy, who paid the last quarter, Mr [*Robert* or *John*] Connould. About this time the Reverend Mr Nathaniel Ganning,[357] rector of Reymerstone, Norfolk, sent into the library as his gift Sir Walter Raleigh's *History of the World*. London, 1677.[358] Sent then into the library Bevereidge's Can[*on*][359] in 2 volumes being the gift of Waller Bacon[360] Esquire.

1708 April 5 Quarter day. Present: Mr [*Robert* or *John*] Connold paid the last quarter,[361] Mr [*Joseph*] Brett, who paid the last quarter, Mr [*John*] Whitefoot, who paid the last quarter, Mr [*John*] Barker, who paid the last quarter, Mr [*William*] Herne, who paid the last quarter.

May 3 1708. Present: Mr [*John*] Paul paid the last quarter, Mr [John] Havett paid the 2 last quarters, Mr [*John*] Clarke paid the last quarter, Mr [*Joseph*] Brett, Mr [*William*] Herne, Mr [*John*] Richardson paid the last quarter, Mr [*Francis*] Fayerman paid the last quarter, Mr [*Edward*] Reveley paid the last quarter, Mr [*Samuel*] Jones paid the last two quarters.

June 7 1708. Present: Mr [*John*] Whitefoot, Dr [*John*] Jefferys paid the last quarter, Mr [*John*] Havett, Mr [*Francis*] Fayerman, Mr [*Joseph*] Ellis.

July 5 Quarter day 1708. Present: Mr [*William*] Herne paid the last quarter, Mr [*John*] Barker paid the last quarter, Dr [*John*] Jeffery paid the last quarter, Mr [*Samuel*] Jones, who paid the last quarter, Mr [*John*] Clarke, who paid the last quarter, Mr [*John*] Whitefoot, who paid the last quarter.

---

[357] Nathaniel Ganning was admitted at Corpus Christi College Cambridge in 1676, graduating BA in 1680 and proceeding MA in 1683. He was ordained in Norwich in 1681 and was rector of Reymerston and of Thuxton until 1728. He died in 1728.

[358] Walter Raleigh: *The history of the world: in five books* (London, 1677)

[359] William Beveridge: *Sunodikon sive Pandectae canonum SS. Apostolorum, et conciliorum ab ecclesia Graeca receptorum* (Oxford, 1672).

[360] Descended from a younger branch of Lord Keeper Bacon's family, Waller Bacon was returned as Whig MP for Norwich for nearly a quarter of a century. He died in 1734.

[361] This is the last time the name Connold appears in the minutes. Since John Connold died in 1708 this strongly suggests that it was he rather than Robert Connold, rector of Bergh Apton, who was the more regular attender. Robert Connold lived until 1715.

August 2 1708. Present: Dr [*John*] Jeffery, Mr Chancelour paid the last two quarters, Mr [*John*] Clarke, Mr [*William*] Herne, Mr [*Henry*] Sheppy, who paid 2 quarters, Mr [*Samuel*] Jones, Mr [*Francis*] Fayerman, who paid the last quarter.

September 6 1708. Present: Mr [*William*] Herne, Mr [*John*] Paul, who paid the last quarter, Mr [*John*] Havett, who paid the last quarter, Mr [*John*] Clarke, Mr [*Francis*] Fayerman, Mr [*Edward*] Rively paid the last quarter. This day was brought into the library by Mr [*John*] Reddington, Fellow of Trinity College in Cambridge, the following books, being the gift of several persons of the said College, videlicet:
Launoij *epistolae*. Cantab., 1689, [362] the gift of Mr Sam[*uel*] Doyley Fellow of the College.
The works of the author of the whole duty of man,[363] the gift of Mr Farewell.[364]
Heylin's *History of the Reformation*[365] the gift of Mr Andrews.[366]
Bennet's *History of prayer*[367] the gift of Mr Foulis.[368]
Gataker's *Antoninus*[369] the gift of Mr [*Thomas*] Hill,[370] Fellow of the aforesaid College.

October 4 1708. Quarter day. Present: Mr [*William*] Herne who paid the last quarter, Mr [*Francis*] Fayerman, who paid the last quarter, Mr [*Joseph*] Brett paid two last quarters, Mr [*John*] Paul paid the last quarter, Mr [*John*] Clarke paid the last quarter, Mr [*Edward*] Rively paid the last quarter, Mr [*John*] Whitefoot, who paid the last quarter, Mr [*Joseph*] Ellis paid all arrears. This day were sent into the library by Mr Brett these following books:
Launoij *Epistolae*,[371] King Charles 1, *Works*.[372] The gift of Mr John

---

[362] Jean de Launoy: *Epistolae omnes: octo partibus comprehensae* (Cambridge, 1689).

[363] Richard Allestree: *The Works of the Author of the Whole Duty of Man*.

[364] Possibly Phillips Farewell of Ware, Hertfordshire, who was admitted pensioner, aged 18, to Trinity College, Cambridge, in May 1708. He was a Fellow of Trinity from 1712 to 1730.

[365] Peter Heylyn: *Ecclesia restaurata, or, The history of the Reformation of the Church of England* (London, 1661)

[366] Perhaps William Andrews, chaplain of Trinity College, Cambridge, in 1706.

[367] Thomas Bennet: *A Brief History of the Joint Use of Precompos'd Set Forms of Prayer* (Cambridge, 1708)

[368] Possibly William Foulis, son of Sir William Foulis of Ingleby, Cleveland, who was admitted Fellow Commoner at Trinity College in July 1705.

[369] *The Emperor Marcus Antoninus his conversation with himself: together with the preliminary discourse of the learned Gataker*

[370] Born in Southfleet, Kent, Thomas Hill graduated BA from Trinity College in 1705. He was appointed a Fellow of his College in 1707. A noted Latin poet, Hill had the distinction of being published by Edmund Curll (*ODNB*).

[371] Jean de Launoy: *Epistolae omnes* (Cambridge, 1689).

[372] *Basilika: the works of King Charles the martyr* (London, 1687).

Lightwin,[373] President of Caius College, Cambridge.

Novum Testamentum ed. Per Joh Gregory.[374] Mason *de ministerio Ecclesiastica Anglicorum.*[375] The gift of Mr Brampton Gurdon, [376] Fellow of Caius College Cambridge.

Hodij Humfredi. *De Bibliorum Textibus Originalibus.*[377] The gift of Mr Roger Hawys,[378] Fellow of <Caius> *Clare* College Cambridge.

Stillingfleet. Bishop. *Origines Sacrae.*[379] The gift of Dr [*Thomas*] Crask[380] in Cambridge.

Unreasonableness of seperation. [381]The gift of Mr [*Samuel*] Dodd,[382] Fellow of <Caius>* Clare * College, Cambridge. Also about this time *also he brought* into the library Dr Mills *Greek Testament,* [383]the gift of William Worts [384]of Cambridge A.M.

November 1 1708. Present: Mr [*William*] Herne, Mr [*John*] Havett, who paid the last quarter, Dr [*John*] Jeffery, who paid the last quarter, Mr [*Edward*] Reveley, Mr [*John*] Richardson paid all arrears, Mr [*John*] Clarke, Mr [*John*] Barker, who paid last quarter.

---

[373] John Lightwine, born at Barford the son of Matthew Lightwine, gentleman, was educated by Mark Purt. He was President of Caius College from 1704 until his death in 1729 (Venn, *Biographical History*, pp. 441–2).

[374] *Novum Testamentum: opera ac studio Joannis Gregorii* (Oxford, 1703).

[375] Francis Mason: *Vindiciae ecclesiae Anglicanae, sive, De legitimo eiusdem ministerio* (1625).

[376] Brampton Gurdon was the elder brother of the antiquary, Thornhagh Gurdon. After attending Wymondham School he matriculated at Caius College in 1688, graduating BA in 1692 and MA in 1695. He was a Fellow of Caius from 1695 to 1721 and Boyle lecturer in 1721–2.

[377] Humphrey Hody: *De Bibliorum textibus originalibus, versionibus Graecis et Latina vulgata* (Oxford, 1705).

[378] Born at Norwich the son of a mercer, Roger Hawys graduated BA from Caius College, Cambridge, in 1696, proceeding MA in 1699. He was a Fellow of his College from 1699 to 1709 and was awarded a DD in 1713. In 1709 he was deputed, 'with Mr Gurdon and the master', to put the library 'in good order'. Instituted rector of Weeting in 1709, he died in 1749 (T. and M. Miller, 'A Seventeenth-Century Medical Family of Wymondham', *Norfolk Ancestor*, 4, 2006, pp. 513–6).

[379] Edward Stillingfleet: *Originae sacrae, or, A rational account of the grounds of Christian faith.*

[380] Thomas Crask was born at Weeting in Norfolk and attended Bury Grammar School. He was admitted to Caius College in 1687 and graduated MB in 1693. He became an MD in 1700, a Senior Fellow, Dean, Registrar, Greek lecturer and Hebrew lecturer. He died at Bury St Edmund's in 1718 (Venn, *Biographical History*, p. 483).

[381] Edward Stillingfleet: *The Unreasonableness of Separation; or, An impartial account of the history, nature, and pleas of the present separation from the communion of the Church of England.*

[382] Samuel Dodd was admitted sizar at Clare College in 1697, graduating BA in 1702 and proceeding MA in 1705. He was a Fellow of his College from 1707 to 1714.

[383] *Novum Testamentum cum lectionibus variantibus. Studio et labore Joannis Milii* (Oxford, 1707).

[384] Born at Landbeach in Cambridgeshire, William Woorts was a graduate of St Catherine's College, Cambridge. On his death in 1709 his estate was bequeathed to the university.

December 6 1708. Present: Mr [*Francis*] Fayerman, Mr [*John*] Havett, Mr [*John*] Clarke, Mr [*William*] Herne.

January 3 Quarter day. 1709. Present: Mr [*Francis*] Fayerman, who paid the last quarter, Mr [*John*] Clarke, who paid the last quarter, Mr [*John*] Havett, who paid the last quarter, Mr [*William*] Herne, who paid the last quarter, Mr [*John*] Paul, who paid the last quarter.

February 7 [*1709*]. Present: Dr [*John*] Jeffery, who paid the last quarter, Mr [*William*] Herne, Mr [*John*] Paul, Mr [*Francis*] Fayerman.

March 7 1709. Present: Mr [*John*] Barker, who paid the last quarter, Mr [*Edward*] Rively, who paid the last quarter, Mr [*John*] Havett, who paid 9s for the 2 last years as library keeper, Mr [*Joseph*] Ellis, Mr [*John*] Paul, Mr [*John*] Whitefoot, who paid the last quarter, Mr [*John*] Clarke. This day Mr [*William*] Herne was chosen library keeper for the two next ensuing yeares.

April 4 1709 Quarter day. Present: Mr [*Francis*] Fayerman, who paid the last quarter, Mr [*Edward*] Reveley, who paid the last quarter, Mr [*Thomas*] Clayton, who paid all arrears, Mr [*John*] Whitefoote, who paid the last quarter, Mr [*Samuel*] Jones, who paid all arrears, Mr [*John*] Clarke, who paid the last quarter, Mr [*Samuel*] Salter,[385] who paid the last quarter, Mr [*William*] Herne.

May 2 1709. Present: Mr [*William*] Herne, who paid the last quarter, Mr [*John*] Havett, who paid the last quarter, Mr [*Edward*] Reveley, Mr [*Joseph*] Ellis, Dr [*John*] Jeffery, who paid the last quarter, Mr [*Samuel*] Salter, Mr Chancellour, who paid all arrears, Mr [*Joseph*] Brett, who paid the two last quarters, Mr [*Samuel*] Jones, Mr [*John*] Clarke, Mr [*Henry*] Sheppey, who paid all arrears. Memorandum. It is this day agreed by us whose names are underwritten that the fourteen shillings & three pence now paid by Mr Herne the present library keeper < *word or words illegible* > to Mr Joseph Brett to clear his disbursements for catalogues &c for the service of the library shal be repaid the said Mr Herne by the succeeding library keeper

---

[385] Samuel Salter graduated BA from Corpus Christi College, Cambridge, in 1701, proceeding MA in 1704 and DD in 1728. He was vicar of St Stephen's in 1708 and vicar of St Saviour's and Earlham in 1712. He married Penelope, the daughter of John Jeffery. He was the author of *A sermon preach'd at the Cathedral-Church of Norwich* (London, 1714). He left Norwich at the age of 70 and went to London, where he became a member of Samuel Johnson's Rambler Club, founded in the winter of 1748–9. According to Hawkins, Salter was 'a man of general reading, but no deep scholar: he was well bred, courteous, and affable, and enlivened conversation by the relation of a variety of curious facts, of which his memory was the only register (Sir John Hawkins, *The life of Samuel Johnson*, ed. B.H. Davies, London, 1962, p. 98). He died in 1756.

upon his election unles paid before. [*signed*]Thomas Tanner. John Jeffery. Jos[*eph*] Ellis. Edw[*ard*] Reveley. Jo[*hn*] Havett.

May 6 1709. Received of the under library keeper fourteen shillings for Sir Walter Raleigh.[386] A supernumerary book sold to Mr [*Samuel?*] Lillington[387] by order of the society which is towards the discharge of the above 14s 3d. paid to Mr [*Joseph*] Brett by me. W[*illiam*] Herne.

June 6 1709. Present: Mr [*John*] Havett, Mr [*John*] Clark, Mr [*John*] Paul, who paid the last quarter, Mr [*William*] Herne, who received of the under library keeper six shillings for Lycophron[388] sold to Dr [*Roger*] Hawys by order of the society being a duplicate.

July 4 [*1709*]. Quarter day. Present: Mr [*John*] Whitefoote, who paid the last quarter, Mr [*Edward*] Reveley, who paid the last quarter, Mr [*John*] Paul, who paid the last quarter, Mr [*John*] Clarke, who paid the last quarter, Mr [*John*] Havett, who paid the last quarter, Mr [*Samuel*] Jones, who paid the last quarter, Dr [*John*] Jeffrey, who paid the last quarter.

August 1 [*1709*]. Present: Dr [*William*] Herne,[389] who paid the last quarter, Mr [*John*] Clarke.

September 5 1709. Present: Mr [*Francis*] Fayerman, who paid the last quarter, Mr [*John*] Whitefoote, Mr [*Edward*] Reveley, Dr [*William*] Herne.

October 3 1709. Quarter day. Present: Dr [*William*] Herne, who paid the last quarter, Mr [*John*] Havet, who paid the last quarter, Mr [*Samuel*] Jones, who paid the last quarter, Mr [*Edward*] Revely, who paid the last quarter, Dr [*John*] Jeffery, who paid the last quarter, Mr [*Samuel*] Salter, who paid the two last quarters, Mr [*Mark*] Purt, who paid the last quarter, Mr [*Joseph*] Ellis, who paid all arrears.

November 7 1709. Present: Mr [*Francis*] Fayerman, who paid the last quarter, Dr [*John*] Jeffery, Dr [*William*] Herne, Sam[*uel*] Salter. Mr [*Thomas*] Clayton paid the library keeper 2s. for Midsummer & Michaelmas quarters this day December 1st.

[386] Sir Walter Ralegh's *History of the World*.

[387] Possibly Samuel Lillington, a worstead weaver, who became sheriff of Norwich in 1730 (Hawes, p. 76).

[388] Lycophron: *Lycophronis Chalcidensis Alexandra: obscurum poema. Cum graeco Isacii, seu potius Joannis, Tzetzae commentario* (Oxford, 1702).

[389] William Herne was awarded a Doctorate in Divinity in 1709.

December 5 1709. Present: Mr [*John*] Richardson, who paid all arrears, Mr [*Francis*] Fayerman, Mr [*Edward*] Reveley, Dr [*William*] Herne, Mr [*Mark*] Purt.

January 2 1710. Quarter day. Present: Mr [*John*] Paul, who paid the two last quarters, Mr [*Francis*] Fayerman, who paid the last quarter, Mr [*John*] Havett, who paid the last quarter, Dr [*William*] Herne, who paid the last quarter and brought in the first volume of Collier's *Ecclesiastical History*,[390] given by Mr James Bedingfeild,[391] Fellow of Gonvile & Caius College in Cambridge. *The Validity of the Orders of the Church of England* [392] *The Life of Mahomet*,[393] & the *Original & Right of Tythes*,[394] these three last by Dr Prideaux, Dean of Norwich, brought in by Mr Paul.
Mr [*Edward*] Revely, who paid the last quarter, Mr [*Samuel*] Salter, who paid the last quarter, Mr [*John*] Clarke, who paid two last quarters, Mr [*Mark*] Purt, who paid the last quarter.

February 6 1710. Present: Dr [*John*] Jeffery paid the last quarter, Mr [*Joseph*] Brett paid the last 3 quarters, Mr [*Samuel*] Salter, Mr [*Joseph*] Ellis, Mr [*Francis*] Fayerman, Mr [*Edward*] Reveley, Mr [*John*] Clarke, Mr [*John*] Havett, Dr [*William*] Herne.

March 6 1710. Present: Mr [*Joseph*] Brett, Mr [*Edward*] Reveley, Dr [*William*] Herne, Mr [*Francis*] Fayerman, Mr [*John*] Clarke.

April 3 1710. Quarter day. Present: Dr [*William*] Herne, who paid the last quarter, Mr [*Edward*] Revely, who paid the last quarter, Mr [*Samuel*] Salter, who paid the last quarter, Mr [*John*] Richardson, who paid the last quarter, Mr [*Thomas*] Clayton paid Christmas & our Lady quarters, Mr [*Francis*] Fayerman paid the last quarter. This day Howel's *Collection of Canons*[395] was

[390] Jeremy Collier: *An ecclesiastical history of Great Britain, chiefly of England: from the first planting of Christianity to the end of the reign of King Charles the Second* (London, 1708–14).

[391] Born at Merton, James Bedingfield, alias James de Grey, was a Junior Fellow at Caius College from 1709 to 1719. He was ordained in 1707 and was instituted rector of Whissonsett in 1718. His will was proved in Norwich in 1745. He asked that his body be carried to the grave by six day labourers and 'very privately' buried at 8 o'clock in the morning with no tolling of any bell, though the minister was to wear a handsome mourning ring, a pair of the best black shammy gloves and a hat band and belt of black silk. His executor was instructed to burn his sermons and all his other written papers (NRO NCC 94 Wright, Will of James Bedingfield, 1745).

[392] Humphrey Prideaux: *The validity of the orders of the Church of England, made out against the objections of the papists* (1688).

[393] Humphrey Prideaux: *The true nature of imposture fully display'd in the life of Mahomet.*

[394] Humphrey Prideaux: *The original and right of tithes: for the maintenance of the ministry in a Christian church truly stated* (Norwich, 1710).

[395] Lawrence Howell: *Synopsis Canonum.* (London, 1708).

brought into the library by Mr [*John*] Reddington, being the gift of Mr John Bennet,[396] gentleman. Mr [*John*] Barker, who paid for a yeare and its quarter all that is due to the under library keeper, Mr Chancellour, who paid a yeare all that is due to the under library keeper.

May 1 1710. Present: Dr [*William*] Herne, Mr [*John*] Havett, Mr [*Edward*] Reveley, Mr [*Francis*] Fayerman, Mr [*John*] Clarke, who paid the last quarter, Mr [*Samuel*] Salter.

June 5 1710. Present: Mr [*Edward*] Reveley, Mr [*John*] Havett, who paid the last quarter, Dr [*William*] Herne, Mr [*John*] Clarke, Mr [*John*] Richardson (tho absent) paid the under library keeper & desired to be discharged, Mr [*Francis*] Fayerman.

July 3 1710. Quarter day. Present: Dr [*William*] Herne, who paid the last quarter, Mr [*Edward*] Revely, who paid the last quarter, Mr [*John*] Paul, who paid the 2 last quarters, Mr Paul, who paid the 2 last quarters, Mr [*Francis*] Fayerman, who paid the last quarter, Mr [*John*] Havett, who paid the last quarter, Mr [*Samuel*] Salter, who paid the last quarter.

August 7 1710. Present: Dr [*John*] Jeffery, who paid the two last quarters, Mr [*Edward*] Reveley, Dr [*William*] Herne, Mr [*Francis*] Fayerman, Mr [*John*] Whitefoote.

September 4 1710. Present: Dr [*William*] Herne.

October 2 1710. Quarter day. Present: Dr [*William*] Herne, who paid the last quarter, Mr [*Edward*] Reveley, who paid the last quarter, Mr [*Francis*] Fayerman, who paid the last quarter, Mr Chancellor, who paid the two last quarters, Mr [*John*] Clarke who paid the two last quarters, Mr [*Thomas*] Clayton, who paid the two last quarters, Dr [*John*] Jeffery, who paid the last quarter.

November 6 1710. Present: Dr [*William*] Herne, Mr [*Joseph*] Ellis, who paid all arrears, Mr [*Edward*] Reveley, Mr [*John*] Paul, who paid the last quarter, Mr [*Francis*] Fayerman, Mr [*Samuel*] Jones, who paid the four last quarters.

December 4 1710. Present: Dr [*William*] Herne, Mr [*Samuel*] Salter, who paid the last quarter, Mr [*Joseph*] Brett, who paid the 3 last quarters, Mr [*John*] Havett, who paid the last quarter, Mr [*Edward*] Reveley.

[396] John Bennet was presumably a friend of John Reddington, Fellow of Trinity College, Cambridge, who had been ordained in Norwich in 1708. Nothing else is known, however.

January 1 1711. Quarter day. Present: Dr [*William*] Herne, who paid the quarter, Mr [*John*] Havett, who paid the last quarter.

February 5 1711. Present: Dr [*William*] Herne, who paid 9s for the 2 last years as library keeper, Mr [*John*] Whitefoot, who paid all arrears, Mr [*Edward*] Reveley, who paid the last quarter, Mr [*John*] Havett, Mr [*John*] Clarke, who paid the last quarter. This day Mr [*Samuel*] Jones was chosen library keeper for the 2 next ensueing years.

March 5 1711. Present: Dr [*John*] Jeffery, who paid the last quarter, Dr [*William*] Hyrne, Mr [*Samuel*] Salter, who paid last quarter, Mr [*John*] Barker, who paid all arrears, Mr [*Edward*] Reveley, Mr [*John*] Whitefoot, Mr [*Francis*] Fayerman, who paid the last quarter.

April 2 1711. Quarter day. Present: Dr [*John*] Jeffery, who paid the last quarter, Dr [*William*] Herne, who paid the last quarter, John Barker, who paid the last quarter, Mr [*John*] Whitefoot, who paid the last quarter, Mr [*Thomas*] Clayton, who paid the two last quarters.

May 7 1711. Present: Mr [*John*] Clarke, Mr [*John*] Barker, Mr [*John*] Whitefoot, Dr [*William*] Herne, Dr [*John*] Jeffery, Mr [*Samuel*] Salter.

June 4 1711. Present: Dr [*William*] Herne, Mr [*Edward*] Reveley, who paid the last quarter.

July 2 1711. Quarter day. Present: Dr [*William*] Herne, who paid the last quarter, Mr [*John*] Havett, who paid the two last quarters, Mr [*Edward*] Reveley, who paid the last quarter, Mr [*John*] Whitefoot, who paid the last quarter, Mr [*Francis*] Fayerman, who paid all arrears, Dr [*John*] Jeffery paid the last quarter July 5.

August 6 [*1711*]. Present: Dr [*William*] Herne, Mr [*Edward*] Revely, Mr [*Samuel*] Jones, who paid all arrears.

September 3 1711. Present: Mr [*Samuel*] Salter, who paid the two last quarters, Mr [*Thomas*] Clayton, who paid the last quarter, Dr [*William*] Herne, Mr [*Edward*] Reveley.

October 1 1711. Quarter day. Present: Mr [*Edward*] Reveley, who paid the last quarter, Dr [*William*] Herne, who paid the last quarter, Mr [*John*] Whitefoot, who paid the last quarter, Mr [*Joseph*] Ellis, who paid all arrears.

November 5 1711. Present: Dr [*William*] Herne, Mr [*Edward*] Reveley.

December 3 1711. Present: Mr [*John*] Whitefoot, Mr [*Edward*] Reveley, Mr [*Joseph*] Brett, who paid all arrears, Mr [*Samuel*] Salter, who paid the last quarter, Dr [*William*] Herne, Dr [*John*] Jeffrey, who paid the last quarter.

January 7 1712. Quarter day. Present: Dr [*John*] Jeffrey, who paid the last quarter, Mr [*John*] Havett, who paid the two last quarters, Dr [*William*] Herne, who paid the last quarter, Mr [*Francis*] Fayerman, who paid all arrears, Mr [*Edward*] Revely, who paid the last quarter.

February 4 1712. Present: Mr [*Edward*] Reveley, Dr [*William*] Herne. February 7. Chancellor[397] paid all arrears.

March 3 1712 [*No entry save for a zero, no doubt indicating a nil attendance*]

March 14 1712. Present: Mr [*Thomas*] Clayton paid all arrears, Dr [*William*] Herne.

April 7 1712. Quarter day. Present: Dr [*William*] Herne, who paid last quarter, Dr [*John*] Jeffery, who paid the last quarter, Mr [*Edward*] Reveley, who paid the last quarter, Mr [*Francis*] Fayerman, who paid the last quarter, Mr [*John*] Barker, who paid the last quarter, Mr [*John*] Havett, who paid last quarter.

May 5 1712. Present: Dr [*William*] Herne.

June 2 1712. Present: Arch Deacon [*John*] Jeffery, Mr [*Joseph*] Ellis, Mr [*Edward*] Revely, Mr [*Joseph*] Brett paid last quarter, Mr [*John*] Barker, Mr [*Samuel*] Jones who paid all arrears, Mr [*Samuel*] Salter who paid all arrears, Mr [*John*] Clarke who paid all, arrears 5s., Mr [*John*] Whitefoot who paid all arrears, Mr [*John*] Havett, Dr [*William*] Herne.

July 7 1712. Quarter day. Present: Dr [*William*] Herne, who paid the last quarter, Mr [*Edward*] Reveley, who paid the last quarter, Mr [*Francis*] Fayerman, who paid the last quarter.

August 4 1712. Present: Mr [*Edward*] Reveley, Dr [*John*] Jeffery, who paid the last quarter, Mr [*Francis*] Fayerman, Dr [*William*] Herne, Mr [*John*] Whitefoot, who paid the last quarter.

---

[397] Thomas Tanner, chancellor of Norwich Diocese.

September 1 1712. Present: Dr [*William*] Herne, Mr [*John*] Clarke paid the last quarter, Mr [*John*] Barker paid the last quarter, Mr [*Thomas*] Clayton paid then all arrears.

October 6 1712. Quarter day. Present: Dr [*William*] Herne paid the last quarter, Mr [*John*] Barker, paid the last quarter, Mr [*Thomas*] Clayton who paid the last quarter, Mr [*Edward*] Reveley, who paid the last quarter, Mr [*Francis*] Fayerman, who paid the last quarter.

October 6 1712. Present: Mr [*John*] Whitefoot paid last quarter, Mr [*Joseph*] Ellis, who paid all arrears, < Mr [*John*] Clarke paid the last quarter >, Mr Clarke paid the last quarter.

November 3 1712. Present: Mr [*Thomas*] Clayton, Mr [*Francis*] Fayerman, Dr [*William*[Herne. November 6. This day the bishop[398] gave Dr [*Thomas*] Brown's *Posthumous Works*[399] to the library.

December 1 1712. Present: Mr [*Joseph*] Brett, who paid the 2 last quarters, Dr [*William*] Herne, Dr [*John*] Jeffery paid last quarter, Mr [*John*] Whitefoote, Mr [*Thomas*] Clayton, Mr [*Francis*] Fairman.

January 5 1713. Quarter day. Present: Mr [*John*] Havett, who paid the 3 last quarters, Mr [*Samuel*] Salter, who paid the 3 last quarters, Mr [*John*] Barker paid the last quarter, Mr [*Thomas*] Clayton paid the last quarter. Mr [*Henry*] Fish, [400] who was this day admitted to the use of the library, Dr [*William*] Herne who paid the last quarter, Mr [*John*] Whitefoote who paid the library.

January 5 1713. This day Mr [*Francis*] Fayerman was chosen library keeper for the two ensuing years.

February 2 1713. Present: Dr [*William*] Herne, Mr [*Joseph*] Brett, who paid the last quarter, Mr [*John*] Barker, Mr [*Edward*] Reveley, who paid the last quarter, Mr [*Francis*] Fayerman, who paid the last quarter. Memorandum.

---

[398] Charles Trimnell, bishop of Norwich from 1708 to 1721. In the same year Trimnell gave three books to the parish library of St James, Bury St Edmund's, and six books to Beccles parish library.

[399] *Posthumous works of the learned Sir Thomas Browne* (London, 1712).

[400] Born at King's Lynn, Henry Fish was admitted sizar at Christ's College Cambridge in 1703, graduating BA in 1708 and proceeding MA in 1711. He was ordained in Norwich in 1709. He was rector of Irstead in 1711, vicar of Scottow in 1713, vicar of Middleton from 1722 to 1737 and rector of Walpole from 1726 to 1743. When he drew up his will he was living in Yarmouth, where he owned considerable amounts of property (NRO ANW 125, Will of Henry Fish, 1743).

Dr Herne paid Mr Fayerman 5s. 9d. in full for dues from him to the library. This day Mr [*Henry*] Fish was admitted to the use of the library.

March 2 1713. Present: Dr [*John*] Jeffery, who paid the last quarter, Dr [*William*] Herne, Mr [*Samuel*] Jones, who paid the under library keeper for the 2 last years *of he being library keeper* and all other arrears, Mr [*John*] Barker, Mr [*Edward*] Reveley.

April 6 1713. Quarter day. Present: John Whitefoot, who paid this quarter.

May 4 1713. Present: Dr [*William*] Herne, who paid the last quarter, Mr [*Francis*] Fayerman, who paid the last quarter, Mr [*Thomas*] Clayton, who paid the last quarter. May 4 1713. Mr [*Samuel*] Salter, who paid the last quarter.

June 1 [*1713*]. Present: Dr [*William*] Herne, Mr [*Joseph*] Brett, who paid the last quarter, Mr [*Francis*] Fayerman, Mr [*John*] Barker, who paid the last quarter, Mr [*Edward*] Reveley, who paid the last quarter, Mr [*Samuel*] Jones, who paid the last quarter, Mr [*Samuel*] Salter, Mr [*John*] Havett, who paid the last quarter, Mr [*John*] Clarke, who paid the two last quarters.

July 6 1713. Quarter day. Present: Mr [*Joseph*] Brett, who paid the last quarter, Mr [*John*] Havett, who paid the last quarter, Mr [*Henry*] Fish, who paid the two last quarters, Mr [*Edward*] Reveley, who paid the last quarter.

August 3 1713. Present: Dr [*John*] Jeffery, who paid the two last quarters, Dr [*William*] Herne, who paid the last quarter, Mr [*Joseph*] Brett.

September 7 [*1713*]. Present: Mr [*Edward*] Reveley, Dr [*William*] Herne, Mr [*Francis*] Fayerman, who paid the last quarter.

October 5 1713. Quarter day. Present: Mr [*Francis*] Fayerman, who paid the last quarter, Mr [*Edward*] Reveley, who paid the last quarter, Dr [*William*] Herne, who paid the last quarter, Mr [*Thomas*] Clayton, who paid the two last quarters.

November 2 1713. Present: Dr [*William*] Herne, Mr [*John*] Havett paid the last quarter, Mr [*Samuel*] Salter paid the 2 last quarters.

December 7 1713. Present: Mr [*John*] Havett, Dr [*William*] Herne, Mr [*Edward*] Revely.

January 4 Quarter day. 1714. Present: Mr [*Edward*] Reveley, who paid the last quarter, Dr [*William*] Herne, who paid the last quarter.

February 1 1714. Present: Mr [*Francis*] Fayerman, who paid all arrears due to the under library keeper to this day. Mr [*Samuel*] Jones, who paid the three last quarters. Mr [*Thomas*] Clayton, who paid the last quarter. Dr [*William*] Herne. This day Mr [*John*] Clark was chosen library keeper for the two years next ensuing.

March 1 1714. Present: Mr [*Thomas*] Clayton, Mr Chancelour, who paid all arrears, Mr [*John*] Clarke, who paid all arrears, Dr [*William*] Herne. Memorandum. Mr [*Francis*] Fayerman paid Mr Clarke 5s. 9d. due from him to the library. This day was brought into the library *Codex Iuris Ecclesiastici Anglicani* [401]in two volumes folio being the gift of John Peck,[402] Esquire, of Brakendale.

April 5 1714. Quarter day. Present: Mr [*Thomas*] Clayton, who paid the last quarter, Mr [*Edward*] Reveley, who paid the last quarter, Dr [*William*] Herne, who paid the last quarter.

May 3 1714. Present: Dr [*William*] Herne, Mr [*Thomas*] Clayton, Mr [*John*] Whitefoote.

June 7 1714. No body.

July 5 1714. Quarter day. Present: Dr [*John*] Jeffery, who paid all arrears to this day, Dr [*William*] Herne, who paid last quarter.

August 4 1714. Present: Dr [*William*] Herne, Mr [*Edward*] Reveley, who paid the last quarter, Mr [*Samuel*] Salter, who paid the 3 last quarters, Mr [*John*] Barker, who paid all arrears.

September 6 1714. Present: Dr [*William*] Herne, Mr [*Thomas*] Clayton, who paid the last quarter, Dr [*John*] Jeffrey, Mr [*John*] Brand[403] this day admitted to the use of the library.

October 4 1714. Quarter day. Present: Mr [*Thomas*] Clayton, who paid the last quarter, Mr [*Edward*] Reveley, who paid the last quarter, Dr [*William*] Herne, who paid the last quarter.

[401] Edward Gibson: *Codex juris ecclesiastici Anglicani* (London, 1713).

[402] John Peck was a rich man. He left his son John over £600 in South Sea stock as well as £250 in cash. His daughter was bequeathed almost £2000 (TNA, PROB 11/658, Will of John Peck, 1733). Peck's second son, Wharton Peck, became Chancellor of Ely (W. Rye, *Norfolk Families*, Norwich, 1913, p. 659)..

[403] John Brand graduated BA from Corpus Christi College, Cambridge, in 1707, proceeding MA in 1710 at King's College. He was rector of St Lawrence's, Norwich, from 1716 to 1728 and ran a school at Chapelfield House (Branford, p. 229).

November 1 1714. Present: Dr [*William*] Herne, Mr [*Joseph*] Brett, who paid all arrears, Mr Tho[*mas*] Clayton, Mr [*John*] Brand, Mr [*Edward*] Reveley, Mr [*John*] Whitefoot, who paid all arrears.

December 6 1714. Present: Dr [*William*] Herne, Mr [*Thomas*] Clayton, John Whitefoot.

< January 3 1714. Quarter day. Dr [*William*] Herne, who paid the last quarter, Mr [*Edward*] Reveley, who paid the last quarter, Mr [*John*] Brand, who paid the last quarter >.

January 3 1715. Present: Mr [*Thomas*] Clayton, who paid the last quarter, Mr [*John*] Clarke, who paid all arrears, Mr [*Samuel*] Salter, who paid the two last quarters, Mr [*John*] Brand, who paid the last quarter, Mr [*Edward*] Riveley, who paid the last quarter, Dr [*William*] Herne, who paid the last quarter.

February 7 1715. Present: Dr [*William*] Herne, Mr [*Samuel*] Jones, who paid all arrears, Mr [*Thomas*] Clayton, John Whitefoot.

March 7 1715. Present: Dr [*Thomas*] Tanner, who paid all arrears, Mr [*John*] Whitefoot, Mr [*Samuel*] Salter, Dr [*William*] Herne.

April 4 1715. Quarter day. Present: Mr [*Edward*] Reveley, who paid the last quarter.

May 2 1715. Present: Dr [*William*] Herne, who paid the last quarter, Mr [*Joseph*] Brett, who paid all arrears, Dr [*John*] Jefery, who paid all areares.

June 6 1715. Present: Mr [*Edward*] Revely, Mr [*John*] Clarke, who paid the last quarter, Dr [*William*] Herne. Memorandum. Peter, the son of Samuel Scott deceased, late under library keeper, was chosen into that place *durante beneplacito societatis.* [404]

July 4 1715. Quarter day. Present: Mr [*John*] Whitefoot, who paid all arrears, Mr [*Edward*] Reveley, who paid the last quarter, Mr [*John*] Brand, who paid the two last quarters, Dr [*William*] Herne, who paid the last quarter.

August 1 1715. Present: Dr [*William*] Herne, Mr [*Henry*] Fysh paid all arrears.

[404] At the pleasure of the society.

September 5 1715. Present: Mr [*Samuel*] Jones, who paid the two last quarters, Mr [*John*] Whitefoot, Dr [*William*] Herne, who this day brought into the library the two first volumes of the *History of the Reformation* by Dr Burnet.[405] The gift of Clement Herne[406] Esquire. Mr [*John*] Brand.

October 3 1715. Present: Mr [*Edward*] Reveley, who paid the last quarter, Mr [*Samuel*] Salter, who paid all arrears, Dr [*William*] Herne, who paid the last quarter.

< October 24 1715. Present: Henry Reeve, surgeon, this day admitted *himself* to the use of the library. > [407]

November 7 1715. Present: Mr [*John*] Brand, who paid the last quarter, Mr [*John*] Barker, who paid all arrears, Mr Chancellor, who paid all arrears, Dr [*William*] Herne, Mr [*John*] Whitefoot.

December 5 1715. Present: Dr [*William*] Herne, Mr [*John*] Brand, Mr [*Thomas*] Clayton, who paid all arrears, Mr [*John*] Whitefoot.

January 2 1716. Quarter day. Present: Mr [*Edward*] Reveley, who paid the last quarter, Mr [*John*] Whitefoot, who paid the 2 last quarters, Dr [*William*] Herne, who paid the last quarter, Mr [*Henry*] Fish, who paid the 2 last quarters.

February 6 1716. Present: Dr [*William*] Herne, Mr [*John*] Whitefoot, Mr [*Edward*] Reveley, Mr [*John*] Clarke, who paid all arrears, Mr [*John*] Brand, who paid the last quarter and was this day chosen library keeper for the 2 ensueing years.

This day Polyglot Bible in 6 volumes valued at	4. 10. 0.
Pool's *Synopsis* in 9 volumes and	3. 0. 0.
Mills' *Greek Testament* folio	1. 5. 0.

Being duplicate agreed to be exchanged with Mr Whitefoot for books of his now in the library to be valued by the society. Memorandum. Mr Clarke paid to Mr Brand 00. 05s. 09 due from him to the library.

---

[405] Gilbert Burnet: *History of the reformation of the Church of England* (London, 1681–3).

[406] Son of Thomas Herne of Metton, Norfolk, Clement Herne was admitted to Caius College, Cambridge, in 1655 and Gray's Inn in 1657.He owned property in Cawston, Brandiston, Felthorpe, Hevingham, Marsham, Erpingham, Metton and Felbrigg (TNA PROB 11/579, Will of Clement Herne, 1721).

[407] This was clearly considered a highly irregular action since Reeve's name does not reappear in the minutes.

March 5 1716. Present: Mr [*Thomas*] Clayton, who paid the last quarter, Mr [*Samuel*] Jones, who paid the two last quarters, Mr [*Joseph*] Brett, who paid all arrears to this day, Mr [*John*] Whitefoot, Mr Chanc[*ello*]r, who paid the last quarter, Mr [*John*] Brand, Dr [*William*] Herne. March 5. This day brought into the library Fabij Quintiliani *opera* 2 volumes Lugd: Batav: 1665[408], the gift of Thomas Seaman,[409] Esquire. This day admitted to the use of the library Mr [*Benjamin*] Mackerell. [410]

April 2 1716. Quarter day. Present: Mr [*Joseph*] Brett, who paid the last quarter, Mr Benj[*amin*] Mackerell, who paid the last quarter, Mr [*John*] Whitefoot, who paid all arrears, Dr [*William*] Herne, who paid all arrears.

April 15 1716. This day was brought into the library Davila's *History of France*[411] folio, Grimston's *History of the Netherlands*,[412] being the gift of Benjamin Mackerell of the city of Norwich, gentl[*eman*].

7 May 1716. Present: Mr [*Joseph*] Brett, Mr [*Thomas*] Clayton, who paid the last quarter, Dr [*William*] Herne, Mr [*John*] Whitefoot, Mr [*John*] Brand, who paid the last quarter. This society having requested the court to give leave that an order might be made to render the library more useful it was accordingly ordered by the court.

[408] Marcus Fabius Quintilianus: *Institutionum oratoriarum libri duodecim: Accesserunt huic renovatae editioni declamationes, quam tam ex P. Pithoei* (Lyon, 1665).

[409] The son of Sir Peter Seaman, Thomas Seaman was educated at Benjamin Nobbs' school in Norwich and at Reepham. He entered Caius College, Cambridge, in 1710. According to William Massey, he had 'an elegant taste of several things that become a gentleman, and a ready facetious view of humour in his conversation, but his conduct was too irregular, and it was thought he ruin'd his constitution, by his manifest neglect of it, and his frequent excesses' (NRO Rye MSS 18, William Massey's Acta Norvicensia). He died in October 1724 aged 31.

[410] Benjamin Mackerell was the second son of alderman John Mackerell, a wealthy merchant and member of the Presbyterian congregation of the Octagon Chapel. Unlike most of the Library members Mackerell did not attend university. His chief passions were antiquities and heraldry. In an introduction to a collection of many thousands of coats of arms, all meticulously drawn and hand-coloured, he revealed that he had used the 'most approved printed books' including Gwillim, Morgan, Leigh, Carter, the *British Compendium* and 'many others'. He probably owned these books since his will mentions a collection of books on heraldry (NRO ANW (13) 25, Will of Benjamin Mackerell, 1762.Thanks are due to Sheila Crickmore for the discovery of this will). He had a whole nexus of friends who provided him with source material: Peter Le Neve, Norroy King of Arms, lent him books on heraldry; Brampton Gurdon, the Boyle lecturer, lent him a manuscript; and John Kirkpatrick lent him a manuscript which had over twenty-thousand coats in it. The arms of the bishops of Norwich were taken from a catalogue that was in the possession of Samuel Salter, vicar of St Stephen's, a fellow member of the library. In 1732 Mackerell produced a printed catalogue of the library, based closely on Joseph Brett's catalogue of 1706.

[411] H.C. Davila: *History of the Civil Wars of France. Translated by William Aylesbury.*

[412] Ed. Grimeston: *A general Historie of the Netherlands.* London, 1627.

Norwich. At an Assembly held the third day of May anno domini 1716:
The petition of the clergy about the books in the library is now agreed to,
so as such care be taken by the library keeper that there be no loss of the
books. Procur[*ator*] Chappell[413]
The articles or conditions of borrowing any book out of the library are
ordered to be written in the first leave of a register to be provided for the
use of the society.

[*The articles were in fact copied into the back of this minute book; see p. 184*]

June 4 1716. Present: Mr [*Edward*] Reveley, who paid the last quarter, Mr
John Whitefoot, Dr [*William*] Herne.

July 2 1716. Quarter day. Present: Dr [*William*] Herne, who paid the last
quarter, Mr [*Edward*] Reveley, who paid the last quarter, Mr [*Samuel*]
Salter, who paid the 3 last quarters, Mr [*John*] Clark, who paid the 2 last
quarters, Mr [*Samuel*] Jones, who paid the 2 last quarters, Mr [*John*]
Whitefoot, who paid the last quarter, Mr [*John*] Barker, who paid all
arrears. July 2 1716. This day was brought into the library Burnet's
Theory,[414] the gift of Nicholas Helwys[415] Esquire.

August 6 1716. Present: Dr [*William*] Herne, Mr [*John*] Whitefoot, Mr
[*John*] Brand, who paid the last quarter, Dr [*John*] Jeffery, who paid all
arrears.

September 3 1716. Present: Dr [*William*] Herne.

October 1 1716. Quarter day. Present: Mr [*Joseph*] Brett, who paid the 2
last quarters, Mr [*Edward*] Reveley, who paid the last quarter, Dr [*William*]
Herne, who paid the last quarter, Mr [*Thomas*] Clayton, who paid all
arrears, Mr [*Samuel*] Salter, who paid the last quarter.

November 7 1716. Present: Dr [*John*] Jeffery, who paid the last quarter,
Mr [*John*] Whitefoot, who paid the last quarter, Dr [*William*] Herne.

[413] John Chappel was town clerk of Norwich from 1687 to 1720 (T. Hawes, *An Index to
Norwich City Officers, 1453–1835* , Norfolk Genealogy, xxi, 1989, p. 35).

[414] Thomas Burnet: *Theory of the Earth; containing an Account of the Original of the Earth, and all the
Changes it has already undergone or is to undergo till the Consummation of all Things* (London, 1691).

[415] Born in Norwich the son of Alderman William Helwys, Nicholas Helwys was admitted
to Caius College in 1679 and to the Middle Temple in 1680. He lived at Morton Hall until his
death in 1724, bequeathing £800 to each of his daughters (NRO NCC 245 Lawrence, Will of
Nicholas Helwys, 1724).

December 3 1716. Present: Mr [*Thomas*] Clayton, Mr [*Edward*] Reveley, Mr John Whitefoot, Dr [*William*] Herne, Dr [*Thomas*] Tanner Chanc[*ello*]r paid all arrears.

January 7 1717. Quarter day. Present: Mr [*Thomas*] Clayton, who paid the last quarter, Mr [*Joseph*] Brett, who paid the last quarter, Mr [*Edward*] Reveley, who paid the last quarter. This day Dr Hicks *Saxon Grammar*[416] 2 volumes, being Dr Peter Parham's[417] gift, was brought into the library. Dr [*William*] Herne paid then the last quarter.

February 4 1717. Present: Mr [*Samuel*] Salter, who paid the last quarter, Mr [*Benjamin*] Mackerell, *who* paid the three last quarters, Mr John Whitefoot, Dr [*William*] Herne, Mr Chancell[*o*]r, who paid the last quarter, Dr [*John*] Jeffery, who paid the last quarter.

March 4 1717. Present: Mr Chancell[*o*]r, Dr [*William*] Herne, Mr [*Edward*] Reveley.

Aprill 1 1717. Quarter day. Present: Dr [*William*] Herne, who paid the last quarter, Mr [*John*] Barker, who paid all arrears, Mr [*John*] Whitefoot, who paid all arrears.

May 6 1717. Present: Mr [*Thomas*] Clayton, who paid the last quarter, Dr [*William*] Herne.

3 June 1717. Present: Dr [*John*] Jeffery, who paid the last quarter. Mr [*Edward*] Reveley who paid the last quarter. Mr [*John*] Clarke who paid all arrears. Mr [*John*] Whitefoot. Mr [*Samuel*] Salter who paid the last quarter. Dr [*William*] Herne. This day was brought into the library by Mr [*John*] Clarke the first volume of Dr [*Humphrey*] Prideaux's *Connection of the Old and New Testament* folio,[418] given by the said Dr Prideaux, dean of Norwich.

July 1 1717. Quarter day. Present: Mr [*Joseph*] Brett, who paid the two last quarters, Dr [*William*] Herne, who paid the last quarter.

---

[416] George Hickes: *Antiquae Literaturae Septentrionalis.* (Oxford, 1705).

[417] Born at Swanton Morley, Peter Parham attended Norwich School and graduated BA from Caius College, Cambridge, in 1657, proceeding MA in 1660. He was a Fellow of his College from 1659 to 1679. He practised medicine in Norwich and married the daughter of the bishop, Anthony Sparrow. When he drew up his will in 1737 he was living in Swanton Morley, where he owned considerable amounts of property, including a blacksmith's and a barber shop (NRO ANW 249, Will of Peter Parham, 1737). He donated a copy of Sir Henry Spelman's *Glossary* to St Margaret's Library, King's Lynn.

[418] Humphrey Prideaux: *The Old and New Testament connected in the history of the Jews and neighbourhood nations from the declension of the kingdoms of Israel and Judah to the time of Christ.* 2 vols. (London, 1718).

August 5 1717. Present: Dr [*William*] Herne, Mr [*Edward*] Reveley, who paid the last quarter.

September 3 1717. Present: Mr [*John*] Whitefoot, who paid the last quarter, Dr [*William*] Herne, Dr [*Thomas*] Tanner, who paid all arrears. Mr John Mompesson[419] and Mr Thomas Gamble[420] were this day admitted to the use of the library. Mr [*Thomas*] Clayton, who paid all arrears.

Quarter day. 7 October 1717. Present: Mr [*Benjamin*] Mackerell, who paid the three last quarters, Dr [*William*] Herne, who paid the last quarter, Mr [*Thomas*] Gamble.

4 November 1717. Present: Mr John Whitefoot, Dr [*John*] Jeffery, who paid the two last quarters, Dr [*William*] Herne.

December 2 1717. Dr [*William*] Herne.

January 6 1718. Quarter day. Present: Dr [*William*] Herne, who paid the last quarter.

February 3 1718. Present: Dr [*William*] Herne, Mr [*Joseph*] Brett, who paid the two last quarters, Mr [*Samuel*] Jones, who paid all arrears, Mr [*Edward*] Reveley, who paid the 2 last quarters, Mr [*Samuel*] Salter, who paid all arrears, Mr [*Thomas*] Clayton, who paid all arrears, Mr [*John*] Brand, who paid all arrears, Dr [*John*] Jeffery, who paid the last quarter.

March 3 1718. Present: Mr John Whitefoot, who paid last 2 quarters, Mr [*Thomas*] Clayton, Dr [*William*] Herne, Mr [*Thomas*] Gamble, Mr [*Samuel*] Salter.

April 7 1718. Quarter day. Present: Dr [*William*] Herne, who paid the last quarter, Mr [*Edward*] Reveley, who paid the last quarter.

[419] Born at Laughton, Yorkshire the son of a clergyman, John Mompesson was admitted pensioner at Peterhouse Cambridge in 1707, graduating BA in 1711 and proceeding MA in 1714. Ordained in 1713, he was rector of Buckenham Ferry and rector of Hassingham from 1717 to 1722. When he drew up his will he was living in the Cathedral Close. He left all his books (the English ones excepted) to his brother and asked his executrix to destroy his sermons and papers and 'not to suffer any person to inspect them' (TNA PROB 11/592, Will of John Mompesson, 1719).

[420] Thomas Gamble was admitted scholar at Trinity Hall Cambridge in 1712, graduating BA in 1716. He was ordained in Norwich in 1715. He was vicar of Wroxham from 1719 to 1731 and rector of Helhoughton from 1723 to 1731. He was living in Wroxham when he made his will (NRO NCC 93 Starbuck, Will of Thomas Gamble, 1731).

May 4 1718. Present: Dr [*William*] Herne. This day brought into the library by Mr [*Thomas*] Clayton *A Compleat History of England* [421] in 3 volumes folio being the gift of Thomas Clarke,[422] Esquire. Mr [*Thomas*] Gamble, who paid the last quarter.

June 2 1718. Present: Dr [*William*] Herne, Mr [*John*] Brand.

July 7 1718. Quarter day. Present: Mr [*Thomas*] Clayton, who paid all arrears. This day was brought into the library Nicolson's *English Historical Library* [423] being the gift of Mr J[*ohn*] Mompesson.[424] Dr [*William*] Herne, who paid this quarter.

August 4 1718. Present: Dr [*William*] Herne, Mr [*Edward*] Reveley, who paid the last quarter, Mr [*Thomas*] Clayton, Mr [*Samuel*] Jones, who paid the 2 last quarters.

September 1 1718. Present: Dr [*William*] Herne, Dr [*John*] Clarke, Mr [*Edward*] Reveley, Mr [*Thomas*] Clayton. This day was brought into the library by Dr Clarke the second volume of Dr Prideaux's *Connexion of the Old & New Testament* folio, given by the said Dr Prideaux, Dean of Norwich.

October 6 1718. Quarter day. Present: Dr [*William*] Herne, who paid this quarter.

November 3 1718. Present: Mr [*Joseph*] Brett, who paid the three last quarters, Dr [*Thomas*] Tanner, who paid all arrears, Dr [*William*] Herne. This day Mr Robert Camell[425] was admitted to the use of the library.

[421] James Tyrrell: *The General History of England* (London, 1697–1704).

[422] A Thomas Clarke, gentleman, of the parish of St Peter Mancroft, was listed in the Norwich Poll Book of 1710.

[423] William Nicolson: *The English historical library, in three parts. Giving a short view and character of most of our historians either in print or manuscript with an account of our records* (London, 1714).

[424] For John Mompesson see above n. 419.

[425] Born at Diss the son of a lawyer, Robert Camell was admitted at Sydney College Cambridge in 1709, graduating LL.B in 1715 and proceeding LL.D in 1723. He was ordained in Norwich in 1716. He was rector of Lound, Suffolk, from 1717 to 1732, rector of Bradwell from 1717 to 1732 and lecturer at St Peter Mancroft, Norwich, in 1731. According to Francis Blomefield, he published several 'ingenious tracts without his name' as well as three sermons. Blomefield added that he could not forbear taking notice of the many helps he received from Camell towards the composition of his *History of Norfolk* (Blomefield, *History of Norfolk*,vol. 1, p. 26). In a sermon preached in St George's Chapel, Great Yarmouth, on 19 September 1725 Camell discoursed on the consequences of disunity, the fatal source of all disasters, using as his example Eusebius' account of the fall of Jesusalem: 'what the Romans could never have brought to pass by their Prowess and Valour, great as it was, was effected by their [*the Jews*]

December 1 1718. Present: Mr [*Edward*] Reveley, who paid the last quarter, Mr [*Robert*] Camell, Dr [*William*] Herne. This day Mr Pexall Forster[426] was admitted to the use of this library.

January 5 1719. Quarter day. Present: Mr [*John*] Brand, who paid all arrears, Mr [*Joseph*] Brett, who paid the last quarter, Mr [*Edward*] Reveley, who paid the last quarter, Mr [*Thomas*] Clayton, who paid the last two quarters. This day Mr Peter Parham[427] was admitted to the use of the library.

January 10. Mr [*Thomas*] Gamble & who paid the three last quarters, Mr [*John*] Mompesson, who paid all arrears.

2 February 1719. Norwich: At the Court of Mayoralty held 28 January 1719. This day a book which has for some years been lodged in the library of this city entituled *The Book of Common Prayer & Administration of the Sacraments & other Rights & Ceremonies of the Church of England*, printed at London by Robert Barker 1632 – wherein are several marginal notes in writing done by the order of King Charles the First, was delivered to Mr [*John*] Brand of this city clerke to be by him transmitted to the Arch-Bishop of Canterbury[428] he having requested the said book might be sent to him.[429] [*Signed*] Procur[*ator*] Chappell.[430]
[*Signed*] Dr [*William*] Herne, who paid the last quarter, Mr [*John*] Brand, Mr [*Pexall*] Forster.

March 2 1719. Present: Dr [*William*] Herne, Mr [*Samuel*] Jones, who paid the 2 last quarters, Mr [*Samuel*] Salter, who paid all arrears, Mr [*John*] Barker, who paid all arrears. 7 quarters. Mr [*Peter*] Parham.

April 6 1719. Quarter day. Present: Mr [*John*] Barker, who paid the last quarter, Mr [*Thomas*] Clayton, who paid the last quarter, Mr [*Francis*] Green,[431] who was this day admitted to the use of the library, Dr [*William*]

own Part-Rage and Fury, by their own enthusiastic Seditions, and unaccountable Divisions' (Robert Camell, *The tender mercies and long suffering of God*, London, 1726, pp. 54–55). Camell died in 1732.

[426] Born in Durham, Pexall Forster was admitted at Lincoln College Oxford in 1710, graduating BA in 1713. He was vicar of Lakenham from 1718 to 1719 and a precentor at Norwich Cathedral. He died in October 1719.

[427] See above n. 417.

[428] William Wake, archbishop of Canterbury (1716–1737).

[429] The book is now part of the Wake Collection at Christ Church College, Oxford. It has the City Library shelfmark, K11 (George Stephen, *Three Centuries of a City Library*, pp. 39–41).

[430] For John Chappell see above n. 413.

[431] The son of a Norwich weaver, Francis Green attended Norwich School and graduated

Herne, who paid the last quarter. This day was brought into the library by Mr [*John*] Barker King Charles 1st *Tumults in Scotland*,[432] given by Mr W[*illia*]m Houghton.[433]

May 4 1719. Present: Mr [*Peter*] Parham, who paid the last quarter, Mr [*Thomas*] Clayton, Dr [*William*] Herne.

June 1 1719. Present: Mr [*Francis*] Green, Dr [*William*] Herne.

9 June. Mr [*Thomas*] Gamble paid the last quarter.

July 6 1719. Quarter day. Present: Dr [*William*] Herne, who paid for Midsummer quarter, Mr [*Francis*] Greene, Mr [*John*] Brand.

August 3 1719. Present: Dr [*William*] Herne, Mr [*Samuel*] Jones, who paid the two last quarters, Mr [*Francis*] Gamble, who paid the last quarter.

September 7 1719. Present: Mr [*Thomas*] Clayton, who paid the Midsummer quarter, Dr [*William*] Herne, Mr [*Joseph*] Brett, who paid all arrears.
October 5 1719. Quarter day. Present: Dr [*William*] Herne, who paid the last quarter, Mr [*Peter*] Parham, who paid the two last quarters.

October 16. Dr [*Thomas*] Tanner paid all arrears.

November 2 1719. Present: Mr [*Francis*] Gamble, who paid the last quarter, Dr [*John*] Jeffery paid all arrears, Mr [*Samuel*] Salter, who paid all arrears, Mr [*John*] Whitefoot, who paid all arrears, Dr [*William*] Herne.

BA from Caius College, Cambridge, in 1714, proceeding MA in 1717. He was a Fellow of his College from 1715 to 1718. He was rector of Little Dunham from 1716 to 1724 and of Erpingham from 1724 to 1738. He bequeathed his printed books and manuscripts ('except such as I order to be burnt') to an unnamed friend along with the manuscripts of the late Samuel Jones (very probably the Samuel Jones who had been a member of the Library) until his son came of age. As he expressed it in his will: 'The printed books I order to be putt into his hands at the age of 21 years. But the manuscripts, no not one of them, to be putt into his hands till he attain the age of 26 years' (NRO NCC 42 Brereton, Will of Francis Green, 1738).

[432] Walter Balcanquall: *A large declaration concerning the late tumults in Scotland, from their first originals. By the king.* (London, 1639).

[433] William Houghton owned property in Gunthorpe, Barningham and Brinton, though latterly he lived in the Cathedral Close in Norwich. He bequeathed £1000 to his wife and almost £2000 in stocks and shares to his kinsman, Thomas Norgate, of Drayton (TNA PROB 11/656, Will of William Houghton).

December 7 1719. Present: Mr [*Edward*] Reveley, who paid all arrears, Mr [*Francis*] Greene, who paid the two last quarters, Mr [*John*] Fox,[434] who was this day admitted to the use of the library, Mr [*Thomas*] Clayton, who paid the last quarter, Dr [*William*] Herne.

January 4 1720. Quarter day. Present: Mr [*Thomas*] Clayton, who paid the last quarter, Mr [*Peter*] Parham, who paid the last quarter, Mr [*John*] Fox, Dr [*William*] Herne, who paid the last quarter.

February 1 1720. Whereas it appears by an order [*sentence incomplete*]
Present: Dr [*Thomas*] Tanner, who paid the last quarter, Mr [*Samuel*] Salter this day chosen library keeper & paid the last quarter, Mr [*Francis*] Green, Mr [*John*] Brand, Dr [*William*] Herne. Memorandum. The order of Court dated January 28 1718 & entered in this book was altered May 9 1718 & the Common Prayer Book there nam'd delivered by Mr Mott[435] the Mayor to Dr John Clarke[436] to be by him sent to the A[*rch*] B[*isho*]p of Canterbury.

March 7 1720. Present: Mr [*Francis*] Greene, who paid the last quarter, Mr [*Edward*] Rively, who paid the last quarter, Mr [*Samuel*] Salter, Mr [*John*] Jeffery[437] & Mr [*Thomas*] Aylmer,[438] who were this day admitted to the use of the library, Mr [*Thomas*] Clayton, Mr [*John*] Fox.

April 4 1720. Quarter day. Present: Dr [*William*] Herne, who paid the last quarter, Mr [*Thomas*] Aylmer.

May 2 1720. Present: Mr [*Thomas*] Aylmer, Dr [*William*] Herne.

June 6 1720. Present: Mr [*Thomas*] Aylmer, Dr [*William*] Herne.

---

[434] Born at Holt, John Fox was admitted sizar at Clare College Cambridge in 1704, graduating BA in 1708 and proceeding MA in 1712. He was vicar of Lakenham, vicar of Catton and a prebend of Norwich Cathedral. When he drew up his will he was living in the Cathedral Close (TNA PROB 11/842, Will of John Fox, 1755).

[435] Richard Mott, mayor of Norwich in 1718.

[436] For Dr John Clarke see above note 356.

[437] John Jeffery, Dr John Jeffery's nephew, was admitted sizar at St Catherine's College, Cambridge, in December 1697, graduating BA in 1702 and proceeding MA in 1705. He was rector of Trunch from 1709 to 1748. Dr John Jeffery bequeathed his manuscripts to his nephew but asked that his library be sold for the benefit of his daughters (NRO NCC 147 Blomefield, Will of John Jeffery, 1720).

[438] A Norfolk man, Thomas Aylmer graduated BA from Corpus Christi College, Cambridge, in 1718, proceeding MA in 1721. He was a Fellow of his College from 1718 to 1732. He was ordained in Norwich in June 1721 and was instituted vicar of St Benet's, Cambridge, in 1722.

July 4 1720. Quarter day. Present: Mr [*John*] Fox, who paid the two last quarters, Dr [*William*] Herne, who paid the last quarter.

August 1 1720. Present: Mr [*Thomas*] Aylmer, who paid the last quarter, Dr [*William*] Herne.

September 5 1720. Present: Mr [*Samuel*] Jones, who paid all arrears, Dr [*William*] Herne, Mr [*Thomas*] Clayton, who paid all arrears.

October 3 1720. Quarter day. Present: Mr [*Edward*] Reveley, who paid all arrears, Mr [*Francis*] Greene, who paid all arrears to this day, Mr [*Samuel*] Salter, who paid all arrears, Dr [*William*] Herne, who paid the last quarter, Mr [*Samuel*] Jones, who paid the last quarter. This day Mr [*John*] Morrant[439] was admitted to the use of the library.

November 7 1720. Present: Mr [*John*] Barker, who paid all arrears, Dr [*William*] Herne, Mr [*Edward*] Reveley, Mr [*John*] Jeffery paid his arrears, Mr [*Thomas*] Aylmer, who paid last quarter, Mr [*Samuel*] Salter, Mr [*Francis*] Green, Mr [*John*] Morrant.

December 5 1720. Present: Mr [*John*] Jeffery, Mr [*Thomas*] Aylmer, Dr [*William*] Herne.

January 2 1721. Quarter day. Present: Mr [*Samuel*] Salter, who paid the last quarter, Mr [*Thomas*] Clayton, who paid all arrears, Mr [*John*] Mompesson, who paid all arrears, Mr [*John*] Morrant, who paid the last quarter, Dr [*William*] Herne, who paid last quarter.

February 5 1721. Present: Mr [*Samuel*] Salter, < who paid the last quarter >, Mr [*Thomas*] Aylmer, who paid the last quarter for himself & Mr [*John*] Jeffery, Dr [*William*] Herne.

March 6 1721. Present: Dr [*William*] Herne, Mr [*Samuel*] Salter, Mr [*Francis*] Greene, who paid the last quarter, Mr [*John*] Fox, who paid the 2 last quarters, Mr [*John*] Jeffery.

April 3 1721. Quarter day. Present: Mr [*Samuel*] Salter, who paid the last quarter, Mr [*Thomas*] Aylmer, who paid the last quarter, Mr [*John*] Jeffery, who paid all arrears, Mr [*Thomas*] Clayton, who paid the last quarter.

[439] Born in Yarmouth, the son of a surgeon, John Morrant was admitted sizar at Caius College in 1707, graduating BA in 1712 and proceeding MA in 1716. He was a Fellow of Caius from 1712 to 1724. Ordained in 1713 he was rector of Hethersett from 1723 to 1736 and rector of St Clement's, Norwich, from 1723 to 1724. He was buried at Hethersett in 1726.

June 5 1721. Present: Dr [*William*] Herne, who paid the last quarter, Mr [*Samuel*] Salter.

July 3 1721. Quarter day. Present: Mr [*Francis*] Greene, Mr [*Samuel*] Jones, who paid all arrears to this day.

August 7 1721. Present: Mr [*John*] Morrant, who paid all arrears, Mr [*John*] Jeffery, who paid the last quarter.

September 4 1721. Present: Mr [*Edward*] Reveley, who paid all arrears, Dr [*William*] Herne, who paid the last quarter.

October 2 1721. Present: Mr [*Samuel*] Jones, who paid the last quarter, Dr [*William*] Herne, who paid Michaelmas quarter, Mr [*John*] Jeffery & Mr [*Thomas*] Aylmer, who both paid all arrears. This day brought into the library by Dr Herne the following books, given by the Reverend Mr John Graile[440] M.A. rector of Blickling in Norfolk & for seven years minister of St George Tombland in Norwich.

Henrici Mori *Opera Theologica*[441] folio
Brochmandi *Systema Universae Theologiae*[442] in 2bis tomis. Quarto
Amyraldi *Specimen Animadversionum in Exercitatione dei gratia.*[443] Quarto
Salmasij *Epistolae* Liber 1mus.[444] Quarto
Vorstij *Tractatus Theologicus de deo*[445] &c Quarto
Tullij S.T.P. *Iustificatio Paulina*[446] Quarto

[440] Despite the fact that he had been presented to the living of Blickling by the Whig Hobarts, the leaders of the Exclusionists in Norfolk, Graile was both a Tory and an anti-Exclusionist. For Graile, the king was 'the Minister of God, and his Power is the Ordnance of God' (John Graile, *Three sermons preached at the cathedral in Norwich and a fourth at a parochial church in Norfolk*, London, 1685, p. 56). The king's power was virtually unfettered. To take up arms against the king is to fight against God, whom the king represents and with whose authority he is invested. Such rebels renounce their human nature and become 'natural Brute beats, made to be taken and destroyed' (Graile, *Three sermons*, p. 52). Republics were the 'natural products of Perfidiousness and Rebellion' and of the dethronement of reason'. All the modern republics, Holland, the Swiss Cantons, Genoa, Geneva and Venice were characterised by discord, jealousy and dilatoriness and all aspired to 'the Name and Shadow of a troublesome Freedom'(Graile, *Three sermons*, pp. 87–91). Graile viewed the Exclusion crisis as evidence of the same anti-monarchical sentiment on the part of a small group of 'horrid Phanaticks'. If the phanaticks were to prove successful and the fundamental right of lineal succession was violated then enslavement and ruin would be the inevitable outcome (Graile, *Three sermons*, p. 118).

[441] Henry More: *Henrici Mori Cantabrigiensis Opera theological* (London, 1675).

[442] Jesper Rasmussen Brochmand: *Universae theologiae systema*. Ulmae Sulvorum: sumptibus Joannis Görlini, bibliopolae, exscripsit litteris Balthasar Kühne, [1638].

[443] Moise Amyraut: *Specimen animadversionum in Exercitationes de gratia universali* (Saumur, 1648).

[444] Claude de Saumaise: *Epistolarum liber primus. Accedunt de laudibus et vita ejusdem, prolegomena Accurante Antonio Clementio* (Lyon, 1656).

[445] Conrad Vorst: *Tractatus theologicus de Deo, sive de natura et attributes Dei* (Steinfurt, 1610).

[446] Thomas Tully: *Justificatio Paulina sive operibus ex mente Ecclesiae Anglicanae* (Oxford, 1674).

Sacra Privata[447]
Youth's Grand Concern[448]
Advice to the Young Gentry.[449] These 3 by the Reverend Mr Graile.

November 6 1721. Present: Mr [*Thomas*] Clayton, who paid all arrears, Mr [*Samuel*] Salter, who paid all arrears, Mr [*Francis*] Greene, who paid all arrears, Mr [*John*] Jeffery. Memorandum. Mr Clayton was paid 13. 6 by duplicate viz Tho[*mas*] Aquinas, Irenaeus & Coslerus being money laid out by him for the board over Mr Nelson's books by the consents of us [*signed*] Fran[*cis*] Greene, Sam[*uel*] Salter, J[*ohn*] Jeffery.

December 4 1721. Mr [*John*] Morrant, who paid the last quarter, Mr [*Edward*] Reveley, who paid the last quarter, Mr [*Samuel*] Salter.

January 1 1722. Quarter day. Mr [*John*] Morrant, who paid last quarter, Mr [*John*] Mompeson, who paid all arrears, Mr [*Thomas*] Clayton, who paid the last quarter.

February 5 1722. Present: Dr [*William*] Herne, who paid last quarter, Mr [*Samuel*] Salter, who paid last quarter, Mr [*John*] Jeffery, who paid last quarter, Mr [*Edward*] Reveley, who paid the last quarter, Mr [*John*] Fox, who paid all arrears.

March 5 1722. Present: Mr [*Thomas*] Clayton, Mr [*John*] Jeffery.

April 2 1722. Quarter day. Present: Dr [*William*] Herne, who paid last quarter, Mr [*John*] Morrant, who paid the last quarter, Mr [*Thomas*] Clayton, who paid the last quarter, Mr [*Samuel*] Jones, who paid the two last quarters, Mr [*John*] Jeffery, who paid all arrears.

May 7 1722. Present: Mr [*Samuel*] Jones, Mr [*Samuel*] Salter, who paid the last quarter & the two year's allowance usual from the library keeper 9s.0d., Mr [*Thomas*] Clayton, Mr [*Francis*] Greene. Memorandum. May 7 1722. Mr John Fox was this day chosen library keeper. [*signed*] Tho[*mas*] Clayton, Franc[*is*] Greene.

June 4 1722. Present: Mr Francis Greene, who paid all arrears to Lady Day, Mr [*John*] Fox, Mr [*John*] Jefferie, Dr [*William*] Herne. Whereas on

---

[447] John Graile: *Sacra private in duas partes distributa* (London, 1699).

[448] John Graile: *Youths grand concern: or, advice to young persons, how to begin betimes to be wise, and good, and happy* (London, 1711).

[449] John Graile: *An essay of particular advice to the young gentry, for the overcoming the difficulties and temptations they may meet with* (London, 1711).

the 7ᵗʰ of May last Mr [*John*] Fox was chosen library keeper & *was* not willing to accept the same as being out of course, Mr [*John*] Morrant being willing to accept of the said place was accordingly chosen library keeper this day by us whose names are above written.

July 2 1722. Quarter day. Present: Dr [*William*] Herne, who paid the last quarter, Mr [*John*] Morrant, who paid the last quarter.

August 5 1722. Present: Thomas Clayton, who paid last quarter, Mr [*John*] Morrant, Dr [*William*] Herne.

September 3 1722. Present: Dr [*William*] Herne. Mr William Herne[450] was this day admitted to the use of the library. Mr [*John*] Morrant, Dr [*Thomas*] Tanner paid all arrears.

October 1 1722. Quarter day. Present: Mr [*Francis*] Greene, who paid all arrears to Michaelmas last, Mr [*John*] Jeffery, who paid all arrears, Mr [*John*] Morrant, who paid all arrears, Dr [*William*] Herne, who paid this quarter.

November 5 1722. Present: Mr [*Samuel*] Jones, who paid all arrears. This day Mr John Mingay[451] was admitted to the use of the library. Dr [*William*] Herne.

December 13 1722. Present: Dr [*William*] Herne, Mr [*Edward*] Reveley, who paid all arrears, Mr [*Samuel*] Jones, Mr [*John*] Morrant.

January 7 1723. Quarter day. Present: Mr [*Edward*] Reveley, who paid the last quarter, Mr [*Thomas*] Clayton, who paid all arrears, Mr [*John*] Jeffery, who paid all arrears, Mr [*John*] Morrant, who paid all arrears, Dr [*William*] Herne, who paid the quarter ending at Christmas, Mr Will[*ia*]m Herne, who paid this last quarter.

February 4 1723. Present: Mr [*John*] Morrant library keeper, Dr [*William*] Herne.

[450] Son of Dr William Herne, William Herne was admitted sizar at Caius College, Cambridge, in 1717, graduating BA in 1721 and proceeding MA in 1725. Ordained in 1722, he was rector of Horningtoft in 1728, vicar of Hemblington from 1729 to 1765, vicar of St James and St Paul, Norwich, from 1735 to 1776 and rector of Garveston from 1744 to 1776.

[451] John Mingay was admitted at Corpus Christi College, Cambridge, in 1718, graduating BA in 1722 and proceeding MA from Clare College in 1736. He was a Fellow of Clare from 1722 to 1726. He was ordained in Norwich in 1725. Master of Yarmouth Grammar School from 1730 to 1741, he was minister of St George's, Yarmouth, from 1731 to 1742 and rector of Heveningham, Sufolk, from 1735 to 1738.

March 4 1723. Present: Mr [*Thomas*] Clayton, Mr [*John*] Jeffery, Mr [*John*] Morrant library keeper, Mr [*John*] Barker, who paid all arrears.

Aprill 1 1723. Quarter day. Present: Mr [*Edward*] Reveley, who paid the last quarter, Mr [*Thomas*] Clayton, who paid the last quarter, Mr [*Samuel*] Salter, who paid all arrears, Mr [*John*] Morrant, who paid all arrears, Dr [*William*] Herne, who paid the last quarter.

May 6 1723. Present: Mr [*Francis*] Green, who paid the 2 last quarters, Mr [*Thomas*] Clayton, Dr [*William*] Herne.

June 3 1723. Present: Mr [*John*] Morrant library keeper, Dr [*William*] Herne.

July 1 1723. Quarter day. Mr [*John*] Mingay, who paid all arrears, Mr [*John*] Morrant library keeper.

August 5 1723. Mr [*John*] Morrant library keeper, Dr [*William*] Herne, who paid the last quarter.

September 2 1723. This day Mr [*Francis*] Johnson[452] was admitted to the use of the library. Present: Mr [*Samuel*] Jones, who paid all arrears, Mr [*John*] Fox, who paid all arrears, Dr [*William*] Herne.

October 7 1723. Quarter day. Present: Mr [*Edward*] Reveley, who paid the 2 last quarters, Mr [*John*] Morrant library keeper. This day Mr [*John*] Francis junior[453] was admitted to the use of the library. Dr [*William*] Herne, who paid last quarter.

---

[452] Born in Norwich, Francis Johnson graduated BA in 1723. He was vicar of Brooke in 1728 and rector of Thwaite from 1733 to 1760, when he drew up his will (NRO ANF 55 66, Will of Francis Johnson, 1760).

[453] John Francis was born in the parish of St Andrew in Norwich, the son of John Francis, the public notary. He was educated at Norwich School under the headmastership of John Reddington and attended Trinity Hall, Cambridge, where he studied law. A member of the Grand Lodge of Norwich Freemasons from 1725, he was not ordained until the following year, when he was presented to the living of Morley. In 1728, on the recommendation of Thomas Tanner, he became rector of St John Maddermarket. In the same year he took his Doctor of Laws degree. He contributed to the combination sermons at Norwich Cathedral on at least two occasions (NRO, NCR N/CCH/3, Swordbearer's Accounts, 1729–30, p. 17; N/CCH/6, 1732–3, p. 7). His views on the advantages of study were clear: 'I am very far from being of their opinion, who either decry human learning in general, or make it such a Moabite or Ammorite, that however it be admitted in civil affairs, it should be forbidden the sanctuary. No: our religion prescribes us rational, not brutish sacrifices, and therefore rejects not any of those advantages which may improve our reason, may exalt the man, and depress the beast in us' (John Francis, *Sermons Preached on Several Occasions*, ii, London, 1773, p. 182–3). In the election of 1734–5 Francis voted for the Tory candidate, Miles Branthwayt.

November 4 1723. Present: Mr [*John*] Morrant library keeper, Dr [*William*] Herne.

December 2 1723. Present: Dr [*William*] Herne.

January 6 1724. Quarter day. Present: Mr [*John*] Jeffery, who paid all arrears, Mr [*Samuel*] Salter, who paid all arrears, Dr [*William*] Herne, who paid the last quarter, Mr [*Francis*] Johnson, who paid the last quarter, Mr [*Thomas*] Clayton, who paid all arrears, Mr [*John*] Francis, who paid the last quarter.

February 3 1724. Present: Mr [*Samuel*] Salter, Mr [*John*] Francis, Mr [*Samuel*] Jones, who paid the *two* last quarters, Mr [*John*] Morrant library keeper.

March 2 1724. Present: Mr [*Samuel*] Jones, Mr [*Thomas*] Clayton, Dr [*William*] Herne.

April 6 1724. Quarter day. Present: Mr [*Thomas*] Clayton paid the last quarter, Mr [*Samuel*] Jones, who paid the last quarter, Mr [*John*] Jeffery, who paid the last quarter, Mr [*John*] Francis, who paid the last quarter.

1 June 1724. Present: Mr [*Thomas*] Clayton, Mr [*Samuel*] Jones, Mr [*John*] Francis, Mr [*Francis*] Greene, who paid all arrears to this day, Mr [*John*] Jeffery. Memorandum: 1 June. Mr Benjamin Makkerel was this day chosen library keeper by the persons above mentioned. Dr [*William*] Herne who paid the last quarter. John Jermy,[454] Esquire, by the consent of the members above mention'd, was admitted to the library.

July 6 1724. Quarter day. Present: Dr [*Thomas*] Tanner paid all arrears, Mr [*Samuel*] Jones, who paid the last quarter, Mr [*John*] Francis, who paid the last quarter, Mr [*Francis*] Johnson paid all arrears, Dr [*William*] Herne, who paid the last quarter.

August 3 1724. Present: Mr [*John*] Francis, Dr [*William*] Herne.

September 7 1724. Present: Mr [*John*] Francis.

October 5 1724. Quarter day. Present: Dr [*Thomas*] Tanner paid the last quarter, Mr [*Benjamin*] Mackerell, who paid all arrears, Mr [*John*] Francis paid the last quarter.

---

[454] Related to the Jermys of Bayfield Hall, John Jermy had a house in the Cathedral Close. When he died he gave his wife 'all the books in her own closet' which included the State Trials, Echard's History and Chambers' Dictionary (TNA, PROB 11/737, Will of John Jermy, 1744).

November 2 1724. Present: Mr [*John*] Francis, Mr Jonathan Thornton,[455] Mr William Massey,[456] who were then admitted to the use of the library. Present: Mr [*John*] Jeffery, who paid all arrears, Mr Benjamin Mackerell. November 5 1724. Mr [*Thomas*] Clayton paid then all arrears.

December 7 1724. Present: Mr [*William*] Massey, Mr [*John*] Jeffery.

January 4 1725. Quarter day. Present: Mr [*Thomas*] Clayton paid the last quarter, Dr [*William*] Herne, who paid all arrears.

February 1 1725. Present: Mr [*William*] Massey paid the last quarter, Dr [*William*] Herne, Mr [*Benjamin*] Mackerell, who paid the last quarter, Mr [*Thomas*] Clayton.

March 1 1725. Present: Mr [*John*] Francis paid the last quarter, Mr Thomas Johnson[457] was this day admitted to the use of the library, Dr [*William*] Herne. Present: Mr [*William*] Massey.

April 5 1725. Quarter day. Present: Mr [*John*] Jeffery, who paid the two last quarters, Mr [*John*] Francis, who paid the last quarter, Mr Tho[*mas*] Johnson, who paid the last quarter, Dr [*William*] Herne, who paid the last quarter.

May 3 1725. Present: Dr [*William*] Herne, Mr Benj[*amin*] Mackerell, who paid the last quarter, Mr Sam[*uel*] Salter, who paid all arrears, Mr William Massey, who paid this last quarter, Mr [*Jonathan*] Thornton, Mr [*Francis*] Greene, who paid all arrears & desired to be dismissed. May 28 1725. This day was given to the Public Library by John Knyvett[458] of this City Esquire Caesaris (Julij) Comentar. *de Bello Gallico.*[459]

[455] Jonathan Thornton graduated BA from Trinity College, Cambridge, in 1722, proceeding MA in 1725. He was vicar of Earlham from 1723 to 1758. He was one of the witnesses to Benjamin Mackerell's will (NRO ANW (13) 25, Will of Benjamin Mackerell, 1762). In 1743, when he drew up his own will, he was living in the parish of St Giles (NRO NCC 375 Smith, Will of Jonathan Thornton, 1753).

[456] William Massey lived in the parish of St Andrew's in Norwich. His diary contains shrewd character sketches of many of his contemporaries (NRO Rye MSS 18, William Massey's *Acta Norvicensia*, 1720–1729).

[457] Thomas Johnson was apprenticed to Valentine Peel, an apothecary, and was made a freeman in 1716. He was Norwich Coroner from 1730 to 1736 and sheriff in 1737 and was one of the founder members of the Grand Lodge of Norwich Freemasons (G.W. Daynes, *Some Records of the Lodge Constituted at The Maids Head, Norwich, in 1724*, Norwich, 1927, p. 44). He produced a continuation of Benjamin Nobbs' manuscript history of Norwich, parts of which survive in the form of rough notes (NRO MS 453). He died in 1758.

[458] John Knyvett owned property in Heigham, which he bequeathed to his brother-in-law, Henry Wilson. He also left £400 to Henry Wilson's son, Edward Knyvett Wilson (NRO NCC 65 Jarvis, Will of John Knyvett, 1741).

[459] Julius Caesar: *Commentariorum de bello Gallico.*

June 7 1725. Present: Mr [*John*] Fox who paid all arrears, Tho[*mas*] [460] Thornton, who paid the last quarter, Mr [*William*] Massey paid the last quarter, Mr [*John*] Francis paid the last quarter.

13 August [*1725*]. Mr John Gardiner[461] was then admitted to the use of the library.

August 16 1725. Mr [*Thomas*] Clayton paid all arrears. August 23. Dr [*William*] Herne, who paid the last quarter.

18 September 1725. Mr John Rolfe,[462] Mr William Crowe[463] were then admitted to the use of the library.

October 4 1725. Quarter day. Present: Dr [*William*] Herne, who paid the last quarter.

October 18 1725. Dr [*John*] Clarke paid all arrears.

November 1 1725. Present: Mr [*Thomas*] Johnson, who paid the last quarter, Mr [*Samuel*] Salter, Mr [*John*] Jeffery, who paid all arrears, Mr [*William*] Massey paid last quarter, Mr [*Francis*] Gardner paid last quarter, Dr [*William*] Herne.

January 3 1726. Quarter day. Present: Dr [*Thomas*] Tanner, who paid all arrears, Dr [*John*] Clarke, who paid last quarter, Mr [*Thomas*] Clayton paid all arrears, Mr [*John*] Barker paid then all arrears, Mr [*Samuel*] Salter paid then all arrears, Dr [*William*] Herne, who paid last quarter.

---

[460] Almost certainly a mistake for Jonathan Thornton.

[461] Admitted sizar at St Catharine's College, Cambridge, in 1718, John Gardiner graduated LL.B in 1724 and became LL.D in 1731. Ordained in Norwich in 1724, he was rector of Little Moulton in 1725, vicar of Hickling from 1728 to 1730, rector of Brumstead in 1729, rector of Great Massingham, rector of St Giles, Norwich, where his daughter enjoyed the 'profits' (NRO ANW 112 149, Will of George Gardiner, 1770) and parish chaplain of St Gregory's Norwich from 1731 to 1770.

[462] John Rolfe was admitted sizar at Corpus Christi College, Cambridge, in 1700, graduating BA in 1704. He was ordained in Norwich in 1705. Vicar of Necton from 1708 to 1718 and rector from 1718 to 1749, he was also rector of Holme Hale. He died in 1749.

[463] William Crowe, a worsted weaver, was a councillor for Wymer Ward from 1724 to 1727 and from 1730 to 1731, sheriff in 1741, alderman from 1742 to 1778 and mayor in 1747. He owned considerable amounts of property in Lakenham, Cringleford, Swardeston, Saxlingham and Yelverton as well as Surrey House in Norwich, and was one of the founder members of the Grand Lodge of Norwich Freemasons (G.W. Daynes, *Some Records of the Lodge Constituted at The Maids Head, Norwich, in 1724*, Norwich, 1927, p. 39). In his will he bracketed his books with his wines and 'spiritous liquors' (NRO NCC 12 Sheppard, Will of William Crowe, 1778).

February 7 1726. Dr [*John*] Clarke, Mr [*Samuel*] Salter, Mr [*Thomas*] Clayton, Mr [*John*] Francis, who paid all arrears, Mr [*Thomas*] Johnson, who paid all arrears & desires to be dismissed, Mr [*John*] Rolfe paid the last quarter.

March 1 [1726]. Mr Tho[*mas*] Johnson, who paid the last quarter, Dr [*William*] Herne.

April 4 Quarter day. Present: Mr John Jermy Esquire paid all arrears, Mr [*Thomas*] Clayton paid this quarter, Mr [*John*] Barker paid the last quarter, Mr [*Jonathan*] Thornton paid all arrears, Mr [*John*] Francis paid the last quarter, Mr [*John*] Gardner paid the last quarter, Dr [*William*] Herne paid all arrears, Mr [*Samuel*] Salter paid the last quarter, Mr [*John*] Fox, who paid all arrears.

May 2 1726. Present: Mr [*John*] Jeffery, who paid all arrears, Mr [*John*] Gardiner, Mr [*Samuel*] Salter, Mr [*Benjamin*] Mackerell.

July 1 [*1726*]. Quarter day. Mr [*Benjamin*] Mackerell paid all arrears, John Barker, who paid the last quarter, Tho[*mas*] Clayton, who paid the last quarter, Mr [*John*] Gardiner paid the last quarter.

August 30 1726. Mr [*John*] Mompesson paid all arrears.

5 September 1726. Present: Dr [*William*] Herne, Mr [*John*] Francis paid the last quarter, Mr [*John*] Gardiner.

October 3 1726. Present: Dr [*Thomas*] Tanner paid all arrears, Mr [*Benjamin*] Mackerell, who paid all arrears, Mr [*John*] Barker, who paid last quarter.

November 7 1726. Present: Dr [*William*] Herne, who paid all arrears, Mr [*Thomas*] Clayton, who paid all arrears, Mr [*John*] Barker, Mr [*Samuel*] Salter, who paid all arrears, Mr [*John*] Francis, who paid the last quarter, Mr [*Jonathan*] Thornton paid all arrears, Mr Chancellor, Mr [*John*] Jeffery, who paid all arrears, Mr [*Benjamin*] Mackerell, Mr [*John*] Gardiner, who paid all arrears.

5 December 1726. Present: Mr [*Thomas*] Clayton, Mr [*Samuel*] Salter, Mr [*John*] Jeffery, Mr [*John*] Gardiner, Mr [*John*] Francis.

December 15 1726. Mr Thomas Johnson paid all arrears and desired to be dismissed.

January 2 1727. Present: Dr [*William*] Herne, who paid the last quarter.

February 6 1727. Present: W[*illia*]m Massey paid all arrears, Mr [*John*] Gardiner, who paid all arrears, Dr [*William*] Herne.

March 6 1727. Present: Mr [*John*] Barker paid the last quarter, Mr [*John*] Francis paid the last quarter, Dr [*William*] Herne.

April 3 1737. Present: Mr [*John*] Morrant paid all arrears, Mr [*John*] Rolfe paid all arrears, Mr [*John*] Barker paid the last quarter, Mr [*Thomas*] Clayton paid all arrears, Dr [*William*] Herne paid the last quarter.

May 1 1727. Present: Dr [*William*] Herne.

June 5 1727. Present: Dr [*William*] Herne, Mr [*Samuel*] Salter, who paid all arrears, Mr [*Jonathan*] Thornton, Mr [*John*] Francis paid last quarter.

July 3 1727. Present: Mr [*Thomas*] Clayton, who paid the last quarter, Dr [*William*] Herne, who paid the last quarter, Mr [*John*] Francis, who paid the last quarter. July 6. Tho[*mas*] Johnson[464] paid all arrears. July 8. W[*illia*]m Harvey[465] was then admitted to the use of the library. July 8. W[*illia*]m Pagan[466] was admitted as above. August 15. Mr [*John*] Gardiner paid all arrears.

October 2 1727. Quarter day. Present: W[*illiam*] Massey paid all arrears, Dr [*William*] Herne, who paid the last quarter, Mr [*John*] Barker, who paid all arrears.

January 1 1728 paid all arrears Mr W[*illiam*] Pagan. Mr [*John*] Francis. Paid all arrears.

February 5 1728. Present: Mr [*John*] Gardiner, who paid all arrears. Mr John Beale[467] who was this day admitted to the use of the library. Mr

---

[464] Thomas Johnson had resigned his membership on 5 December 1726.

[465] Born at Beechamwell, William Harvey was admitted sizar at Caius College in 1713, graduated BA in 1718 and proceeded MA in 1726. He was ordained in Norwich in 1720. He was rector of West Winch from 1732 to 1786, vicar of Crimplesham from 1735 to 1785 and rector of Fincham from 1745 to 1786. He was buried at Crimplesham in 1786.

[466] William Pagan was a wealthy schoolmaster who left over £3000 in bequests including £200 to twenty poor dissenting ministers (TNA, PROB 11/1034, Will of William Pagan, 1769). He was an Anglo-Saxon scholar and possessed a library of 'rare books' in Anglo-Saxon. One of his pupils was the surgeon, Philip Meadows Martineau, who was instrumental in establishing the Norwich Subscription Library in 1784 (*A Memoir of the Late Philip Meadows Martineau, Surgeon,* Norwich, 1831, p. 3).

[467] Born in Norwich, John Beale was admitted sizar at Caius College, Cambridge, in 1715, graduating BA in 1719 and proceeding MA in 1730. Ordained in London in 1720, he was

Tho[*mas*] Manlove,[468] who was this day admitted to the use of the library.

March 4 1728. Present: Mr [*John*] Gardiner, Dr [*William*] Herne, who paid the last quarter, Mr [*John*] Beale. March 7 1728. Mr [*John*] Jermy paid all arrears to Christmas last inclusive.

1 April 1728. Present: Mr [*John*] Francis, who paid the last quarter, Mr [*Thomas*] Clayton, who paid all arrears, Mr [*William*] Harvey, who paid all arrears, W[*illiam*] Massey paid all arrears.

May 6 1728. Present: Mr [*John*] Gardiner, who paid the last quarter.

June 3 1728. Present: Mr [*John*] Beale, Mr [*William*] Pagan, who then paid last quarter, Mr [*John*] Francis.

July 1 1728. Mr [*Thomas*] Manlove, who paid the last quarter, Mr [*William*] Harvey.

5 August 1728. Present: Mr [*John*] Beale, Mr [*John*] Francis, Mr [*William*] Harvey, Mr [*William*] Pagan paid the last quarter, Mr [*Jonathan*] Thornton paid all arrears.

October 7 1728. Mr [*John*] Fox, who paid all arrears, Mr [*John*] Francis, who paid all arrears, Mr [*William*] Pagan, who paid all arrears.

November 7 1728. Present: Mr [*Thomas*] Manlove, who paid all arrears, Mr [*John*] Gardiner, who paid all arrears, W[*illiam*] Massey paid all arrears.

January 6 1729. William Pagan, who paid all arrears.

February 3 1729. Present: Mr [*Thomas*] Clayton, who then paid all arrears, Mr [*John*] Beale, who then paid all arrears.

March 3 1729. Dr [*William*] Herne, who paid all arrears, Mr [*John*] Gardiner, who paid all arrears & desires to be dismissed.

---

rector of Salthouse from 1742 to 1778 and rector of Kelling from 1745 to 1778. A friend of Benjamin Mackerell's, he was a witness to his will (NRO ANW (13) 25, Will of Benjamin Mackerell, 1762). He died in 1778.

[468] Baptised at Longstanton in Cambridgeshire in 1698, Thomas Manlove was admitted sizar at Emmanuel College in 1714, graduating BA in 1718 and proceeding MA in 1727. He was ordained in 1720 and was instituted vicar of Surlingham in 1725 and vicar of St Stephen's Norwich in 1729. When he drew up his will in 1746 he was rector of Caistor St Edmund (NRO NCC 84 Gostling, Will of Thomas Manlove, 1746).

April 8 1729. W[*illiam*] Massey paid all arrears, W[*illia*]m Pagan paid all arrears.

May 5 1729. Present: Mr [*Thomas*] Clayton, who paid the last quarter, Mr [*John*] Beale.

2 June 1729. Present: Mr [*John*] Francis, who paid all arrears, Mr [*William*] Harvey, W[*illia*]m Pagan. June 4 1729. Mr [*John*] Barker then paid all arrears to the summer & took his name out the list. Dr [*Samuel*] Salter, who did the same.

1729. September 16. William Massey paid all arrears and desires his name may be put out of the list.

October 6 1729. W[*illia*]m Pagan paid off all arrears.

January 5 1730. Mr [*John*] Fox paid all arrears & took his name out of the list.

January 5. Present: Mr [*Thomas*] Clayton, W[*illia*]m Pagan paid all arrears.

February 2 [*1730*]. Present: Mr [*Thomas*] Clayton, who then paid all arrears.

March 2 [*1730*]. Dr [*John*] Francis, who paid all arrears, Mr [*Jonathan*] Thornton paid all arrears & took his name out of the list.

April 6 [*1730*]. Dr [*John*] Clarke, who paid all arrears, Dr [*Thomas*] Tanner, who paid all arrears, Mr W[*illia*]m Harvey paid all arrears & asked his name to be taken out of the list. April 6 1730. Gilbert Benet[469] was this day admitted to the use of the library. W[*illiam*] Pagan paid all arrears.

May 4 1730. Dr [*John*] Francis, who paid all arrears.

June 1 1730. Present: Dr [*John*] Francis.

August 3 1730. Gilbert Benet paid the last quarter. August 6 1730. Mr [*Thomas*] Clayton paid then all arrears. Dr [*John*] Francis paid all arrears.

---

[469] The son of a clergyman from Reepham in Lincolnshire, Gilbert Bennet graduated BA from Merton College, Oxford, in 1727 and proceeded MA from St Catherine's in 1733. He was vicar of Surlingham from 1731 to 1736.

October 5 1730. William Pagan paid off all arrears, Dr [*Thomas*] Tanner paid all arrears.

6 December 1731. Present: Mr Official Clayton paid all arrears, Mr [*William*] Herne paid all arrears, Mr [*Gilbert*] Bennett paid all arrears, Dr [*John*] Francis paid all arrears. Mr [*William*] Pagan. Mr [*Thomas*] Clayton brought in the *History of Parliaments* & *Court Baron & Court Leet* by Thornagh Gurdon Esquire being the gift of the author.[470] Memorandum: It was then ordered by the persons whose names are above written that Peter Scott [471] wait upon Mr [*Benjamin*] Mackerell, library keeper, and desire him to meet them the next library day; they intending to proceed to the election of a new one, the time for such election being long since lapsed.

11 January 1732. Present: Mr Official Clayton, who paid the last quarter, Dr [*William*] Herne, who paid the last quarter, Mr [*Gilbert*] Bennet paid all arrears, Mr [*William*] Pagan paid all arrears. Dr [*Benjamin Joseph*] Ellis,[472] Dr [*William*] Herring,[473] Mr [*John*] Reddington,[474] Mr [*David*] Flemming[475] and Mr [*Francis*] Spendlove[476] were then at their request admitted members.

7 February 1732. Present: Mr [*Thomas*] Clayton, Dr [*Benjamin Joseph*] Ellis, paid the last quarter, Mr [*David*] Flemming, Mr [*William*] Herne, Dr [*John*] Francis, Mr [*Gilbert*] Bennett, Dr [*Robert*] Cammell. Mr [*Robert*] Cory,[477]

---

[470] Thornhaugh Gurdon: *The history of the High Court of Parliament: its antiquity, pre-eminence and authority: and the history of Court Baron and Court Leet* (London, 1731). Gurdon was born at Letton in Norfolk in 1663. He was educated at schools in Wymondham and Earl Stonham and was admitted as a commoner to Gonville and Caius Cambridge in 1681. He received his MA *comitiis regis* in 1682. After he was appointed Receiver General of Norfolk he lived mainly in Norwich in the Cathedral Close. Besides *The history of the High Court of Parliament* he published anonymously an *Essay on the antiquity of the castel of Norwich* (1728). He died in 1733, leaving almost £4000 in bequests (TNA PROB 11/664, Will of Thornhaugh Gurdon, 1733).

[471] The Scott family were, in effect, hereditary under keepers.

[472] The son of Joseph Ellis, minister of St Andrew's, Benjamin Joseph Ellis graduated BA from Corpus Christi College, Cambridge, in 1707, proceeding MA in 1710. He was awarded a Doctorate of Divinity in 1725. He was usher at Norwich School from 1709 to 1713 and was curate of St Peter Hungate in 1715. He died in 1767.

[473] William Herring graduated LL.B from Trinity Hall, Cambridge, in 1713 and was awarded a Doctorate of Laws in 1722. He was rector of Intwood and Keswick from 1720 to 1743. He became Chancellor of York diocese in 1748.

[474] For John Reddington see above n. 316.

[475] For David Fleming see above n. 353.

[476] Although a rich man, the extent of Francis Spendlove's wealth is not revealed in his will (TNA PROB 11/905, Will of Francis Spendlove, 1765).

[477] Robert Cory, son of a Norwich weaver, was admitted sizar at Caius College, Cambridge, in 1708, graduating BA in 1713 and proceeding MA in 1716. He was a master at Norwich School from 1713 to 1737, vicar of St. Michael Coslany from 1715 to 1716 and

*Mr [*John*] Kirkby*[478] and Mr Samuel Killet[479] were then at their request admitted members, as was also Mr Brooks.[480] Memorandum: It was then unanimously agreed that the members meet for the future on the first Tuesday in every Month at two o'clock in the afternoon. John Jermy Esquire paid all arrears. Mr William Pagan was then elected library keeper by the persons < above > under mentioned. Dav[*id*] Fleming, Fran[*cis*] Spendlove, John Brooke, Tho[*mas*] Clayton, Dr [*Benjamin Joseph*] Ellis, John Francis, Gilb[*ert*] Benet, Robert Cammell, W[*illiam*] Herne, Sam[*ue*]ll Killet.

7 March 1732. Present: Mr [*William*] Pagan, library keeper, Mr [*John*] Reddington, Mr [*David*] Flemming, Mr [*Samuel*] Killet, Mr [*Gilbert*] Bennet, Mr [*John*] Kirkby, Dr [*John*] Francis. Whereas the Reverend Mr Francis Johnson[481] took some time since the Works of Bishop Bull[482] in 4 volumes 8vo out of this library, & has returned only the 1st, 3rd & 4th volumes instead of the 2nd Sherlock on providence,[483] it was then order'd that that should be returned him again & that hee be required either to send back the said 2nd volume or take the remaining three & send an entire sett. Order'd likewise that Mr [*John*] Morrant be required to return Bishop Stillingfleet's *Origines sacrae* *being the 2nd volume of his works* [484] long since taken out by him. Mr [*Gilbert*] Benet gave to the library *The Phenix*[485] in two volumes.

April 4 1732. Mr [*William*] Pagan library keeper paid the last quarter, Mr [*William*] Herne paid the last quarter, Mr [*Francis*] Spendlove paid the last quarter, Mr [*Gilbert*] Benet paid the last quarter.

rector of St. Edmund's from 1737 to 1750. He wished to be buried at St Edmund's and asked that his books be sold, along with his household goods, plate and linen, to pay for a gravestone 'of the same goodness and dimension' as that of his wife (NRO ANW 6 223, Will of Robert Cory, 1751).

[478] John Kirkby was admitted sizar at St. John's College Cambridge in 1723, graduating BA in 1727 and proceeding MA in 1745. Venn suggests he was vicar of Stoke Holy Cross and Trowse from 1729 to 1754. He died on 21 May 1754.

[479] Born at Gorleston, Samuel Killet attended Norwich School while John Reddington was headmaster. He graduated LL.B. from Trinity College, Cambridge, in 1731 and was ordained in 1732. He was instituted rector of Bradwell, Suffolk, in 1733.

[480] John Brooke graduated LL.B from Pembroke College, Cambridge, in 1732. He was rector of St Augustine's from 1733 to 1790 and vicar of St Peter Southgate from 1738 to 1789.

[481] For Francis Johnson see above n. 452.

[482] George Bull: *Opera omnia, quibus duo praecipui Catholicae fidei articuli, de S. Trinitate et justificatione...* (London, 1703). Bull (1634–1710) was bishop of St. David's.

[483] William Sherlock: *A Discourse Concerning the Divine Providence.*

[484] Edward Stillingfleet: *The works of that eminent and most learned prelate, Dr Edw. Stillingfleet. Together with his life and character. In six volumes* (London, 1709–10).

[485] John Dunton: *The phenix: or, a revival of scarce and valuable pieces from the remotest antiquity down to the present times* (London, 1707).

May 2 [*1732*]. W[*illia*]m Pagan paid the last quarter, D[*avid*] Fleming. Paid the last quarter. J[*ohn*] Kirkby.

June 6 1732. Mr [*Thomas*] Clayton paid the last quarter, Mr [*Gilbert*] Bennet, Mr [*William*] Pagan, Mr [*John*] Reddington paid the last quarter, Dr [*John*] Francis paid the last quarter, Mr [*John*] Brooke paid the last quarter.

July 4 1732. Mr [*Gilbert*] Benet then paid the last quarter.

August 1 1732. Present: Mr [*Thomas*] Clayton, who paid the last quarter, Mr [*William*] Pagan, who paid the last quarter, Mr [*Gilbert*] Benet, who paid the last quarter.

September 5 1732. Mr [*David*] Flemming paid the last quarter, Dr [*John*] Francis paid the last quarter, Mr [*John*] Kirkby paid the last quarter, Mr John Brooke present.

October 3 1732. Present: Mr [*John*] Brook, who paid the last quarter, Dr [*John*] Francis, who paid the last quarter, Mr [*John*] Reddington, who paid the 2 last quarters, W[*illia*]m Pagan.

November 7 1732. Mr [*John*] Riddington, Dr [*John*] Francis, Dr [*William*] Herring paid all arrears, Mr [*William*] Pagan, Mr [*John*] Kirkby paid the last quarter.

December 5 1732. Present: Mr [*Thomas*] Clayton, Mr [*William*] Pagan paid all arrears to Michaelmas, Mr [*David*] Fleming paid last quarter.

January 3 1733. Mr [*David*] Fleming paid last quarter. All Dr [*Robert*] Camel's arrears were paid by his widow, Mr [*Gilbert*] Bennet paid last quarter.

January 2 1733. B[*enjamin Joseph*] Ellis paid all arrears to Christmas, Gilbert Benet paid Christmas quarter. January 2 1733. Mr [*William*] Pagan paid all arrears, Mr [*William*] Herne paid all arrears.

February 6 1733. J[*ohn*] Jermy paid all arrears, J[*ohn*] Francis paid the last quarter, Tho[*mas*] Clayton paid all arrears, L[*ynne*] Smear,[486] C[*harles*] Ray[487] admitted to the use of the library.

[486] Lynne Smear was admitted sizar at Trinity College in 1704, graduating BA in 1712 and proceeding MA in 1727. He was ordained in Norwich in 1711 and was rector of St Augustine's until 1730 and vicar of Eaton from 1735 to 1761. When he drew up his will in 1761 he was living in the Cathedral Close. His books he bequeathed to his executrix, Mary Oliver (NRO DCN VI 69, Will of Lynne Smear, 1761).

[487] Charles Ray was admitted sizar at Corpus Christi College in 1727, graduating BA in

March 6 1733. Present: Dr [*John*] Francis, Mr [*John*] Reddington, who paid the Christmas quarter, Mr [*William*] Pagan.

3 April 1733. Present: Mr John Whaley[488] at his request was then admitted a member of the library. Mr [*Gilbert*] Bennet who paid the last quarter. Mr [*John*] Brooke paid all arrears.[489]

Rules in the form of a declaration, drafted by the Court of Common Council on 16 January 1657

[Transcribed at the back of the minute book, presumably in February 1657 when the minute book was purchased].

We whose names are hereunto annexed upon our admission to the use of the Publick Library in the City of Norwich, in Complyance with an Act of the Common Council of the said City dated the 16th January 1656, do faithfully engage & promise,
/Imprimis/That we will not at any time carry out of the said Library any booke belonging to it.
/ 2ly /That we will not leave any books belonging to the said Library (after our using it) out of its due place, nor write anything in any of the bookes, nor leave them with any leaves turned down.
/ 3ly /That we will not prejudice any other person by our use of the said Library, to which purpose, we shall not at any time delay our going to the Library after the receipt of the Keyes from the Keeper, nor the restoring them when we come out of the said Library.
/ 4ly /That we shall as to all these Articles be responsall for our friends who shall goe with us to the said Library, as for our selves.

1731 and proceeding MA in 1734. He was a Fellow of the College from 1733 to 1735. Ordained in Norwich in 1731, he was a minor canon of Norwich Cathedral and vicar of Calthorpe and Thwaite from 1734 to 1739. He died in 1754.

[488] Born in the parish of St Andrew's, Norwich, in April 1710, John Whaley attended Eton College before entering King's College, Cambridge, graduating BA in 1732 and proceeding MA in 1735. He was a Fellow of his College from 1731 to 1745. 'A good jolly companion, a singer of a good song, and rather a genteel person, [Whaley's] company was sought after, and he spent his time in a continual scene of jovial amusements and mirthful society' (W.S. Lewis and J. Riely, eds, *Horace Walpole's Miscellaneous Correspondence*, i, Oxford, 1980, p. 3n). His first volume of poetry was published in 1732. In around 1735 he became tutor to Horace Walpole. A number of letters from Whaley to Walpole survive describing a journey he made around England in the summer of 1735. Whaley was ordained in 1745 and in the same year published *A Collection of Original Poems and Translations*, consisting of imitations of Horace, Tibullus and Martial (*ODNB*).

[489] The minutes end at this point.

/ 5ly /We shall (being duly chosen thereto) not above once in seaven yeares, discharge the office of Library-Keeper.

/ 6ly /We shall faithfully pay our proportions to the under Keeper of the said Library quarterly, & also our equall share with the rest of our brethren in all charges they shall be at for the better preserving of the said Library. All these things we shall endeavour faithfully to observe & keep. If through our negligence we shall fail in any of them, we Agree to subject our selves to the penalties mentioned in the orders confirmed by the Court of Common Councill in the said City.

Articles of 1716

[These articles of 7 May 1716 were also copied into the back of the minute book]

The articles upon which this request or petition was grounded were:

First, that every person taking out any book shall enter the same into a book to be provided for the purpose.

Secondly, that he shall be obliged to return the same book or books in one month from the time of borrowing and enter the return of the said book in a column of the register opposite to that wherein the borrowing of the said book is mentioned,

Thirdly, that no person shall have above the number of three books from this library at one time unless the leave of the society be first asked and obtained.

Fourthly that if any damage be done to any book he in whose hands it is shall make it good and to prevent disputes if the book be damaged before taken out of the library it shall be shown to the under library keeper.

Fifthly, that there be some persons appointed to assist the upper library keeper in calling over the said books the first Monday of January next and so yearly and every year and that the library keeper shall have power to send for and call in such books as are all abroad and every person in whose hands any books have been above the limit or time of one month at such days of calling over the said books shall forfeit two shillings and six pence to be applied to such use as the society shall adjudge proper.

Sixthly, that no person shall be admitted to the use of this library (those of this court excepted) nor have the liberty of borrowing any book from the said library who are not already or shall not hereafter be admitted to the use of the said library according to the usages and customs of the society.

[A record of members c.1666–1733 and a catalogue of authors whose books illustrated sacred scripture in whole or in part are not included in this edition].

The Donation Book 1608–1737
(MS 4228)

Introduction

Although a 'catalogue of benefactours' was already in existence when the library was re-established in 1657, a new donation book – no doubt drawing on its predecessor – was composed and submitted for approval to the members of the library on 11 July 1659.[1] Sir John Pettus' status as the founder was celebrated in an elaborately designed title page that is very reminiscent of the memorial panel to Sir Peter Reade that survives with the collection of Norwich civic portraits. The designer of the title page (or 'clearke' as he was described) who signed his initials, 'JS', in the border, has not been identified. Inside the top border was inscribed '*verbum dei manet in aeternam*', the motto of the Stationers' Society but also sometimes found on surviving Jacobean pulpits in Norfolk such as, for example, North Elmham.

Along with an entry in the donation book some at least of the donors were assigned book plates, or 'printed pages' as they were called. The books bought with the money given by Sir Joseph Paine were allocated a plate with the inscription, *ex dono Domini Josephi Paine militis civitatis praetoris*. Edmund Anguish's bookplate included his parish of residence as well as the year of the donation, *Donum Edmundi Anguish de parochial S. Petri de Mancroft in Noruica. Ann. Dom. 1617.* Robert Garsett included the dramatic flourish *Patriae & Posteritati.*

There is no discernible pattern to the confessional identity of the donors. Some, like Susanna Downing, Thomas Hirne, Joseph Payne and Sir Thomas Browne, appear to have held 'conservative' views. Others, like Thomas Atkins, Thomas Allen and Thomas Corbett, were more radical. But the views of the majority are impossible to uncover. It is perhaps safer to ascribe the motives of the donors to Christian humanism. As well as providing the library Sir John Pettus also built a conduit at a spring near Bishopgate bridge. This was not only the action of a canny politician –

---

[1] 'The library keeper brought in a catalogue of the bookes & benefactors' names fairley written in a parchment booke, for the wrighting whereof hee paid to the clerk 7s. For the repayment of which monye it was agreed every minister should pay 8d. which money was paid by as many as were then present (NRO MS 4226, Norwich City Library Minute Book, p. 8).

Bishopgate was in the city ward Pettus represented as alderman – it was also the action of a man who exhibited all the characteristics of Cicero's *vir civilis*, the civic man, the humanist provider. The granting of benefits to the citizen was widely recognised as one of the characteristics of the man (or woman) who led a truly humane life.

The most significant change in the pattern of donations occurred in the period 1707 to 1709, shortly after the publication of Joseph Brett's catalogue. Brett, who had been a Fellow of Caius College from 1689 to 1699, must have circulated copies of the catalogue at Cambridge University since over twenty academics, most of whom were Fellows of Trinity College, donated books. Donations continued to be received after 1737. For example, there is a note on the half-title of Elkanah Settle's *Eusebia Triumphans. The Hanoverian Succession to the Imperial Crown of England, an Heroic Poem* (London, 1704) which records that the book was given to the Library by John Hilyard in 1745.

The Donation Book

Bibliotheca publica Norvicensis communi studiosorum bono instituta incaepta, et inchoate fuit an[n]o domini MDCVIII JOHANNE PETTUS milite, huius tunc civitatis praetore.
[*Norwich Public Library was set up, begun and put together in the year 1608 by John Pettus knight, at that time mayor of this city, for the common use of those devoted to learning.*]

CATALOGUS librorum et nomenclatura benfactorum (memoriae & gratitudinis ergo) quorum liberalitate, talibus monumentis, nova haec bibliotheca Norvicensis aucta indies, et quotannis adornata fuit.
[*A list of the books and (in memory and gratitude) the names of the benefactors through whose generosity this new Norwich library has daily increased and every year has been adorned with such memorials.*]

[1] **A. D. 1608. Johannes Pettus**[2] Miles [*knight*], D[*ono*] D[*edit*] [*granted by gift*].
Concilia omnia, Collectore Binio Tom: 4: vol: 5. Impress: Coloniae: 1606.
[1.1] Severinus Binius: *Concilia generalia et provincialia.* Coloniae Agrippinae: Apud Ioan Gymric. & Anton. Hierat, 1606.
Centuriatores Magdeburgenses: 7: vol: Impress: Paris: 1608.

---

[2] It has been suggested that the Pettus family, because they had recusants among their relatives, were sympathetic to Catholicism, but this is purely speculative (Reynolds, p. 61). What is certain is that Sir John was closely connected with the Norfolk élite. One of his friends was Sir Henry Hobart, the founder of the Hobart family fortune and the builder of Blickling Hall (TNA PROB/11/123, Will of Sir Thomas Pettus, 1613).

[1.2] Matthias Flacius: *Ecclesiastica Historia, integram Ecclesiae Christi…per aliquot studiosos et pios viros in urbe Magdeburgica.* Basileae, [1560] – 1574.
[2] **A.D.1608. 23 November. Susanna Downing**[3] uxor Georgii Downing Aldermanum D.D. [*wife of alderman George Downing*] Opera Zanchii: 8 Tomis: 3: vol: impress: Per Stephan: Gammonetum. 1605.
[2.1] Hieronymus Zanchius: *Operum theologicorum.* Genevae: Excudebat Stephanus Gamonetus, 1605.
[3] **A.D. 1609. 17 October. Thomas Corye**[4] **Mercator** [*merchant*] **D.D.**
Opera Lutheri: 7: vol: Impress: Wittiberg:
[3.1] Martin Luther: *Opera omnia.* Wittenberg, 1554–83.
Opera Lavateri: 3 vol: Impress: Tiguri.
[3.2] Ludwig Lavater: *Liber Iobi homilijs CXLI.* Tiguri: Excudebat Christophorus Froschouerus, 1585.
[4] **A. D. 1609. October 19. Thomas Hirne**[5] **miles** [*knight*] **D.D.**
Biblia Vatabli: Hebr: Gr: & Lat: vol: 2:
[4.1] Bible. Polyglot: *Sacra Biblia Hebraica, Graece, et Latine.*Heidelberg, 1599.
Opera Calvini: 10: vol.
[4.2] Jean Calvin: *Tractatus Theologici Omnes, in vnvm volvmen certis classibus congesti.* Genevae: Apud Patrum Santandreanum, 1597.
[4.3] Jean Calvin: *Quinque libros Mosis, commentarii.* [Genevae]: In officina Santandreanum, 1595.
[4.4] Jean Calvin: *Commentarius in Librum Psalmorum.* Genevae: Apud Evstathivm Vignon, 1578.
[4.5] Jean Calvin: *Praelectiones in Librum Prophetiarum Jeremiae, et Lamentationes.* Genevae: Apud Haered. Evstath. Vignon, 1589.

[3] Susanna Downing was the wife of George Downing, mayor in 1607. Margaret, one of her daughters, was married to alderman Robert Debney. Another, Hester, was married to alderman Bassingbourne Throckmorton. The family lived in the Laudian parish of St. Gregory's and contributed to the restoration scheme at St. Gregory's Church in 1623. It has been tentatively suggested that the fact that Susanna owned a painting of 'our Ladye' is evidence of her allegiance to Laudian ceremonialism (Reynolds, pp. 139–40; NRO, NCC Belward 66, Will of Susanna Downing, 1625).
[4] Alderman Thomas Corie, surveyor of the children's hospital, was a close friend of mayor John Tooley, who acted as the executor of his will. Corie left money to various named Norwich preachers. John Ward received £3. 6s. 8d., Mr Dawson, vicar of St Michael at Plea, received 40s., and Ralph Furnace 26s. 8d. John Carter, William Bridge, George Cock, Daniel Claydon and John Walker were each given 26s. 8d. He also left 40s. for the repair of St Michael at Plea (TNA PROB 11/180, Will of Thomas Corie, 1638).
[5] Reynolds emphasises Hyrne's ceremonialist leanings and points to his gift of £10 towards a new organ at the Cathedral in 1607. He was one of the largest contributors (Reynolds, pp. 128, 132).

[4.6] Jean Calvin: *Praelectiones in librum prophetiarum Danielis.*
Genevae, 1591.

[4.7] Jean Calvin: *Commentarii in omnes Pauli Apostoli Epistolas,*
atque in epistolam ad Hebraeos. Genevae: Apud Haeredes Eustathii
Vignon, 1600.

[4.8] Jean Calvin: *Epistolae et responsa.* Genevae: Apud Petrum
Santandreanum, 1575.

[4.9] Jean Calvin: *Harmonia ex evangelistis tribus.* Genevae: Apud
Evstathivm Vignon, 1592.

[4.10] Jean Calvin: *Harmonia ex evangelistis tribus.* Genevae:
Apud Haeredes Evstathii Vignon, 1595. (Adams C 353)

[5] **A. D. 1609: Jan: 12 Thomas Corbett**[6] Armiger [*Esquire*] D.D.
Opera Augustini: 6: vol: Impress: Basil: 1569

[5.1] Saint Augustine: *Opera.* Basileae: per Ambrosium
& Aurelium Frobenios, 1569.

[6] **A.D. 1609. Henricus Doyly**[7] Armiger D.D.
Opera Bernardi: 2: vol: Impress: Paris: 1586.

[6.1] Saint Bernard: *Opera omnia.* Paris, 1586.

[7] **A.D. 1610. May 8.Carolus Doyly**[8] Generosus [*gentleman*] D.D.
Opera Ambrosii: 2: vol:

[7.1] St. Ambrose: *Omnia quotquot extant opera.* Basileae, 1567.
Opera Petri Martyris: 7: vol:

[7.2] Pietro Martire Vermigli: *Loci communes D. Petri Martyris Vermilii.*
Heidelbergae: Apud Johannem Lancellottum, 1603.
Opera Fran: Junii: 2: vol:

[7.3] Francois Du Jon: *Opera theologica.* Heidelberg, 1608.

[8] **A. D. 1610 Junii: 17. Robertus Sedgwick**[9] Mercator [*merchant*]
D.D.
Opera, S. Hieronymi: 3 vol: Impress: Paris.

[8.1] Saint Jerome: *Opera omnia quae reperiri potuerunt, ex antiquiis exemplaribus*
diligentia et labore Mariana Victorii Reatini…emendata. Parisiis: Apud Bibliopolas
urbis Parisiensis consortes, 1609.

---

[6] Thomas Corbett of Sprowston left instructions to be buried in the chancel of Sprowston
Church 'without any funeral pomp or dole'. His executors were to give to 'certain preachers of
God's word at their disposition' the sum of £20. Robert Gallard, the editor of Thomas
Newhouse's posthumous sermons (one of which was dedicated to Corbett and his wife, Anne),
was to have £5 (TNA PROB 11/131, Will of Thomas Corbett, 1617). Gallard had offended
the diocesan authorities in 1614 while chaplain of St Andrew's by praying 'not for archbishops
and bishops according to the prescript form of the canon' but for the ministry and clergy
(Reynolds, p. 103).

[7] Henry Doyly was the son of Edmund Doyly of Shotesham, sheriff of Norfolk in 1602 and
1603 (M. Riviere, 'A note on the D'Oylys of Shotesham', *Norfolk Archaeology*, 32, 1961, pp.
47–9).

[8] Charles Doyly was the third son of Henry Doyly.

[9] Robert Sedgewick was sheriff of Norwich in 1623.

Opera Tertulliani, Impress: Basil.

[8.2] Tertullian: *Opera omnia.* Basilieae, 1562.

Opera Origenis lat. 2: vol: Impress: Basil.

[8.3] Origen: *Opera, quae quidem extant omnia, per Des. Erasmus Roterodamum partim versa.* Basileae, 1545.

Opera Irenei: Impress: Parisiis.

[8.4] Irenaeus: *Diui Irenaei...in libri quinque aduerus portentoses haereses Valentini & aliorum.* [Geneva & Paris], 1570.

Opera Cyprian, Impress: Parisiis. 1504.

[8.5] Saint Cyprian: *Opera diui Caecilii Cypriani Episcopi Carthaginensis.* Basileae: Ex Officina Frobeniana, 1521.

Opera Athanasii, lat: Impress: Basil. 1504.

[8.6] Saint Athanasius: *Athanasii magni Alexandrini episcopi, graviss, scriptoris, et sanctiss, martyris, opera.* Basileae: ex officina Episcopiana, 1564.

Opera Cyrilli, lat. Impress: Basil. 1560.

[8.7] Saint Cyril: *Divi Cyrilli Alexandrini episcopi theology praestantissimi opera quae hactenus haberi potuere.* Basileae, 1566.[10]

Opera Hilarii. Impress: Basil.

[8.8] Hilarius Pictaviensis: *D. Hilarii pictavorum episcopi Lucubrationes quotquot extant.* Basle: Froben, 1550.

Martyrologia Johannis Fox: Angl:

[8.9] John Foxe: *Actes and monuments of matters most speciall and memorable, happening in the Church with an universall history of the same.* London: printed by Peter Short, [1596].

[9] **A. D. 1610 May 22. Michael Peade** [11] Notarius publicus et Registrarius Archidiaconis Norvicensis D.D. [*public notary and registrar to the Archdeaconry of Norwich*]

Decreta Gratiani. Impress: Paris.

[9.1] Possibly Gratian: *Apostoli describentis episcoporum, presbyterorum, et diaconorum mores semeiosis, ex viginti quinque Gratiani Distinctionibus excerpta. Decretorum parte prima.* Parisiis: apud Andream Wechelum, 1559.

Opera Aneae Silvii. Impress: Basil.

[9.2] Pope Pius II: *Aeneae Sylvii Piccolominei Senensis, qui post adeptum pontificatum Pius eius nominis secundus appellatus est, opera quae extant omnia.* Basle: per Henrichum Petri, 1551.

---

[10] Listed as such in Brett's 1706 catalogue.

[11] Michael Pead was rated as a property owner in the parish of St. Michael at Plea in 1633–4 (W. Rye, *The Norwich Rate Book*, London, 1903, p.52). His rate was the second highest. Only alderman Thomas Cory paid more. According to his will, where he is described as a gentleman 'late of Syderstone', he owned a house called the Friars in Conesford Street. He died in 1641 (NRO NCC 129 Brampton, Will of Michael Pead, 1641).

[10] A. **D. 1610. Johannes Mingay**[12] Generosus: D.D.
Hemingium in Epistolas
[10.1] Niels Hemmingsen: *Commentaria in omnes epistolas apostolorum.*
Argentorati: Theodosius Rihelius, 1586.
Hemingii Opuscula
[10.2] Niels Hemmingsen: *Opuscula theological...additis variis indicibus notis, &*
praefationibus necessariis. Genevae: E. Vignon, 1586.
[11] **A. D. 1610: 1 Octob: Augustinus Pettus** [13] filius et heres prae-
dicti Johannis D.D. [*son and heir of the aforesaid John*]
Theatrum vitae humanae Collectore Zuingero. Impress: Basil: 4 vol.
[11.1] Theodor Zwinger: *Theatrum humanae vitae.* Basileae: per Sebastianum
Henricpetri, 1604.
[12] **Laurentius Howlett**[14] S.T.B.Pastor Ecclesiae S. Andreae D.D.
Opera Theophilacti, Latine.
[12.1] Possibly *Theophylacti in quatuor Euangelistas.*[15]
[13] **A. D. 1611 Aug: 16. Thomas Newhouse**[16] in Artibus Magister et
verbi Divini Minister D. D. [*Master of Arts and minister of God's word*]
Opera Chrystomi: lat: 4 vol: Impress Basil.
[13.1] John Chrysostom: *Opera quae hactenus versa sunt omnia, ad Graecorum*
codicum collationem multis in locis emendata. Basle: in officina Frobeniana,
1530.
[14] **An: D: 1611. Willelmus Hannam**[17] Generosus in Artibus
Magister D.D.
Opera Theodor Beza: 2 vol. Impress: Genevae[18]
[14.1] Theodore Beza: *Theodore Beza...volumen tractationum theologicarum, in*

[12] Mingay gave money to the rogation at St Stephen's and to the minister, Matthew
Stonham, for preaching a sermon at his burial (NRO NCC 335 Belward, Will of John Mingay,
1625).

[13] Augustine Pettus gave a copy of Matthieu's *Histoire de France* (1605) to St John's College,
Cambridge, stamped with his arms and the initials A.P. on the vellum covers is reference to
William Pettus IV.

[14] Howlett was a fellow of Emmanuel College, Cambridge, from 1613 to 1621 and lecturer
at St. Andrew's from 1622 to 1626. He died in 1626.

[15] Not listed in Brett's 1706 catalogue. Tilley points out that a copy of Theophylact on the
Evangelists, belonging to the City Library, was recorded by Beecheno as being in the library in
St Andrew's Church in 1883 (J. Tilley, *A catalogue of the donations made to Norwich City Library,*
1608–1656, Cambridge, 2000, p. 71).

[16] Newhouse left a nuncupative will in 1611 in which his donation of four volumes of
Chrysostom to the City Library is recorded. The remainder of his books he left to Robert
Gallard, minister of St. John's Ber Street (NRO, NCC 135 Stywarde, Will of Thomas
Newhouse, 1611).

[17] Born in Somerset, William Hannam was educated at Eton and was a Fellow of King's
College, Cambridge, from 1562 to 1575. He returned to Somerset in later life and died there
(TNA PROB 11/120, Will of William Hannam, 1611).

[18] Listed in Brett's 1706 catalogue as in one volume.

NORWICH CITY LIBRARY 193

quibus pleraque Christianae religionis dogmata adversus haereses. Genevae, 1582.
Peresium Traditionibus.
[14.2] Martin Perez de Ayala: *De diuinis, apostolicis, atque ecclesiasticus tradi-tionibus, deque authoritate ac vi earum sacrosancta, adsertiones ceu libri decem.*
[15] An. Dm. 1612 Feb: 9. Robertus Garsett[19] Armiger D.D.
Annales Caesaris Baronii: 6 vol.
[15.1] Caesar Baronius: *Annales ecclesiastici.*Coloniae Agrippinae: sumptibus
I. Gymnici & A. Hierati, 1609.
Effigies presantium aliquot Theologorum qui Antichristum Oppugnarunt,
una cum Elogiis Librorumque Catalogis.
[15.2] Jacobus Verheiden: *Praestantium aliquot Theologorum qui Rom.*
Antichristum praecipue oppugnarunt. Effigies; quibus addita
elogia. librorum catalogi. Hagae Comitis: Ex officina Bucoldi Cornelii
Nieulandii, 1602.
[16] An: D: 1613: Aprilis 5. Joanna Blowe[20] **vidua** [*widow*] D.D
Buntingi Chronologiam
[16.1] Heinrich Bunting: *Chronologia, hoc est, omnium temporum et annorum series*
ex sacris Bibliis. Servestae: Impressum typis
Bonaventurae Fabri, 1590.
Calepini Dictionarium: 8 linguar
[16.2] Ambrosius Calepinus: *Dictionarium octo linguarum.* Basileae, 1584.
Micropresbyticon
16.4] *Mikropresbutikon: veterum quorundam brevium theologorum, sive episcoporum,*
sive presbyterorum, aut sacri ordinis aliorum qui aut tempore Apostolorum aut non
multo post vixerunt, elenchus. Basileae: Apud Henrichum Petri, 1550.
Author Romanas Antiquitates: Rosini
[16.5] Johannes Rosinus: *Romanorum Antiquitatum libri decem, ex variis*
scriptoribus...collecti. Basileae: ex officina haeredum Petri Pernae, 1583.
Sanctorum Catalogum a Petro de Natalibus
[16.6] Petrus de Natalibus: *Catalogus sanctorum et gestorum eorum ex diversis*
voluminibus collectus. Lugduni: Venundantur ab Stephano Gueynard, 1514.
[17] An: Dm: 1613: April 20. Hammondus Thurston[21] Mercator D.D.

[19] Alderman Robert Garsett bequeathed to the preachers of the city of Norwich the sum of £3, to be bestowed at the 'discretion' of his executors. He gave Nicholas Bownde, minister of St Andrew's, 20s. 'over and besides', and 40s. 'to the reparation of St Andrew's church where I now dwell'. He also remembered his constituents. He gave £100 to the ward of West Wymer (TNA, PROB 11/119, Will of Robert Garsett, 1609).

[20] Joan Blowe was the daughter of alderman Thomas Corie, who donated books to the library in 1609. Her husband, Augustine Blowe, died in 1604. A wealthy property owner, he left £200 to his daughter Mary (NRO, NCC 29 Cockes, Will of Augustine Blowe, 1604).

[21] A supralapsarian Calvinist and friend of alderman William Browne, Sir Thomas Browne's uncle, alderman Thurston left money to the Norwich ministers Fulke Roberts, John Yates, Robert Gallard, Robert Kent and John Ward and made a contribution of £10 to Thomas Anguish's fund for establishing a children's hospital (TNA PROB 11/133, Will of Hammond Thurston, 1618).

Summam Aquinatis

[17.1] Thomas Aquinas: *S. Thomae Aquinatis Summa totius theologiae.* Coloniae Agrippinae: Ex officina Anthonij Hierati, 1604.

Historiam Eusebii, Ruffini, Socratis, Theodoreti, Sozomeni, et Aliorum.

[17.2] Eusebius: *Eusebii Pamphili, Ruffini, Socratis, Theodoriti, Sozomeni, Theodori, Evagrij & Dorothei Ecclesiastica Historia.* Basileae: per Sebastianum Henricpetri, 1611.

Biblia nova translationis Angl[*icis*]

[17.3] The Holy Bible, Conteyning the Old Testament, and the New: Newly Translated out of the Original tongues. London: Printed by Robert Barker, 1612

[18] **A: D: 1613: Julij 12. Matheue Peckouer**[22] nuper Vicecomes Norwici: D.D. [*formerly sheriff of Norwich*]

Opera Magistri Gulielmi Perkins 3 vol.

[18.1] William Perkins: *The works of that famous and worthy minister of Christ in the Universitie of Cambridge, Mr William Perkins.* London: printed by John Legatt, 1612.

[19] **A: D: 1614: Junij 8. Petrus Launaeus**[23] **Pastor** Ecclesiae Galliobelgicae D.D. [*minister of the French church*]

Concordantiam Magistri Petri de Besse

[19.1] Pierre De Besse: *Concordantiae Bibliorvm vtrivsque testamenti generales.* Parisiis, 1611.

Liturgiam Ecclesiae Anglicanae Gallice reddita ab ipso Petro Launaeo

[19.2] La liturgie angloise, ou Le Liure des priers publiques. A Londres: par Iehan Bill, 1616.

[20] **Willielmus Welles**[24] Theologiae Baccalaureus. D.D.

Nicholas de Lyra in Veterum Testamentum 4: vol.

---

[22] Alderman Matthew Peckover left an explicit Calvinistic will: 'before all things I commit my soul into the merciful hands of my lord and only Saviour Jesus Christ assuredly trusting that through his merits, death and passion I shall after this life ended be received amongst the number of his elect children into his everlasting kingdom' (NRO, NCC 171 Belward, Will of Matthew Peckover, 1625).

[23] Born in 1574, the son of a Huguenot divine and physician, Peter de Laune became pastor of the French Church in Norwich in 1599. His translation of the Book of Common Prayer into French, a copy of which he presented to the City Library, was published in 1616. In 1629 he provoked much controversy by agreeing to be instituted rector of Harleston and Redenhall while retaining his pastorship of the French Church. The young Isaac Clement was appointed his coadjutor in December 1655. De Laune died in October 1657 (NRO MS 20576, A.L. Gowans' Biographical notes on Peter de Laune).

[24] William Wells was such a popular preacher that in 1594 the city assembly decided that in consideration of the diligence and great pains that he took weekly in preaching the word of God he should have an annuity of £6. 6s. 8d. (NRO, NCR Norwich Assembly Book, 1565–1613, fol. 136v). Judging by the provisions of his will, he was a man who was convinced of the merits of education and of the part books could play. He bequeathed all his books and writings to his son William but only if he became a scholar and had taken his MA or was

[20.1] Biblia Latina cum glosa ordinaria et expositione Nicolai de Lyra. Basileae: Johann Froben & Johann Petri, 1498.

Concordantiam Hebraeam.

[20.2] Isaac Nathan ben Kalonymus: *Concordantiarum Hebraicarum Capita, quae sunt de vocum expositionibus a doctissimo Hebraeo Rabbi Mardochai Nathan.* Basileae: per Henrichum Petri, 1518.

[21] **Bassingbourne Throkmorton** [25] D.D.

Biblia Hieronymi Manuscripta.

[21.2] A thirteenth-century copy of the Vulgate.[26]

Richardum vicum Basinstoke De origine Insulae Britanniae.

[21.3] Richard White: *Ricardi Viti Basinstochi, comitis Palatini, historiarum Britanniae insulae, ab origine muni ad annum Christi octingentesimum, libri novem priores.* Duaci, 1598–1602.

[22] **A: D: 1614: Johannes Cropp** [27] Medicus et Chirurgus. D.D. [*doctor and surgeon*]

Willet in Genesin.

[22.1] Andrew Willet: *Hexapla in Genesin.* Cambridge: printed by John Legat, 1605.

Missale Romanum.[28]

[22.2] An unidentified service book for the Mass.

Jacobum de valentia in Psalm.

[22.3] Jacobus Perez de Valentia: *Expositiones in psalmos Davidicos.*

Kantzii Chronica Daniae.

[22.4] Albertus Krantz: *Chronica Regnorum Aquilonarium, Daniae, Suetiae, Norvagiae.*

chosen a Fellow of a college or else was a beneficed clergyman (NRO, NCC 100 Williams, Will of William Wells, 1620). One of the witnesses of the will was Richard Gammon, rector of St Lawrence and St Giles who, in 1636, was an active supporter of bishop Matthew Wren (Reynolds, p. 130). Another witness to the will was alderman Robert Debney, the man who made the single largest donation towards the refurbishment of St Gregory's in 1623 (Reynolds, p. 147).

[25] Alderman Throckmorton left money towards the repair of the churches of Holy Trinity, Bungay, and St Paul's in Norwich (TNA PROB 11/178, Will of Bassingbourne Throckmorton, 1638). He also left 20s. to John Burnham, the minister at St Paul's, who was suspended by Bishop Wren in 1636 (Reynolds, p. 191), and 20s. to Richard Gamon, minister of St Lawrence's, who was an active supporter of Wren (Reynolds, p. 130n).

[26] Ker, *Medieval Manuscripts*, p. 553.

[27] The son of an immigrant from Flanders, John Cropp was born in 1572, possibly in Norwich. In 1605 he was described as 'practitioner in physic, licentiate of the City of Norwich'. Two years later he became a freeman and a warden of the Norwich Barber-Surgeons Company. An account of his practice was given by Katherine Paston: 'I am very glad to see he [Tom Hartston, a neighbour's son] has so much strength in his arm, for I did fear he had been stark lame of it...on Monday Mr Crope I think will take it in hand, first by physic and after by applying strenghy things to it' (M. Pelling and C. Webster, 'Medical practitioners' in, C. Webster, ed., *Health, Medicine and Mortality in the Sixteenth Century*, Cambridge, 1979, pp. 224–5).

[28] Not listed in Brett's 1706 catalogue.

[23] **An. D: 1614. Henricus Bird** [29] D.D.
Pagnini Thesaurum Linguae Sacrae.
[23.1] Sanctes Pagninus: *Thesaurus Linguae sanctae; sive Lexicon Hebraicum.*
Lugduni, 1575.
[24] **A:. D: 1615: Richardus Ross** [30] Generosus Nuper Norvici
Vicecomes D.D.
Nicholaum de Lyra in Vet & Novum Testamentum.
[24.1] Nicolaus de Lyra: *Postilla super Biblia.* Nurnburgen: Anthonii
Koburger, 1481.
[25] **A: D: 1614: Gabriel Barbar** [31] Generosus, Nomine Societatis
Virginiae [*in the name of the Society of Virginia*].
Musculi opera: 9 vol: Impress: Basil:
[25.1] Wolfgang Musculus: *In Davidis Psalterium sacrosanctum Commentarii.*
Basileae: per Sebastianum Henricpetri, 1599.
[25.2] Wolfgang Musculus: *In Esaiam Prophetam commentarii.* Basileae: Ex
officina Heruagiana, 1570.
[25.3] Wolfgang Musculus: *Commentarii in Matthaeum Evangelistam.* Basileae:
per Sebastianum Henricpetri, 1611.
[25.4] Wolfgang Musculus: *Commentariorum in Evangelistam Ioannem.* Basileae,
1545.
[25.5] Wolfgang Musculus: *In Epistolam D. Apostoli Pauli ad Romanos
commentarij.* Basileae: per Sebastianum Henricpetri, 1600.
[25.6] Wolfgang Musculus: *In Apostoli Pauli ambas Epistolas ad Corinthios
commentarij.* Basileae: per Sebastianum Henricpetri, 1611.
[25.7] Wolfgang Musculus: *In Epistolas Apostoli Pauli, ad Galatas & Ephesios
Commentarij.* Basileae: ex officina Hervagiana, 1569.
[25.8] Wolfgang Musculus: *In Divi Pauli Epistolas ad Philippenses, Colossenses,
Thessalonicenses ambas, & primam ad Timotheum.* Basileae: ex officina
Hervagiana, 1575.
Clem[ent] Alexandrinum. Gr. L. Impress: Lugd; Batar.
[25.9] Titus Flavius Clemens: *Clementis Alexandrini opera, Gr. et Lat.* Lugduni
Batavorum. 1616.
Fulgentium Impress: Basil
[25.10] Saint Fulgentius, Bishop of Ruspa: *Beati Fulgenti episcopi Ruspensis in
Aphrica, priscorum ecclesiae doctorum nulli non conferendi, opera.* Basleae: Per
Sebastianum Henricpetri, 1587.

[29] In his will Henry Bird asked that his books be sold to pay his debts and to help his three
grandchildren (NRO NCC 41 Gibson, Will of Henry Bird, curate of Seething, 1640).

[30] Richard Ross owned property in the Norwich parishes of St Mary, St Martin at Oak and
St Peter Southgate (NRO NCC 4 Burlye, Will of Richard Ross, 1645).

[31] One of the most generous contributors to the Feoffees for Impropriations, Gabriel
Barbour was a member of the Providence Island Company as well as the Virginia Company
(C. Hill, *Economic Problems of the Church from Archbishop Whitgift to the Long Parliament*, Oxford,
1955, p. 255). He donated a copy of the works of Charles I to St Margaret's Library, King's
Lynn (NHC KL 018.2, 'Catalogue of the Library of St Margaret's, King's Lynn', p. 28).

[26] **An. D. 1616 Feb: 5. Edwardus Nutting** [32] nuper Norvici
Vicecomes D.D. [*Lately Sheriff of Norwich*]
Opera Martini Chemnitii: 3 vol.
[26.1] Martin Chemnitz: *Examinis Concili Tridentini, per D.D. Martinum
Chemnicium scripti.* Genevae: Excudebat Stephanus Gamonetus, 1614.
[26.2] Idem: *Loci theologici.* Witenbergae: Typis Wolffgangi Meisneri, 1615.
[26.3] Idem: *Harmoniae evangelicae, a praestantissimo theologo D. Martino
Chemnitio.* Brunswigae, 1615.
Opera Amandi Polani: vol.
[26.4] Amandus Polanus: *Symphonia Catholica.* Genevae: Ex Typographia
Iacobi Stoer, 1612.
[26.5] Idem: *Sylloges Thesium theologicarum.* Basileae: per Conradum
Waldkirch, 1600.
[26.6] Idem: *Sylloges Thesium Theologicarum.* Basileae: per Conradum
Waldkirch, 1602.
[26.7] Idem: *De ratione legendi cum fructu auctores.* Basileae: Typis Conradi
Waldkirch, 1611.
[26.8] Idem: *De concionum sacrarum methodo institutio.* Basileae: Typis Conradi
Waldkirchii, 1604
[26.9] Idem: *Analysis libri Hoseae prophetae tradita.* Basileae: per Conradum
Waldkirch, 1601.
[26.10] Idem: *In Danielem prophetam visionum.* Basileae: Typis Conradi
Waldkirchii, 1606.
Catologum Testium.
[26.11] Matthias Flacius: *Catalogus testium veritatis, qui ante nostram aetatem
reclamarunt papae.* Genevae: in officina Iacobi Stoer, 1608.
[27] **Willielmus Batho**[33] Theologiae Baccalaureus D.D. [*Bachelor of Theology*]
Opera Gregorii Magni.
[27.1] Pope Gregory I: *Sancti Gregori Magni…opera olim diversis tomis dispersa,
nunc vero beneficio…Bertholdi Rembolt in unum sunt volumen redacta.* Parrhisiis: in
edibus Joannis Parvi, 1518.

[32] Edward Nutting, the first husband of Prudence Blosse, another important donor, owned
property in Norwich, Drayton, Taverham, Thorpe Hamlet and Wymondham. In his will he
left 'to every of the preachers of Norfolk and Suffolk that shall come to preach at the common
place in the cathedral church of Norwich 2s. 6d. To the minister of the said parish of St
Saviour being a preacher licensed 40s. every year. To a preacher to preach a sermon there
yearly upon the Sunday next after the day of my burial 6s. 8d. every year'. Nutting left £5 to
the library and gave 20s to 'every preacher in Norwich'. Prebendary Fulke Roberts and Mr
[*Robert*] Allison, chaplain of St George Colegate, were left 40s. each (NRO, NCC 99 Sayer,
Will of Edward Nutting, 1616).

[33] William Batho gave all his books to his brother Toby 'except some particulars which I
have bound and engaged my self to leave to the parvetical library of the city of Norwich'. He
also gave Mr [*Robert*] Kent 'an other book to his study because of his ancient acquaintance with
me' (NRO, NCC 103 Gente, Will of William Batho, 1624). Robert Kent, chaplain of St
Martin at Oak, preached a sermon in 1601 in which he complained that 'bribery and corruption were of prelates and church government' (Reynolds, p. 172).

[28] **A: D: 1617: Johannes Anguish** [34]Generosus & Civis [*citizen*] D.D. Opera Hospiniani; 5 vol.

[28.1] Rodolphus Hospinianus: *Historia sacramentaria: hoc est libri Quinque.* Tiguri: apud Iohannem Wolphium, 1598.

[28.2] Ibid: *Historiae sacramentariae pars altera.* Tiguri: apud Iohannem Wolphium, 1602.

[28.3] Ibid: *De Templis: hoc est De Origine, progressu, usu et abusu templorum.* Tiguri: in officina Wolfian, 1603.

[28.4] Ibid: *Concordia Discors: De origine et progressu formulae concordiae Bergensis.* Tiguri: in officina Wolphiana, 1608.

[28.5] Ibid: *Festa Christianorum. Hoc est de origine, progressu, ceremoniis et ritibus festorum dierum christianorum.* Tiguri: apud Joh. Rodolphum Wolphium, 1612.

Basilii magni opera lat.1: vol.

[28.6] Saint Basil, Bishop of Caesarea: *Opera omnia: iam recens per Wolfgangum Musculum partim locis aliquot castigata, partim luculentis accessionibus aucta.* Basle, 1565.

Epiphanii opera lat. 1 vol.

[28.7] Saint Epiphanius, Bishop of Constantia: *D. Epiphanius episcopi Constantiae Cypri, contra octaginta haereses opus, Pannarium, sive Arcula, aut Capsula medica appellatum, continens libros tres, & tomos sive sectiones ex toto septem.* Parisiis, 1544.

[29] **An: D: 1617: Edmundus Anguish**[35] Generosus D.D.

Justini Martyris opera Graecolat.

[29.1] Saint Justin Martyr: *Opera.* Heidelberg: ex typographeio Hieronymi Commelini, 1593.

Stellam in Lucam.

[29.2] Diego de Estella: *Eximii verbi diuini concionatoris, in sacrosanctum Iesu Christi Domini nostri Euangelium secundum Lucam enarrationem.* Antuerpiae, 1608.

Whitakeri opera.

[29.3] William Whittaker: *Praelectiones..G. Whitakeri…in quibus tractatur contro-versia de Ecclesia, contra Pontificios, inprimis R. Bellarminum, in septem Quaestiones distributa.* Cambridge, 1599.

Photii Bibliothecam.

[29.4] Saint Photius: *Photii Bibliotheca: sive lectorum a Photio librorum recensio.* Augustae Vindelicorum, 1606.

[34] John Anguish was one of the highest rated inhabitants of the parish of St George Tombland in 1633 (WRye, ed., *The Norwich rate-book. From Easter 1633 to Easte 1634*, Norwich, 1904, p, 56).

[35] The will of Edmund Anguish of Great Moulton near Long Stratton was proved in 1616. It had a strongly Calvinist preamble. Anguish 'trust[ed] to be made partaker of the heavenlie inheritance prepared by Allmightie God for his elect' (NRO ANW 33, f. 65, Will of Edmund Anguish, 1616).

Molerum in Psalmas.

[29.5] Heinrich Moller: *Enarrationis Psalmorum Dauidis, ex praelectionibus D. Henrici Molleri Hamburgensis…* Geneuae: Apud Petrum & Iacobum Choet, 1610.

Theophilactum in N: T: 2 vol: 8o lat.

[29.6] Perhaps *In omnes d. Pauli Epistolas enarrationes* or *In quatuor Euangelia enarrationes.*[36]

Prosperi opera: 8o

[29.7] Saint Prosper of Aquitaine: *Diui Prosperi Aquitanici, Episcopi Rhegiensis, viri eruditissimi, Opera.* Coloniae Agrippinae: Excudebat Arnoldus Kempensis, sumptibus Ioannis Crithii, 1609.

Viguerii Institutiones Theologiae: 8o

[29.8] Joannes Viguerius: *Institutiones theologicae, ex sacris literis.* Coloniae Agrippinae: apud Bernardum Gualtherium, 1607.

[30] **A: D: 1617: Thomas Catelyn**[37] Armiger. D.D.

Dictionarium Johannis Minshei

[30.1] John Minsheu: *Ductor in linguas: cum illarum harmonia, & etymologiis, originationibus, rationibus, & derivationibus in omnibus his undecim linguis.* London: printed by William Stansby, 1617.

Anatomiam Helkiae Crooke

[31.2] Helkiah Crooke: *Mikrokosmographia: a description of the body of man.* London: Printed by William Iaggard dwelling in Barbican, 1615.

Purkase Pilgrimage

[31.3] Samuel Purchas: *Purchas his pilgrimage, or Relations of the world and the religions observed in all ages and places discovered, from the creation to the present.* London: printed by William Stansby, 1617.

Lexicon Pentaglotton Schindler

[31.4] Valentin Schindler: *Lexicon pentaglotton, Hebraicum, Chaldaicum, Syriacum, Talmudico-Rabbinicum, et Arabicum.* Francofurti ad Moenum: typis Joannis Jacobi Hennei, 1612.

Scapulae

[31.5] Johann Scapula: *Lexicon Graeco-Latinum nouum in quo es primitiuorum & simplicium fontibus deriuata…deducuntur Ioannis Scapulae opera & studio.* Basiliae: per Sebastianum Henricpetri, [1604].

Damasceni opera: gr: Lat.

[31.6] John of Damascus: *Ioan Damasceni viri suo tempore in divinis primatum tenentis, omnia quae hactenus & a nobis & ab aliis haberi potuerunt opera, ad vetustiora Graecorum exemplaria collata atque emendata.* Basileae: excudebat Henricus Petrus, 1535.

---

[36] Probably the copy 'in 2 little octavos' purchased on 13 April 1662 by John Collinges for 2s.

[37] When he made his will Thomas Catlyn was living in Bracondale in Norwich (NRO NCC 348 Spendlove, Will of Thomas Catlyn, 1636). His grandson, also Thomas, a captain in the royalist army, was killed at the battle of Naseby in 1644 (Venn).

REGIS IACOBI opera.

[31.7] James I, King of England: *The workes of the Most High and Mightie Prince James.* London: printed by Robert Barker and John Bill, 1616.

*[32]***Anna Corbett,**[38] **vidua** Thomae Corbett Armigeri. D.D.
Chronica Anglica Johannis Speed.

[32.1] John Speed: *The theatre of the empire of Great Britaine: presenting an exact geography of the kingdomes of England, Scotland, Ireland, and the iles adioyning: with the shires, hundreds, cities and shire-townes, within ye kingdome of England.* London: sold by I. Sudbury and G. Humble, 1611.

[33] **A: D: 1618. Thomas Atkins**[39] Mercator Norvicensis D.D.
Melancthonis opera; vol: 4: Impress: Witteberg.

[33.1] Philipp Melanchthon: *Operum omnium reverendi viri Philippi Melanchthonis.* Witebergae: Typis Simonis Gronenburgij, 1601.
Arcam Noae

[33.2] Marcus Marinus: *Arca Noe thesaurus linguae sanctae nouus.* Venetiis: Apud Iohannem Degarum, 1593.
Richardus in Apocalipsin: Manuscript.

[33.3] Berengaudus: *In Apocalypsin;* Richard of Wethersett: *Qui bene presunt.*[40]
A Defence of Priests Marriage.

[33.4] Thomas Martin: *A Defence of priestes marriages, stablysshed by the imperiall lawes of Englande against a Ciuilian, naming himself T. Martin.* Londini: J. Kinston for R. Jugge, 1562.
Unacum quinque libris ad libros emendos [*together with five pounds for buying books*].

[34] **A: D: 1621. Augustinus Scottowe** [41] D.D.
Opera Piscatoris in omnes, V: T: Libros: 14: vol.

[34.1] Johannes Piscator: *Commentarius in Genesin.* Herbornae Nassoviorum, 1611.

[34.2] Ibid.: *Commentarius in Exodum.* Herbornae Nassoviorum, 1605.

[34.3] Ibid.: *Commentarius in Leviticum.* Herbornae Nassoviorum, 1615.

[34.4] Ibid.: *Commentarius in librum Josuae.* Herbornae Nassoviorum, 1607.

---

[38] Anne Corbett was the dedicatee of one of Thomas Newhouse's sermons, published posthumously by Robert Gallard, minister of St Andrew's (Robert Gallard, *Two Sermons, Preached by that Reuerend and Iudicious Diuine Master Thomas Newhovse* (London, 1614). For Thomas Corbett see above note 6.

[39] Atkins served as a Norwich councillor between 1613 and 1616 and again between 1618 and 1627. He was sheriff in 1627–8 and alderman in 1629–38. One of the feoffees for impropriations, he presented the petition against bishop Wren to the Short Parliament. He took the covenant in 1645 and criticised the employment of non-ordained preachers, strong evidence that his sympathies were with the Presbyterians (*ODNB*).

[40] Ker, *Medieval Manuscripts*, pp. 552–3.

[41] Scottowe, a member of the Norwich Grocers' Company, was another of the feoffees for impropriations (Reynolds, pp. 162–3).

[34.5] Ibid.: *Commentarius in libros duos Samuelis.* Hebornae Nassoviorum, 1610.

[34.6] Ibid.: *Commentarius in duos libros Regum.* Hebornae Nassoviarum, 1611.

[34.7] Ibid.: *Commentarius in duos libros Chronicorum.* Hebornae Nassoviarum, 1616.

[34.8] Ibid.: *Commentarius in librum Jobi.* Hebornae Nassoviorum: Ex officina typographica Christophor Corvini, 1612.

[34.9] Ibid.: *Commentarius in librum Psalmorum.* Hebornae Nassoviorum, 1618.

[34.10] Ibid.: *Commentarius in Proverbia Salomonis, itemque in Canticum Canticorum.* Hebornae Nassoviorum, 1617.

[34.11] Ibid.: *Commentarius in Prophetam Esaiam.* Hebornae Nassoviorum, 1612.

[34.12] Ibid.: *Commentarius in Prophetam Jeremiam, & ejusdem Lamentationes.* Hebornae Nassoviorum: Ex officina typographica Christophori Corvini, 1614.

[34.13] Ibid.: *Commentarius in Prophetam Ezechielem.* Hebornae Nassoviorum, 1614.

[34.14] Ibid.: *Commentarius in duocecim prophetas quos nominant minores.* Hebornae Nassoviorum, 1615.

Eiusdem opus in N: T: vol: 1

[34.15] Johannes Piscator: *Commentarii in omnes libros Novi Testamenti.* Herbornae Nassoviorum, 1621.

Opera Aretij in Novum Testamentum:

[34.16] Benedictus Aretius: *In Novum Testamentum domini nostri Jesu Christi commentarii doctissimi.* Genevae: Apud Petrum & Iacobum Chouët, 1618.

Ejusdem Loci communes.

[34.17] Benedictus Aretius: *Theologiae problemata, Hoc est, loci communes christianae religionis methodice explicati.* Bernae Helvetiorum: Excudebat Ioannes le Preux, 1604.

[35] **Robertus Gallardus** [42] D.D. olim Pastor parochiae Sancti Andreae [*formerly minister of the parish of St Andrew*]:
Synopsin Papismi Doctoris Willetti.

[35.1] Andrew Willet: *Synopsis papismi, that is, A generall view of papistrie.* London: imprinted by Felix Kyngston, 1614.

[36] **A: D: 1625. Feb: 1. Franciscus Page** [43] D. D.
B. Babingtons Workes.

[36.1] Gervase Babington: *The workes of the right reverend father in God Gervase*

[42] A protégée of Thomas Newhouse, whose posthumously published sermons he edited, Gallard was presented in 1614 for praying 'not for archbishops and bishops according to the prescript form of the canon but for the ministrie and clergie' (Reynolds, pp. 162–3).

[43] A Francis Page is recorded as having paid a rate in the parish of St Andrew's in 1633 (Rye, *Norwich Rate Book*, p. 50).

Babington, late Bishop of Worcester. London: printed by George Eld, 1615.
[37] **A: D: 1628: Civitas Norwici**: D.D.
Dictionarium Minshai 11: Linguarum, 2 nd Editionis
[37.1] John Minsheu: *Minshaei emendatio, vel a mendis expurgatio, seu augmentatio sui Ductoris in linguas. The guide into tongues.* London: printed by Iohn Haviland, 1627.
[38] **Nathaniell Remington** [44]Aldermannus: D: D:
Alexandri Alensis Summas in 3: vol.
[38.1] Alexander of Hales: *Universae theologiae summa: in quatuor partes ab ipsomet authore distributa.* Coloniae Agrippinae: Sumptibus Ioannis Gymnici, 1622.
Flavii Ilyrici Clavem Scripturae.
[38.2] Matthias Flacius Illyricus: *Clavis Scripturae Sacrae, seu de sermone sacrarum literarum.* Basileae: apud Henripetrinos, 1629.
Eiusdem Glossarum in Novum Testamentum.
[38.3] Matthias Flacius Illyricus: *Nouum Testamentum Iesu Christi filii Dei: ex versione Erasmi, innumeris in locis ad Graecam veritatem genuinumque sensum emendata. Glossa compendiaria M. Matthiae Flacij Illyrici Albonensis.* Basileae: impressum per Petrum Pernam et Theobaldum Dietrich, 1570.
[39] **A: D: 1631: July 14: Johannes Borage** [45] D: D:
Opera Salmeronis: 7: vol.
[39.1] Alfonso Salmeron: *Commentarii in Evangelicum historiam et in Acta Apostolorum nunc primum in lucem editi.* Coloniae Agrippinae: apud Antonium Hierat, et Ioan. Gymnicum, 1602–04.
[40] **A: D: 1633: Decemb: Samuell Chapman**[46] Mercator: D: D:
Opera Bannez: 2: vol.
[40.1] Domingo Banes: *Scholastica commentaria in primam partem Summae theologicae S. Thomae Aquinatis.* Duaci: ex typographia Petri Borremans, 1614–15.
[41] **A: D: 1633: Thomas Barret**[47] Mercator: D: D:
Opera Epiphanii Greek, Latin. 2 vol. Idem
[41.1] Saint Epiphanius: *Opera omnia in duos tomos distributa. Dionysius Petauius*

[44] Nathaniel Remington, Alderman of Colegate Ward, was extremely well connected. Augustine Scottowe was a brother-in-law, as was Dr Robert Lane, President of St John's College, Cambridge. Scottowe and Alderman Thomas Atkins, another important donor, acted as his executors (TNA PROB 11/159, Will of Nathaniel Remington, 1631). He left 20s. each to Fulke Robarts, William Allison, Ralph Furness, Robert Gallard, Peter de Laune, Robert Kent, John Ward and John Carter, 'all preachers of God's word'.

[45] Born at North Barsham, John Burrage was admitted to Caius College in 1581 and to the Middle Temple in 1584. He founded a Fellowship at Clare College (NRO NCC 135 Parke, Will of John Burrage, 1637; Blomefield, vii, p. 51).

[46] The son of John Chapman, gentleman, Samuel Chapman, a worstead weaver, was enrolled as a freeman in October 1615. By 1633 he was the second highest ratepayer in the parish of St Simon and St Jude (Rye, *Norwich Rate Book*, Norwich, 1903, p. 55).

[47] For Thomas Barrett see the minutes, n. 84.

Aurelianensis. Parisiis: Sumptibus M. Sonnii, Cl. Morelli et S. Cramoisy, 1622.

[42] **Idem Thomas Barrett** 11 Novembris 1661 D: D:
Stephani Thesaurum Linguae Grecae eum Glossario
[42.1] Henri Estienne: *Thesaurus Graecae linguae ab Henrico Stephano constructus.* [Genevae]: excudebat H. Stephanus, [1572].
[42.2] Henri Estienne: *Glossaria duo, e situ vetustatis eruta.* [Genevae]: Excudebat Henr. Stephanus, 1573.

[43] **An: D: 1634: Antonius Mingay** [48] Generosus D.D.
Opera Bedae 3 volumes folio
[43.1] The Venerable Bede: *Opera quotquot reperiri potuerunt omnia. Hac ultima impressione ornatius in lucem edita.* Coloniae Agrippinae: sumptibus Anton. Hierati et Ioan Gymnici, 1612.
Opera Bonaventura 4 volumes
[43.2] Saint Bonaventura: *Opera...diligentissime emendata, libris eius multis undique conquisitis aucta.* Moguntiae: sumptibus Antonij Hierati, 1609.
Martini Lexicon Philologicum
[43.3] Matthias Martinius: *Lexicon philologicum, praecipue etymologicum, in quo Latine et a Latinis auctoribus usurpatae.* Bremae:
impensis M. Johannis Willii & Georgii Hoismanni, 1623.
Lorichii opera
[43.4] Jodocus Lorich: *Thesaurus novus utriusque theologiae theoricae et practicae.* Friburgi Brisgoiae: excudebat Martinus Böckler, 1609.
Draudij Bibliothecam 2 volumes quarto
[43.5] Georg Draudius: *Bibliotheca classica, siue catalogus officinalis, in quo singuli singularum facultatum ac professionum libri.* Francofurti: impensis Balthasaris Ostern, 1625.

[44] **Mingay Vidua** [49] D.D.
Cornelii a Lapide Comment in 6 volumes[50]
[44.1] Cornelius a Lapide: *In Pentateuchum Mosis Commentaria.* Lutetia Parisiorum: Ex Officina Typographica Edmundi Martini, 1630.
[44.2] Cornelius a Lapide: *Ecclesiasticus Jesu Siracidis expositus accurate commentario.* Lugduni, 1633.
[44.3] Cornelius a Lapide: *Commentaria in duodecim prophetas minores.* Parisiis: Apud Hervetum du Mesnil, 1630.

---

[48] One of the sons of John and Susan Mingay, Anthony Mingay was among the largest contributors to the city rate in St Stephen's parish in 1633 (Rye, p. 26).

[49] The wife of Alderman John Mingay, a donor in 1610, Susan Mingay clearly saw herself as one of God's 'elect children'. A reference in her will to a 'preacher's chamber' suggests that the Mingays had a resident chaplain. As well as leaving books to the City Library, she also bequeathed £5 each to the 'libraryes of the preachers' at St Andrew's and St Peter Mancroft to buy books (NRO NCC 148 Sone, Will of Susan Mingay, 1642).

[50] In fact there were 8 volumes.

[44.4] Cornelius a Lapide: *Commentaria in Acta Apostolorum*. Parisiis, 1631.

[44.5] Cornelius a Lapide: *Commentaria in Epistolas Canonicas*. Parisiis, 1631.

[44.6] Cornelius a Lapide: *Commentaria in Apocalypsin S. Iohannis Apostoli*. Parisiis, 1631.

[44.7] Cornelius a Lapide: *In omnes Divi Pauli Epistolas commentaria*. Parisiis, 1631.

[44.8] Cornelius a Lapide: *Commentaria in quatuor prophetas maiores*. Parisiis, 1622.

Gesneri Bibliothecam.

[44.9] Konrad Gesner: *Bibliotheca universalis*. Tiguri: apud Christophorum Froschouerum, 1545.

[45] **A: D: 1634: Aug: 5: Johannes Freeman**[51] D.D.
Mappam sive Chartam terrae in Canaan a Magistro Johanne
More descriptam.[52]
[*Map or chart of the land of Canaan drawn by Master John More*]

[46] **Anno Dm. 1634: Prudentia Blosse** vidua. Relicta Thomae Blosse Aldermannij D.D.
Biblia Regis Hispania edita opera Ariae Montanij: 8: vol.

[46.1] *Biblia Sacra Hebraice, Chaldaice, Graece, & Latine*. Antuerpiae: Christoph Plantinus, 1569–72.

[47] **Johannes Chappell**[53] S. Theolog. Bach. Ecclesiae S. Andreae Pastor. D.D.
Biblia Hebraica et Chaldaica cum Masorals – magna
et parua, multis Rabbinorum Commentarijs, 2: vol.

[47.1] *Biblia sacra Hebraica & Chaldaica cum Masora…magna et parva, ac selectissimis Hebraeorum interpretum commentariis…studio fide et labore indefesso Johannis Buxtorfi*. Basileae: Sumptibus & typis Ludovici König, 1620.

Kirkeri Concordantias, Hebr. Graec. 2: vol.

[47.2] Conrad Kircher: *Concordantiae Veteris Testamenti Graecae: ebraeis vocibus respondentes*. Francofurti: apud Claudium Marnium & Iohannis Aubrii, 1607.

[48] **Josephus Payne** Aldermanus D.D.

[51] John Freeman, churchwarden of St Gregory's, was cited in the Norwich Consistory Court for having erected 'divers piles…of Images, pictures or portreytures, which had an Image mounted above all the rest…to be called and known to be the Image of our Saviour Christ and the others to be the Image of the Saynts or Apostles' (Reynolds, p. 148).

[52] John More (c1542–1592), the 'apostle of Norwich', was minister of St Andrew's from 1573 until his death. Thomas Fuller recorded that More made an 'excellent' map of Canaan, possibly based on Humfrey Cole's double-page engraved map of Canaan that appeared in the Bishop's Bible or the earlier map by Abraham Ortelius in his *Theatrum orbis terrarium*, published in 1570.

[53] In 1633 William Bridge accused Chappell of Arminianism for preaching that 'God doth truly intend and will the salvation of all men and that Christ died for all men according to the holy scriptures conditionally that they repent, believe and obey the terms of the Gospel' (Reynolds, p. 177).

Ravanelli Bibliothecam

[48.1] Petrus Ravanellus: *Bibliotheca sacra, seu Thesaurus Scripturae Canonicae.*
Genevae: Sumptibus Petri Chouet, 1650.

Item xx librae ad emendos libros [*£20 for buying books*]

[49] **Johannes Thornback**[54] Ecclesiae Sancti Andreae Pastor D.D.

Newmans Concordance

[49.1] Samuel Newman: *A large and complete concordance to the Bible in English,
according to the last translation.* London: printed for Thomas Downes and
James Young 1643.[55]

*[50]***Guilielmus Stinettus** S: Theologiae B. Ecclesiae Sancti Johannis de
Madermarket Rector D.D. [*Bachelor of Sacred Theology. Rector of St John
Maddermarket*]

Bibliothecam Bodliana.

[50.1] Thomas James: *Catalogus universalis librorum in bibliotheca Bodleiana.*
Oxoniae: Excudebant Ioannes Litchfield & Iacobus Short, 1620.

Institutiones Justiniani

[50.2] Possibly, Justinian: *A. Vinnii…in quatuor libros Institutionum Imperialium
commentarius.* Amstelaedami: Apud L. & D. Elzevinos, 1659.

Aromatum Historiam

[50.3] Carolus Clusius: *Caroli Clusii Atreb. Aliquot notae in Garciae Aromatum
historiam.* Antuerpiae: Ex officina Christophori Plantini, 1582.

Fosteri Lexicon

[50.4] Johann Forster: *Dictionarium hebraicum novum.* Basileae: Froben, 1564.

Ainsworths workes

[50.5] Henry Ainsworth: *Annotations upon the five bookes of Moses, the booke of
Psalmes, and the Song of Songs, or Canticles.* London: Printed for John
Bellamie, 1627.

Summa Sylvestrina

[50.6] Silvestro Mazzolini: *Sylvestrinae summae: quae summa summarum merito
nuncupator.* Lugdunum, 1593.

Vueckeri Antidotarium

[50.7] Johann Jacob Wecker: *Antidotarium speciale…ex optimorum authorum tam
veterum quam recentiorum scriptis fideliter congestum, methodiceque digestum.* Basileae:
per Eusebium Episcopium, 1574.

[51] **Johannes Collinges:** [56] S: Theolog: Dr. D.D.

Hugonis Cardinalis opera in 6 volumes folio

[51.1] *Prima (-Sexta) pars huius operis: continens textum biblie cum postilla domini*

---

[54] John Thornback succeeded Henry Hall, a member of the Assembly of Divines, as
minister of St Andrew's. A contributor to *Vox populi, or the peoples cry against the clergy* (1646), he
threatened to tread out his Independent opponents, cut them to pieces and turn their houses
into latrines. He died in March 1647.

[55] The surviving copy was donated by Thomas Nelson in 1707.

[56] For information on the donors after 1657 see the footnotes to the minutes above.

Hugonis Cardinalis. Basileae: Johann Froben 1504.
Item in money 20s. Jan 24 1658
[52] **Johannes Whitefoot** Rector de Heigham juxta Norwicum D.D.
[*Rector of Heigham near Norwich*]
Bacon, Jo[hannes], in Sententias 2 vol fol.
[52.1] John Baconsthorpe: *Doctoris resoluti Io. Bachonis Angl. Carmelitatae theology celeberrimi, & canonistae praccipuli. Quaestiones in quatuor libros Sententiarum, & Quodlibetales...*Cremonae, 1618.
Pugio fidei Raymundi Martinin fol:
[52.2] Ramon Marti: *Adversus Mauros, et Judaeos.* Parisiis: apud Mathurinum Henault, 1651.
His 2 sermons
[52.3] John Whitefoot: *[Israel Anchithanes]: death's alarum: or, the presage of approaching death.* London: printed by W. Godbid, 1656.[57]
Sayrj Casus Conscientiae, Fol:
[52.4] Gregory Sayer: *Clavis regia sacerdotum, casuum conscientiae sive theologiae moralis thesauri locos omnes aperiens.* Monasterii Westfaliae: Sumptibus Michaelis Dalii & Bernardi Raesfelt, 1628.
[53] **Anno Domini 1659:** Decemb: 12: **Thomasina Brooke:** Vidua et relicta Gulielmi Brooke Generosi D.D. [*Widow and relict of William Brooke gentleman*]
Calvini Lexicon Juridicum 1 vol. fol.
[53.1] John Calvin: *Lexicon juridicum juris Caesarei simul, et canonici: feudalis item, civilis, criminalis, theoretici, ac practici*
Bonacina
[53.2] Martino Bonacina: *Opera omnia.* Lutetiae Parisiorum: Sumptibus Petri Billaine, 1633.
Azorii Institutiones Morales 3 vol fol.
[53.3] Johannes Azorius: *Institutiones morales: in quibus universae quaestiones ad conscientiam recte.* Coloniae Agrippinae, 1613.
Cameronis Opera 1 vol. fol.
[53.4] John Cameron: *Ta Sozomena, sive opera partim ab auctore ipso edita, partim post eius obitum vulgata, partim nusquam hactenus publicata.* Genevae: P. Chouët, 1658.
Arminii Opera 1 vol. 4to.
[53.5] Jacobus Arminius: *Iacobi Arminii Veteraquinatis Bataui, ss. theologicae doctoris eximij, opera theologica, nunc denuo conjunctim recusa.* Prostant Francofurti: apud Wolfgangum Hoffmannum, 1635.
Tolletti Casus conscientiae 1 vol. 8ctavo
[53.6] Francisco de Toledo: *Francisci Toleti Societatis Iesu, S.R.E. Presb. Card. Instructio sacerdotum in libros octo distincta.* Rothomagi: Apud Manassem de Preaulx, 1619.

[57] Another edition was printed in 1657.

Navarri Enchyridion
[53.7] Martin de Azpilcueta: *Enchiridion, sive manuale
confessariorum, et poenitentium.*
Cornelium â Lapide in Evangelium 1 vol. fol.
[53.8] Cornelius a Lapide: *Commentaria in IV Evangelia.* Lugduni: Sumptibus
Iacobi & Petri Prost, 1638.
Filucii Qu. Moralis
[53.9] Vincentius Filliucius: *Moralium quaestionum de Christianis officiis et
casibus conscientiae.* Coloniae Agrippinae: apud Antonium & Arnoldum
Hieratos, 1629.
Schmidii Concordantiam
[53.10] Erasmus Schmid: *Novi Testamenti Iesu Christi
Graeci, hoc est, originalis linguae tameion aliis
concordantiae.* Wittebergae: impensis haeredum C. Bergeri, 1638.
Suidas in 2 vol. fol.
[53.11] Suda: *Suidas, cuius integram Latinam interpretationem, & perpetuam Graeci
textus emendationem Aemilius Portus.* Coloniae Allobrogum: Apud Petrum &
Iacobum Chouët, 1619.
Josephi Historiam Grae. Col. Lat.
[53.12] Flavius Josephus: *Flavii Iosephi Opera.* Genevae: apud Iacobum
Crispinum, 1634.
Sanctii Opera 9 vol. 7 in fol. 2 in 4to
[53.13] Gaspar Sanctius: *Gasparis Sanct…in duodecim prophetas minores &
Baruch commentarij cum paraphrasi.* Lugduni, 1621.
[53.14] Ibid: *In Ezechielem & Danielem prophetas commentarij cum paraphrasi.*
Lugduni, 1619.
[53.15] Ibid: *In Ieremiam prophetam commentarij cum paraphrasi.* Lugduni, 1618.
[53.16] Ibid: *In Isaiam prophetam commentarij cum paraphrasi.* Lugduni, 1615.
[53.17] Ibid: *In libros Ruth, Esdrae, Nehemiae, Tobiae, Iudith, Esther,
Machabaeorum commentarij.* Lugduni, 1627.
[53.18] Ibid: *In Canticum canticorum commentarij, cum expositione Psalmi LXVII.*
Lugduni, 1616.
[53.19] Ibid: *In librum Iob commentarij cum paraphrase.* Lugduni, 1625.
*Commentarii in Actus Apostolorum…Accessit disputatio de Sancti Jacobi et Pauli
Apostolorum in Hispaniam adventu.* Lugduni, 1616.
[53.20] Ibid: *In quatuor libros Regum, & duos Paralipomenon, commentarij.*
Lugduni, 1623.
Paraei Opera omnia 2 vol. fol.
[53.21] David Pareus: *D. Davidis Parei S. Litterarum olim in antiquissima
Academia Archipalatina Heidelbergensi Doctoris & professoris primarij Operum theo-
logicorum exegeticorum.* Francofurti: Apud viduam Ionae Rosae, 1647.
Rivetti Opera 3 vol. fol.
[53.22] André Rivet: *Andrae Riveti operum theologicorum quae Latine edidit.*

Roterodami: ex officina typographica Arnoldi Leers, 1651–60.
[54] **Thomas Allen:** D.D.
His Chaine of Scripture Chronologie.
[54.1] Thomas Allen: *A chain of scripture chronology, from the creation of the world to the death of Jesus Christ.* London: printed by Thomas Roycroft, 1659.
[55] **Civitas Norwici:** D.D.
Biblia Polyglotta 6 vol. fol.
[55.1] Biblia sacra polyglotta, complectentia textus originales, Hebraicum, cum Pentateucho Samaritano, Chaldaicum, Graecum, edidit Brianus Waltonus.
[56] **Anno: D: 1661: Josephus Payne** Miles nuper huius Civitatis Maior D.D. *[late mayor of this city]*
Ravanelli Bibliothecam.
[56.1] Petrus Ravanellus: *Petri Rauanelli Vticensis Occitani Bibliotheca sacra, seu, Thesaurus scripturae canonicae amplissimus.* Geneuae: Sumptibus Petri Chouet, 1650.
Anno 1634 12 Sep. Presentis Anni D.D.
Critica Sacra. Edit Cornelij Bee. 9 vol. fol.
[56.2] Critici sacri: sive Doctissimorum vivorum in ss. Biblia annotationes, & tractatus. Opus summa cura recognitum, & in novem tomos divisum. Londini: Excudebat Jacobus Flesher, Prostant apud Cornelium Bee…1660.
Gerrardi Loci Communes 4 vol. fol.
[56.3] Johann Gerhard: *Loci theologici, cum pro adstruenda veritate, tum pro destruenda quorumvis contradicentium falsitate, per theses nervose, solide & copiose explicati.* Francofurti & Hamburgi: Sumptibus Zachariae Hertelii, 1657.
Eiusdem Supplementum Harm. Evang. 1 vol. fol.
[56.4] Johann Gerhard: *Harmoniae Euangelistarum Chemnitio-Lyserianae continuatio a Ioh. Gerhardo SS.* Roterodami: Ex bibliopolio Arnoldi Leers, 1646.
Eiusdem Harmonia Passionis 1 vol. fol.
[56.5] Johann Gerhard: *In harmoniam historiae euangelicae de passione, crucifixione, morte et sepultura Christi saluatoris nostri, ex quatuor euangelistis contextam.* Francofurti: Sumptibus Ioannis Iacobi Porsij, 1622.
[57] **Augustinus Scottowe:** Mercator D.D.
Basilii Opera Graec. Col. Lat. 2 vol. fol.
[57.1] Saint Basil: *Opera omnia.* Parisiis: Apud Michaelem Sonnium, 1618.
Oecumenii Opera Graec col. Lat. 2 vol. fol.
[57.2] Oecumenius: *Commentaria in Novi Testamenti tractatus.* Lutetiae Parisiorum: sumptibus Claudii Sonnii, 1631.
Theophilacti Opera Graec. Col. Lat. 2 vol. fol.
[57.3] Possibly *Commentarii in quatuor Euangelia.*
Philonis Judaei Opera 1 vol. fol.
[57.4] Philo Judaeus: *Omnia quae extant opera.* Lutetiae Parisiorum: cum Regis privilegio, 1640.
[58] **Johannes Smyth:** Rector Ecclesiae Sancti Michaelis in Coslania

D.D. [*Rector of the church of St Michael in Coslany*]
Doctor Fulke upon the Rhemish Testament 1 vol. fol.
[58.1] William Fulke: *The text of the New Testament translated out of the vulgar Latine by the Papists of the traitorous Seminarie at Rhemes. With arguments...Whereunto is added the translation...used in the Church of England. With a confutation of all such arguments...as conteine manifest impietie.* London: Printed by Augustine Mathewes, 1633.
[59] **Anno: D: 1662: Franciscus Norris:** Ciuis et Aldermannus D.D.
Opera omnia Tostati 14 vol. fol.
[59.1] Alphonsus Tostatus: *Commentaria in Genesim.* Venetiis, 1615.
[59.2] Alphonsus Tostatus: *Commentaria in Primam Partem Exodi.* Venetiis, 1615.
[59.3] Alphonsus Tostatus: *Commentaria in Leviticum.* Venetiis, 1615.
[59.4] Alphonsus Tostatus: *Commentaria in Primam Partem Nvmerorvm.* Venetiis, 1615.
[59.5] Alphonsus Tostatus: *Commentaria in Primam Partem Iosve.* Venetiis, 1615.
[59.6] Alphonsus Tostatus: *Commentaria in Primum Partem 1 Regvm.* Venetiis, 1615.
[59.7] Alphonsus Tostatus: *Commentaria in Librum Tertivm Regvm.* Venetiis, 1615.
[59.8] Alphonsus Tostatus: *Commentaria in Primam Partem Matthaei.* Venetiis, 1615.
[59.9] Alphonsus Tostatus: *Commentaria in Tertiam Partem Matthaei.* Venetiis, 1615.
[59.10] Alphonsus Tostatus: *Commentaria in Quintam Partem Matthaei.* Venetiis, 1615.
[59.11] Alphonsus Tostatus: *Commentaria in Septimam Partem Matthaei.* Venetiis, 1615.
[59.12] Alphonsus Tostatus: *Index Rervm Omnivm Praecipvarvm, quae in commentariis ac operibus omnibus Alphonsi Tostati.* Venetiis, 1615.
[59.13] Alphonsus Tostatus: *Index Qvaestionvm ex omnibus operibus Alphonsi Tostati.* Venetiis, 1615.
[60] **Thomas Morley:** curatus Sancti Petri de Hungate D.D. [*curate of St Peter Hungate*]
Ludolphum de vita Christi 1 vol folio.
[60.1] Ludolphus of Saxony: *Vita Iesu Christi e quatuor Evangeliis et scriptoribus orthodoxis concinnato.* Antwerpiae: apud Ioannem Keerbergium, 1618.
Musculum in Sanctum Johannem 1 volume folio
[60.2] Wolfgang Musculus: *Commentarii in Evangelium Ioannis.* Basileae: ex officina Ioannis Hervagii, 1564. Or possibly *Commentariorum in Evangelistam*

Ioannem. Basileae: Apud Bartholomaeum Westhemerum: Apud [per] Ioannem Hervagium, 1545.

[61] **Anno: D: 1664:** Junii 13 **Johannes Mann:** Ciuis et Aldermannus D.D.

Vasquez in Thomam 7 vol. fol.

[61.1] Gabriel Vasquez: *Opera omnia.* Antuerpiae: apud Petrum & Ioannem Belleros, 1621.

Buxtorfii Lexicon Rabinneum 1 vol. fol.

[61.2] Johann Buxtorf: *Johannis Buxtorfi Lexicon Hebraicum et Chaldaicum.* Basileae: Sumptibus Ludovici König, 1631.

Chrysostomi Opera Edit. Saviliana 8 vol. fol.

[61.3] Saint John Chrysostom: *Tou en Hagiois Patros hemon Ioannou Archiepiskopou Konstantinoupoleos tou Chrysostomou ton heuriskomenon.* Etonae: in Collegio Regali, excudebat Ioannes Norton, 1613.

Gomarum in 3 vol. fol.

[61.4] Franciscus Gomarus: *Francisci Gomari Brigensis viri clariss. Opera theologica omnia.* Amstelodami: Ex officina Joannis Janssonii, 1644.

Sillburgii Etymologi Magn. 1 vol. fol.

[61.5] Friedrich Sylburg: *Etymologicon magnum: seu magnum grammatica penu.* [Heidelberg]: E typographeio Hieronymi Commelini, 1594.

Sigonii Opera 5 vol. fol.

[61.6] Carolus Sigonius: *Historiarum de regno Italiae libri viginti.* Francofurti, 1591.

[61.7] Ibid.: *Historiae de rebus Bononiensibus libri VIII.* Francofurti, 1604.

[61.8] Ibid.: *Fasti consulares, ac triumphi acti a Romulo rege usque ad Ti. Caesarem.* Basileae, 1559.

[61.9] Ibid.: *Historiam de Occidentali imperio libri XX.* Francofurti, 1593.

[61.10] Ibid.: *De antiquo iure civium Romanorum, Italiae, provinciarum, ac Romanae iurisprudentiae iudicis, libri XI.* Francofurti, 1593.

Gualtheri Comment 12 vol. fol.

[61.11] Rudolph Gualther: *In Acta Apostolorum per divum Lucam descripta, homiliae CLXXV.* Tiguri, 1562.

[61.12] Ibid.: *In Evangelium Iesu Christi secundum Marcum homiliae CXXXIX.* Tiguri, 1570.

[61.13] Ibid.: *In Prophetas duodecim, quos vocant minores Rodolphi Gualtheri Tigurini homiliae.* Tiguri: Excudebat Chri. Froschouerus, 1572.

[61.14] Ibid.: *In D. Pauli apostoli Epistolam ad Romanos homiliae.* Tiguri…

[61.15] Ibid.: *In Priorem D. Pauli apostoli ad Corinthios epistolam homiliae XVX.* Tiguri…

[61.16] Ibid.: *In Evangelium Iesu Christi secundum Lucam homiliae CCXV.* Tiguri, 1573.

[61.17] Ibid.: *In D. Pauli apostoli Epistolam ad Galatas homiliae LXI.* Tiguri…..

[61.18] Ibid.: *In Isaiam prophetam homiliae CCCXXVII.* Tiguri, 1583.

[61.19] Ibid.: *Homiliarum in Evangelium Iesu Christi secundium Matthaeum.*
Tiguri, 1583.

[61.20]. Ibid.: *Homiliarum in Evangelia Dominicalia a vigilia Nativitatis Domini*
Nostri Iesu Christi, usque ad Festum Paschatis. Lugduni Batavorum, 1583.
Funcii Chronologiam 1 vol. fol.

[61.21] Johann Funck: *Chronologia: Hoc est, omnium temporum et annorum ab*
initio mundi. Witebergae: typis Zachariae Lehmanni, 1601.

[62] **Anno. Dom. 1665 Samuel Fromentell** Civis D.D.
An old Concordance in Edward 6ᵗʰ Reigne in one Vol. Fol.

[62.1] John Marbeck: *A concordance, that is to saie, a worke where in by the ordre*
of the letters of the A.B.C. ye maie redely finde any worde conteigned in the whole Bible.
London: R. Grafton, 1550.

[63] **Anno. Dom. 1666. Joshua Meene** olim Curat Ecclesiae Sancti Pet
per Montergate D.D. [*former curate of the church of St Peter Permountergate*]
Catenam Graecorum Patrum in Jobum.

[63.1] *Catena Graecorum patrum in beatum Iob.* Londini: Ex typographio regio,
1637.
Collect Niceta 1 vol. Fol.

[63.2] Nicetas of Heracleia: *Catena Graecorum patrum in beatum Iob.* Londini:
Ex typographio regio, 1637.
Gregorii de Valentia Vol. 1 Fol

[63.3] Gregorius de Valentia: *De rebus fidei hoc tempore controversis libri, qui*
extant omnes, cum nonnullis aliis nondum antea editis. Lutetia Parisiorum: e
typographia Rolini Theoderici & Petri Cheualerii, 1610.
Eusebii Eccle. Historiam 1 Vol. Fol.

63.4] Eusebius: *Autores historiae ecclesiasticae.* Basileae: In officina
Frobeniana, 1535.

[64] **Anno Dom. 1666 Thomas Browne** [58] Med. Professor D.
Dedicavit
Justii Lipsii Opera 8to vol 9 4to
[64.1] Justus Lipsius: *Epistolarvm Selectarvm Centvria Singularis.*
Antverpiae: Ex officina Plantiniana, 1613.

[64.2] Justus Lipsius: *De Crvce libri tres.* Antverpiae:
Ex officina Plantiniana, 1606.

[64.3] Justus Lipsius: *De Constantia Libri Dvo.* Antverpiae:
Ex officina Plantiniana, 1615.

[64.4] Justus Lipsius: *Epistolarvm selectarvm centvria*
prima Miscellanea. Antverpiae: Ex officina Plantiniana, 1614.

---

[58] Sir Thomas Browne settled in Norwich in 1636 and spent the rest of his life in the city.
He knew several members of the Library very well. He sat on a committee that included Dr
John Collinges, George Cock, Robert Harmer and John Whitefoot which considered the suit-
ability of Mark Lewis' scheme to establish a school in rivalry with the Grammar School (H.W.
Saunders, *A History of the Norwich Grammar School*, Norwich, 1932, p. 360).

[64.5] Justus Lipsius: *Admiranda, sive De Magnitvdine Romana*. Antverpiae: Ex officina Plantiniana, 1617.

[64.6] Justus Lipsius: *De Militia Romana*. Antverpiae: Ex officina Plantiniana, 1614.

[64.7] Justus Lipsius: *V.C. opera omnia*. Antverpiae: ex officina Plantiniana, 1614.

[64.8] Justus Lipsius: *Politicorum sive Civilis Doctrinae*. Antverpiae: Ex officina Plantiniana, 1610.

Opera sua, viz Religio medici, Vulgar Errors, &c

[64.9] Sir Thomas Browne: *Religio medici: with annotations never before published, upon all the obscure passages therein: also, observations by Sir Kenelm Digby, now newly added*. London: printed by Tho. Milbourn, 1659.

[64.10] Ibid.: *Pseudodoxia Epidemica*. London: J.R. for Nath Elkins, 1672.

*[65]***Anno Dom. 1668. Guilielmus Oliver** Bibliopola [*bookseller*] D.D. Pererii Commentar in Gen. 1 vol. Fol.

[65.1] Benedictus Pererius: *Commentariorum et disputationum in Genesim*. Coloniae Agrippinae: ex officina Anthonij Hierati, 1606.

1673 Senecae Opera Gruteri, Jureti & aliorum notis Folio Parisijs. Anno Dom. 1602.

[65.2] Lucius Annaeus Seneca: *Philosophi scripta quae extant: hac postrema editione doctissimorum virorum, praecipuevero Iani Gruteri et Fr. Iureti notis, et observationibus aucta.*
Parisiis: apud Marcum Orry, 1602.

[66] 1673 **Georgius Cock** Sancti Petri de Mancroft in civitate Norvic.Curatus D.D. [*Curate of St Peter Mancroft in the city of Norwich*] Suarezii Opera omnia in 18 vol. Fol.

[66.1] Francisco Suarez: *Opera omnia*. Mogvntiae: Sumptibus Hermanni Mylij Birckmanni Excudebat Balthasar Lippius, 1621.

[66.2] Francisco Suarez: *Commentariorvm ac Dispvtationvm in Primam Partem Divi Thomae. Pars II*. Mogvntiae: Sumptibus Hermanni Mylij Birckmanni Excudebat Balthasar Lippius, 1621.

[66.3] Francisco Suarez: *Commentariorvm ac Dispvtationvm in Primam Partem Divi Thomae. Pars II*. Mogvntiae: Sumptibus Hermanni Mylij Birckmanni Excudebat Balthasar Lippius, 1622.

[66.4] Francisco Suarez: *Tractatus de Legibus, ac Deo Legislatore*. Mogvntiae: Sumptibus Hermanni Mylij Birckmanni Excudebat Balthasar Lippius, 1619.

[66.5] Francisco Suarez: *De Divina Gratia Pars Prima*. Mogvntia: Sumptibus Hermanni Mylij Birckmanni Excudebat Balthasar Lippius, 1620.

[66.6] Francisco Suarez: *Opus de Triplici Virtvte Theologica*. Parisiis: Typis Edmundi Martini, 1621.

[66.7] Francisco Suarez: *De Virtvte et Statv Religionis.*
Tomis Tertivs. Mogvntiae: Sumptibus Hermanni Mylii,
Birckman. Excudebat Hermannus Meresius, 1625.
[66.8] Francisco Suarez: *De Virtvte et Statv Religionis.*
Tomus II. Mogvntiae: Sumptibus Hermanni Mylii, Birckman.
Excudebat Hermannus Meresius, 1623.
[66.9] Francisco Suarez: *De Virtvte et Statv Religionis.*
Quo Qvid Contineatvr, Index proximus indicabit.
Mogvntiae: Sumptibis Hermanni Mylii, Birckman.
Excudebat Hermannus Meresius, 1624.
[66.10] Francisco Suarez: *Commentariorvm ac Dispvtationvm*
in Tertiam Partem Divi Thomae. Tomus Secvndvs.
Mogvntiae: Sumptibus Hermanni Mylii Birckman.
Excudebat Hermannus Meresius, 1616.
[66.11] Francisco Suarez: *Commentariorvm ac Dispvtationvm*
in Tertivm Partem Divi Thomae. Tomvs Tertivs.
Mogvntiae: Sumptibus Hermanni Mylii Birckman.
Excudebat Hermannus Meresius, 1619.
[66.12] Francisco Suarez: *Commentariorvm ac Dispvtationvm*
in Tertivm Partem Divi Thomae. Tomvs Qvartvs.
Mogvntiae: Ex officina Typographica Balthasari Lippij,
sumptibus Hermanni Mylii, 1616.
[66.13] Francisco Suarez: *Tractatvs Quinqve, ad primam*
secvndae D. Thomae. Mogvntiae: Sumptibus Hermanni
Mylii Birckmanni, Excudebat Hermannus Meresius, 1629.
[66.14] Francisco Suarez: *Dispvtationvm De Censvris*
in Commvni Excommvnicatione, suspensione, & Interdicto,
itemque de Irregularitate. Tomvs Quintvs. Mogvntiae:
Ex officina Typographica Balthasari Lippij, 1617.
[66.15] Francisco Suarez: *Commentariorvm ad Dispvtationvm,*
in Tertiam Partem Divi Thomae. Tomi Quinqve.
Mogvntiae: Ex officina Typographica Balthasari Lippij, 1617.
[66.16] Francisco Suarez: *Defensio Fidei Catholicae*
et Apostolicae Adversvs Anglicanae Sectae Errores.
Mogvntiae: Ex officina Typographica Balthasari Lippij, 1619.
[66.17] Francisco Suarez: *Operis De Religione Tomvs Qvartvs,*
et Vltimvs. Lugduni: Sumptibus Iacobi Cardon & Petri Cauellat, 1625.
[66.18] Francisco Suarez: *Metaphysicarvm Dispvtationvm.*
Coloniae: Excudebat Franciscus Heluidius, 1614.
[67] An. Dom. 1671 **Johannes Barnham Civis** Bibliothecis Norvicensis
[*Member of Norwich Library*]
Matthaei Poli Synops. Criticorum volumen Primum. Fol.
[67.1] Matthew Poole: *Synopsis criticorum aliorumque sacrae scripturae inter-*

pretum. Londini: Typis J. Flesher, 1669.

[67.2] Anno Dom. 1672.Volumen Secundum Folio.

[67.3] Anno Domini 1673.Volumen Tertium

[67.4] 1674.Volumen Quartum.

[67.5] 1676.Volumen Quintum.

[68] **Anno. Dom: 1673: Anthony Norris** Mercator Norvicensis D.D.
Dr. Jackson's Works in 3 volumes London 1673.

[68.1] Thomas Jackson: *The works of the reverend and learned divine Thomas Jackson.* London: printed by Andrew Clark, 1673.

[69] **Johannes Ellsworth Medicinus** [*doctor*] D.D Dedicat.

Fran. Georgii Veneti problemata in S S Scripturam

[69.1] Francesco Giorgio: *Francisci Georgii Veneti...in scripturam sacram problemata.*

Eiusdem Harmonia Mundi

[69.2] Francesco Giorgio: *Francisci Georgii Veneti Minoritanae familiae, De harmonia mundi totius cantica tria. Cum indice eorum, quae inter legendum adnotatu digna visa fuere, nunc recens addito.* Parisiis: Apud Andream Berthelin, 1546.

[70] **Thomas Tenison S S TB**

Dat Dedicat Bibliothec Norvic: Libros sic vocatos viz.

Codinus de officiia et officialibus Ecclesiae et Aulae Constantin op. Fol.
Parisiiae 1625

[70.1] George Codinus: *De officiis et officialibus magnae Ecclesiae, et Aulae Constantinopolitanae.* Parisiis: Apud Sebastianum Cramoisy, 1625.

Herbert de Relig. Gentilium 4to

[70.2] Edward Herbert: *De religione Gentilium, errorumque apud eos causis.*
Amstelaedami: typis Blaeviorum, 1663.

Heylens Historia Quinquaris 4to

[70.3] Peter Heylyn: *Historia quinqu-articularis: or, A declaration of the judgement of the Western Churches, and more particularly of the Church of England, in the five controverted points, reproached in these last times by the name of Arminianism.*
London: printed by E.C. for Thomas Johnson at the Key in St Paul's
Church-yard, 1660.

Usserii Cronologia Sacra 4to

[70.4] James Ussher: *Chronologia sacra sive Chronologia annorum regum Israelis & Judae, ad calculum redacta et illustrata per Jacobum Usserium Armachanum.*
Oxoniae: typis Guil. Hall...impensis Rich. Davis, Edw. & Jo. Forrest,
1660.

Racovian Catechismua 8vo

[70. 5] Matthias Flacius: *Ecclesiastica Historia, integram ecclesiae Christi ideam quantum ad locum.* Basiliae: per Ioannem Oporinum, [1562] -74.

[71] / 1675 / **Nathaniel Cock Mercator** Londinensis Bibliothec.
Norvic Libros D.D. 33 qui sic se habent

Fratres Poloni 6 vol. Fol. 1656

[71.1] *Bibliotheca fratrum polonorum qui unitarii appellantur*
continens opera omnia, Johannis Crellii Francii, Ludovici
Wolsogenii, Fausti Socini senensis & exegetica Jonae Schlichtingii
a Bucowiec. Irenopoli, 1656.
Medes works 2 Vol
[71.2] Joseph Mede: *The works of the pious and profoundly learned Joseph Mede,*
B.D. London: printed by Roger Norton, for Richard Royston, 1677.
Sancti Cyrilli et Synesuu Opera Graecol in 1 vol. Fol. Paris 1631
[71.3] Saint Cyril: *Opera.* Lutetiae Parisiorum: Apud Hieronymum
Drouart, 1631.[59]
Sancti Athanasii Opera Graecol 2 Vol. Fol. 1627
[71.4] Saint Athanasius: *Opera quae reperiuntur omnia.* Parisiis: Sumptibus
Michaelis Sonnii, Claudii Morelli, & Sebastiani Cramoisy, 1627.
Estius in Epist omnes Fol. Paris 1623
[71.5] Willem Hesselszoon van Est: *In omnes Beati Pauli et aliorum Apostolorum*
epistolas commentaria. Parisiis: Apud Iacobum Quesnel, 1623.
History of the Council of Trent Fol.
[71.6] Servita Paolo: *The history of the Council of Trent...written in Italian by*
Pietro Soave Polano, and faithfully translated...by Sr Nathanael Brent, Knight.
London: Printed by J. Macock for Samuel Mearne, 1676.
Cypriani Opera per Rigalt 1648
[71.7] Saint Cyprian: *Sancti Caecilii Cypriani opera: Nicolai Rigalti observation-*
ibus ad veterum exemplarium fidem recognita et illustrata. Lutetiae Parisiorum:
Apud viduam Mathurini du Puis via Iacobaea, 1649.
Eusebii &c Histor. Ecclesiast Graecol per Christopher Sonum 1612
[71.8] John Christopherson: *Historiae ecclesiasticae scriptores*
Graeci nempe Eusebij. Coloniae Allobrogum: excudebat Petrus
de la Rouiere, 1612.
Espencaei Opera Fol. Paris. 1619.
[71.9] Claude D'Espence: *Opera omnia quae superstes adhuc edidit.* Lutetiae
Parisiorum: Sumptibus Claudi Morelli, 1619.
Maldonat in pap. Lib. Fol
[71.10] Juan de Maldonado: *Ioannis Maldonati Sapharensis, e Societatis Iesu,*
Commentarii in praecipuos Sacrae Scripturae libros Veteris Testamenti. Parisiis:
Sumptibus Sebastiani Cramoisy, 1643.
Justinian in Omnes Epistolas 3 vol. Fol. Lugduni 1621
[71.11] Benedetto Giustiniani: *Benedicti Iustiniani Genuensis...in omnes b. Pauli*
apost. Epistolas explanationum. Lugduni: Sumptibus Horatij Cardon,
1612–13.
[71.12] Benedetto Giustiniani: *Benedicti Iustiniani Genuensis Societatis Iesu In*

---

[59] Half-title reads: *Sancti Patris nostri Cyrilli Hierosolymitani, et Synesii Cyrenensis Episcoporum opera*
Graec. Lat.

omnes Catholicas Epistolas explanationes. Lugduni: Sumptibus Iacobi Cardon et Petri Cauellat, 1621.

Hesychii Lexicon 1668

[71.13] Hesychius of Alexandria: *Hesychii Lexicon cum variis doctorum virorum notis vel editis antehac vel ineditis.* Lugduni Batavorum et Roterod: Ex officina Hackiana, 1668.

Sixti Senensis Bibliothec Sancta 4to

[71.14] Sisto da Siena: *Bibliotheca sancta a F. Sixto Senensi ordinis praedicatorum.* Coloniae Agrippinae: Ex officina Choliniana, 1626.

Arnobius Lugd. Batav. 4to 1651

[71.15] Afer Arnobius: *Arnobii...adversus Gentes libri VII. Cum recensione viri celeberrimi & integris omnium commentariis.* Lugduni Batavorum: I. Maire, 1651.

Is. Casaub. Exercit de rebus Sacris 1615

[71.16] Isaac Casaubon: *Isaaci Casauboni De rebus sacris & ecclesiasticis exercitationes XVI.* Francofurti: Curantib. Ruland, typis Ioan. Bring, 1615.

Vossii Theses et Hist. Pelag. 2 Vol. 4to

[71.17] Gerardus Joannes Vossius: *Gerhardi Iohannis Vossii historiae de controversiis, quas Pelagius eiusque reliquiae moverunt.* Lugduni Batavorum: excudit Ioannes Patius, 1618.

[71.18] Ibid: *Gerardi Ioh. Vossii V. CL. Theses theologicae et historicae: de varijs doctrinae Christianae capitibus.* Bellositi Dobunorum: Excudebat W.T. impensis W.W., 1628.

Heylin on the Creed Fol.

[71.19] Peter Heylyn: *Theolgia veterum: or, The summe of Christian theologie, positive, polemical, and philological; contained in the Apostles Creed.* London: Printed by S. Simmons, for A.S., 1673.

Usserii Annales Fol. 2 vol. Lond.

[71.20] James Ussher: *Annales Veteris Testamenti, a prima mundi origine deducti.* Londini: Ex officina J. Flesher, & prostant apud L. Sadler, 1650.

John Reynolds praelect in lib. Apoc 2 vol. 4to

[71.21] John Rainolds: *Censura librorum apocryphorum Veteris Testamenti, adversum pontificios, imprimis Robertum Bellarminum.* In nobili Oppenheimio: sumtibus viduae Levini Hulsii & Henrici Laurentii, 1611.

Sancti Clementis Ep. Ad Corin Oxon 1633

[71.22] Pope Clement I: *Klementos pros Korinthious epistole prote Clementis ad Corinthios epistola prior.* Oxonii: excudebat Iohannes Lichfield Academiae Typographus, 1633.

Dr James treatise of the Corruption of the Script. Counc. & Fathers 4to

[71.23] Thomas James: *A treatise of the corrvptions of Scripture, councils, and fathers by the prelates, pastors, and pillars of the church of Rome, for the maintenance of popery and irreligion.* London: Printed by H.L. for M. Lownes, 1611.

[72] Anno Dom 1676 **Edwardus Episcopus** Norvicensis D.D. [*Edward bishop of Norwich*]
Leunclavii Ius Graeco-Latinum fol.
[72.1] Johannes Leunclavius: *Iuris Graeco-Romani tam canonici quam civilis tomi duo.* Francofurti: Impensis heredum Petri Fischeri, 1596.
Diogenem Laertium. Fol. Gr-Lat
[72.2] Laertius Diogenes: *Laertii Diogenis De vitis dogmatis et apopthegmatis eorum qui in philosophia claruerunt.* Londini: Typis Tho. Ratcliffe impensis Octaviani Pulleyn, 1664.
Virgilium Servio Donato &c
[72.3] Publius Vergilius Maro: *Pub. Vergilii Maronis Opera, quae quidem exstant, omnia: cum iustis et doctis in Bucolica, Georgica, & Aeneida.* Basileae: per Sebastianum Henricpetri, 1613.
Ferarii Lexicon Geograph. Fol.
[72.4] Philippus Ferrarius: *Lexicon geographicum: in quo universi orbis oppida, urbes, regiones, provinciae, regna, emporia, academiae, metropoles, fontes, flumina, & maria antiquis recentibusque nominibus appellata.* Londini: Ex officina Rogeri Danielis, 1657.
Scaligerum in Eusebii Chronicon. Fol.
[72.5] Eusebius: *Thesaurus temporum Eusebij…Chronicorum canonum omnimodae historiae libri duo, interprete Hieronymo…Eiusdem Iosephi Scaligeri notae & castigationes in Latinam Hieronymi interpretationem…*Amstelodami: Apud Joannem Janssonium, 1658.
Chamieri Panthratia Catholic 4 vol. Fol.
[72.6] Daniel Chamier: *Danielis Chamieri Delphinatis Panstratiae Catholicae, siue Controuersiarum de religione aduersus pontificios corpus.* Geneuae: Typis Rouerianis, 1626.
Pindarum Notis Quarto
[72.7] Pindar: *Pindari Olympia, Pythia, Nemea, Isthmia, Iohannes Benedictus…ad metri rationem, variorvm exemplarium fidem, scholiastae ad verisimiles coniecturas directionem, totum authorem innumeris mendis repurgauit.* Salmurii: Ex typis Petri Piededii, 1620.
Erasmi, Mori &c Epistolas. Fol.
[72.8] Desiderius Erasmus: *Epistolarum D. Erasmi Roterodami libri XXXI. Et P. Melancthonis libri IV. Quibus adjiciuntur Th. Mori & Lud. Viuis epistolae.* Londini: excudebant M. Flesher & R. Young, 1642.
Originem contra Celsum. Graeco-lat. Quarto.
[72.9] Origen: *Contra Celsum libri octo…Philocalia. Gulielmus Spencerus…utriusque operis versionem recognovit, et annotationes adjecit.* Cantabrigiae: excudebat Joan. Hayes, 1677.
Episcopii Opera. 2 vol. Fol.
[72.10] Simon Episcopius: *Opera theologica.* Amstelodami: ex typographeio Ioannis Blaeu, 1650–1665.

Spanhemii Dubia 2 vol.
[72.11] Friedrich Spanheim: *Dubia Evangelica in tres partes distributa.*
Genevae: sumptibus Petri Chouet, 1651–55.
Hensii Notas in Novum Testamentum Aristarcho. Fol.
[72.12] Daniel Heinsius: *Danielis Heinsii Sacrarum exercitationum ad Novum
Testamentum libri XX.* Lugduni Batavorum: ex officina Elseviriorum, 1639.
Volkelium de Vera resone. Quarto.
[72.13] Joannes Volkelius: *De vera religione libri quinque; quibus praefixus est
Johannis Crelli liber de Deo et ejus attributis.* Racoviae: Typis Sebastiani
Sternacii, 1630.
Laud against Fisher. Fol.
[72.14] William Laud: *A relation of the conference betweene William Lawd, then
Lrd. Bishop of St David's, now Arch-Bishop of Canterbury, and Mr Fisher the Jesuite,
by the command of King James of ever blessed memory.*
Pearson on the Creed. Fol.
[72.15] John Pearson: *An Exposition of the Creed.* London: J.F. for John
Williams, 1669.
Heylins Geography. Fol.
[72.16] Peter Heylyn: *Cosmographie in four books: containing the chorographie and
historie of the whole world, as all the principal kingdoms, provinces, seas, and isles
thereof.* London: Printed for Anne Seile, 1669.
Rawleigh's History of the World. Fol.
[72.17] Sir Walter Raleigh: *The historie of the world.*
Bakers Chronicle
[72.18] Sir Richard Baker: *A Chronicle of the Kings of England...unto the death
of King James.* London: Printed for George Sawbridge & Thomas Williams,
1674.
History of the Council of Trent
[72.19] Paolo Sarpi: *The history of the Council of Trent, written in Italian by
Pietro Soave Polano; and faithfully translated into English by Nathanael Brent.*
London: printed by J. Macock for S. Mearne 1676.
[73] Anno Dom. 1678 **Johannes Watson**, Vicarius apud Wroxham
D.D. [*Vicar at Wroxham*]
Barradii Commentaria. 2 vol. Fol.
[73.1] Sebastiao,Barrados: *R.P. Sebastiani Barradii, Olisiponsensis, e Societate
Iesu doctoris theologi, in Eborensi Academia quondam sacrarum literar. professoris,
Commentaria in concordiam et historiam Euangelium.* Moguntiae: Sumptibus
Arnoldi Mylii: Excudebat Balthasar Lippius, 1601.
[74] /1680/ **Samuel Clark** Rector of Rainham D.D.
Librum Cronicarum
[74.1] Hartmann Schedel: *Registrum hujus operas libri cronicarum cum figuris et
imagibus ab inicio mundi.* Nuremberge: A. Koberger, 1493.

[75] /1681/ **Franciscus Gardiner** Civis et Aldermannus D.D.
Bocharii Hierozoicon in fol.
[75.1] Samuel Bochart: *Hierozoicon: sive bipertitum opus de animalibus S.*
Scripturae. Francofurti ad Moenum: impensis Johannis Davidis Zunnen,
typis Balthas. Christophori Wustii, 1675.
Eiusdem Phaleg in 4to.
[75.2] Ibid.: *Geographia sacra: cujus pars prior Phaleg de dispersione gentium &*
terrarum divisione facta in aedificatione turris Babel. Francofurti ad Moenum, 1647.
[76] **Guillielmus Nurce** Clericus D.D.
Ciceronis Opera in 2 vol.
[76.1] Cicero: *Opera omnia quae extant, a Dionysio Lambino*
Monstroliensi ex codicibus manuscriptis emendata, & aucta.
Londini: per Ioh. Iackson & Edm. Carpenter, 1585.
[77] **Humphridus Prideaux** S. Theol. Professor et Prebendarius D.D.
Partem Maimonidis a se Latine reddita cum viginti solidis qua pecunia et
alia ex mulctis empti sunt [*part of Maimonides translated by him from the Latin*
together with twenty shillings, bought with this and with other money from fines][60]
[77.1] Moses Maimonides: *De jure pauperis et peregrine apud Judaeos.* Oxonii:
E Theatro Sheldoniano, 1679.
Swiceri Thesaurus Ecclesiasticis in 2 vol. fol.
[77.2] Johann Kaspar Suicer: *Thesaurus ecclesiasticus, e patribus graecis ordine*
alphabetico exhibens. Amstelaedami: Apud J.H. Wetstenium, 1682.
Hofmanni Lexicon in 2 Vol. fol.
[77.3] Johann Jacob Hofmann: *Lexicon universale: historico-geographico-chrono-*
logico-poetico-philologicum. Basileae: impensis Iohan. Herman. Widerhold,
typis Jacobi Bertschii & Joh. Rodolphi Genathii, 1677.
[78] /**1691**/ **Guillielmus Adamson** Rector St. Johannis in
Maddermarket
Corpus Iuris Civilis in 2 vol fol. cum notis Gothofredi 1650
[78.1] Justinian: *Corpus juris civilis cum notis integris repetitae quantum praelectionis*
Dionysii Gothofredi.
[79] /**1678**/ **Augustine Brigges** Civis et Aldermannus D.D. quinque
libras [*five pounds*]
[80] **Thomas Wisse** Civis et Aldermannus D.D. tres libras [*three pounds*]
  [81] **Bernardus Church** Civis et Aldermannus D.D. tres Libras
simul undecim Libras. Qua pecunia empti sunt Libri Sequentes [*Three*
pounds together with eleven pounds. With which moneys were bought the following
books]
Mathaei Paris Opera
[81.1] Matthew Paris: *Matthaei Paris monachi Albanensis Angli. Historia major.*
Londini: excudebat Richardus Hodgkinson, 1640.

---

[60] That is, 77.1 was donated by Prideaux and 77.2 and 77.3 were bought with 20s. given by
him and money from fines.

Aristotelis Opera Gr. Lat.

[81.2] Aristotle: *Opera omnia quae extant, Graece et Latine.* Lutetiae Parisiorum: typis Regiis, 1629.

Plutarchii Opera in 2 Vol. Gr. Lat.

[81.3] Plutarch: *Plutarchi Chaeronensis quae exstant omnia cum Latina interpretatione Hermanii Cruserij: Gulielmi Xylandri.* Francofurti: In officina Danielis as Dauidis Aubriorum, 1620.

Huetii Demonstratio Evangelica

[81.4] Pierre-Daniel Huet: *Demonstratio evangelica. Ad serenissimum Delphinum.* Parisiis: apud Stephanum Michallet, 1679.

Photii Epistolae

[81.5] Saint Photius: *Patriarch of Constantinople, Photii, sanctissimi patriarchae Constantinopolitani epistolae. Per...Richardum Montacutium Norvicensem nuper episcopum.* Londini: Ex officina Rogeri Danielis, 1651.

Philostorgii Historia Ecclesiastica

[81.6] Theodoret, Bishop of Cyrrhus: *Theodoriti Episcopi Cyriet Euagrii Scholastici Historia ecclesiastica. Item excerpta ex Historiis Philostorgii et Theodori Lectoris.* Parisiis: typis Petri Le Petit, 1673.

Johannes Bona de rebus Liturgicis

[81.7] Giovanni Bona: *Rerum liturgicarum libri duo.* Coloniae Agrippinae: Apud Joan. Wilhelmum Friessem Juniorem, 1674.

Johannis Meursii Glossarium Gro Barb.

[81.8] Joannes Meursius: *Glossarium Graeco-Barbarum.* Lugduni Batavorum: apud Ludovicum Elzevirium, 1614.

Megiseri Institutiones Linguae Turcica

[81.9] Possibly Franciszek Meninski: *Thesaurus linguarum orientalium Turcicae, Arabicae, Persicae.* Viennae Austriae, 1680.

[82] Anno Dom. 1696. **Benjaminus Penning** Artium Magister et Ecclesiae Sancti Clementis Apud Norvicenses Rector D.D. Sculptas delineations Collegiorum et Aularum Utriusque Academiae, viz. Cantabrigiensis et Oxoniensis.

[82.1] David Loggan: *Oxonia illustrata.* Oxoniae: e Theatro Sheldoniana, [1675].

[82.2] David Loggan: *Cantabrigia illustata.* Cantabrigia, 1688.

[83] **/1692/ Mr Richard Ireland**

Formerly Rector of Beeston and sometime also of St. Edmonds in the Citty of Norwich where he was born, gave by his last will all his bookes to the publick library of the Citty where they are set up on shelves and accordingly specified in the catalogue of the library, viz. the folios on classis 16 and the smaller bookes on classis 20 and 21 with some others of the old citty library distinguished in the said catalogue.

Memorandum. Some of Mr Ireland's bookes which the library was furnished with before are set up in the outward library to be sold and exchanged for others, as he gave leave.

[84] / **Anno 1700 / William Adamson** Rector of St. John Maddermarket gave to this Library three shelves full of bookes viz. classis 17, 18 and 19, the first in folio, the second in quarto, the third in octavo, and are specified in the catalogue of the library.

*[85] /***Anno 1704/ Dr Charles Trimnell Archdeacon of Norfolk & Prebend of Norwich** Gave to the Library
Dr Watson's Clergymans Law folio
[85.1] William Watson: *The clergy-man's law, or, The complete incumbent: collected from the 39 articles, canons, decrees in Chancery and Exchequer, as also from all the acts of Parliament, and common-law cases, relating to the church and clergy of England.* London: Printed by the assigns of R. and E. Atkins, for J. Place, 1701.
Archbishop Bramhall's Works in 1 vol folio.
[85.2] John Bramhall: *The works of the Most Reverend Father in God, John Bramhall...collected into one volume, in four tomes: to which is prefixt, the authour's life.* Dublin: Printed at His Majesties printing-house, 1676.
Index Expurgatoris in Quarto.
[85.3] Index librorum expurgatorum, illustrissimi ac reverendis D.D. Gasparis Quiroga, Cardinalis & Archiep. Toletani Hispan. generalis Inquisitoris iussu editus. Salmuri: Apud Thomam Portau, 1601.

*[86] /***Anno 1704/ Stephen Gardiner,**[61] **Esquire, Recorder** of this Citty gave to this Library
Marmora Oxoniensia Edita per Humphredum Prideaux 1676
[86.1] Humphrey Prideaux: *Marmora Oxoniensia, ex Arundellianis, Seldenianis, aliique conflata.* Oxonii: E theatro Sheldoniano, 1676.

[87] / **Anno 1706 / Thornaugh Gurdon Esquire**
Gave to this Library
L[or]d Bacon's Natural History
[87.1] Francis Bacon: *Historia naturalis & experimentalis de ventis, &c.* Lugd. Batavorum: Apud Franciscum Hackium, 1648.
H. Stephani Concordantia N.T.
[87.2] Henricus Stephanus: *Concordantiae Graeco-Latinae Testamenti Novi.*

[88] / **Anno 1706 / Mr [***Benjamin***] Resbury** Rector of Cranworth cum Letton gave to this Library
Ammiani Marcellini Histor. Paris 1681.
[88.1] Marcellinus Ammianus: *Ammiani Marcellini Rerum gestarum qui de XXXI. supersunt. libri XVIII. Ope MSS, codicum emendati ab Henrico Valesio.* Parisiis, ex officina Antonii Dezallier, 1681.

*[89] /***Anno 1706/ Mr Archibald Adams**

---

[61] Born at Mendham, Suffolk, Stephen Gardiner was educated at Norwich Grammar School and the Middle Temple. He was Recorder of Norwich from 1703 to 1727.

Gave to this Library
Galileus Galileus his System of the World
[89.1] Galileo Galilei: *The systeme of the world in four dialogues wherein the two grand systems of Ptolemy and Copernicus are largely discoursed of...*London: printed by William Leybourne, 1661.

[90] /**Anno 1706/ John** [*Moore*] **Lord Bishop of Norwich**
Gave to this Library Eusebii, Socratis, Sozomeni, Theodoriti & Evagrii Hist. Ecclesiast. In 3 Vol. Paris. 1678

[90.1] Eusebius: *Ecclesiasticae historiae libri decem.*
Parisiis: typis Petri Le Petit, 1678.

[90.2] Socrates: *Socratis Scholastici et Hermiae Sozomeni historia ecclesiastica.* Parisiis: excudebat Antonius Vitré, 1668.

[90.3] Theodoret: *Theodoriti Episcopi Cyri et Evagrii Scholastici Historia ecclesiastica.* Parisiis: Typis Petri Le Petit, 1673.

[91] /**Anno 1706/ Thomas Tanner D.D Chancellor of Norwich**
Gave to this Library Binii Bibliotheca Patrum. 5 Vol. Paris 1588.

[91.1] Marguerin de La Bigne: *Sacra bibliotheca sanctorum patrum.* Parisiis: Apud Michaelem Sonnium, 1589.

[92] /**Anno 1706/ Waller Bacon** Esquire
Gave unto this Library Dr Beveridge his Cannons
[92.2] William,Beveridge: *Synodikon sive pandectae canonum SS. Apostolorum, et conciliorum ab ecclesia Graeca receptorum.* Oxonii: E Theatro Sheldoniano, 1672.

[93] /**Anno 1706/ Michael Beverley Esquire Citizen and Alderman of Norwich** Gave to this Library
Callius Rhodiginus
[93.1] Lodovicus Coelius Rhodiginus: *Lectionum antiquarum libri triginta.* [Frankfurt]: Apud heredes Andreae Wecheli, Claudium Marnium, & Ioannem Aubrium, 1599.
Athenaei de Sophista
[93.2] Naucratites Athenaeus: *Athenaei Deipnosophistarum libri xv: Isaacus Casaubonus recensuit.* [Heidelbergae]: Commelinus, 1597.
Lloyd's Memoirs
[93.3] David Lloyd: *Memoires of the lives, actions, sufferings & deaths of those...personages: that suffered...for the Protestant religion.* London: Printed for Samuel Speed, and sold by him and by John Wright, John Symmes and James Collins, 1668.
Suetonius with Casaubon's Commentaries
[93.4] Suetonius: *Caius Suetonius Tranquillus cum Isaaci Casauboni animadversionibus, et dissertationibus politicis Ioh. Henr. Boecleri, itemque uberrimo indice.* Argentorati: Ex offici Ioh. Philippi Mulbii, 1647.
Jacob Bohm's Works in four Quartos.
[93.5] Jakob Böhme: *Signatura rerum, or the signature of all things.* London: printed by John Macock, for Gyles Calvert, 1651.

[93.6] Ibid.: *Concerning the election of grace. Or of Gods will towards man. Commonly called predestination.* London: Printed by John Streater, for Giles Calvert and John Allen, 1655.

[93.7] Ibid.: *Aurora, that is, the day-spring, or dawning of the day in the Orient.* London: Printed by John Streater, for Giles Calvert, 1656.

[93.8] Ibid.: *Several treatises of Jacob Behme: not printed in English before, according to the catalogue here following.* London: printed for L. Lloyd, 1661.

[94] /**Anno 1707**/ **Algernon Potts Esquire**
Gave Tacquetti Opera Mathematica.

[94.1] André Tacquet: *Opera mathematica...demonstrata et propugnata a Simone Laurentio Veterani.* Antverpiensis, 1668.

[95] /**Anno 1707**/ **Mr Thomas Nelson** Rector of Morston in Norfolk gave to this Library
Vossii (Gerhardi Johannis) Aristarchus, sive de Arte Grammatica. Amstel 1685.

[95.1] Gerardus Joannes Vossius: *Aristarchus, sive De arte grammatica libri septem.* Amstelodami: Ex typographia P. & I. Blaeu, 1695.
Erasmi Adagia 1629.

[95.2] Desiderius Erasmus: *Adagia, id est: proverbiorum, paroemiarum et parabolarum omnium, quae apud Graecos, Latinos, Hebraeos, Arabas, &c. in usu fuerunt, collectio absolutissima in locos communes digesta.*
[Frankfurt am Main]: Typis Wechelianis, sumptibus Clementis Schleichii, & Petri de Zetter, 1629.
Woodall's Surgeon's Mate. London 1655.

[95.3] John Woodall: *The surgeons mate, or, Military & domestique surgery.* London: Printed by John Legate for Nicholas Bourne, 1655.

[96] /**Anno 1707**/ **Sir William Cook Baronet** gave to this Library Du Perron's Works in three volumes French. Paris 1620.

[96.1] Jacques Davy Du Perron: *Les ambassades et negotiations de l'illustrissime & reverendissime Cardinal Du Perron.* A Paris: par Antoine Estiene a l'olivier de Robert Estiene, 1623.

[96.2] Ibid.: *Replique a la response du serenissime roy de la Grand Bretagne.* A Paris: Par Antoine Estiene, 1620.

[96.2] Ibid.: *Les diverses oeuvres de l'illustrissime cardinal Du Perron.* A Paris: Par Antoine Estiene, 1622.
Aquinatis Tho. Summa contra Gentiles. Paris 1587.

[96.4] Saint Thomas Aquinas: *Summa contra Gentiles, quatuor libris comprehensa: commentariis...Francisci de Sylvestris, Ferrariensis...illustrata...*Parisiis, 1552.
Sigonii Opera de Antiquo Jure Civium Romanorum. Franc. 1593.

[96.5] Carlo Sigonio: *De antiquo iure civium Romanorum...Libri xi...De republica Atheniensium...Libri quinque, quibus adiecti nunc sunt...De republica Hebraeorum, libri septem.* Frankfurt: Marnius de Aubriis, 1593.

Maffei Historia Indicor[um] cum Ignatii Loyola Vita Col. Agrip. 1589.
[96.6] Giovanni Pietro Maffei: *Historiarum Indicarum libri xvi. Selectarum, item, ex India epistolarum, eodem interprete, libri iv. Accessit Ignati Loiolae vita.* Coloniae Agrippinae: off. Birckmannica for A. Mylius, 1589.
Mason de Ministerio Ecclesiae Anglicana 1638
[96.7] Francis Mason: *Vindiciae Ecclesiae Anglicanae: siue De legitimo eiusdem ministerio: id est, de episcoporum successione, consecratione, electione, & confirmatione: item, de presbyterorum, & diaconorum ordinatione…*Londini: [Printed by Felix Kingston, 1638.
Morton's Catholick Appeal for Protestants 1610
[96.8] Thomas Morton: *A Catholike appeale for Protestants, out of the confessions of the Romane doctors; particularly answering the mis-named Catholike apologie for the Romane faith.* Londini: printed for Richard Field, 1610.
Commentarius de Bestia Apocalypta. Delphis 1621.
[96.9] [William Alabaster]: *Commentarius de Bestia Apocalyptica.* Delphis, 1621.
[97] /**Anno 1707**/ **Mr Henry Eden** Fellow of Trinity College Cambridge. Gave to this Library as follows
Josephus his Works translated by Sir Roger L'Estrange. London 1702.
[97.1] Flavius Josephus: *The Works of Flavius Josephus, translated by Sir Roger L'Estrange.* London: printed for Richard Sare, 1702.
Hugo Grotius de jure Belli. Amstel 1689
[97.2] Hugo Grotius: *De jure belli as pacis libri tres.* Amstelodoami: Janssonio-Waesbergiorum, 1689.
Mr Young's Sermons Dean of Sarum 2 vol. London 1703.
[97.3] Edward Young: *Sermons on several occasions.* London: printed by J.H. for Walter Kettilby, 1703–1706.
[98] /**Anno 1707**/ **Mr John Laughton** of Trinity College in Cambridge and Library Keeper to the University gave to this Library viz.
Hodius de Textibus Originalibus Bibliorum. Oxonii, 1705.
[98.1] Humphrey Hody: *De Bibliorum textibus originalibus, versionibus graecis, & latina vulgata.* Oxoniis: E Theatro Sheldoniano, 1705.
Father Simon's Critical History Old Testament. London, 1682.
[98.2] Richard Simon: *A Critical History of the Old Testament. Written originally in French…and since translated into English, by a Person of Q uality.* London: printed by W. Davis, 1682.
Critical Inquiries. London, printed 1684.
[98.3] Richard Simon: *Critical enquiries into the various editions of the Bible printed in divers places and at several times.* London: Printed by Tho. Braddyll. 1684.
Nectarius contra Imperium Papae. Latin, translated by Dr Alix. London, printed 1702.
[98.4] Nectarius, patriarch of Jerusalem: *Confutatio imperii papae in Ecclesiam.* Londini, 1702.

[99] /**Anno 1707**/ **Mr Edward Rudd** Fellow of Trinity College in Cambridge. Gave to this Library
Catalogus Librorum Bibliothecae Bodleianae. Oxon 1694
[99.1] Thomas James: *Catalogus universalis librorum in Bibliotheca Bodleiana.* Oxoniae: excudebant Johannes Lichfield & Jacobus Short, 1620.
Dr Plot's History of Oxfordshire. Oxford 1705
[99.2] Robert Plot: *The natural history of Oxfordshire; being an essay towards the natural history of England.* Oxford: pr. By Leon Lichfield, 1705.
Hooker's Ecclesiastical Polity. 5 books. London
[99.3] Richard Hooker: *Of the Lawes of Ecclesiasticall Politie.* London: Iohn Windet, [1593] - 1597.
[100] **Mr Samuel Bradshaw**[62] A.B. of Trinity College Cambridge
Aeschili Tragediae per Henry Stephanum. 1557
[100.1] Aechylus: *Aeschyli Tragoediae VII. Quae cum omnes multo quam antea castigatiores eduntur, tum vero una, quae mutila & decurtata prius erat, integra nunc profertur.* Genevae: Ex officina Henrici Stephani, 1557.
[101] **Mr Gilbert Granger** A.B. of Trinity College Cambridge
Lycophron Oxford 1702
[101.1] Lycophron: *Lycophronis Chalcidensis Alexandra, obscurum poemo. Cum Graeco Isaacii, seu potius Joannis, Tzetzae commentario.* Oxonii: e Theatro Sheldoniano, impensis Joannis Oweni, 1702.
[102] **Mr Matthew Snow** of Trinity College Cambridge
Another Lycophron
[103] **Mr William Chamberlain** Fellow of Trinity College Cambridge
Chillingworth's Protestants Safe Way. Oxford 1638
[103.1] William Chillingworth: *The religion of Protestants a safeway to salvation, or, An answer to a book entituled Mercy and truth, or, Charity maintain'd by Catholiques, which pretends to prove the contrary: to which is added The apostolical insitution of episcopacy.* London: Printed by Andrew Clark for Richard Chiswell, 1674.
[104] **Mr Ralph Bourchier** of Trinity College Cambridge
Pearsonii Opera Posthumia London, 1688
[104.1] John Pearson: *Opera Posthuma Chronologica.* Londini: Typis S. Roycroft, 1688.
[105] **Mr Roger Cotes**, Fellow of Trinity College Cambridge
Bennet's Abridgement of the London Cases. Cambridge 1700
[105.1] Thomas Bennet: *An answer to the dissenters pleas for separation, or, An abridgment of the London cases: wherein the substance of those books is digested into one short and plain discourse.* London: Printed at the University Press, for Alexander Bosvile, 1700.

[62] A Derbyshire man, Samuel Bradshaw was educated at Westminster School and Trinity College, Cambridge, graduating BA in 1707 and proceeding MA in 1710. He was ordained in 1709.

Confutation of Popery. Cambridge, 1701.

[105.2] Thomas Bennet: *A confutation of popery, in III parts. Wherein. I. The controversy concerning the rule of faith is determined. II. The particular doctrines of the Church of Rome are confuted. III. The popish objections against the Church of England are answer'd.* Cambridge: Printed at the University Press, for E. Jeffery, 1701.

A Discourse of Schism. Cambridge 1702.

[105.3] Thomas Bennet: *A Discourse of Schism...Written by way of letter to three Dissenting Ministers in Essex, viz. Mr Gilson and Mr Gledhill of Colchester, and Mr Shepherd of Braintree.* Cambridge: Edmund Jeffery, 1702.

[106] **Mr Lawrence Eusden** of Trinity College Cambridge
Virgilii Opera in usum Delphini. London, 1695

[106.1] Virgil: *P. Virgilii Maronis opera: interpretatione et notis illustravit Carolus Ruaeus, Soc. Jesu, jussu Christianissimi regis, ad usum serenissimi Delphini.*
Londini: Impensis A. Swalle, 1696.

Flori Annaei Hist in usum Delphini. London, 1692.

[106.2] Lucius Annaeus Florus: *L. Annaei Flori Rerum Romanorum epitome. Interpretatione & notis illustravit Anna Tanaquilli Fabri filia, iussu Christianissimi regis, in usum serenissimi Delphini.* Londini: Impensis R. Clavell, 1692.

Salustii Crisp Hist in usum Delphini. London, 1697.

[106.3] Sallust: *C. Sallusti Crispi quae extant: In usum Delphini, diligenter resensuit, et notulas addidit Daniel Crispinus.* Londini: impensis Abelis Swall, 1697.

Lucani Pharsaliae

[106.4] Lucan: *M. Annei Lucani Cordubensis...Pharsaliae.*

The Father's Counsel to his Children. London 1678.

[106.5] The fathers legacy: or, Counsels to his children. London: printed for Henry Brome, 1678.

[107] **Mr Edward Smith** of Trinity College Cambridge
Thysii Anton Roma Illustrata. Amstelod. 1657

[107.1] Justus Lipsius: *Roma illustrata, sive Antiquitatum Romanorum breviarium ex nova recensione Antonii Thysii.* Amstelodami: Apud Ludovicorum & Danielem Elzevirios, 1657.

Cicero M. Tullius de Officiis per Graevium. Amstel. 1691

[107.2] Marcus Tullius Cicero: *M. Tullii Ciceronis De officiis.* Amstelaedami: Apud Henricum Westenium, 1691.

Grotius Hugo de Veritate Religionis Christianae. Paris 1640.

[107.3] Hugo Grotius: *De veritate religionis Christianae.* Parisiis: Sumptibus Seb. Cramoisy, Typographi Regii, 1640.

[108] **Mr David Fleming** A.B. of Trinity College Cambridge
Juvenalis & Persius in Usum Delphini. Paris 1684

[108.1] Juvenal: *D. Junii Juvenalis et A. Persii Flacci satirae.*
Parisiis: Ex typographia Frederici Leonard, 1684.

[109] **Mr Nathaniel Ganning**, Rector of Reymerston in Norfolk

Sir Walter Rawleigh's History of the World. London 1677.
[109.1] Sir Walter Raleigh: *The history of the world, in five books.* London: Printed for R. White, T. Basset, J. Wright [et al.], 1677.
[110] **Anno 1708 Mr Samuel Doyly,**[63] Fellow of Trinity College Cambridge
Launoii Epistolae. Cantabrigiensis, 1689.
[110.1] Jean de Launoy: *Joannis Launoii constantiensis, parisienesis theologi, Epistolae omnes, octo partibus comprehensae, nunc demum simul editae.* Cantabrigiae: Ex officina Joan. Hayes…impensis Edwardi Hall, 1689.
[111] **Mr** *[Phillips]* **Farewell**[64]
The Works of the Author of the Whole Duty of Man.
[111.1] William Perkins: *The workes of that famous and worthy minister of Christ in the Vniuersitie of Cambridge, Mr William Perkins.* Printed at London and Cambridge: By Iohn Legatt, printer to the Vniuersitie of Cambridge, 1612.
[112] **Mr** *[William]* **Andrews**[65]
Heylin's History of the Reformation
[112.1] Peter Heylyn: *Ecclesia restaurata; or, The history of the reformation of the Church of England.* London: Printed for H. Twyford, T. Dring, J. Place, W. Palmer, 1661.
[113] **Mr** *[William]* **Foulis** [66]
Bennet's History of Prayer.
[113.1] Thomas Bennet: *A brief history of the joint use of precompos'd set forms of prayer.* Cambridge: Printed at the University Press, for Edmund Jeffery, 1708.
[114] **Mr** *[Thomas]* **Hill,**[67] Fellow of Trinity College Cambridge
Gataker's Antoninus
[114.1] Probably Marcus Aurelius: *The Emperor Marcus Aurelius his conversation with himself. Together with the preliminary discourse of the learned Gataker.* London: Printed for Richard Sare, 1708.

---

[63] Samuel Doyly was descended from the D'Oylys of Shottesham. He graduated BA at Trinity College, Cambridge, in 1704 and proceeded MA in 1707, the year in which he was made a Fellow. In 1730 he published *An historical, critical, geographical, chronological and etymological dictionary of the Holy Bible.*

[64] Born at Ware, Hertfordshire, Phillips Farewell was educated at Westminster School and Trinity College, Cambridge, graduating BA in 1710 and proceeding MA in 1713. He was a Fellow of his College from 1712 to 1730.

[65] Born in 1682, William Andrews was educated at Merchant Taylor's School and Trinity College, Cambridge, graduating BA in 1703 and proceeding MA in 1706. Rector of Meesden, Hertfordshire, he died in 1750.

[66] Born at Ingleby in Yorkshire the son of a baronet, William Foulis was educated at Enfield, Middlesex, and Trinity College, Cambridge. He succeeded his father in 1741.

[67] Born in Southfleet, Kent, Thomas Hill was educated at Westminster School and Trinity College, Cambridge, graduating BA in 1705 and proceeding MA in 1708. He was elected a Fellow of his College in 1707. A published poet, his most famous work was the *Nundinae Sturbrigienses*, which describes a visit to Stourbridge Fair.

[115] **Mr John Lightwin**, President of Caius College Cambridge
Launoii Epistolae
[115.1] Jean de Launoy: *Joannis Launoii Constantiensis, Parisiensis theologi, Epistolae omnes, octo partibus comprehensae, nunc demum simul editae.*
Cantabrigiae: ex officina Joan. Hayes, 1689.
The Works of King Charles the First
[115.2] *Basilika: the works of King Charles the martyr*
London: printed for Richard Chiswell, 1687.
[116] **Anno 1708 Mr Brampton Gurdon**, Fellow of Caius College
Cambridge
Novum Testamentum. Ed. J. Gregory
[116.1] *Novum Testamentum una cum scholiis Graecis, e Graecis scriptoribus, tam ecclesiasticis quam exteris, maxima ex parte desumptis. Opera ac studio Joannis Gregorii.* Oxonii: E Theatro Sheldoniano, 1703.
Mason de Ministerio Eccl Anglican
[116.2] Francis Mason: *Vindici Ecclesi Anglican; siue De legitimo eiusdem ministerio.* Londini: Impressum per Felicem Kyngstonum, 1625.
[117] **Mr Roger Hawys**, Fellow of Caius College Cambridge
Hodii de Bibl. Textib. Originalibus.
[117.1] Humphrey Hody: *Humfredi Hodii linguae Graecae professoris regii et archidiaconi Oxon. de Bibliorum textibus originalibus, versionibus Graecis, & Latina vulgata.* Oxonii: e Theatro Sheldoniano, 1705.
[118] **Dr [Thomas] Crask** of Cambridge
Stillingfleet's Origin Sacrae
[118.1] Edward Stillingfleet: *Origines sacrae: or, a rational account of the grounds of natural and reveal'd religion.*
[119] **Mr [Samuel] Dodd**, Fellow of Clare Hall
Unreasonableness of Separation
[119.1] Edward Stillingfleet: *The unreasonableness of separation, or, An impartial account of the history, nature, and pleas of the present separation from the communion of the Church of England.*
[120] **Mr William Worts** A.M. of Cambridge
Dr Mills' Greek Testament
[120.1] *Novum Testamentum: Cum lectionibus variantibus MSS exemplarium, versionum, editionum, SS Patrum & scriptorum ecclesiasticorum; & in easdem notis...Studio et labore Joannis Millii.* Oxonii: E. Theatro Sheldoniana, 1707.
[121] **Anno 1709 Mr James Bedingfield** alias James de Grey, Fellow of Gonville & Caius College Cambridge
Collier's Ecclesiastical History Vol. 1st
[121.1] Jeremy Collier: *An ecclesiastical history of Great Britain, chiefly of England: from the first planting of Christianity, to the end of the reign of King Charles the Second. With a brief account of the affairs of religion in Ireland.* London: printed for Samuel Keble, and Benjamin Tooke, 1708–1714.

[122] **Humphrey Prideaux D.D. & Dean of Norwich**
The Validity of the Orders of the Church of England
[122.1] Humphrey Prideaux: *The validity of the orders of the Church of England made out against the objections of the papists, in several letters to a gentleman of Norwich, that desired satisfaction therein.* London: printed by John Richardson for Brabazon Aylmer, 1688.
The Life of Mahomet
[122.2] Humphrey Prideaux: *The True Nature of imposture fully display'd in the Life of Mahomet: with a discourse annex'd for the vindicating of Christianity from this charge, offered to the consideration of the deists of the present age.*
The Original and Right of Tythes
[122.3] Humphrey Prideaux: *The original and right of tithes: for the maintenance of the ministry in a Christian church truly stated.* London: Printed for Maurice Atkins, 1710.
[123] **Anno 1712 Charles [*Trimnell*] Lord Bishop** of Norwich
Dr Browne's Posthumous Works
[123.1] Sir Thomas Browne: *Posthumous works of the learned Sir Thomas Browne, kt. M.D. late of Norwich: printed from his original manuscripts.* London: Printed for E. Curll at the Dial and Bible; and R. Gosling at the Mitre in Fleetstreet, 1712.
[124] **Anno 1713 John Peck Esquire of Bracondale**
Codex Juris Ecclesiastic Anglican. 2 Vol. Folio.
[124.1] Edmund Gibson: *Codex Juris Ecclesiastici Anglicani: or, the Statutes, Constitutions, Canons, Rubricks and Articles of the Church of England, methodically digested under their proper heads, with a commentary.* London: J. Baskett, 1713.
[125] **Anno 1714 Mr Thomas Nelson**, late rector of Morston in the county of Norfolk gave by his last will and testament all his books unto the public library of this city where they are placed upon six shelves by themselves in the inner room belonging to the said library with his name over them in gold letters.
[126] **Anno 1715 Clement Herne** Esquire of Haveringland
Burnet's History of the Reformation, the two first volumes in folio.
[126.1] Gilbert Burnet: *The history of the reformation of the Church of England: in two parts.* London: Printed by T.H. for Richard Chiswell, 1681–3.
[127] **Thomas Seaman** Esquire of Heigham
Fabii Quintiliani Opera in 2 volumes. Lugduni Batav. 1665.
[127.1] Marcus Fabius Quintilianus: *Institutionum oratoriarum libri duodecim. Accesserunt huic renovatae ed. declamationes, quae tam ex P. Pithoei, quam aliorum bibliothecis & editionibus colligi potuerunt.* Lugd. Batav. et Roterodami: ex officina Hackiana, 1665.
[128] **Anno 1716 Benjamin Mackerell** of the city of Norwich gentleman gave Davila's History of France, folio.
[128.1] Arrigo Caterino Davila: *The historie of the civil warres of France, written*

in Italian by H.C. Davila. Translated out of the original by CC and WA. London: Printed by R. Raworth, and are to be sold by W. Lee, D. Pakeman, and G. Bedell, 1647.

Grimston's History of the Netherlands. Folio.

[128.2] Jean Francois Le Petit: *A generall histories of the Netherlands. Newly reuewed, corrected, and supplied with sundrie necessarie obseruations omitted in the first imprssion. By Ed. Grimeston Sergeant at Armes. Continued from the yeare 1608 till the yeare of our Lord 1617 by William Crosse Mr of Arts.* London: Printed by Adam Islip, 1627.

[129] **Nicholas Helwys Esquire, Citizen and Alderman of Norwich**

Burnet's Theory of the Earth.

[129.1] Thomas Burnet: *The theory of the earth: containing an account of the original of the earth, and of all the general changes which it hath already undergone, or is to undergo till the consummation of all things.* London: printed by R. Norton, for Walter Kettilby, 1691.

[130] **Anno 1717 Humphrey Prideaux D.D. and Dean of Norwich** sent in the first volume of the Connection of the Old and New Testament in folio written by himself the year after he sent in his 2nd volume in folio.

[131.1] Humphrey Prideaux: *The Old and New Testament connected in the history of the Jews and neighbouring nations: from the declension of the kingdoms of Israel and Judah to the time of Christ.* London: For R. Knaplock and J. Tonson, 1718.

[132] **Anno 1718 Thomas Clark Esquire** gave A Compleat History of England in three volumes folio by Tyrrel 1706.

[132.1] James Tyrrell: *The general history of England, both ecclesiastical and civil: from the earliest accounts of time, to the reign of His present Majesty, King William III.* London: W. Rogers, 1697–1704.

[133] **Humphrey Prideaux D.D.**

The second volume of the Connection of the Old & New Testament in folio written by himself.

[133.1] Humphrey Prideaux: *The Old and New Testament connected in the history of the Jews and neighbourhood nations from the declension of the kingdoms of Israel and Judah to the time of Christ.* London: printed for R. Knaplock and J. Tonson, 1718.

[134] **Anno 1719 Mr William Houghton**

King Charles the First's Tumults in Scotland

[134.1] Walter Balcanquhall: *A large declaration concerning the late tumults in Scotland, from their first originals: together with a particular deduction of the seditious practices of the prime leaders of the Covenanters…By the King.* London: printed by Robert Young, His Majesties printer for Scotland, 1639.

[135] **Anno 1721 Mr John Grayle**, rector of Blickling

Henrici Mori Opera Theologica Folio

[135.1] Henry More: *Henrici Mori Cantabrigiensis Opera theologica, anglice quidem primitus scripta, nunc vero per autorem Latine reddita.* Londini: typis J. Macock, impensis Johan. Martyn & Gualteri Kettilby, 1675.
Rochmandi Systema Univers Theol. 2 tomibus quarto
[135.2] Caspar Erasmus Brochmand: *Systematis universae theologicae.* Lipsiae: Sumptibus Joannis Hallervordii & Joachimi Moltkenii, 1638.
Amyraldi Specimen Animadvers Exercitat de Gratia quarto
[135.3] Moyse Amyraut: *Specimen animadversionum in exercitationes de gratia universali.* Salmurii: apud Ioh. Lesnerium, 1648.
Salmasii Epistola Liber Primus quarto
[135.4] Claudius Salmasius: *Claudii Salmasii, viri ill. Epistolarum liber primus. Accedunt de laudibus et vita ejusdem prolegomena accurante Antonio Clementio.* Lugduni Batavorum: Ex typographia Adriani Wyngaerden, 1656.
Vorstii Tractatus Theologicus de deo &c quarto
[135.5] Conradus Vorstius: *Tractatus theologicus de Deo, sive De natura & attributis Dei, Omnia fere ad hanc materiam pertinentia (saltem de quibus utiliter & religiose disputari potest) decem disputationibus, anti hac in illustri Schola Steinfurtensi, diverso tempore, publice habitis…comprehendens.* Steinfurti: excudebat Theophilus Caesar, 1610.
Tulii S.T.P. Justificatio Paulina quarto
[135.6] Thomas Tully: *Justificatio Paulina sive operibus ex mente Ecclesiae Anglicanae…asserta & illustrata. Accessit Dissertatiuncula de seusa Pauli, Rom. 7.* Oxoniae, 1674.
Sacra Privata
[135.7] John Graile: *Sacra privata in duas partes distributa: quarum una tractatum continet de religiligiosa[sic] solitudine, privatis precibus aliisque officiis piis, cum doctrinae studio conjugendis.* Londini: typis J.L. impensis autem Gualteri Kettilby, 1699.
Youth's Grand Concern
[135.8] John Graile: *Youths grand conern: or, advice to young persons, how to begin betimes to be wise, and good, and happy.* London: printed by J.H. for John Wyat, 1711.
Advice to the Young Gentry
[135.9] John Graile: *An essay of particular advice to the young gentry, for the over-coming the difficulties and temptations they may meet with.* London: printed for John Wyat, 1711.
N.B. The 3 last books were written by himself.
[136] **Anno 1725 John Knyvett** of this city esquire D.D.
Julii Caesaris Commenta de Bello Gallico, quarto.
[136.1] Julius Caesar: *Commentariorum de bello Gallico.*
[137] **Anno 1726 Thomas Tanner S.T.P.** and Chancellor of the Diocese of Norwich this year added more than an hundred books to those which he had formerly given to this public library which are particularly inserted in the catalogue with his name before each book.

[138] **Anno 1727 Mr Edward Reveley** gave four books to this library
with his name before each book

[139] **Anno 1728 Mr John Kirkpatrick** merchant and treasurer to the
Great Hospital in this city did by his last will and testament give (note the
following are the very words of his will) to the mayor, sheriffs, citizens &
commonalty aforesaid all my ancient manuscripts and all my medals and
ancient coins of silver & brass to be reposited in their library at the New
Hall. Also all my printed books in the Anglo-Saxon language & all such of
my books which were printed before the year of our Lord 1600 as are not
already in the said library together with Mountfaucon's Antiquities[68] &
Maddox's Firma Burgi[69] lately printed; and I will & desire that all these
things be kept there for public use as the other books in the said library
are (thus far his will). Some time after the decease of the said Mr John
Kirkpatrick there was more than two hundred books sent to this library
according to his will and desire which are inserted in the catalogue with
his name before each book.

/N.B./ The medals and coins are not yet delivered but are still in the
hands of John Custance[70] esquire.

[140] **Anno 1729 John Jermy** esquire sent & given to this library several
law books and others which are particularly inserted in the catalogue with
his name before each book.

[141] **Anno 1730 Edmund Prideaux**[71] Esquire gave to this library
more than three score books which are all of them inserted in the catalogue with his name before each book.

[142] **Anno 1730 Robert Wingfield** [72] writing master gave thirteen
books to this library, which are all inserted in the catalogue with his name
before each book.

[143] **Anno 1731 Mr William Pagan** gave seven books to this library
which are all inserted in the catalogue with his name before each book.

[144] **Thornaugh Gurdon** Esquire have added to those books which he

---

[68] Bernard de Montfaucon: *Antiquity explained, and represented in sculptures, by the learned Father
Montfaucon; translated into English by David Humphreys.* London: Printed by J. Tonson and J. Watts,
1721–1722.

[69] Thomas Madox: *Firma burgi: or, An historical essay concerning the cities, towns and boroughs [sic] of
England.* London: Printed by W. Bowyer, 1726.

[70] John Custance was sheriff of Norwich in 1723 and mayor in 1726. The purchase of the
Weston Longville Estate cost him £5,000.

[71] Son of Humphrey Prideaux, Dean of Norwich, Edmund Prideaux was called to the bar
in 1718. The Norwich physician, Sir Benjamin Wrench, was his father-in-law.

[72] A wealthy man, Robert Wingfield ran a writing school complete with 'desks, forms,
cupboards and closets'. He left all his music books and papers to Charles Lulman and his
books and papers on grammar, arithmetic, mensuration, surveying, accountancy and short-
hand to his servant, John Massingham. His wife, Sarah, was given his books of divinity in
English, to be 'enjoyed to her own use' (NRO NCC 104 Woodrofe, Will of Robert Wingfield,
1742).

formerly gave to this library & which are inserted in the catalogue with his name before each book.

[145] **Mr Reuben King,**[73] premier English school master in this city gave this, viz. A scholastical discourse against the sign of the cross, 1607.

[145.1] Robert Parker: *A scholasticall discourse against symbolizing with Antichrist in ceremonies especially in the signe of the crosse.* Middleburg: Printed by Richard Schilders, 1607.

[146] **Anno 1731 Benjamin Mackerell** the present library keeper have added thirteen books to those which he formerly sent, which are particularly inserted in the catalogue with his name before each book.

[147] **Anno 1733 Mr John Whaley** gave to this library Demosthenes' Select Orations published by R. Mounteney.

[147.1] Demosthenes: *Demosthenis Selectae orationes...recensuit, textum, scholiasten, et versionem...castigavit, notis insuper illustravit Ricardus Mounteney.* Cantabrigiae: typis academicis, 1731.

[148] **Mr Gilbert Bennet** gave to this library
The Phoenix in two volumes.

[148.1] *The Phenix: or, a revival of scarce and valuable pieces from the remotest antiquity down to the present times. A collection of manuscripts and printed tracts, no where to be found but in the closets of the curious.* London: Printed for J. Morphew near Stationers Hall, 1707.

[149] **April 26 1733 John Jermy** Esquire gave this day to this library forty books viz. 4 folios, 8 quartos & 28 octavos which are inserted in the catalogue.

[150] **1 May 1732 Dr Benjamin Joseph Ellis** minister of St. Andrew's in Norwich gave to this library
Tyrrell's Bibliotheca Politica

[150.1] James Tyrrell: *Bibliotheca politica: or, An enquiry into the antient constitution of the English government, with respect to the just extent of the regal power.* London: printed for D. Browne, 1718.

Stephani Dictionarium Historicum & auctum &c per Nicolo Loyd

[150.2] Charles Estienne: *Dictionarium historicum, geographicum, poeticum.* Genevae: Typis I. Stoer, 1650.

[151] 1737 **John Jermy Esquire** gave to this library fourteen books viz. 3 folios, 5 quartos, 6 octavos which are all inserted in their proper places in this interleaved catalogue belonging to this library.

---

[73] Reuben King, who is described as a 'gentleman' in his will, owned considerable amounts of property in St Stephen's parish. His executors were William Brooke, esquire, and Isaac Preston of Lincoln's Inn (NRO NCC 30 Tetsall, Will of Reuben King, 1733).

[74] A Londoner, Robert Nash attended Merchant Taylor's school and matriculated at Wadham College, Oxford, where he was a Fellow. He was created Doctor of Laws in 1734. Blomefield pays him a fulsome tribute, referring to Nash's 'many encouragements' (Blomefield, v, p. 637).

[152] **Anno 1737 Robert Nash**[74] Esquire, chancellor of this diocese, gave to the City Library
Burnet's Abridgement of the sermons preached at the lectures founded by the Honourable Robert Boyle Esquire in four volumes, which are inserted in the written copy of the catalogue.
[152.1] Gilbert Burnet: *A Defence of Natural and Revealed Religion: being an abridgment of the sermons preached at the lecture founded by the Honble. Robert Boyle, Esq.* London: A. Bettesworth & C. Hitch, 1737.

Library Catalogue c.1707
(MS 4227)

Introduction

The loss of the early fourteenth-century catalogue of Norwich Cathedral Priory Library[1] is partly compensated by the survival of a remarkable catalogue of the contents of the City Library, whose full significance becomes apparent if it is compared with the first catalogue of St. Margaret's Library, King's Lynn.[2] The earliest part of the St. Margaret's catalogue dates from around 1632. The first eleven leaves contain a list of the books bought from the £53 collected by the mayor and burgesses, plus the £20 donated by Joan and Thomas Atkins. The entries are very abbreviated, so much so that they resemble the book lists in probate inventories. Then at leaf twelve the catalogue metamorphoses into a donation book. In style the subsequent entries are very similar to the entries in the Norwich donation book.

The Norwich catalogue is of a very different order. It begins with a brief account, written in Latin, of the physical layout of the library, which was in two halves, an east side (*bibliotheca orientalis*) and a west side (*bibliotheca occidentalis*). Within this configuration the books were shelved in classes by format, ten classes in folio and four classes in quarto, octavo and duodecimo. As in other institutional libraries, folios were regarded as being far more important than smaller books. The folios were arranged by subject, as follows (the quartos, octavos and duodecimos had no subject classification):

1 Bibles
2–3 Bible commentaries
4 Theology and history
5 Theology and canon law
6 Writings of the Church Fathers
7 Dictionaries and concordances
8 Protestant commentaries
9 Ecclesiastical History
10 Miscellaneous

[1] N. Ker, 'Medieval manuscripts from Norwich Cathedral Priory', *Cambridge Bibliographical Society*, i (1949) p. 28.
[2] NHC, KL 018.2, St Margaret's Church Library Catalogue.

After the classified catalogue there is an author catalogue arranged in alphabetical order of author or, where there is no author, by title. As in the classified catalogue, each volume is given a class number and a shelf mark. The books on the west side of the library were numbered from the top shelves to the bottom, those on the east side from the bottom to the top.

Most impressive of all is the third section, the 'catalogue of commentators', in effect an analytical catalogue. The compiler may have been inspired by Thomas James' catalogue of the Bodleian Library, published in 1605, which also included a catalogue of commentators. At Cambridge University Library in the 1650s the under librarian, Jonathan Pindar, also produced a catalogue of commentators, again possibly based on James' original.[3] A similar 'catalogue of commentators' was composed at Sion College Library in 1650 by the Reverend John Simpson, the librarian. The compiler (or compilers) of the Norwich catalogue scanned each volume in the collection and noted which book of the Bible that volume glossed. No doubt they used concordances and commonplace books to assist them in their work but, even so, it was an impressive achievement. At least initially, each section of the analytical catalogue was in two parts. The first part related to those works that dealt with whole books of the Bible (*in librum integrum*), the second with works that dealt with parts of books (*in aliquam partem*). In both instances class and shelf marks were included. What is clear is that the analytical catalogue was compiled under John Collinges' direct supervision. There is an entry in the minutes of 13 December 1657 to the effect that the 'catalogue of commentators' had been commenced and would be 'perfected by his [Collinges] own hand'.

It was formerly assumed that MS 4227 was the catalogue produced in 1658,[4] but this is not the case. The first entry, the Wycliffite Bible, was not donated until 1692. William Adamson's donation of 1700 was incorporated, as was Martin Jubb's of 1706 and Edward Rudd's of 1707. Since there is no evidence that any of these entries were later interpolations, the catalogue must have been produced some years after the appearance of Joseph Brett's printed catalogue of 1706. There is no reference in the minutes to its production so its purpose can only be understood from the way it was constructed. It was designed as a research tool. The King's Lynn catalogue was a simple shelf-list, an inventory of the town's intellectual and cultural property. The Norwich catalogue was designed for use by a group of serious scholars who were clearly focussed on exploiting the collection they had inherited as a key to the Bible, 'the most worthy writing that ever saw the light'.

[3] J.C.T. Oates, *Cambridge University Library: a history from the beginnings to the Copyright Act of Queen Anne* (Cambridge, 1986) p. 264.

[4] Stephen, p. 45; D. Norris, *A History of Cataloguing and Cataloguing Methods, 1100–1850* (London, 1939) p. 169.

Note on style of entry

Catalogue entry.
Donor's name. Date. NCL classmark.
Note on binding and fore-edge marks.
[*Editor's serial number*] Author: *Title*.
Publication details. Bibliographical reference.
Notes

The Catalogue

/Norvicensi/ praecognita ad usum catalogi sequentis bibliothecarii.
Duae sunt partes bibliothecae 1. Orientalis. 2. Occidentalis.

In orientali parte duplex est librorum gaza major & minor

Major divisa est in decem classes, fol: -
Minor habet tantum quatuor classes librorum in 4to & 8o
Quarum omnium classium enumeratione semper
incipiendum est ex imo. –

In parte occidentali simplex est librorum
gazophylacium in quinque largiores classes
dispositum. Quarum si quaeras ordinem, semper ex alto sunt recensendae.

Introduction to the use of the following catalogue of Norwich library.
There are two parts to the library 1. East 2. West

The wealth of books in the eastern part is two-fold: large and small.
The large part is divided into ten classes, folio.
The small has only four classes of books, in quarto and octavo.
The numbering of all which classes always begins at the bottom.
In the western part the treasury of books is straightforwardly arranged in five main
classes. If the order is sought they are always numbered from the top.

Ex parte orientali

Catalogus librorum in bibliotheca
Nordovicensi secundum classes dispositorum

Classis 1a in folio		Librorum

English Bible M.S. unto the Proverbes   1
Richard Ireland   1692   I. h. 20
Nineteenth-century rebind with sixteenth-century
leather relaid on front and back boards.
[1] Wycliffe Bible containing the Books of the Old Testament
from Genesis to Proverbs. On vellum written in double
columns in a hand of the xv century with decorated capitals
at the beginning of each book.
On fol. 2v: liber Iacobi Boolene manens in Blickling
Ker *MMBL*, pp. 557–8.

Biblia sacra excusa sumptibus Philippi Regis
Hispaniensis edita per Ariam Montanum.

Antuerpiae 1658	1 Vol.	2
	2 Vol.	3
	3 Vol.	4
	4 Vol.	5
	5 Vol.	6
	6 Vol.	7
	7 Vol.	8
	8 Vol.	9

Prudence Blosse   1634   F. h. 7–14
Foredge: PB.   Rebound.
[2] Biblia Sacra Hebraice, Chaldaice, Graece,
et Latine,Philippi II Reg.Cathol.[Edited by]
Benedictus Arias Montanus. Antverpiae: Excudebat
Christophorus Plantinus, 1572.
Ex dono Prudentie Blosse vidue.

Biblia sacra Heb. Gr: Lat. cum annotationibus	1 Vol.	10
Francisci Vatabli in duos volumines ex typis		
Commelianis	2 Vol.	11

Sir Thomas Hyrne   1609   F.g. 4–5
Vol. 2 rebound in quarter leather. Modern endpapers.
[3] Sacra Biblia: Hebraice, Graece et Latine cum annotationibus Francisci Vatabli
Hebraicae. [Heidelberg]: ex officina commeliniana, [1599].

Biblia sacra Heb. Cald. cum Massora per Johannem Buxtorfium in duos
volumines impressa Basileae 1620.   1 Vol.   12
John Chappel   1634   F. g. 2–3   2 Vol.   13
Seventeenth-century calf.
[4] Biblia Sacra Hebraica & Chaldaica: cum Masora... Johannis Buxtorfi.
Basileae: Sumptibus & typis Ludovici Konig, 1620.

Biblia Polyglotta   1 Vol.   14
Norwich City Assembly   1658   F. h. 1–6   2 Vol.   15
                                             3 Vol.   16
                                             4 Vol.   17
                                             5 Vol.   18
                                             6 Vol.   19
Vol.1 rebound with original covers relaid.
[5] Biblia sacra polyglotta, complectentia textus originales,
Hebraicum, cum Pentateucho Samaritano, Chaldaicum,
Graecum, edidit Brianus Waltonus. Londini: Imprimebat
Thomas Ryecroft, 1655–57. (W 2797)

Critici Sacri   1 Vol.   20
                2 Vol.   21
                3 Vol.   22
                4 Vol.   23
                5 Vol.   24
                6 Vol.   25
                7 Vol.   26
                8 Vol.   27
                9 Vol.   28

Sir Joseph Payne   1661   G. h. 1–9
Rebound
[6] Critici sacri: sive Doctissimorum vivorum in ss. Biblia annotationes, & tractatus.
Opus summa cura recognitum, & in novem tomos divisum. Quid in hoc opere
praestitum sit praefatio ad lectorem ostendit.
Londini: Excudebat Jacobus Flesher, Prostant apud Cornelium Bee,
Guilielmum Wells, Richardum Royston, Samuelum Thomson [in]
Londini. Thomam Robinson [in] Oxonii. Guilielmum Morden [in]
Cantabrigiae, 1660.
Bookplate: Ex dono Domini Josephi Payne militis   civitatis praetoris

Classis 2a in Folio	Librorum	
Bedae opera impressa Col: Agr: 1612.	1 Vol.	1
	2 Vol.	2
	3 Vol.	3

Anthony Mingay   1634   E. g. 10–12
Vol. 1 Foredge: Opera V. Bedae   I   II   III
Vol. 2 Foredge: 4   5   6
[7] Bede: *Venerabilis Bedae Presbyteri Anglo-Saxonis
viri sua aetate doctissimi opera quotquot reperiri potuerunt omnia.*
Coloniae Agrippinae: Sumptibus Anton. Hierati et Ioan. Gymnici, 1612.

Bonaventurae opera impressa Moguntiae 1609	1 Vol.	4
	2 Vol.	5
	3 Vol.	6
	4 Vol.	7

Anthony Mingay   1634   G. g. 10–13
Seventeenth-century calf.
[8] Saint Bonaventura: *Opera:... diligentissime emendata, libris eius multis
undique conquisitis aucta... Nunc primum in Germania post correctissimam Roman.
Vaticanum editionem prodeunt in lucem.*
Moguntiae: Sumptibus Antonij Hierati bibliopolae Coloniensis, 1609.

Cornelius a Lapide in Pentateucum impress. Lutet. 1630		8
In Evangelistas	In 4 Proph: majores Paris	9
	In 12 Proph: minores Paris	10
	In Ecclesiasticum Lugd	11
	In Epistolas Pauli Paris	12
	In Proverbia Paris	13
	In Acta Paris	14

Anthony Mingay's widow   1634   A. k. 1
Foredge: C A Lapide Pentateuch
Front free endpaper: Mistress Susan Mingay Widd. Gave
Cornelius a Lapide in 6 volumes
[9] Cornelius Cornelii a Lapide: *In Pentateuchum Mosis commentaria.*
Lutetiae Parisiorum: Ex officina typographica Edmundi Martini, via
Iacobaea, 1630.

In 4 proph: majores Paris   9
Foredge: Cornel a Lap. In 4 Prophet Maiores   A. k. 8

Classis 2a in Folio   Librorum

Rebound.
[10] Ibid: *Commentaria in quatuor Prophetas maiores.* Parisiis, 1622.

In 12 proph: minores Paris   10
A. k. 4
[11] Ibid: *Commentaria in duodecim prophetas minores.* Parisii, 1630.

In Ecclesiasticum Lugd   11
Foredge: Eccl.   Rebound.   A. k. 3
[12] Ibid: *Ecclesiasticus Iesu Filii Sirach.* Lugduni: ex Officina Landriana
Sumptibus Claudij Dufour & Claudij Gapaillon, 1633.

In Epistolas Pauli Paris   12
Foredge: Epistolas Paul.   Rebound.   A. k. 7
[13] Ibid: *In omnes divi Pauli Epistolas commentaria.* Parisiis: Sumptibus
Ioannis Brachv, 1631.

In Proverbia Paris   13
Foredge: Proverbs.   Rebound.   A. k. 2
[14] Ibid: *Salomon sive Commentarius in Proverbia Salomonis.* Lutetiae
Parisiorum: Sumptibus Sebastiani Cramoisy, 1635.

In Acta Paris   14
Foredge: Acta.   Rebound.   A. k. 6
[15] Ibid: *Commentaria in Acta Apostolorum.* Parisiis, 1631.

/ Tho /Aquinat: Catena aurea In Evangelia   15
Hammond Thurston   1613   C. g. 15
Title page: Tho. Allen.   Rebound in quarter leather.
[16] Thomas Aquinas: *Catenam vere avream dicvnt in Qvatvor evangelia,
Matthaevm, Marcvm, Lvcam et Ionnem.* Parisiis: Apud Michaëlem Sonnium,
1611.
Maldonatus in Evangelia   16
Nathaniel Cock   1675   B. i. 12
Rebound.

[17] Joannes Maldonatus: *Commentarii in quattuor
Evangelistas.* Mussiponti: Ex Typographia Stephani
Mercatoris eiusdem Ducis Typographi, 1612

Classis 2a in Folio	Librorum

Hemingius in Epistolas Argentor   17
John Mingay   1610   B. k. 15
Foredge: Hemingius in Epistolas.
[18] Niel Hemmingsen: *Commentaria in omnes epistolas Apostolorum,*
Pauli, Petri, Iudae, Johannis, Iacobi, et in eam quae ad Hebraeos inscribitur.
Argentorati: Excudebat Theodosius Rihelius, 1586.
Name plate on front cover: Hemmingius in Epistol. Johannes Mingeius
martij 10 1618.

Stella in Lucam Antuerpiae
Edmund Anguish   1617   C. l. 1   18
[19] Diego de Estella: *R[everend] di Patris Fratris Didaci Stellae, Minoritani*
Regularis Observantiae Provinciae Sancti Iacobi, eximii verbi diuini Concionatoris, in
sacrosanctum Iesu Christi Domini nostri Euangelium secundum Lucam enarrationum.
Antverpiae: Sumptibus Viduae & Haeredum Petri Belleri, 1608.
Bookplate: Donum Edmundi Anguish de parochia S. Petri
de Mancroft in Noruica. Ann. Dom. 1617

Hieronimi ab Oleastro Com. In Pentateucum 1588   19
Augustine Scottowe   1621   B. k. 1
[20] Jeronimo Azambuja: *Commentaria in Pentateuchum Mosi: hoc est, in quinque*
primos Bibliorum libros: quibus iuxta M. Sanctis Pagnini Lucensis… interpretationem,
Hebraica veritas cum ad genuinum literae sensum, tum ad mores informandos, ad
vnguem enucleatur a R.P. Fratre Hieronymo ab Oleastro… in lucem edita. Ludguni:
Apud Petrum Landry,
1588.

Oecumenius in epistolas Pauli   20
In epistolas Catholicus   21
Augustine Scottowe   1661   D. k. 13–14
Vol. 1 Rebound. Modern endpapers.
[21] Oecumenius: *Commentaria in Hosce Novi Testamenti tractatus. In Acta*
Apostolorum. In omnes Pauli Epistolas. In Epistolas catholicas omnes. Accesserunt
Arethae Caesareae Cappadociae episcopi explanationes in Apocalypsin. Opus nunc
primum Graece et Latine editum… Interprete Ioann. Hentenio, Emendatore et praelec-
*tore huius editionis Fed. Morello.*Lutetiae Parisiorum: Sumptibus Claudii Sonii,
1631.

Catena Graecorum Patrum in Job   22
Joshua Meene   1666   E. 1. 12

Classis 2a in Folio	Librorum

Seventeenth-century calf.
*[22]*Nicetas: *Catena Graecorum patrum in beatum Iob collectore Niceta Heracleae Metropolita ex duobus MSS Bibliothecae Bodleianae codicibus.* Londini, 1637. (STC 18527)

Gregorius de Valentia   23
Joshua Meene   1666   D. g. 4
Foredge: Greg. Val.
[23] Gregorio dè Valencia: *De rebus fidei hoc tempore controversis libri, qui hactenus extant omnes, cum nonnulis aliis nondum antea editis, ab ipso auctore recogniti, et certa ratione ac methodo distributi, eodemque volumine comprehensi.* Lutetiae Parisiorum: e Typographia Rolini Theoderici & Petri Chevalerii, 1610.

Willet in Genesin   24
John Cropp   1614   C. g. 5
Foredge: Willet in Gen.
[24] Andrew Willet: *Hexapla in Genesin: that is, a sixfold commentarie upon Genesis, wherein sixe seuerall translations, that is, the Septuagint, and the Chalde, two Latin, of Hierome and Tremellius, two English, the great Bible, and the Geneva edition are compared, where they differ, with the originall Hebrew, and Pagnine, and Montanus interlinearie interpretation: together with a sixfold vse of euery chapter, etc.* Cambridge: Iohn Legat, 1605. (STC 25682)

Philo Judaeus. Gr. Lat.   25
William Stinnett   1658   A. k. 9
Rebound
[25] Philo Judaeus: *Omnia quae extant opera.* Lutetiae Parisiorum, 1640.

Azorii Institutiones. 3 vol.   1 vol   26
                                                 2 vol   27
                                                 3 vol   28

Richard Ireland   1692   B. F. 10–12
Nineteenth-century repair. Red leather title label.
[26] Johannes Azorius: *Institutiones morales: in qvibus vniuersae qvaestiones ad conscientiam recte, aut praue factorum pertinentes, breuiter tractantur.* Coloniae Agrippinae: Apud Antonium Hierat. Sub Monocerote, 1613.

Classis 3a in Folio	Librorum	

Lyra. In Vetus Test. cum glossa ordinaria. 1498.   1 vol   1
2 vol   2
3 vol   3
4 vol   4

William Welles   1614   F. f. 3–5
3 volumes only. Rebound by Riley, Dunn and Wilson.
[27] Nicolaus de Lyra: *Biblia Latina cum glosa ordinaria*
et expositione Nicolai de Lyra. Basileae, 1498.
(Hain 3172)

Lavaterus. In Job. Prov: Eccles: et Ezech   5
Thomas Corye   1609   E. i. 7
Foredge: Iob. Pro. Eccles et Ezech
[28] Ludwig Lavater: *Liber Iobi homilijs CXLI.*
Tiguri: Excudebat Christophorus Froschouerus, 1585. (Adams L 314)

Ejusdem Secundum Volumen In Jos. Jud: Paralip. Esther   6
Thomas Corye   1609   E. i. 6
Foredge: Ios. Iud. Paral. et Est
[29] Ibid: *In librum Iosve inuictissimi Imperatoris Israelitarum Homiliae.* Tiguri:
Excudebat Christophorus Froschouerus, 1586.

Junij opera theologica   1 vol   7
Charles Doyly   1610   B. k. 5–6   2 vol   8
Foredge: 1 Tom   2 Tom
[30] Franciscus Junius: *Opera theologica.* Heidelburg:
In officina Sanctandreana, 1608.

Bezae annotationes in N. Test.   9
William Hannam   1611   F. f. 11
Foredge: Theod Bezae No. Testam.   Rebound.
*[31] Iesu Christi Domini Nostri Nouum Testamentum, siue, Nouum foedus: cuius
Graeco contextui respondent interpretations duae: vna, vetus: altera, Theodori Bezae.*
[Geneva]: Sumptibus Haered. Evst. Vignon, 1598.

Ejusdem Tractat. Theologici   10
William Hannam   1611   D. k. 15
Foredge: Theod: Bezae Tractationum Theologicarum
[32] Theodore de Beze: *Tractationum Theologicarum: In Quibus
Pleraque Christianae Religionis dogmata aduersus haereses*

Classis 2a in Folio	Librorum

nostris temporibus renouatas solide ex Verbo Dei defenduntur.
Genevae: Apud Eustathius Vignon, 1582.

Zanchij opera. 1605.	1 vol	11
	2 vol	12
	3 vol	13

Susanna Downing   1608   E. G. 7–9
Vol. 1 Foredge: 1   2   3   TOM.
Vol. 2 Foredge: 4   5   6   TOM
Vol. 3 Foredge: 7   8   TOM
Boards detached.
[33] Hieronymus Zanchius: *Operum theologicorum.*
[Geneva]: excudebat Stephanus Gamonetus, 1605.

Lutheri opera Wittebergae	1 vol	14
	2 vol	15
	3 vol	16
	4 vol	17
	5 vol	18
	6 vol	19
	7 vol	20

Thomas Corye   1609   E. l. 1–7
Rebound
[34] Martin Luther: *Opera omnia...cum praefationibus*
Philippi Melancthonis.
Witterbergae: Typis Zachariae Lehmani, 1554–82.

Salmeronis Comment in N. Test. impr' 1605	1 Vol	21
	2 Vol	22
	3 Vol	23
	4 Vol	24
	5 Vol	25
	6 Vol	26
	7 Vol	27

John Borrage   1631   A. f. 1–7
Rebound
[35] Alfonso Salmeron: *Commentarii in Evangelicum historiam et*
in Acta Apostolorum nunc primum in lucem editi. Addita est auctoris
vita. Coloniae Agrippinae: Apud Antonium Hierat, et Ioan. Gymni, 1604.

Classis 4a in Folio	Librorum

Polani. Syntagma Theologiae Hanoviae   1
Bernard Church   1678   B. h. 5
Foredge: Instit
[36] Amandus Polanus: *Syntagma theologiae Christianae.*
Hanoviae: Typis Wechelianis, 1615.

Calvini Institut per Le Proux   2
Sir Thomas Hyrne   1609   C. f. 6
Foredge: Instit.
[37] John Calvin: *Institutio Christianae religionis Iohanne Calvino authore; que ad*
superiors editions hac postrema, omnium emendatissima locupletissimaque, recens
addita... Genevae: Apud Iohannem le Preux, 1607.

Musculi Loc: Comm: Basilea   3
William Adamson   1700   A. l. 10
Foredge: Muscul: Loci:
Rebound in quarter leather.
[38] Wolfgang Musculus: *Loci communes Sacrae Theologiae,*
jam recens recogniti et emendati... Adjectus est...multo
quam antea copiosior index. Basileae, 1599.

Chemnitij Loc. Com. Wittebergae   4
Edward Nutting   1616   D. g. 6
Foredge: Loci Theolog.
[39] Martinus Chemnitius: *Loci theologici... quibus et loci*
communes D. Philippi Melanchthonis... explicantur...
editi opera & studio Polycarpi Leyseri D.
Wittebergae: Typis Wolffgangi Meisneri, 1615.
Front free endpaper: 'Quinto Februarij 1616 Dono dedit
Mr Edward Nutting huic incipirit Biblioth'.

P. Martyris Loc. Comm: Heidelbergae   5
Charles Doyly   1610   A. g. 10
Foredge: Loci communes
[40] Pietro Martire Vermigli: *Loci communes Petri Martyris*
Vermilii Florentini, Sacrarum Literarum in schola Tigurina
Professoris: ex variis ipsius authoris scriptis, in
vnum librum collecti, & in quatuor classes distributi.
Heidelbergae: Apud Iohannem Lancellotum, 1603.

Classis 4a in Folio	Librorum

Hemingij opuscula per Vignon   6
John Mingay   1610   B. k. 16
[41] Niels Hemmingsen: D. Nicolai Hemmingii... Opuscula
Theologica... additis varijs indicibus notis, & praefationibus
necessarijs. Genevae: Excudebat Evstathius Vignon, 1586.
Name plate on front cover: Iohannis E. Mingei munusculo Hemmingii
opuscula March 10 1618

Lorichij thesaurus Theolog Brisgoiae   7
Anthony Mingay   1634   A. i. 10
Rebound. Modern endpapers.
[42] Jodocus Lorich: *Thesaurus novus utriusque theologiae theoricae et practicae.*
Friburgi Brisgoiae: Excudebat Martinus Bockler, 1609.

Gerrhardi Loci Communes in quat vol		
	1 Vol	8
	2 Vol	9
	3 Vol	10
	4 Vol	11

Joseph Payne   1661   B. i. 1–4
Vols. 1 and 2 rebound. Modern endpapers.
[43] Johann Gerhard: *Loci theologici, cum pro adstruenda*
veritate, tum pro destruenda quorumvis contradicentium
falsitate, per theses nervose, solide & copiose explicati.
Francofurti et Hamburgi: Sumptibus Zachariae Hertelii, 1657.

Bonacinae opera   12
Thomasina Brooke   1659   A. k. 11
Rebound
[44] Martino Bonacina: *Opera omnia.* Parisiis: Sumptibus Ioannis Branchv,
1633.

Fosteri Lexicon Hebraicum   13
Rebound
William Adamson   1700   D. k. 5
[45] Johann Forster: *Dictionarium Hebraicum nouum:*
non ex Rabinorum commentis, nec nostrarium doctorum
stulta imitatione descriptum, sed ex ipsis thesauris Sacrorum
Bibliorum, & et eorundem accurate locorum collatione

Classis 4a in Folio	Librorum

depromptum, cum phrasibus Scripturae Veteris & Noui
Testamenti diligenter annotates.
Basileae: Per Frobenium et Episcopium, 1564. (Adams F 784)
Much marginal annotation

Filiucij Moralia   14
Thomasina Brooke 1659   E. h. 5
Binding crudely repaired. Detached boards.
[46] Vincent Filiucci: *Moralivm quaestionvm de Christianis officijs,*
et casibvs conscientiae, ad formam cursus, qui praelegi solet
in eiusdem Societatis Collegio Romano.
Coloniae Agrippinae: Apud Antonium & Arnoldum Hieratos
fratres, 1629.

Matthai Parisiensis opera   15
Bernard Church   1678   D. i. 5
Seventeenth-century calf.
[47] Matthew Paris: *Matthaei Paris monachi Albanensis*
Angli, historia major: juxta exemplar Londinense 1571,
verbatim recusa. Et cum Rogeri Wendoveri, Willielmi
Rishangeri, authorisque majori minorique historiis
Chronicisque MSS. editore Willielmo Wats.
Londini: Excudebat Richardus Hodgkinson, 1640. (STC 19210)

< Speeds History and Mapps London>   <1>   <15>
Ann Corbett   1617   I. h. 1–2
Rebound
[48] John Speed: *The theatre of the empire of Great Britaine: presenting an exact*
geography of the kingdom of England, Scotland, Ireland, and the Iles adjoyning.
London: Printed for Thomas Basset... and Richard Chiswel, 1611. (STC
23041)

Plinii Historia naturalis Lat. Francofurti   <2>   16
Richard Ireland   1692   B. h. 6
Foredge: C. Plinius
[49] Pliny the Elder: *Historia mundi naturalis. C. Plinii Secundi:*
hoc est amplissimum, lucidissimum, perspicacissimumque,
nec non plane mirandum totius vniversi, rervmque natvralium
speculum. Typis excudebatur Francoforti ad Moenum, a partu
Deipar & virginis, 1582. (Adams P 1579)

Classis 4a in Folio	Librorum

Plutarchi vitae Lat. Francofurti   <3>   17
Bernard Church   1678   C. h. 4
Foredge: Plutarchi
[50] Plutarch: *Plutarchi Chaeronensis, summi philosophi &*
Historici, parallela. Francoforti ad Moenum: Impensis Sigismundi
Feyrabendium, 1580.
Heavily annotated.

Polidori Virgilij historiae Anglicanae   <4>   18
William Adamson   1700   D. g. 10–11
Vol. 2 comprehensively rebound.
[51] Polydore Vergil: *Polidori Vergilii Urbinatis Anglicae historiae*
libri XXVI: indices rerum singularum copiosos et usui
egregrio futuros, adiecimus. Basileae: Apud Io. Bebelium,
1534. (Adams V 446)
Johannes Brewster verus possessor huis libri.
Vol. 1 front free endpaper in an eighteenth century hand:
'There is no doctrine so absurd in itself, but that it has at some
time or other been embraced with no ordinary zeal by the greatest
scholars in the age they liv'd in nor has any historian been so free
from humane imperfections as never to have mixd amongst the most
shining parts of their history some thing that is effete and trivial, and
now and then absurd and nonsensical – witness the learned author'.
Heavily annotated.

Rosini Antiquitates Romanae   <5>   19
Joanna Blowe   1613   B. e. 14
[52] Johannes Rosinus: *Romanorum antiquitatum libri decem ex*
variis scriptoribus summa fide singularique diligentia
collecti a Ioanne Rosino. Basileae: ex officina Haeredum Petri
Pernae, 1583. (Adams R 798)

Heroologia Anglicana   <6>   20
William Adamson   1700   Not found
[53] Henry Holland: *Her[o]ologia Anglica: hoc est clarissimorum*
et doctissimorum, aliquot Anglorum, qui floruerunt ab anno
Cristi. M.D. vsque ad presentem annum M.D.C.XX viuae effigies
vitae et elogia. Arnhem: Impensis Crispini Passaei calcographus et
Jansonii bibliopolae Arnhemiensis, [1620].

Classis 4a in Folio		Librorum

Purchas his Pilgrimage pars ia   7   21
Thomas Catlyn   1617   D. e. 8
Rebound
[54] Samuel Purchas: *Purchas his pilgrimage, or Relations of
the world and the religions observed in all ages and places
discouered, from the Creation vnto this present.*
London: Printed by William Stansby for Henry Fetherstone,
1617. (STC 20507)

Historiae rerum et urbis Amstelodamensis Auth.
Pontano   8   22
Richard Ireland   1692   H. c. 21
[55] Johannes Isacius Pontanus: *Rerum et urbis Amstelodamensium
historia: In qua Hollandiae primum atque inde Amstelandiae,
oppidiq[ue], natales, exordia, progressus, privilegia, statuta
eventaq[ue] mirabilia cum novis urbis incrementis commercijsque
ac navigationibus longinquis, aliaque ad politiam spectantia,
additis suo loco tabulis aeri incisis, ad haec usque tempora,
observata annorum serie accurate omnia dedicuntur.*
Amsterodami: excudit J. Hondius, 1611.

Dreyton's Polyalbion   9   23
Anthony Mingay   1634   D. l. 5
Front board detached.
[56] Michael Drayton: *Polyolbion. Or a chorographicall description of…Great
Britaine…digested in a poem.* London: printed by H.L. for
Mathew Lownes, 1613. (STC 7227)

/Reperiendum in folio   /Refere ad sequentem classem/
   sequentis classis/

<Chronica Regnorum Asquilonarius>   <10>
John Cropp   1614   Not found
[57] Albert Krantz: *Chronica regnorum aquilonarium. Daniae, Suetiae, Norvagiae.*

<Legenda per Jacobum de Voragine>   <11>
Edward Reynolds   1676   G. e. 19
Spine repaired.
[58] Jacobus de Voragine: *Legenda hec aurea nitidis excutitur*

Classis 4a in Folio	Librorum

formis. Lugduni: per Gilbertum de villiers, 1514.
'John Kirkpatrick 1712' on rear endpaper.
Did Kirkpatrick borrow this book and not return it?

<Catalogus sanctorum per Petrum de natalis> <12>
Joanna Blowe   1613   A. g. 18
[59] Petrus de Natalibus: *Catalogus sanctorum et*
gestorum eorum ex diuersis voluminibus collectus.
Lugduni: Jacobum saccon, 1514. (Adams P 46)
<Bartholomeus Anglius de rerum proprietat> <13>
John Watson   1678   C. e. 1
Binding much worn.

[60] Bartholomeus Anglicus: *De rerum proprietatibus*
inscriptum ad communem studiosorum. Nuremberg:
Joannis Koberger, 1519. (Adams B 264)

Effigies et elogia praestantus theologoris qui Rom <14>   24
Antichristo praecipuae oppugnarunt
Robert Garsett   1612   C. l. 17
Gold blocked device in centre of covers with initials 'RG'.
[61] Jacobus Verheiden: *Praestantium aliquot theologorum,*
qui Rom. Antichristum praecipue oppugnarunt, effigies: quibus
addita elogia, librorumque catalogi. Hagae-Comitis: ex officina
Bucoldi Cornelii Nieulandii, 1602,

Glossa Illyrici Flacci
Richard Ireland   1692   F. f. 9   <15>   25
Foredge: Gloss Flacii
[62] *Novum Testamentum… ex versione Erasmi, innumeris in locis ad Graecam veri-*
tatem, genuinumque sensum emendata. Glossa compendiaria M. Matthiae Flacii Illyrici
Albonensis
in novum Testamentum. Basileae: Per Petrum Pernam et Theobaldum
Dietrich, 1570. (Adams F 1702)

A concordance in English made in K. Edward ye vi time
Samuel Fromanteel   1665   Not found   <16>   26
[63] John Marbeck: *A concordance, that is to saie, a worke*
wherein by the ordre of the letters of the A.B.C. ye maie redely
finde any worde conteigned in the whole Bible. London: R. Grafton, 1550.

Classis 4a in Folio	Librorum

Doctor Jacksons Works compleat 3 Fol: London: 1673
Anthony Norris   1673   E. i. 9–11   28 29 27
[64] Jackson, Thomas: *The works of the Reverend*
and Learned Divine,Thomas Jackson. London:
Printed by J. Macock for John Martyn, 1673. (W 90)
Vol. 1 front free endpaper: 9 May 1673:
'If any imperfection be in the bindinge of these 3 volumes of Dr Jackson
I oblige my selfe to make it good. William Oliver bibliopola Norvicensis'.

Gregorij Sayrj Casus conscientiae
John Whitefoot   1658   D. g. 9 31   <16>   31a
[65] Gregory Sayer: *Clavis regia sacerdotum, casuum conscientiae,*
sive theologiae moralis thesauri locos omnes aperiens: et
canonistarum atque summistarum difficultates, ad communem
praxim pertinentes doctissime decidens, & copiosissime explicans.
Monasterii Westfaliae: Sumptibus Michaelis Dalii & Bernardi
Raesfelt, 1628.
Note on title page: pretium £1. 5s.

Sylburgij Etymologicon Magnum
Richard Ireland   1692   D. f. 18   31
Rebound.
[66] Fridericus Sylburgius: *Etymologicon magnum; seu Magnum grammaticae*
penu: in quo & originum & analogiae doctrina
ex veterum sententia copiosissime proponitur: historiae item & antiquitatis monumenta
passim attinguntur… opera Friderici Sylburgii veter.[Heidelberg]: E typographeio
Hieronymi Commelini, 1594. (Adams S 2133)

Classis 5a in Folio	Librorum

Codicis Justiniani Libr. 9   1
[67] Justinian I, Emperor of the East: *Codicis*
Justiniani priores libri nouem.   Not found

Decretalia per Bartholoum   1614   C. h. 11   2
Rebound by Riley, Dunn and Wilson, 1995
[68] Decretalium hac Georgicanam compilationem
cum apparatu domini Barnhardi. Nuremberge:
Antonius Koberger, 1496.

Classis 5a in Folio	Librorum

Compilatio Decretalium   3
Foredge: Decretales.   Rebound.
I. h. 11
[69] Decretales cum summariis suis et textuum
divisionibus ac etiam rubricarus continuationibus.
Venetijs: per Baptistam de Torris, 10 October 1496.

Archidiaconus super Decretalia 1496   4
Richard Ireland 1692   C. h. 11
Rebound by Riley Dunn and Wilson, 1996
[70]Decretales cum summarijs suis et textuum
divisionibus ac etiam rubricarum continuationibus.
Nuremberg: Anton Koberger, 10 June 1496.
Occasional annotations

Lyrae opera absque glossa   1 Vol.   5
    2 Vol.   6

Richard Ross   1615   F. g. 6–7
[71] Nicholas de Lyra: *Postilla super Biblia cum*
additionibus Pauli Burgensis. Nuremberg: impensis
Anthonij Koburger, 1481.   (Hain 10369)
Volume 2 annotated.

Zuingeri theatrum vitae humanae in 4 Volumin
    1 Vol.   7
    2 Vol.   8
    3 Vol.   9
    4 Vol.   10

Augustine Pettus   1610   E. i. 1–4
[72] Theodor Zwinger: *Theatrum humanae vitae Theodori Zuingeri Bas.tertiatone*
novem voluminibus locupletatum, interpolatum, renovatum Jacobi Zvingeri fil. recogni-
tione plurium inprimis recentiorum
exemplorum auctario, titulorum et indicum certitudine ampliatum
cum quadrigemino elencho.
Basileae: per Sebastianum Henricpetri, 1604.
In volume 2 on half-title: Augustine Pettus pretiam £4. 5. 0

Classis 5a in Folio	Librorum

Schindleri Lex: Pentaglott   11
Richard Ireland   1692   B. h. 3
Foredge: Lexicon Pentaglot   Rebound.
[73] Valentin Schindler: *Lexicon pentaglotton, hebraicum, chaldaicum, syriacum,*
talmudico-rabbinicum, & arabicum. In quo omnes voces...
sub suis singulae radicibus digest[a]e continentur... Collectum, et concinnatum a
...Valentino Schindlero... Opus novum, nunc post
Authoris obitum, ex ipso autographo... editum
Francofurti ad Moenum: typis Joannis Jacobi Hennei, 1612.

Suidae opera Gr: & Lat   1 Vol.   12
                                                   2 Vol.   13
Thomasina Brooke   1659   D. g. 2–3
Marbled endpapers.
[74] Suidas: *Cuius integram Latinam interpretationem, & perpetuam Graeci textur*
emendationem. Coloniae Allobrogum: Apud Petrum &
Jacobum Chouet, 1519.

Schmidij Concord. Graec: 14
Thomasina Brooke   1659   E. f. 6
Seventeenth-century calf.
[75] Erasmi Schmidii: *Novi Testamenti Iesu Christi Graeci, hoc est, originalis*
linguae tameion alijs Concordantiae. Wittebergae: Apud heredes Clementis
Bergeri, 1638.

Calvini Lexicon Juridicum   15
Thomasina Brooke   1659   C. f. 1,2 or 3
[76] Jean Calvin: *Lexicon iuridicum: ivris Caesarei simvl, et canonici:*
Fevdalis item civilis, criminalis: theoretici, ac practici: et in schola
et in foro vsitatarvm...vocum penvs...Stvdio et opera Ioannis Calvini,
alias Kahl.

Josephi opera Graec: & Latine   16
Thomasina Brooke   1659   C. h. 10
Marbled endpapers.
[77] Flavius Josephus: *Flavii Iosephi Opera quae extant.*
Genevae: Apud Petrum Aubertum, 1634.

Theophilacti opera   1 Vol.   17
                                                   2 Vol.   18

Classis 5a in Folio   Librorum

Augustine Scottowe   1661
[78] Theophylact: *Commentarii in quatuor Euangelia.*
Lutetiae Parisiorum: Apud Carolum Morellum, 1635.
Note on front free endpaper: 'Bought in Paules Churchyard
at the Signe of the Kings Armes and I doe warrant it perfect
or to make it perfect by me Richard Whitaker 18 May 1636'.

[79] Theophylact: *In D. Pauli Epistolas Commentarii.*
Londini: E. Typographeo Regio, 1636. (STC 23948)

Reymundi Mar: Pugio fidei   19
John Whitefoot   1658   A. k. 14
Binding repaired. Modern endpapers.
[80] Ramon Marti: *Pugio fidei Raymundi Martini Ordinis Praedicatorum Aduersus*
*Mauros, et Iudaeos: Nunc primum in lucem editus.*Parisiis: Apud Mathurinum
Henault, via Iacoboea sub signo
Angeli custodies: Apud Ioannem Henault, via Iacobaea sub signo
S. Raphaelis, 1651.

Merceri Thesaurus lingua Heb   20
Bernard Church   1678   G. g. 9
Rebound.
[81] Sanctes Pagninus: *Thesaurus linguae sanctae,*
sive Lexicon Hebraicum... Lugduni:
Apud Bartholomaeum. Vincentium, 1575. (Adams P 38)

Ludolphus de vita Christi   21
Thomas Morley   1663   G. g. 13
[82] Ludolf von Sachsen: *Vita Iesu Christi e quatuor Euangeliis*
et scriptoribus orthodoxies concinnata per Ludolphum de
Saxonia ex ordine Carthusianorum.
Antuerpiae: Apud Ioannem Keerbergium, 1618.

Ainsworth's works   22
William Stinnett   1658   D. k. 6
[83] Henry Ainsworth: *Annotations upon the five*
bookes of Moses, the Booke of the Psalmes,
and the Song of Songs or Canticles.
London: printed for John Bellamie, 1627. (STC 219)

Classis 5a in Folio	Librorum

Damasceni opera   23
Thomas Catlyn   1617   B. e. 19
Rebound.
[84] John of Damascus: *Ioan Damasceni viri suo tempore in divinis primatum tenentis, omnia quae hactenus & a nobis & ab aliis haberi potuerunt opera, ad vetustiora Graecorum exemplaria collata atque emendata.*
Basileae: Excudebat Henricus Petrus, 1535.

Photij Bibliotheca   24
Edmund Anguish   1617   C. l. 19
[85] Photius: *Photii Bibliotheca: sive lectorum a Photio librorum recensio, censura atque excerpta philologorum, oratorum, historicorum, philosophorum, medicorum, theologorum. ex Graeco Latine reddita, scholiisque illustrata.*
Augustae Vindelicorum: Ad insigne pinus, 1606.

Bartholomae Anglius de rerum proprietatibus &c   25
John Watson   1678   C. e. 1

[86] Bartholomaeus Anglicus: *Venerandi patris Bartholomei Anglici, ordinis Minoru[m]: viri eruditissimi: opus: De reru[m] proprietatibus inscriptum…iam denuo summa cura labore ac industria recognitu[m]: chalcographieq[ue] demandatum: atq[ue] ad fabre politu[m].*
Nurembergii: Joannis Koberger, 1519.
Duplicate entry of *[60]*.

Catalogij Sanctorum per Petrus de Natalibus Venetiis   26
Joanna Blowe   1613   A. g. 18
Remains of clasps.
[87] Petrus de Natalibus: *Catalogus sanctorum et gestorum eorum ex diversis voluminibus collectus.* Lugduni, Jacobum Saccon, 1514.

Legenda per Jacobum de Voragine   27
Edward Reynolds 1676   G. e. 19
[88] Jacobus de Voragine: *Legenda aurea nitidis excutitur formis.* Lugduni: Gilbertum de Villiers, 1514.
Note on sig. Bii: A Book worthy to be preserved by all Protestants to manifest the abominable lies & foolish superstitions of the Papists religion – printed before the Reformation as at the end appeareth videlicet AD 1514
Duplicate entry of *[58]*

Chronica regnorum Aquiloniarium vide class Occid: C [5]   28
John Cropp   1614   Not found
[89] Albertus Krantz: *Chronica Regnorum Aquilonarium, Daniae, Suetiae, Norvagiae.*

Classis 6a in Folio	Librorum	
Bernardi opera Parisiis 1586	Vol. 1	1
	Vol. 2	2

Henry Doyly   1609   F. i. 15–16
Vol. 1 Foredge: Bern Tom 1
Vol. 2 Foredge: Tom 2
Front board detached, vol. 1.
[90] St. Bernard of Clairvaux: *Diui Bernardi Claraeuallensis abbatis primi religiosissimi ecclesiae doctoris...Opera omnia.*
Parisiis: cum signo Magnae navis, 1586.

Hieronimi opera Parisiis 1609	Vol. 1	3
	Vol. 2	4
	Vol. 3	5

Robert Sedgwick   1610   G. h. 10–12
Foredge: S. Hieron. Rebound.
[91] Saint Jerome: *Opera omnia quae reperiri potuerunt, ex antiquis exemplaribus diligentia et labore Mariani Victorii Reatini...*
emendata, atque argumentis et scholijs illustrata.
Parisii: Apud Bibliopolas urbis Parisiensis Consortes, 1609.

Augustini opera edita Basileae 1526	Vol. 1	6
	Vol. 2	7
	Vol. 3	8
	Vol. 4	9
	Vol. 5	10
	Vol. 6	11

Thomas Corbett   1609   G. g. 3–8
[92] Saint Augustine: *Opera omnia.*
Basiliae: per Ambrosium et Aurelium Frobenios, 1569.

Gregorij magni opera Paris 1580   12
William Batho   1616   E. g. 3
Foredge: Opera Gregorii

---

[5] Clearly, the book stock on the western side of the Library was classified.

Classis 6a in Folio	Librorum

[93] Saint Gregory: *Sancti Gregorii Magni...Opera...beneficio Bertholdi Rembolt in unum volumen redacta.*
Parisiis: In edibus Joannis Parvi, 1518.
'W[*illiam*] Batho' on title page

Chrysostomi opera latine ex editione	Vol. 1	13
Erasmi Basileae 1530	Vol. 2	14
	Vol. 3	15
	Vol. 4	16

Thomas Newhouse   1611   I. h. 14–18
[94] Saint John Chrysostom: *D. Joannis Chrysostomi archiepiscopi Constantinopolitani opera: quae hactenus versa sunt omnia, ad Graecorum codicum collationem multis in locis per utriusque linguae peritos emendata.*
Basiliae: in officina Frobeniana, 1530. (Adams C 1514)
Much marginal annotation

Cyrilli opera latine		17

Robert Sedgwick   1610   A. k. 12
Boards detached.
[95] Saint Cyril: *Divi Cyrilli Alexandrini Episcopi theologi praestantissimi opera qvae hactenvs haberi potvere, in tomos qvinqve digesta.* Basileae: per Haeredes Ioannis Hervagii, 1566. (Adams C 3169)

Basilij opera in 2 vol: Graec collat: Graece-Lat:	1 Vol.	<18>18
Paris 1618.	2 Vol.	19

Augustine Scottowe   1621   C. h. 8–9
Rebound.
[96] Saint Basil: *Opera omnia, quae reperiri potuerunt. Nunc primum Graece et Latine coniunctim edita, in duos tomos distributa...Cum in Graeco textu, tum in Latina versione correcta et illustrata, ac ducentis quatuordecim epistolis aucta. Accessit appendix, quae seorsim conciones a Symeone Magistro excerptas, et notas continet, quibus varia eiusdem auctoris loca emendatur.* Parisiis: Apud Michaelem Sonnium, 1618.

Ambrosij opera edita Basileae 1527	1 Vol.	<19> 20
	2 Vol.	<20> 21

Charles Doyly   1610   C. g. 7–8
Vol. 2 Rebound. Modern endpapers.

Classis 6a in Folio	Librorum

[97] Saint Ambrose: *Omnia opera, per eruditos viros.*
Basileae: 1567. (Adams A 942)

/Graeco-lat/
Epiphanij opera Graec: Collat. Edit Paris 1622   <21>   22
in 2 Vol.   <22>   23
Thomas Barrett   1633   C. i. 14–15
[98] Saint Epiphanius: *Opera omnia in duos tomos distributa. Dionysius Petauius*
Aurelianensis…ex veteribus libris recensuit, Latine vertit, et animadversionibus, illus-
travit. Parisiis: sumptibus Michaelis Sonnii, 1622.
Note of the price (56s. 8*d.*) on the half-title.

/Graeco-lat/
Iustini Martyris opera Graec. Collat. Ex typis   <23>   24
Commelianis
Anne Corbet   1617   H. c. 2
Foredge: Just Martyr
Rear board detached.
[99] Saint Justin Martyr: *S. Iustini, philosophi et martyris, opera, qvae*
vndeqvaqve inveniri potvervnt. [Heidelberg]: ex typographeio Hieronymi
Commelini, 1593. (Adams J 498)

/Graeco-lat/
Clementis Alexandrini opera Graec.   <24>   25
Collat: Ludg. Bat. 1616.
Gabriel Barber   1614   Not found
[100] Saint Clement of Alexandria: *Clementis Alexandrini*
Opera graece et latine quae extant. Daniel Heinsius
textum graecum recensuit, interpretationem veterem
locis infinitis meliorem reddidit.
Lugduni Batavorum: 1616.

Origenis opera edita Basileae 1537 in 2 vol.   <25>   26
                                                  <26>   27
Robert Sedgwick   1610   G. g. 1–2
Rebound.
[101] Origen: *Opera, quae quidem extant omnia, per Des. Erasmum Roterodamum*
partim versa, partim vigilanter recognita, cum praefatione de vita, phrasi, docendi
ratione, et operibus illius, adiectis epistola Beati Rhenani nuncupatoria, quae pleraque

Classis 6a in Folio	Librorum

de uita obituque ipsius Erasmi cognitu digna continet.
Basileae: Ex officina Frobeniana, 1545.
Much marginal annotation

Irenej opera per Le Proux 1570   <27>   28
Robert Sedgwick   1610   Not found
[102] Saint Irenaeus: *Libri quinque aduersus*
portentosas haereses Valentini & allorum...
[Paris]: Apud Ioannem le Preux, 1570. (Adams I 157)

Hilarij opera edit. Basileae   <28>   29
Robert Sedgwick   1610   E. i. 15
Foredge: D. Hila
Binding repaired. Modern endpapers. Evidence of clasps.
[103] Hilarius, bishop of Poitiers: *Lvcvbrationes quotquot extant,*
olim per Des. Erasmum Roterod. Haud mediocribus sudoribus emendate, nunc
denuo uigilantissime & ad plura exemplaria per D. Martinum Lypsium
collatae & recognite. Earum catalogum reperies uersa hac pagina.
Basileae: Froben, 1550. (Adams H 555)
Binding signed RP.

Athanasij opera Latine edit: Basileae 1564   30
Robert Sedgwick   1610   E. f. 10
Remains of clasps.
[104] Saint Athanasius: *Opera, in qvatuor tomos distributa: quorum tres sunt a*
Petro Nannio Alcmariano, ad Graecorum exemplarium fidem iam primum conuersi.
Basileae, 1564. (Adams A 2084)

Tertulliani opera edita Basileae 1562 vide Classem 9am   30
Robert Sedgwick   1610   Not found
[105] Tertullian: *Opera omnia. Non omissis accuratis B. Rhenani*
annotationibus. Basileae, 1562. (Adams T 411)

Theophilactij com. in Evangelia Lat. 1536 et in Epistolas   31
Coloniae vide classem 5am
[106] Theophylactus: *In quatuor Euangelia, enarrationes*
luculentissimae diligenter iam Tandem atq[ue] adamussim
recognitae. Coloniae, 1536. (Adams T 591)

[107] Theophylactus: *In D. Pauli Epistolas commentarii: studio...Augustini*

Classis 6a in Folio   Librorum

Lindselli Episc. Herefordensis, ex antiques manuscriptis codicibus descripti, et castigati,
et nunc primum Graece editi. Londini, 1636. D. h. 15
Duplicate of *[75]*.

Jo: Damasceni opera edita Basileae 1535 vide class. 5a   32
Damascene.
Thomas Catlyn   1617   B. e. 19
Rebound.
[108] John of Damascus: *Ioan Damasceni viri suo tempore in divinis primatum*
tenentis, omnia quae hactenus & a nobis & ab aliis haberi potuerunt opera, ad vetus-
tiora Graecorum exemplaria collata atque emendata. Basileae: Petrus, 1535.

Classis 7a in Folio   Librorum

Minshaei Dictionarium undecim ling. Lond: 1617   1
Thomas Catlyn   1617   F. k. 7
[109] John Minsheu: *The Guide into the Tongues.* London:
apud Ioannem Browne, 1617. (STC 17944)

Emendatio ejusdem 1627   2
Norwich Corporation   1628   F. k. 8
Rebound.
[110] John Minsheu: *Minshaei emendatio, vel à mendis expurgatio, seu*
augmentatio sui Ductoris in linguas.
London: printed by John Haviland, 1627. (STC 17947)
Inscription on front free endpaper: This Booke was given to the
Library by the City in the time of the Maioralty of Mr Thomas Cory

Concord. Lat: Biblioth. Utriusq Test. 1611   3
Peter Laune   1614   G. h. 3
[111] Pierre de Besse: *Concordantiae Bibliorvm vtrivsque testamenti generales.*
Parisiis: Apud Michaelem Sonnivm, 1611.
Inscribed 'Anno 1614. Petrus Lavnaevs pastor ecclesiae Gallo belgicae
quae est Nordoviciam die 8 vus mensis Junij peregrinatione
in Galliam suspicions do: de: hunc librum Bibliothecae publicae
Nordouicanae in perpetuo erga theologicas eiusdem ciuitatis
(eu quibus erat coniunctissimus) Christianissimi amoris
testimonium'.

Classis 7a in Folio	Librorum

Concord. Hebr: per Rabbi Mordecay Nathan   4
William Wells   1614   G. h. 7
Rebound. Modern endpapers.
[112] Mordecai Nathan: *Concordantiarum Hebraicum capita*
*quae sunt de vocum expositionibus.*Basileae: per Henrichum
Petri, 1556. (Adams N 188)

Marini Arca Noae Venetijs 1593   5
Thomas Atkins   1618   A. i. 8
Foredge: Thesaurus Linguae Sanctae
[113] Marcus Marinus: *Arca Noe thesaurus linguae sanctae nouus.*Venetiis:
Apud Iohannem Degarum, 1593. (Adams M 597)

Calepini Dictionariu[m] octo Ling: Basileae 1584   6
Joanna Blowe   1613   D. g. 1
Binding repaired. Modern endpapers.
[114] Ambrosius Calepinus: *Dictionarium*
octo linguarum..Respondent autem vocabulis Latinis,
Hebraica, Graeca, Gallica, Italica, Germanica, Belgica,
Hispanica. Basileae: per Sebastianum Henricpetri, 1584.

Ravanelli Bibliotheca 1650   7
Joseph Payne   B. h. 4
Binding repaired. Modern endpapers.
[115] Petrus Ravanellus: *Petri Rauanelli Vticensis Occitani*
Bibliotheca sacra, seu Thesaurus scripturae canonicae
amplissimus: In quo ea, qvae in vtroqve foedere extant.
Genevae: Sumptibus Petri Chouet, 1650.

Scapulae Lexicon Graec. Lat. Basileae. 1615   8
Thomas Catlyn   1617   A. i. 11
Detached front boards.
[116] Johann Scapula: *Lexicon Graeco-Latinum nouum*
in quo ex primitivorum & simplicium fontibus
derivata atque composita ordine non minus naturali,
quam alphabetico, breuiter & dilucide deducuntur.
Basileae: Per Sebastianum Henricpetri, [1615].

Illyrici. Clavis scripturae 1629   9
Nathaniel Remington   1629   B. f. 1

Classis 7a in Folio   Librorum

Binding repaired. Modern endpapers.
Foredge: Cla. Scrip. per Math. Illyricis
[117] Matthias Flacius Illyricus: *Clavis Scripturae Sacrae*
seu, De sermone Sacrarum Literarum. Basileae:
Apud Heinricpetrinos, 1629

Neumans Concordance London. 1643   10
Thomas Nelson   A. i. 13
Remains of clasps.
[118] Samuel Newman: *A large and complete concordance*
to the Bible in English, according to the last translation.
First collected by Clement Cotton, and now much enlarged
and emended by Samuel Newman. London: printed for Thomas Downes
and James Young, 1643. (W 929)
Front free endpaper: Tho. Nelson oweth this booke
Given him by his Grandmother Mrs Hutton
May 11 1663

Martinij Lexicon Philologicum 1623   11
Anthony Mingay   1634   E. f. 9
Rebound
[119] Matthias Martini: *Lexicon philologicum, praecipue*
etymologicum: in quo Latinae et a Latinis auctoribus
usurpatae tum purae tum barbarae voces ex originibus
declarantur. Bremae: Typis Villerianis, 1623.

Gesneri Bibliotheca 1545   12
Mrs Mingay   C. g. 2
Detached boards.
[120] Konrad Gesner: *Bibliotheca universalis: sive catalogus*
omnium scriptorum locupletissimus, in tribus
linguis, Latina, Graeca et Hebraica.
Tiguri: apud Christophorum Froschouerum, 1545. (Adams G 516)

Aquinatis summae Col. Agrip. 1604   13
Hammond Thurston   1613   F. i. 4
Rebound.
[121] Thomas Aquinas: *S. Thomae Aquinatis, summa totius theologiae.* Coloniae
Agrippinae: Ex officina Antonij Hierati, 1604.

Classis 7a in Folio	Librorum

Halensis. Summae Col. Agrip:

	Vol. 1	14
	Vol. 2	15
	Vol. 3	16

Nathaniel Remington   1629   Not found
[122] Alexander of Hales: *Universae theologiae summa: in quatuor partes
ab ipsomet authore distributa.* Coloniae Agrippinae: Sumptibus Ioannis
Gymnici, 1622.

Bannesij Comment: in Tho: Aquin. Duaci 1614.

	Vol. 1	17
	Vol. 2	18

Samuel Chapman   1633   E. g. 13–14
Binding repaired. Modern endpapers.
[123] Domingo Banez: *Scholastica commentaria in primam
partem Summae theologicae S. Thomae Aquinatis.*
Duaci: Ex typographia Petri Borremans, 1614.

Durandus in Sententias Lugdun 1587   19
William Adamson   1700   C. i. 7
[124] Durandus of Saint-Purcain: *In sententias
theologicas Petri Lombardi commentariorvm
libri quatuor primum quidem per Nicolaum a Martimbos.*
Lvgdvni: Apvd Gvlielmvm Rovillivm, 1587.
Note of price (5s.) on title page

Bellarmini opera Parisijs 1608

	Vol. 1	20
	Vol. 2	21
	Vol. 3	22

Henry Doyly   1609   B. k. 2–4
Vol. 3 Foredge: 3 TOM
Vol. 4 Foredge: 4 TOM

[125] Roberto Bellarmino: *Disputationes...de controversies
Christianae fidei adversus huius temporis haereticos, quatuor tomis
comprehensae.* Parisiis: ex officinis Tri-Adelphorum
bibliopolarum, 1608.

Classis 7a in Folio	Librorum

Whitakeri Disputationes et praelectiones Genevae 1610   23
Edmund Anguish   1617   Not found
[126] William Whitaker: *Opera theologica.*. Opera theologica. Geneuae:
Sumptibus Samuelis Crispini, 1610

Chemnitij examen Concilij Tridentini 1614   24
Edward Nutting   1616   I. h. 12
[127] Martinus Chemnitius: *Examinis Concilii Tridentini...*
opus integrum, quatuor partes, in quibus praecipuorum
capitum totius doctrinae Papisticae...refutatio.
Geneuae: Excudebat Stephanus Gamonetus, 1614.

Willets Synopsis Papismi London 1614   25
Robert Gallard   C. g. 6
Seventeenth century calf.
[128] Andrew Willet: *Synopsis papismi, that is, a generall*
view of papistrie: wherein the whole mysterie of
iniquitie, and summe of anti-Christian doctrine is set
downe, which is maintained this day by the synagogie
of Rome, against the church of Christ.
London: Imprinted by Felix Kyngston, for Thomas Man,
1614.   (STC 25699a)
Note on front free endpaper: Robert Gallard in Artibus
Magister nuper unus praedicator parochiae St Andraeae
in Civit Norvici dono dedit huic librum Civi Bib.
6 Nov 1623[6]

Bacon in Sententias

	Vol. 1	26
	Vol. 2	27

John Whitefoot   1658   B. h. 16–17
Vol. 1: Front board detached.
[129] John Baconsthorpe: *Doctoris resoluti Io. Bachonis Angl. Carmelitae theologi*
celeberrimi, & canonistae praecipui. Quaestiones in quatuor libros Sententiarum, &
Quodlibetales... Cremonae: Apud Marc Antonium Belpierum, 1618.

---

[6] Robert Gallard MA, lately a preacher in the parish of St Andrew's in the City of Norwich, gave this book by gift to the City Library 6 November 1623.

Classis 8a in Folio	Librorum

Marloratus in Novum Testamentis 1585   1
Thomas Atkins   1618   G. k. 6
Rebound.
[130] Augustin Marlorat: Novi Testamenti Catholica
expositio ecclesiastica: Ex Probatis Theologis...
excerpta, & diligenter concinnata.
Geneuae: Apud Petrum Sanctandreanum, 1585. (Adams M 620)

Chemnitij Harmonia 1615   2
Edward Nutting   1616   D. g. 7
Foredge: Harmonia
[131] Harmoniae evangelicae, a praestantissimo theologo
D. Martino Chemnitio. Primum in choatae, & per
D. Polycarpum Lyserum continuatae, libri quinque,
uno hoc volumine comprehensi, & emendatiores
editi. Brvnsvigae: Excudebat Petrus Aubertus, 1615.
Front free endpaper: Quinta Februarij 1616
Ex dono Mr Edwardi Nuttinge

Aretius in Novum Testamentis 1618   3
William Stinnett   1658   A. h. 7
Foredge: Aretius No: Testam:
[132] Benedictus Aretius: *In Novum Testamentum*
domini nostri Iesu Christi commentarii
doctissimi Benedicti Aretii Bernensis.
Geneuae: Apud Petrum & Iacobum Chouet,
1618.

/Opera/
Calvini Comment. In 9 Volumin. 1597

	Opuscula	Vol. 1	4
	Epistola	Vol. 2	5
		Vol. 3	6
		Vol. 4	7
		Vol. 5	8
		Vol. 6	9
		Vol. 7	10
		Vol. 8	11
		Vol. 9	12

Sir Thomas Hyrne   1609   C. f. 5, 7–8, 10–15

Classis 8a in Folio   Librorum

[133] Jean Calvin: *Tractatus Theologici Omnes, in vnvm volvmen certis classibus congesti.* Genevae: Apud Patrum Santandreanum, 1597. (Adams C 384)

[134] Jean Calvin: *Quinque libros Mosis, commentarii.* [Genevae]: In officina Santandreanum, 1595. (Adams C 278)

[135] Jean Calvin: *Commentarius in Librum Psalmorum.* Genevae: Apud Evstathivm Vignon, 1578. (Adams C 291)

[136] Jean Calvin: *Praelectiones in Librum Prophetiarum Jeremiae, et Lamentationes.* Genevae: Apud Haered. Evstath. Vignon, 1589.

Foredge: Dan & 12 prophet
[137] Jean Calvin: *Praelectiones in librum prophetiarum Danielis.* Genevae, 1591.

Foredge: Epist Pauli   Rebound.
[138] Jean Calvin: *Commentarii in omes Pauli Apostoli Epistolas, atque in epistolam ad Hebraeos.* Genevae: Apud Haeredes Eustathii Vignon, 1600. (Adams C 324)

[139] Jean Calvin: *Epistolae et responsa.* Genevae: Apud Petrum Santandreanum, 1575.

[140] Jean Calvin: *Harmonia ex evangelistis tribus.* Genevae: Apud Evstathivm Vignon, 1592.

Foredge: Evang
[141] Jean Calvin: *Harmonia ex evangelistis tribus.* Genevae: Apud Haeredes Eustathii Vignon, 1595. (Adams C 353)

Melancthonis opera Wittebergae		
	Vol. 1	13
	Vol. 2	14
	Vol. 3	15
	Vol. 4	16

Thomas Atkins   1618   A. f. 8–11
Foredge: Vol. 1: Melanchton, Vol. 2: 2, Vol. 3: 3, Vol. 4: 4
[142] Philipp Melanchthon: *Operum omnium.* Witebergae: Typis Simonis Gronenbergij, 1601.

Classis 8a in Folio		Librorum	

Musculi opera Basileae in 8 Volum. 1611

In Math	1 Vol.	<16>	20
In Epist. ad Corinth	2 Vol.	<17>	23
In Genesin	3 Vol.	<18>	17
In Psalmos	4 Vol.	<19>	18
In Philip. Col. Thes. Tim.	5 Vol.	<20>	25
In Epist. ad Roman	6 Vol.	<21>	22
In Epist. ad Gal. & Eph	7 Vol.	<22>	24
In Isaiam	8 Vol.	<23>	19
In St Johannem	9 Vol.		21

Gabriel Barber   1614   A. l. 1–9
Foredge: In Mathaeam   Rebound.
[143] Wolfgang Musculus: *Commentarii in Matthaeum Evangelistam.* Basileae: per Sebastianum Henricpetri, 1611.

Foredge: Ad Corinth
[144] Wolfgang Musculus: *In Apostoli Pauli ambas Epistolas ad Corinthios commentarij.* Basileae: per Sebastianum Henricpetri, 1611.

Foredge: Psalmos   Rebound.
[145] Wolfgang Musculus: *In Davidis Psalterium sacrosanctum commentarii.* Basileae: per Sebastianum Henricpetri, 1599.

Foredge: Esaim   Rebound.
[146] Wolfgang Musculus: *In Esaiam prophetam commentarii.* Basileae: Ex officina Heruagiana, 1570.

Foredge: In St. Johannem
[147] Wolfgang Musculus: *Commentariorum in Evangelistam Ioannem.* Basileae, 1545.

Foredge: In Romanos
[148] Wolfgang Musculus: *In Epistolam D. Apostoli Pauli ad Romanos commentarij.* Baslieae: per Sebastianum Henricpetri, 1600.

Foredge: Ad Galatos & Ephes
[149] Wolfgang Musculus: *In Epistolas Apostoli Pauli, ad Galatos & Ephesios Commentarij.* Basileae: ex officina Hervagiana, 1569.

Classis 8a in Folio   Librorum

Foredge: Ad Philipp: Coloss: Thess: ? Tim: 1
[150] Wolfgang Musculus: *In Divi Pauli Epistolas ad Philippenses, Colossenses, Thessalonicenses ambas, & primam ad Timotheum.* Basileae: ex officina Hervagiana, 1578.

< Illyrici Glossa in No: Test: Basil: 1570 vide class 4tam >   24
Nathaniel Remington   F. f. 9
Foredge: Glossa Flacii
[151] Matthias Flacius Illyricus: *Nouum Testamentum Iesu Christi Filii Dei: ex versione Erasmi, innumeris in locis ad Graecum veritatem genuinumque sensum emendata. Glossa compendiaria M. Matthiae Flacij Illyrici Albonensis.* Basileae, 1570.

Petri Martyris Com[m]ent: in 6 Volum
In Epist. ad Roma	1 Vol.	<25>	30
In Libros Regum	2 Vol.	<26>	29
In Libros Samuel	3 Vol.	<27>	28
In Genesin	4 Vol.	<28>	25
In Epist.ia ad Cor.	5 Vol.	<29>	31
In Libris Judicis	6 Vol.	<30>	27

Charles Doyly   1610   A. g. 12–16

[152] Pietro Martyris Vermigli: *In Epistolam S. Pauli Apostoli ad Romanos.* Basileae: Apud Petrum Pernam. 1558. (Adams P 784)

Foredge: Regum 1 & 2
[153] Pietro Martyris Vermigli: *Melachim id est, Regum libri duo posteriores cum commentariis.* Heidelbergae: Ex Officina Andreae Cambieri, 1599. (Adams P 783)

Foredge: Sam 1 & 2
[154] Pietro Martyris Vermigli: *In Samuelis Prophetae libros duos.* Tiguri: Apud Joannem Wolphivm, 1595. (Adams P 779)

Foredge: Gen
[155] Pietro Martyris Vermigli: *In primum librum Mosis, qui vulgo Genesis dicitur, Commentarii.* Heidelbergae: E Typographeio Ioannis Lancelloti, 1606

Foredge: Iud
[156] Pietro Martyris Vermigli: *In librum Iudicum.* Tiguri: Apud Christophorum Froschoverum, 1582 (Adams P 775)

Classis 7a in Folio	Librorum

Mollerus in Psalmos Genevae 1610   <31>   32
Edmund Anguish   1611   D. h. 18
[157] Heinrich Moller: *Enarrationis Psalmorum Dauidis, ex praelectionibus D.*
Henrici Molleri Hamburgensis... Geneuae: Apud Petrum & Iacobum Chouet,
1610.

Babingtons Workes 1615   32   33
Francis Page   1625   B. l. 13
Seventeenth-century calf.
[158] Gervase Babington: *The workes of the Right Reuerend*
Father in God Gervase Babington, late Bishop of Worcester:
containing comfortable notes upon the fiue bookes of Moses...
London: Printed by George Eld, dwelling in Fleete-lane,
1615. (STC 1078)
Front free endpaper: Ex dono Magistri Francisci Page.

Fulke upon the Rhemish Testament   33   34
John Smith   1661   F. f. 10
Rebound.
[159] William Fulke: *The text of the New Testament translated*
out of the vulgar Latine by the Papists of the traiterous
Seminarie at Rhemes. With arguments...Whereunto is added
the translation...used in the Church of England. With a
confutation of all such arguments...as conteine manifest
impietie. London: Printed by Augustine Mathewes, 1633. (STC 2947)
Front free endpaper: Ex libris Thomas Nelson.
Presumably, the Thomas Nelson who was rector of Morston.

Eusebij aliorum Gr Historia Ecclesiast Latine   35
Nathaniel Cock   1675   C. i. 16
Rebound.
[160] John Christopherson: *Historiae ecclesiasticae scriptores Graeci, nempe*
Eusebij. Coloniae Allobrogum: excudebat Petrus de la Rouiere, 1612

Classis 9a in Folio	Librorum

Foxes Martyrology: London. 1596   1
Robert Sedgwick   1610 F. i. 6
[161] John Foxe: *Actes and monuments of matters most speciall and memorable,*
happening in the Church with an vniuersall history of the
*same...*London: Printed by Peter Short, 1596. (STC 11226)

Baronij Annales Col. Agrip: 1609	1 Vol.	2
	2 Vol.	3
	3 Vol.	4
	4 Vol.	5
	5 Vol.	6
	6 Vol.	7

Robert Garsett   1612 E. h. 11–16
[162] Caesar Baronius: *Annales ecclesiastici.*
Coloniae Agrippinae: Sumptibus Ioannis Gymnici, 1609. (Adams B 239)
Bookplate in every volume except the rebound vol. 1: Patriae, &
Posteritatj. Robertus Garsett, 1612

Concilia. Gen: per Bineum Lat. Col. Agrip 1606	1 Vol.	8
	2 Vol.	9
	3 Vol.	10
	4 Vol.	11
	5 Vol.	12

Sir John Pettus   1608 E. h. 6–10
[163] Concilia generalia et provincialia: quotquot reperiri potuerunt;
item epistolae decretales, et Romanor. Pontific. Vitae. Omnia
studio et industria R.D. Severini Binii.
Coloniae Agrippinae: I. Gymnicum et A. Hierat, 1606.

Acta Synodi Dordraconae Lugd: Bat   13
Richard Ireland   1692 D. i. 8
Seventeenth-century calf.
[164] Synod of Dort. Acta synodi nationalis, in nomine Domini
Nostri Iesu Christi, autoritate illustr. et praepotentum.
Lugduni Batavorum: typis Isaaci Elzeviri, Societatis
dordrechtanae sumptibus, 1620.
Title page: 'Sumptibus Theologon Norwici Anno 1620
Decembris 2o pretium 15s. 6d'.

Classis 9a in Folio	Librorum

Eusebij Historia Eccles. Lat: Basileae. 1611   14
Hammond Thurston   1613   Not found
[165] Eusebius of Caesarea: *Eusebii Pamphili... Ecclesiastica Historia.*
Basileae: Per Sebastianum Henricpetri, 1611.

Illyrici Catalogus testium Veritatis. Edit: 1608   <14>   15
Edmund Nutting   1616   E. f. 14
[166] Matthias Flacius Illyricus: *Catalogus testium veritatis, qui, ante nostram*
aetatem, Pontificum Romanorum primatui variisque Papismi superstitionibus, erroribus,
ac impiis fraudibus reclamarunt. Genevae: In officina Iacobi Stoer, 1608.
On front free endpaper: 'Quinto die Febr. Ao 1616
hunc librum dd: Mr Edw: Nutting huic Bibliothecae'.

Centur: Magdeburg: Basileae 1574	1 Vol.	<15>	16
	2 Vol.	<16>	17
	3 Vol.	<17>	18
	4 Vol.	<18>	19
	5 Vol.	<19>	20
	6 Vol.	27	21
	7 Vol.	28	22

Sir John Pettus   1608   B. f. 2–8
Vol. 2 foredge: 4 Cen   Vol. 3 foredge: 6 Cent
Vol. 4 foredge: 8 Centur   Vol. 5 foredge: 9,10,11 Cent
Vol. 6 foredge: 12 Cent   Vol. 7 foredge: 13 Cen
[167] Matthias Flaccius Illyricus: *Ecclesiastica Historia, integram Ecclesiae*
Christi ideam quantum ad locum, propagationem, persecutionem, tranquillitatem,
doctrinam, haereses, ceremonias, gubernationem, schismata, synodos, personas, miracula,
martyria, religiones extra Ecclesiam, et statum Imperii politicum attinet, secundum
singulas centurias...complectens...Per aliquot studiosos et pios viros in urbe
Magdeburgica.
Basileae: per Ionannem Oporinum, [1560]–1574.

Peretius de divinis et Apostolicis trad: 1549   23
William Hannam   1611   Not found
[168] Martin Perez de Ayala: *De divinis, apostolicis*
atque ecclesiasticis traditionibus, de que authoritate
ac ui earu[m] sacrosancta, adsertiones ceu libri decem:
in quibus fere uniuersa ecclesiae antiquitas, circa dogmata
apostolica orthodoxe elucidatur.
Coloniae: excudebat Iaspar Gennepaeus, 1549. (Adams P 676)

Classis 9a in Folio	Librorum		

Rodolphi Hospiniani opera 1503

De templis 1503	1 Vol.	<23>	24
Histor Sacram 1562	2 Vol.	<24>	25
Histor Sacram 1598	3 Vol.	<25>	26
De Festis Christ 1612	4 Vol.	<26>	27
Concord. Discors. 1607	5 Vol.	<27>	28

John Anguish   1617   A. l. 11–15
Foredge: Hospin
[169] Rodolphus Hospinianus: *De templis: Hoc est, de origine, progressu, usu et abusu Templorum...* Tiguri: in officina Wolfiana, 1603.

Foredge: Hospin
[170] Rodolphus Hospinianus: *Historia sacramentaria: hoc est Libri Quinque.* Tiguri: apud Iohannem Wolphium, 1598. (Adams H 1042)

Foredge: Hospin
[171] Rodolphus Hospinianus: *Historia sacramentariae pars altera.* Tiguri: apud Iohannem Wolphium, 1602. (Adams H 1042)

Foredge: Hosp
[172] Rodolphus Hospinianus: *Festa Christianorum. Hoc est De origine, progressu, ceremoniis et ritibus festorum dierum christianorum.* Tiguri: apud Joh. Rodolphus Wolphium, 1612.

Foredge: Hospin
[173] Rodolphus Hospinianus: *Concordia Discors: De Origine et Progressu formulae concordiae Bergensis.* Tiguri: in officina Wolphiana, 1608.

Tertulliani opera   28   29
Robert Sedgwick   1610   B. l. 12
Detached front board.
[174] Tertullian: *Opera adhuc reperiri potuerunt omnia: ex editione Iacobi Pamelii Brugensis. Quibus seorsum additae sunt annotationes Beati Rhenani...itemque castigationes...Francisci Junii.*
Franekerae: Excudebat Aegidius Radaeus, 1597. (Adams T 416)
Much marginal annotation

Classis 10a in Folio	Librorum	

King James his workes London 1616   1   1
Thomas Catlyn   1617   B. i. 16
[175] James 1, King of England: *The workes of the Most High
and Mightie Prince, Iames by the grace of God, King of
Great Britaine, France and Ireland, Defender of the Faith.*
London: Printed by Robert Barker and Iohn Bill, printers to
The Kings Most Excellent Maiestie, 1616. (STC 14344)

Crookes Anatomy. London. 1615   2   2
Thomas Catlyn   1617   Not found
[176] Helkiah Crooke: *Mikrokosmographia: a description of the body
of man. Together with the controuersies thereto belonging.
Collected and translated out of all the best authors of anatomy,
especially out of Gasper Bauhinus and Andreas Laurentius.*
London: Printed by William Iaggard dwelling in Barbican,
1615. (STC 6062)

Buntingi Chronologia 1590   3   3
Joanna Blowe   1613   H. c. 17
Rebound.
[177] Heinrich Buenting: *Chronologia hoc est, omnivm temporvm
et annorum Series: ex sacris Bibliis, aliisqve fide dignis scriptoribvs, ab
Initio mvndi ad nostra usq[ue] tempora…collecta, & calculo
Astronomico exactissime demonstrate.*
Servestae: Impressvm typis Bonaventvrae Fabri, sumtibus Ambrosij
Kirchneri bibliopolae Magdeburgensis, 1590. (Adams B 3154)

Scaliger de Emendat: temporum: 1629   4   4
Richard Ireland   1692   F. e. 1
[178] Joseph Justus Scaliger: *De emendatione temporum:
Addita veterum Graecorum fragmenta selecta.*
Coloniae Allobrogum: Typis Roverianis, 1629.
Title page: Tho: Allen.
Possibly the author of *A chain of scripture chronology* (1658).

Aeneae Sylvij Picolom. Opera 1551 Basileae   5   5
Michael Pead   1610   B. l. 5
Foredge: Opera Aeneae Sylvij:
[179] Pope Pius II: *Aeneae Sylvii Piccolominei Senesis,
opera quae extant omnia.* (Adams P 1333)

Classis 10a in Folio	Librorum

Basileae: Per Henrichum Petri, mense Augusto anni 1551.
Binding signed with the initials B. I.

<Hookers Ecclesiast: Polity. London 1597>   <6>
Edward Rudd   1707   C. e. 30
Rebound.
*[180] Richard Hooker: Of the Lawes of Ecclesiasticall
Politie.* London: Printed by Iohn Windet, [1593]–97.
Much marginal annotation. (STC 13712 and 13712.5)

Hugonis Cardinaliis opera			
	1 Vol.	<7>	6
	2 Vol.	<8>	7
	3 Vol.	<9>	8
	4 Vol.	<10>	9
	5 Vol.	<11>	10
	6 Vol.	<12>	`11

John Collinges   1658   D. k. 7–12
Volumes 1 and 2: Marbled enpapers
Volumes 3 to 6: Modern endpapers
*[181]Bible. Prima (-Sexta) pars huius operas: contines textum
Biblie cu postilla domini Hugonis Cardinalis &c.
(Repertorium apostillarum...Hugonis Cardinalis
[compiled by G. Eppius]*
Basle: Iohann Amorbach, 1504. (Adams B 984)
On title page of vol. 1: Jo. Hassall emit Lugdum Batavorum
18. Junij 1625 pretio 16 Fl. pro 6 voll.

Perkins his workes			
	1 Vol.	<14>	12
	2 Vol.	<15>	13
	3 Vol.	<16>	14

Matthew Peckover   1613   B. h. 8–10
Boards detached
[182] William Perkins: *The workes of that famous and worthy
Minister of Christ in the Vniuersitie of Cambridge, Mr.
William Perkins.* London [and Cambridge]: By Iohn Legatt, printer to
the Vniuersitie of Cambridge, 1612. (STC 19650)

Classis 10a in Folio	Librorum		

Paraei opera

	1 Vol.	<17>	15
	2 Vol.	<18>	16

Thomasina Brooke   1659   G. h. 8–9
Marbled endpapers
[183] David Pareus: *D.D. Parei…Operum theologicorum
Exegeticorum.* Francofurti: Impensis viduae Ionae Rosae, 1647.

Gerrhardi Continuatio in Harmon	Vol. 1	<19>	17
	Vol. 2	<20>	18

Sir Joseph Payne   B. i. 5
Boards detached
[184] Johann Gerhard: *Harmoniae Euangelistarum
Chemnitio-Lyserianae continuatio a Ioh. Gerhardo SS.
Theolog. D. et in Academia Ienensi professore, iusto
commentario illustrata, cum indicibus capitum,
rerum & verborum utilissimis.*
Roterodami: Ex bibliopolio Arnoldi Leers, 1646.

Riveti opera

	1 Vol.	<20>	19
	2 Vol.	<21>	20
	3 Vol.	<22>	21

Thomasina Brooke   1659   H. a. 1–3
Volume 1: Mutilated
Volumes 2 and 3: Boards detached
[185] Andre Rivet: *Operum theologicorum quae Latine edidit.* Roterodami: Ex
officina typographica Arnoldi Leers, 1652–60.

Stephani Thesau Grae. Linguae

	1 Vol.	<23>	22
	2 Vol.	<24>	23
	3 Vol.	<25>	24
	4 Vol.	<26>	25
	5 Vol.	<27>	26

Thomas Barrett   1633   A. i. 3–7
Bindings repaired. Modern endpapers.
[186] Henri Estienne: *Thesaurus Graecae linguae
ab Henrico Stephano constructus.*
Paris, 1572. (Adams S 1790)

Classis 10a in Folio	Librorum	

Cameronis opera	<28>	27

Thomasina Brooke   1659   D. f. 15
Binding crudely repaired
[187] John Cameron: *Ioannis Cameronis Scoto-Britanni*
Theologi eximij [Ta sozomena], siue Opera partim
ab auctore ipso edita, partim post eius obitum vulgata,
partim nusquam hactenus publicata, vel e Gallico
Idiomate nunc primum in Latinam linguam translata.
Genevae: sumptibus Petri Chouet, 1658.

Pererius in Genesin	28

William Oliver   1668   G. k. 9
[188] Benedictus Pererius: *Commentariorum et disputationum*
in Genesim. Coloniae Agrippinae: Ex officina Antonij
Hierati, 1606.
On front free endpaper: Pretium 20s.

Memorandum. That all these bookes in 4to & 8o placed in 4 classes or on
4 short shelves are removed to others of the like size in the west side of
the library

Classis 2a in Quart. & Octavo	Librorum

[The whole of class 1a is cancelled]

Vigueri Institut Theolog: Col. Agrip. 1607	1

Edmund Anguish   1617   C. d. 4
Binding crudely repaired
[189] Jean Viguier: *Institutiones theologicae, ex sacris literis...*
Coloniae Agrippinae: Apud Bernardum Gualtherium, 1607.
Bookplate on rear pastedown: 'Donum Edmvndi Angvvish de parochia
S. Petri de Mancroft in Noruico. Ann. Do. 1617'.

An English Bible London: 1612	2

Hammond Thurston   1613   Not found
[190] The Holy Bible, Conteyning the Old Testament, and the New: Newly
Translated out of the Original tongues. London: Printed by Robert Barker,
1612.   (STC 2219 or 2220)

Classis 2a in Quart. & Octavo	Librorum

Lavater in Nehemiam et Esdram 1586   3
Thomas Corye 1609
[191] Ludwig Lavater: *Nehemias: Liber Nehemiae*
qui et secundus Ezrae dicitur, homiliis LVIII.
Tiguri: ex officina Froschouiana, 1586 (Adams L 312).

Sculteti Medulla Patrum Neapoli 1605   4
William Adamson   1700   K. a. 19
[192] Abraham Scultetus: *Abrahami Sculteti...Medullae*
Theologiae patrum: in qua theologia clarissimorum veteris ecclesiae
doctorum Athanasii magni, et epiphanii polyhistoris, analytica &
synthetica methodo expressa. Neapoli Nemetum: excudebat
Nicolaus Schrammius, 1605.

Pelargi Bibliotheca Theolog Francof.   5
Not found
[193] Christophorus Pelargus: *Bibliotheca theologica, hoc est,*
index bibliorum praecipuorum...qui in numero Rabbinorum,
Patrum, Lutheranorum, Pontificiorum, aut Cinglio-Calvinianorum
contineantur. Francofurti Marchionum: Sumtibus Ioannis
Thymii, [1608?].

Cartwrighti Harmon: Evangeliorum 1627   6
Thomas Toft [7]   I. b. 17
Detached front board.
[194] Thomas Cartwright: *Harmonia evangelica per analysin logicam,*
et metaphrasin historicam quatuor evangelistas explicans &
concinnans. Amsterodami, 1627.
Title page: DD Tho: Toft in Artibus Magister
Theological notes on front and rear endpapers.

Jamesij Catalogus librorum in Biblioth: Bodleiana 162   7
Richard Ireland   1692   A. c. 12
Rebound. Modern endpapers.
[195] Thomas James: *Catalogus universalis librorum in*
Bibliotheca Bodleiana omnium librorum, linguarum,

---

[7] Thomas Toft graduated BA at Corpus Christi College, Cambridge, in 1629, proceeding
MA in 1632. As rector of St Michael at Plea he 'never wore the surplice...nor observed other
ceremonies' (*Vox Norwici: or the cry of Norwich, vindicating their ministers,* 1646, p. 12). His gift is not
recorded in the donation book.

& scientiarum genere refertissima, sic compositus.
Oxoniae: Excudebant Iohannes Lichfield, & Iacobus
Short, Academiae typographi, impensis Bodleianis,
1620. (STC 14450)

Martins defense of Priests marriages   8
Thomas Atkins   1618   C. c. 8
Rebound.
*[196]A Defence of priestes marriages, stablysshed by the imperiall lawes of
England...* London: J. Kinston for R. Jugge, 1562. (STC 17518)

Broughton on the Revelat. 1610   9
William Adamson   1700   Not found
[197] Hugh Broughton: *A reuelation of the holy Apocalyps.*
[Amsterdam]: Printed [by Giles Thorp], 1610. (STC 3883)

Clusij Historia Aromatum   10
[198] Garcia de Orta: *Aromatum et simplicium aliquot
medicamentorum apud Indos nascentium historia...illustrata
a Carolo Clusio Atrebate.* Not found

Fulgentij opera   11
William Adamson   1700   D. a. 11
Binding in a distressed state.
[199] Saint Fulgentius: *Opera, quae extant, omnia:
diligenter conquisita.* Basileae:
Per Sebastianum Henricpetri, 1587. (Adams F 1141)

Viti Historia Insul. Britan   12
Bassingbourn Throckmorton   Not found
[200] Richard White: *Ricardi Viti Basinstochi comitis Palatini
historiarum Britanniae insulae libri nouem priores.* Duaci:
Apud Carolum Boscardum, 1598–1602. (Adams W 89)

Pagnini epitome Rad: Heb: 13
Henry Bird   1614   G. g. 9
Comprehensively rebound.
[201] Santes Pagninus: *Hoc est, Thesaurus Linguae sanctae: sive Lexicon
Hebraicum.* Lugduni, 1595.

Classis 2a in Quart. & Octavo	Librorum

Erasmi Test: Graec. Collat.   14
F. f. 9
Foredge: Glossa Flacii
Seventeenth-century calf.
[202] Tes Tou Giou Theou Kaines Diathekes Hapanta:
Novvm Testamentvm Jesv Christi Filii Dei Ex
Versione Erasmi, Innvmeris in Locis ad Graecam
veritatem, genuinumque sensum emendata.
Basileae: Per Petrvm Pernam et Theobaldum
Dietrich, 1570. (Adams B 1702)

Prosperi opera Colon Agrip 1609   15
Edmund Anguish   1617
[203] Saint Prosper of Aquitaine: *Diui Prosperi Aquitanici,*
Episcopi Rhegiensis, viri eruditissimi, Opera.
Accurata exemplarium vetustorum collatione
a mendis pene innumeris repurgata. Quid vero
in hac editione praeter ditissimum indicem, tam
scripturarum quam rerum accesserit, versa pagina
demonstrat. Coloniae Agrippinae: Excudebat Arnoldus Kempensis,
sumptibus Ioannis Crithii, 1609.

Mr Whitefoot 2 sermons
John Whitefoot   1658   Not found
[204] John Whitefoot: [*Israel Anchithanes*]: *death's alarum: or the presage of*
approaching death. London: printed for W. Godbid
for Edward Dod, 1656. (W 1863 and 1864A)
Probably two editions of the same sermon. The second edition
was published in 1657. Both copies possibly transferred to Norwich Public
Library stock.

Manuale confessariorum   16
Thomasina Brooke   1659
[205] Martin de Azpilcueta: *Enchiridion, sive manuale*
confessariorum, et paenitentium.   Not found

Classis 2a in Quart. & Octavo	Librorum

In folio. Large volumes on a short shelfe in the East side of the library

Pitts English Atlas Volumen 1   1
Martin Jubbs[8]   1706   Not found
[206] Moses Pitt: *The English Atlas. 5 vols.* Oxford:
printed at the Theatre, 1680–2.
(W 2306, 2306A, 2306B, 2306C)
On 7 May 1681, 'at the request of the ministers', the City
Assembly agreed to buy Moses Pitt's proposed 12–volume
English Atlas by subscription.[9] By the time Brett's catalogue
was printed 4 volumes had been acquired, though one was
already missing. Perhaps Martin Jubbs replaced the missing
volume.

Speeds Maps & Cronicle   2
Ann Corbett   1617   I. h. 1–2
Rebound
[207] John Speed: *The theatre of the empire of Great Britaine: presenting an exact
geography of the kingdomes of England, Scotland, Ireland, and the iles adioyning: with
the shires, hundreds, cities and shire-townes, within ye kingdome of England.* London:
William Hall, 1611. (STC 23041)

Liber Cronicarum ab initio mundi cum imaginibus 1493   3
Samuel Clark   1680   I. h. 3
Binding repaired. Modern endpapers.
[208] Hartmann Schedel: *Liber chronicarum.* Nuremberg: A. Koberger,
1493.

Loggan Cantabrigia et Oxonia Illustrata 1675   4
Benjamin Penning   1696   Not found
[209] David Loggan: *Oxonia illustrata.* Oxoniae:
e Theatro Sheldoniano, [1675] (W 2838)
[209.1] David Loggan: *Cantabrigia illustrata.*
Cantabrigia, 1688. (W 2836)
Described in Benjamin Penning's will as 'the prints of the Colleges &
other buildings in the universitys of Cambridge & Oxford done by
Loggan'.

---

[8] Born at Wymondham in 1664, the son of John Jubbs, gentleman, Martin Jubbs was
admitted to Lincoln's Inn in 1681. He died in 1732.
[9] NRO NCR Case 16d/8, Assembly folio book of proceedings, 1668–1707, f. 85.

Classis 2a in Quart. & Octavo	Librorum

English Bible MS to the psalmes   5
Richard Ireland   1692   I. h. 20
[210] Wycliffite Bible
Duplicate entry of *[1]*.

Classis 3a in Quarto	Librorum
2a	

2a
[The whole of class 3a in quarto is cancelled]

Eccles: Belgicarum Leiturgia Graec: Linguae conversa   1
[211]Belgicarum Ecclesiarum doctrina & ordo. Hoc est confession, catechesis, liturgia,
canones ecclesiastici, graece & latin: interpretibus Friderico Sylburgio…& Jacobo
Revio. Hardervici: Excudebat Nicolaus à Wieringen, 1627.

Biblia: Ma[*nu*]sc[*ript*]a   2
Bassingbourn Throckmorton   C. a. 30
Comprehensively rebound by Riley, Dunn and Wilson
[212] Thirteenth-century manuscript copy of the Vulgate
Ker, *MMBL*, p. 553.
On f. 4v: Bassingbonus Throckmorton generosus D.D.
Bibliothecae publicae Nordouicanae

Junij et Tremellij Biblia cum Annotationibus   3
Richard Ireland   1692   F. f. 8
Rebound. Modern endpapers.
[213] Testamenti Veteris Biblia sacra, siue, Libri canonici priscae Iudaeorum
ecclesiae a Deo traditi Latini recens ex Hebraeo facti, breuibus[que] scholiis illustrati
abImmanuele Tremellio, & Francisco Iunio.
Geneuae: Sumptibus Matthaei Berjon, 1617.

An English Bible with the Geneva Notes 1560   4
Hammond Thurston   1613   F. f. 16
Comprehensively rebound by Riley, Dunn and Wilson.
[214] The Bible and Holy Scriptures conteyned in the Olde and Newe
Testament. Translated according to the Ebrue and Greke, and
conferred with the best translations in diuers languages. With
moste profitable annotations vpon all the hard places, and other things
*of great importance as may appeare in the epistle to the reader.*Geneva: Printed by
Rouland Hall, 1560. (STC 2093)

Classis 2a in Quart. & Octavo	Librorum	
Weemes his Workes	1 Vol.	5
	2 Vol.	6
	3 Vol.	7

Thomas Toft   A. c. 19–21
Rebound. Modern endpapers.
[215] John Weemes: *The workes of M. Iohn Weemes of Lathocker
in Scotland*. London: by T. Cotes for Iohn Bellamie, 1633. (STC 25207)
Title page vols 2 and 3: DD Tho: Toft

Kircheri Concord: Heb: Graec. Francofurti 1607	1 Vol.	8
	2 Vol.	9

John Chappel   1634   C. d. 15
Nineteenth-century red leather title label.
[216] Conrad Kircher: *Concordantiae Veteris Testamenti Graecae: ebraeis vocibus
respondentes*. Francofurti: Apud Claudium Marnium
& heredes Johannis Aubrii, 1607.

Draudij Bibliotheca	1 Vol.	10
	2 Vol.	11

Anthony Mingay   1634   K. c. 19–20
Rebound. Modern endpapers.
[217] Georg Draudius: *Bibliotheca classica, siue catalogue officinalis, in quo
singuli singularum facultatum ac professionum libri…*
Francofurti ad Moenum: impensis Balthasaris Ostern, 1625.

Dr de Lawnes translation of the English Liturgy Gallicae   12
Peter de Laune   1614   B. d. 3
Nineteenth-century red leather title label.
*[218]La liturgie angloise. Ou le liure des prieres publiques, de l'administration des
sacremens, & autres orders & ceremonies de l'eglise d'Angleterre. Nouuellement traduit
en francois.* Londres: par Iohan Bill, 1616. (STC 16431)
Inscription on title page: 'Liber bibliothecae publicae Nordouicensis ex
dono pastoris Petri Launaei quo authore Anglicanae haec ecclesiae
liturgia facta est Gallicana'. With a letter from A.W. Pollard to George
Stephen, the Norwich City Librarian, dated 7 February 1917, tipped in.

Mr Allens chaine of scripture chronologie   13
Thomas Allen   1660   Not found
[219] Thomas Allen: *A chain of Scripture chronology: from
the creation of the world to the death of Jesus Christ:
in VII periods.* London: Ekins, 1658 or 1659. (W 1047A or 1048)

2a

Classis in Quarto et Octavo 3a   Librorum

[*The whole of class 3a is cancelled*]

Piscator	In Totum Novum Test: Herbornae 1621	1
	In Psalmos	2
	In Jobum	3
	In Isaiam	4
	In Prophetas minores	5
	In Jeremiam	6
	In Ezechiellem	7
	In Proverbia	8
	In Paralip Lib: 1 et 2	9
	In Reg: Lib: 1 et 2	10
	In Samuelem Lib: 1 et 2	11
	In Josuam	12
	In Leviticum	13
	In Exodum	14
	In Genesin	15

In totum Novum Testamentum: Hebornae 1621
Augustine Scottowe   1621   E. a. 1– 16
[220] Johannes Piscator: *Johan. Piscatoris Commentarii in omnes libros Novi
Testamenti*… Hebornae Nassoviorum, 1621.

In Psalmos
Augustine Scottowe
[221] Johannes Piscator: *Commentarius in librum Psalmorum.*
Hebornae Nassoviorum, 1618.

In Jobum
Augustine Scottowe
[222] Johannes Piscator: *Commentarius in librum Jobi.*
Hebornae Nassoviorum: Ex officina typographica Christophor
Corvini, 1612.

In Isaiam
Augustine Scottowe
[223] Johannes Piscator: *Commentarius in Prophetam Esaiam.*
Hebornae Nassoviorum, 1612.

Classis in Quarto et Octavo 3a

In Prophetas minores
Augustine Scottowe
[224] Johannes Piscator: *Commentarius in duodecim prophetas quos nominant minores.* Hebornae Nassoviorum, 1615.

In Jeremiam
Augustine Scottowe
[225] Johannes Piscator: *Commentarius in Prophetam Jeremiam, & ejusdem Lamentationes.* Hebornae Nassoviorum: Ex officina typographica Christophori Corvini, 1614.

In Ezechiellem
Augustine Scottowe
[226] Johannes Piscator: *Commentarius in Prophetam Ezechielem.* Hebornae Nassoviorum, 1614.

In Proverbia
Augustine Scottowe
[227] Johannes Piscator: *Commentarius in Proverbia Salomonis, itemque in Canticum Canticorum.* Hebornae Nassoviorum, 1617.

In Paralip.
Augustine Scottowe
[228] Johannes Piscator: *Commentarius in duos libros Chronicorum.* Hebornae Nassoviorum, 1616.

In Reg: Lib: 1 et 2
Augustine Scottowe
[229] Johannes Piscator: *Commentarius in duos libros Regum.* Hebornae Nassoviorum, 1611.

In Samuelem
Augustine Scottowe
[230] Johannes Piscator: *Commentarius in libros duos Samuelis.* Hebornae Nassoviorum, 1610.

In Josuam
Augustine Scottowe
[231] Johannes Piscator: *Commentarius in librum Josuae.* Hebornae Nassoviorum, 1607.

Classis in Quarto et Octavo 3a

In Leviticum
Augustine Scottowe
[232] Johannes Piscator: *Commentarius in Leviticum.*
Hebornae Nassoviorum, 1615.

In Exodum
Augustine Scottowe
[233] Johannes Piscator: *Commentarius in Exodum.*
Hebornae Nassoviorum, 1605.

In Genesin
Augustine Scottowe
[234] Johannes Piscator: *Commentarius in Genesin.*
Hebornae Nassoviorum, 1611.

Classis 4a In 4o 8vo & 12o

[*The whole of class 4a is cancelled*]

Polani Comment.		
	In Ezechielem. 1608	1
	In Danielem: 1606	2
	In Hoseam: 1601	3
	Syphonia Catholica 1612	4
	De incarn: mort. et resur. Christi et in Psal	5
	De methodo concionandi	6
	Mellificium	7
	De ratione legendi scripturas et in psalmos 1611	8
	De eterna dei praedestinatione 1600	9
	Syllog. disputation[ib]u[s]oppos: Bellar. 160	10

Polani Comment   In Ezechielem 1608
Edward Nutting   1616   Not found
[235] Amandus Polanus: *In librum prophetiarum Ezechielis commentarii*
Basileae, 1608.

Classis in Quarto et Octavo 3a

In Danielem 1606
Edward Nutting   1616   B. a. 6
Rebound in quarter leather. Modern endpapers.
[236] Amandus Polanus: *In Danielem prophetam visionum.* Basileae:
Typis Conradi Waldkirchi,1606.

In Hoseam 1601
Edward Nutting   1616   B. a. 5
Foredge: Hoseae
Nineteenth century red leather title label.
[237] Amandus Polanus: *Analysis libri Hoseae prophetae tradita.*
Basileae: per Conradum Waldkirch,1601.

Symphonia Catholica 1612
Edward Nutting   1616   B. a. 1
Rebound. Modern endpapers.
[238] Amandus Polanus: *Symphonia catholica seu consensus catholicus et
orthodoxus dogmatum hodiernae ecclesiae ex praescripto verbi Dei reformatae,
et veteris apostolicae catholicae...* Genevae: ex typographia Iacobi Stoer, 1612.

De ineann: mort: et iesu Christi et in Psal
Edward Nutting   1616   Not found
[239] Amandus Polanus: *Exegesis analytica illustrium aliquot
vaticinorum Veteris Testamenti de incarnatione, passione, morte et
resurrectione domini nostri Jesus Christi, in praelectionibus publicis tradita.*
Basileae, 1606.

De methodo Concionandi
Edward Nutting   1616   B. a. 4
Rebound. Nineteenth century red leather title label.
[240] Amandus Polanus: *De concionum sacrarum methodo insitutio.*
Basileae: Typis Conradi Waldkirchii, 1604.

Mellificium
Edward Nutting   1616   Not found
[241] Amandus Polanus: *Mellificium, in quo articuli
praecipui symboli apostolici de dn.nostri Jesu Christi:
incarnatione, nativitate [&c] enarrantur.*
Ambergae: typis Schönfeldionis, 1613.

Classis in Quarto et Octavo 3a	Librorum

De ratione legendi scripturas et in Psalmos 1611
Edward Nutting   1616   B. a. 3
Rebound. Modern endpapers.
[242] Amandus Polanus: *De ratione legendi cum fructu autores, inprimis sacros…tractatus. Cui adjuncta est analysis logica & exegesis theologica psalmorum tredecim.* Basileae, 1611.

De eterna dei praedestinationes 1600
Edward Nutting   1616   Not found
[243]De aeterna Dei praedestinatione didascalia. Basileae:
Typis Conradi Waldkirchii, 1600. (Adams P 1731)

Syllog. disputationu oppos. Bellar. 1600
Edward Nutting   1616   B. a. 2
Rebound. Modern endpapers.
[244]Sylloges thesium theologicarum, ad methodi leges conscriptarum et disputationibus Roberti Bellarmini praecipue oppositarum atque in vetusta Academia Basiliensi ad disputandum propositarum. Basileae:
Per Conradum Waldkirch, 1600.

In: 12o	Librorum

Psalterum Graec. Collat Paris 1557   12o   11
[245] Unidentified psalter in duodecimo.

Justiniani Institutiones   12o   12
William Stinnett   c1658   Not found
[246] Justinian: *Institutionem juris civilis libri iiii*

Toleti instructio sacerdot in 8vo   13
Thomasina Brooke   1659   D. a. 16
Foredge: Tollet
Rebound in quarter leather. Modern endpapers.
[247] Franciscus Toletus: *Instrvctio Sacerdotvm in libros octo. distincta.* Rothomagi: Apud Manassem de Preavlx, 1619.

Usserij de Macedonum et Asianorum anno solari   14
dissertat   8o

Classis in Quarto et Octavo 3a	Librorum

Richard Ireland 1692   Not found
[248] James Ussher: *Jacobi Vsserii Armachani de*
Macedonum et Asianorum anno solari dissertatio.
Londoni: Typis M. Flesher & prostant apud Cornelium
Bee, 1648.
Catachysm Racovian   8o   15

[249] Matthias Flacius: *Ecclesiastica Historia, integram*
Ecclesiae Christi ideam quantum ad locum,
propagationem, persecutionem tranquillitatem,
doctrinam, haereses, ceremonias, gubernationem,
schismata, synodos, personas, miracula, martyria,
religiones extra Ecclesiam... Basileae, [1560]–74.
Duplicate of *[167]* B. f. 2–8

Classis 2 decima	Lib[*rorum*]

Buxtorfij Lex Rabbinic	1

John Mann   1664   F. i. 14
Rebound in quarter leather. Modern endpapers.
[250] Johannes Buxtorfius: *Lexicon chaldaicum talmudicum*
et rabbinicum. Basileae: sumptibus & typis Ludovici
König, 1640.

Sanctij opera in Lib. Reg.	2
In Esdr, Nehem et Apoc	3
In lib Jobi	4
In Isajam	5
In Jer	6
Ezech. Et Dan	7
Min. Prophet	8
Cantic. Cantic	9
Act Apost	10

Thomasina Brooke   1659   B. k. 12
Rebound in quarter leather. Modern endpapers.
[251] Gasparus Sanctius: *In quatuor libros Regvm, & duos*
Paralipomenon, commentarij. Lugduni: sumpt. Iacobi
Cardon et Petri Cavellat, 1623.

Rebound in quarter leather. Modern endpapers.   B. k. 13

Classis 2 decima   Lib[*rorum*]

[252] Gaspar Sanctius: *In libros Rvth, Esdrae, Nehemiae, Tobiae, Ivdith, Esther, Machabaeorum commentarij.* Lugduni: sumptibus
Iacobi Cardon, 1628.

Rebound in quarter leather. Modern endpapers.   B. k. 14
[253] Gaspar Sanctius: *In librvm Iob commentarij cum paraphrasi.*
Lugduni: sumpt. Iacobi Cardon et Petri Cavellat, 1625.
Rebound in quarter leather. Modern endpapers.   B. k. 11

[254] Gaspar Sanctius: *In duodecim prophetas minores & Baruch commentarij cum paraphrasi.* Lugduni: sumpt.
Iacobi Cardon et Petri Cavellat, 1621.

[255] Gaspar Sanctius: *In Canticum canticorum commentarij, cum expositione Psalmi LXVII.* Lugduni: Apud Horatium Cardon,
1616.   Not found

Nineteenth-century red leather title label. Modern endpapers.
[256] Gaspar Sanctius: *In Ieremiam prophetam commentarij cum paraphrasi.*
Lugduni: sumptibus Horatii Cardon, 1618.   B. k.9

Front board detached. Seventeenth century calf.
[257] Gaspar Sanctius: *In Ezechielem & Danielem prophetam commentarij cum paraphrasi.* Lugduni: Sumptibus Horatii Cardon, 1619.
B. h. 10

Nineteenth-century red leather title label.
[258] Gaspar Sanctius: *In Isaiam prophetam commentarij cum paraphrasi.*
Lugduni: Sumptibus Horatii Cardon, 1615.   B. k. 8

Tostati opera In Gen.	11
Exod	12
Levit	13
Num et Deut	14
Josh. Jud. Et Ruth	15
Sam. 1 et 2	16
Reg. 1 et 2	17
Paralip	18
Mark	19
Math. 2 vol.	20
Mat. 3 vol.	21

Classis 2 decima	Lib[*rorum*]
Mat. 4 vol.	22
Index huius operas	23
Index quest[*ionum*]	24

Francis Norris 1662 D. f. 1
Rear board detached.
[259] Alphonsus Tostatus: *Commentaria in Genesim.*
Venetiis, 1615.

Seventeenth-century calf.
[260] Alphonsus Tostatus: *Commentaria in Primam
Partem Exodi.* Venetiis, 1615. D. f. 2

Seventeenth-century calf.
[261] Alphonsus Tostatus: *Commentaria in Leviticvm.*
Venetiis, 1615. D. f. 3

Rebound in quarter leather. Modern endpapers.
[262] Alphonsus Tostatus: *Commentaria in Primam
Partem Nvmerorvm.* Venetiis, 1615. D. f. 4

Rebound in quarter leather. Modern endpapers.
[263] Alphonsus Tostatus: *Commentaria in Primam
Partem Iosve.*Venetiis, 1615. D. f. 5

Seventeenth-century calf. Wormed.
[264] Alphonsus Tostatus: *Commentaria in Primum Partem 1 Regvm.*
Venetiis, 1615. D. f. 6

Seventeenth-century calf. Water stained.
[265] Alphonsus Tostatus: *Commentaria in Librum Tertivm Regvm.*
Venetiis, 1615.

Crudely repaired. Water stained.
[266] Alphonsus Tostatus: *Commentaria in Primam Partem Matthaei.* Venetiis,
1615. D. f. 9

Seventeenth-century calf.
[267] Alphonsus Tostatus: *Commentaria in Primam Partem
Parlipomenon.* Venetiis, 1615. D. f. 8

Classis 2 decima

Seventeenth-century calf.
[268] Alphonsus Tostatus: *Commentaria in Tertiam Partem Matthaei.*
Venetiis, 1615.   D. f. 10

Front board detached.
[269] Alphonsus Tostatus: *Commentaria in Quintam Partem Matthaei.*
Venetiis, 1615.   D. f. 11

Rear board detached. Water stained.
[270] Alphonsus Tostatus: *Commentaria in Septimam Partem Matthaei.*
Venetiis, 1615.   D. f. 12

Rebound in quarter leather. Modern endpapers.
[271] Alphonsus Tostatus: *Index Rervm Omnivm Praecipvarvm, qvae
in commentariis ac operibvs omnibvs Alphonsi Tostati.*
Venetiis, 1615.   D. f. 13

Rebound in quarter leather. Modern endpapers.
[272] Alphonsus Tostatus: *Index Qvaestionvm ex omnibvs operibvs
Alphonsi Tostati.* Venetiis, 1615.   D. f. 14

Chrysostomi opera Editioni Savilian in 8 vol.
John Mann   1664   H. a. 6–13
Vols. 7–9   not found
[273] John Chrysostom: *Opera graece.* Etonae: In Collegio Regali,
Excudebat Ioannes Norton, 1613.

Vasquez in Tho. Aquin. 7 vol.
John Mann   1664
Rebound in quarter leather. Modern endpapers.
[274] Gabriel Vasquez: *Commentariorvm, ac dispvtationvm
in primam partem Sancti Thomae tomvs primvs.*
Antverpiae: apud Petrum & Ioannem Belleros, 1621.   A.g. 1

Rebound in quarter leather. Modern endpapers.
[275] Gabriel Vasquez: *Commentariorvm, ac disputationvm in primam
partem Sancti Thomae tomvs secundvs.*
Antverpiae: apud Petrum & Ioannem Belleros, 1621.   A. g. 2

Rebound in quarter leather. Modern endpapers.
[276] Gabriel Vasquez: *Commentariorvm, ac disputationvm in primam
secvndae Sancti Thomae tomvs secundvs.*
Antverpiae: apud Petrum & Ionannem Belleros, 1621.   A. g. 3

Classis 2 decima   Lib[*rorum*]

Rebound in quarter leather. Modern endpapers.
[277] Gabriel Vasquez: *Commentariorvm ac disputationvm in tertiam partem Sancti Thomae tomvs primvs.*
Antverpiae: apud Petrum & Ioannem Belleros, 1621.   A. g. 4

Rebound in quarter leather. Modern endpapers.
[278] Gabriel Vasquez: *Commentariorum ac disputationum in primam secundae Sancti Thomae tomus primus.*
Antverpiae: apud Petrum & Ioannem Belleros, 1621.   A. g. 5

Rebound in quarter leather. Modern endpapers.
[279] Gabriel Vasquez: *Commentariorvm ac disputationvm in tertiam partem Sancti Thomae tomvs secundvs.*
Antverpiae: apud Petrum & Ioannem Belleros, 1621.   A. g. 6

Rebound in quarter leather. Modern endpapers.
[280] Gabriel Vasquez: *Commentariorvm ac disputationvm in tertiam partem Sancti Thomae tomvs quartvs.*
Antverpiae: apud Petrum & Ioannem Belleros, 1621.   A. g. 7

Gomari opera 3 vol.
John Mann   1664   B. k. 17
Crudely repaired.
[281] Franciscus Gomarus: *Opera theologica omnia.*
Amstelodami: Ex officina Joannis Janssonii, 1644.
Signature of J. Lloyd on title page.

Damaged binding.
[282] Franciscus Gomarus: *Operum pars secvnda.*
Amstelodami: Ex officina Joannis Janssonii, 1644.   B. k. 18

Nineteenth century red leather title label.
[283] Franciscus Gomarus: *Opervm pars tertia.*
Amstelodami: Ex officina Joannis Janssonii, 1644.   B. k. 19

Funcij Chronologia   43
John Mann   1664   D. f. 17
Lacks spine. Front board detached.
[284] Johann Funck: *Chronologia, hoc est, omnivm temporvm et annorvm ab initio mvndi, usque ad annvm a nato Christo.* Witebergae: Typis Zachariae Lehmanni, Impensis Andreae Hoffmanni Bibliopolae, 1601.

Classis 2 decima Lib[*rorum*]

In 4 class. Sylburgij Etimolog. Magn. 44
Richard Ireland 1692 D. f. 8
Rebound in quarter leather. Modern endpapers.
[285] Fridericus Sylburgius: *Etymologicon Magnvm; seu Magnvm
Grammaticae Penv.* Heidelberg: E Typographeio
Hieronymi Commelini, 1594.

Sigonij opera in vol. 5
John Mann 1664 B. l. 6
Vellum binding
[286] Carolus Sigonius: *Historiarum de regno Italiae
libri viginti.* Francofvrti: Apud heredes Andreae
Wecheli, 1591. (Adams S 1124)

Rebound in quarter leather. Modern endpapers.
[287] Carolus Sigonius: *Historiae de rebvs Bononiensibvs libri VII.*
Francofurti: Apud Claudiam Marniam, 1604. B. l. 7

Binding repaired. Modern endpapers.
[288] Carolus Sigonius: *Fasti consvlares, ac trivmphi acti à Romulo rege
Usque ad Ti. Caesarem.* Basileae: Apud Nicolaum Episcopium Iuniorem,
1559. (Adams S 1116) B. l. 8

Binding crudely repaired. Water stained.
[289] Carolus Sigonius: *Historiarvm de Occidentali imperio libri xx.*
Francofurti: Apud heredes Andreae Wecheli, 1593. B. l. 9

Nineteenth-century red leather title label.
[290] Carolus Sigonius: *De antiqvo iure civivm Romanorvm…
Libri xi, de republica atheniensium…Libri
quinque, quibus adiecti nunc sunt eiusdem
de republica hebraeorum, libri septem.*
Francofurti: Apud Heredes Andreae Wecheli, 1593.
(Adams S 1101) B. l. 10

Gualtheri opera 12 vol.
John Mann 1664 A. h. 10
Foredge: Gualter in Isaiam
Nineteenth century red leather title label. Detached front board.
[291] Rudolf Gualther: *Isaias in Isaiam prophetam.* Tigvri:
Excudebat Christophorvs Froschovervs, 1583. (Adams G 1361)

Classis 2 decima

Nineteenth-century red leather title label.
[292] Rudolf Gualther: *In Prophetas Dvodecim, Qvos vocant minores.*
Tigvri: excudebat Chri. Froschouerus, 1572.
(Adams G 1364)   A. h. 11
Title page signed Thomas Scot.

Rebound in quarter leather. Modern endpapers.
[293] Rudolf Gualther: *D. Matthaevs Evangelista. Pars prima.*
Tigvri: Excudebat Christophorvs Froschovervs, 1583.   A. h. 12
Title page has 'Hoc age Tho: Scot'.

Rebound in quarter leather. Modern endpapers.
[294] Rudolf Gualther: *D. Marcvs Evangelista.* Tigvri: Excudebat
Christophorvs Froschovervs, 1570. (Adams G 1373)   A. h. 13

Nineteenth-century red leather title label. Detached front board.
[295] Rudolf Gualther: *D. Lvcas Evangelista.* Tigvri: Excudebat
Christophorvs Froschovervs, 1573. (Adams G 1377)   A. h. 14

Nineteenth-century red leather title label.
Foredge: Gualther Hom
[296] Rudolf Gualther: *Homiliarvm in Evangelia.* Lvgdvni Batavorvm,
1585. (Adams G 1368)   A. h. 15

Foredge: Gualtheri Hom
Nineteenth century red leather title label. Detached front board.
[297] Rudolf Gualther: *Homiliarvm in Evangelia. Pars II.* Lvgdvni
Batavorvm, 1585. (Adams G 1368)   A. h. 16

Rebound in quarter leather. Modern endpapers.
[298] Rudolf Gualther: *In Acta Apostolorum per Diuum Lucam descripta.*
Tigvri: Excudebat Christoph. Froschovervs, 1569.
(Adams G 1388)   A. h. 17

Rebound in quarter leather. Modern endpapers.
Foredge: Head: Gualt in Roma & St Johannis Epistolas
[299] Rudolf Gualther: *In D. Pauli Apostoli Epistolam ad Romanos
Homiliae.* Tiguri: Excudebat Christophorvs Froschovervs,
1572. (Adams G 1393)   A. h. 18

Classis 2 decima	Lib[*rorum*]

Rebound in quarter leather. Modern endpapers.
Foredge: Head: Gualt. Gala
Rebound in quarter leather. Modern endpapers.
[300] Rudolf Gualther: *In D. Pavli Apostoli Epistolam ad Galatas.*
Tigvri: Excudebat Christophorvs Froschovervs, 1576.
(Adams G 1399)   A. k. 19

Nineteenth-century red leather title label. Detached front board.
Foredge: Head: Gualt Johannis
[301] Rudolf Gualther: *D. Ionnes Evangelista.* Tigvri: Excudebat
Christophorvs Froschovervs, 1568. (Adams G 1381)   A. k. 20

Rebound in quarter leather. Modern endpapers. Trimmed.
[302] Rudolf Gualther: *In Priorem D. Pavli ad Corinthios Epistolam
Homiliae.* Tigvri: Excudebat Christophorvs Froschovervs, 1572.
(Adams G 1396)   A. h. 21

Pererius in Gen.
William Oliver 1668
[303] Benedictus Pererius: *Commentariorvm et dispvtationvm
in Genesim.* Coloniae Agrippinae: Ex officina Anthonij Hierati, 1606.
G. k. 9

Euseb. Cum alijs de hist
John Moore 1706
[304] Eusebius: *Ecclesiasticae historiae libri decem.*
Parisiis: typis Petri Le Petit, 1678.
'Cum alijs' probably refers to the two other works
donated by Bishop John Moore.

Seneca opera
William Oliver 1668
Marbled endpapers.
[305] Lucius Annaeus Seneca: *Philosophi scripta
qvae extant hac postrema editione doctissimorvm
vivorum, praecipue vere Iani Gruteri et Fr. Iureti
notis, et obseruationibus aucta.* Parisiis: apud
Marcvm Orry, 1602.   A. i. 9

Classis 2 decima Lib[*rorum*]

Poole's Critic 3 vol.
John Barnham 1671–6 G. k. 1–5
Volume 1: Rebound in quarter leather. Modern endpapers.
Volume 2: Front board detached.
Volume 3: Quarter leather. Modern endpapers.
Volume 4: Quarter leather. Modern endpapers.
Volume 5: Quarter leather. Modern endpapers.
[306] Matthew Poole: *Synopsis criticorum aliorumque*
Sacrae scripturae interpretum. Londini: Typis J. Flesher & T. Roycroft,
1669–76.

In 5 cla. Dr Jackson's works 3 vol. E. i. 9–11
[307] Thomas Jackson: *The works of the Reverend and Learned*
*Divine, Thomas Jackson.*London: Printed by J. Macock for John Martyn,
1673.
Duplicate entry of *[64]*.

Suarez 18 vol.
George Cock 1673
Seventeenth century calf.
[308] Francisco Suarez: *Opera omnia.* Mogvntiae: Sumptibus
Hermanni Mylij Birckmanni Excudebat Balthasar Lippius,
1621 E. k. 1

Crudely repaired.
[309] Francisco Suarez: *Commentariorvm ac Dispvtationvm in Primam*
Partem Divi Thomae. Pars II. Mogvntiae: Sumptibus
Hermanni Mylij Birckmanni Excudebat Balthasar Lippius,
E. k. 2

Crudely repaired.
[310] Francisco Suarez: *Commentariorvm ac Dispvtationvm in Primam*
Partem Divi Thomae. Partis II. Mogvntiae: Sumptibus
Hermanni Mylij Birckmanni Excudebat Balthasar
Lippius, 1622. E. k. 3

Seventeenth-century calf.
[311] Francisco Suarez: *Tractatvs de Legibvs, ac Deo Legislatore.*
Mogvntiae: Sumptibus Hermanni Mylij Birckmanni
Excudebat Balthasar Lippius, 1619. E. k. 4

Classis 2 decima

Seventeenth-century calf.
[312] Francisco Suarez: *De Divina Gratia Pars Prima.* Mogvntia: Sumptibus
Hermanni Mylij Birckmanni Excudebat Balthasar Lippius,
1620.   E. k. 5

Spine crudely repaired.
[313] Francisco Suarez: *Opvs de Triplici Virtvte Theologica.* Parisiis: Typis
Edmundi Martini, 1621.   E. k. 6

Quarter leather. Modern endpapers.
[314] Francisco Suarez: *De Virtvte et Statv Religionis. Tomvs Tertivs.*
Mogvntiae: Sumptibus Hermanni Mylii, Birckman.
Excudebat Hermannus Meresius, 1625.   E. k. 7

Spine crudely repaired.
[315] Francisco Suarez: *De Virtvte et Statv Religionis. Tomvs II.*
Mogvntiae: Sumptibus Hermanni Mylii, Birckman.
Excudebat Hermannus Meresius, 1623.   E. k. 8

Crudely repaired.
[316] Francisco Suarez: *De Virtvte et Statv Religionis. Qvo Qvid
Contineatvr, Index proximus indicabit.* Mogvntiae:
Sumptibus Hermanni Mylii, Birckman. Excudebat
Hermannus Meresius, 1624.   E. k. 9

Crudely repaired.
[317] Francisco Suarez: *Commentariorvm ac Dispvtationvm in Tertiam
Partem Divi Thomae. Tomvs Secvndvs.* Mogvntiae:
Sumptibus Hermanni Mylii Birckman, Excudebat
Hermannus Meresius, 1616.   E. k. 10

Crudely repaired.
[318] Francisco Suarez: *Commentariorvm ac Dispvtationvm in Tertivm
Partem Divi Thomae. Tomvs Tertivs.* Mogvntiae:
Ex officina Typographica Balthasaris Lippii, 1619.   E. k. 11

Seventeenth-century calf.
[319] Francisco Suarez: *Commentariorvm ac Dispvtationvm in Tertivm
Partem Divi Thomae. Tomvs Qvartvs.* Mogvntiae:

Classis 2 decima

Ex officina Typographica Balthasari Lippij, sumptibus
Hermanni Mylii, 1616. E. k. 12

Seventeenth-century calf.
[320] Francisco Suarez: *Tractatvs Quinqve, ad primam secvndae
D. Thomae.* Mogvntiae: Sumptibus
Hermanni Mylii Birckmanni, Excudebat
Hermannus Meresius, 1629. E. k. 13

Seventeenth-century calf.
[321] Francisco Suarez: *Dispvtationvm De Censvris in Commvni,
Excommvnicatione, suspensione, & Interdicto,
itemque de Irregularitate. Tomvs Quintvs.*
Mogvntiae: Ex officina Typographica Balthasari
Lippij, 1617. E. k. 14

Front board detached.
[322] Francisco Suarez: *Commentariorvm ac Dispvtationvm, in
Tertiam Partem Divi Thomae. Tomi Quinqve.*
Mogvntiae: Ex officina Typographica Balthasari
Lippij, 1617. E. k. 15

Seventeenth-century calf.
[323] Francisco Suarez: *Defensio Fidei Catholicae et Apostolicae
Adversvs Anglicanae Sectae Errores.* Mogvntiae:
Ex officina Typographia Balthasari Lippij,
1619. E. k. 16

Early repair to spine.
[324] Francisco Suarez: *Operis De Religione Tomvs Qvartus, et
Vltimvs.* Lugduni: Sumptibus Iacobi Cardon & Petri
Cauellat, 1625. E. k. 17

Seventeenth-century calf.
[325] Francisco Suarez: *Metaphysicarvm Disputationum.* Coloniae:
Excudebat Franciscus Heluidius, 1614. E. k. 18

Sir Thomas Brown's Vulgar Errors & relig. med. in 4to
Sir Thomas Browne   1666
[326] Sir Thomas Browne: *Pseudodoxia Epidemica.*

Classis 2 decima

London: J.R. for Nath. Elkins, 1672. [A. e. 23]
A later addition to Browne's Justus Lipsius donation recorded
in a different hand.

Sir Thomas Browne 1666
[327] Sir Thomas Browne: *Religio medici: with annotations*
never before published, upon all the obscure passages therein:
also, observations by Sir Kenelm Digby, now newly added.
London: printed by Tho. Milbourn, 1659.
A later addition to Browne's Justus Lipsius donation recorded
in a different hand.

Lipsij opera 8 vol. in 4to
Sir Thomas Browne 1666
[328] Justus Lipsius: *Epistolarvm Selectarvm Centvria Singvlaris.*
Antverpiae: Ex officina Plantiniana, 1613. H. d. 1
Preliminaries damaged.

[329] Justus Lipsius: *De Crvce libri tres.* Antverpiae: Ex officina
Plantiniana, 1606. H. d. 2
Note tipped in: 'This book belongs to the City Library,
borrowed 5 August 1728'.

Spine crudely repaired. Preliminaries damaged.
[330] Justus Lipsius: *De Constantia Libri Dvo.* Antverpiae:
Ex officina Plantiniana, 1615. H. d. 3

Spine crudely repaired.
[331] Justus Lipsius: *Epistolarvm selectarvm centvria prima*
Miscellanea. Antverpiae: Ex officina Plantiniana, 1614. H. d. 4

Spine crudely repaired.
[332] Justus Lipsius: *Admiranda, sive De Magnitvdine Romana.*
Antverpiae: Ex officina Plantiniana, 1617. H. d. 5

Spine crudely repaired.
[333] Justus Lipsius: *De Militia Romana.* Antverpiae: Ex officina
Plantiniana, 1614. H. d. 6

Classis 2 decima

Spine crudely repaired.
[334] Justus Lipsius: *V. C. opera omnia.* Antverpiae: Ex officina
Plantiniana, 1614. H. d. 7

Spine crudely repaired.
[335] Justus Lipsius: *Politicorvm sive Civilis Doctrinae.* Antverpiae:
Ex officina Plantiniana, 1610. H. d. 8

Summa Sylvestrina
William Stinnet c. 1658 C. d. 25
Rebound in quarter leather. Modern endpapers.
[336] *Svmmae Sylvestrinae, quae svmma svmmarvm merito nvncvpatvr.*
Lvgduni: Svmptibus Petii
Landry, 1593.

Weckeri Antidotar
William Stinnet c. 1658 A. d. 10
Nineteenth century red leather title label.
[337] Johann Jacob Wecker, *Antidotarium speciale*
(Basle, 1574). A. d. 10
Note of the price (6s. 8d.) on the title page.
Prolific marginalia and much underlining

Ex parte Occidentali

Catalogue librorum in Occidentali parte Bibliotheca Norvicensis
secundum classes dispositorum

Classis prima in folio

[*The compiler of the catalogue does not continue his description of the east side of the
library beyond this point.*]

Catalogus librorum in Bibliotheca Nordovicensi Alphabetice dispositorum.
Prior numerus marginalis Classem. Secundus librum denotat:

A		Class	Librorum
[Col. 1]			
Acta Synodi Dordraconae fol.		19	13
Barth Anglus de reru[m] proprietate		5	14
Aeneae Sylvii opera. fol.		10	5
Ambrosii opera fol.		6	29
Tomus secundus		6	
Aquinatis Catena aurea fol.		2	16
Aquinatis Summae		7	13
Archidiaconis super decret		6	4
Aretij Commentar in Novum Test		11	13
Arca Noae fol.		8	5
Athanasii opera fol.		9	34
Augustini opera fol. 1 vol		7	6
	2 vol	7	7
	3 vol	7	8
	4 vol	7	9
	5 vol	7	10
	6 vol	7	11
Ainsworths workes		6	22
T[*homas*] Allen's chaine of scripture chronologie 4to		1	17
Azorii institutions morales 3 vol folio			
Arminii opera folio		1	15

B			
Babington's Workes		9	32
Bannes in Thomam	1 vol	8	17
	2 vol	8	18

		Class	Librorum
Baronii Annales	1 vol	9	2
	2 vol	9	3
	3 vol	9	4
	4 vol	9	5
	5 vol	9	6
	6 vol	9	7
Basilii opera Graec. Lat.	1 vol	7	18
folio	2 vol	7	19
Bedae opera folio	1 vol	2	1
	2 vol	2	2
	3 vol	2	3
Bartholdi Decret		6	2
Bernardi opera folio	1 vol	7	1
	2 vol	7	2
Bellarmini Controvers. folio	1 vol	8	20
	2 vol	8	21
	3 vol	8	22
Bezae Annot. in Novum Test.		3	9
Tractatus Theologici folio		3	10
Biblia MS folio		1	13
Biblia Regis Hispan folio	1 vol	1	2
	2 vol	1	3
	3 vol	1	4
	4 vol	1	5
	5 vol	1	6
	6 vol	1	7
	7 vol	1	8
	8 vol	1	9
Biblia Fr. Vatabli folio	1 vol	1	10
	2 vol	1	11
Biblia Buxtorfij cum	1 vol	1	12
Comment Rabbin folio	2 vol	1	13
Bible English 4to		1	2
Bible MS English 4to		1	2
Bible English with the Geneva notes		2	4
Bonaventura folio	1 vol	2	4
	2 vol	2	5
	3 vol	2	6
	4 vol	2	7
Broughton on the Revelation 4to		1	9

		Class	Librorum
Buntingi Chronologia folio		11	3
Jo. Bacon in sententias folio	1 vol	8	26
	2 vol	8	27
Jo. Buxtorfi Lexicon Chaldaicum Talmudicum et Rabbinicum		12	1
Bartholomeus Anglicus de rerum proprietatem		5	24

[Col. 2]

Bonacinae opera fol.		4	13
Sir Thomas Browne M.D. his Vulgar Errors & his Relig. Medici 1 Vol.			

C

[Col. 1]

		Class	Librorum
Calvini Dictionarium Octoling.		7	6
Calvini Institut		4	12
Calvini Comment.	1 vol	8	4
	2 vol	8	5
	3 vol	8	6
	4 vol	8	7
	5 vol	8	8
	6 vol	8	9
	7 vol	8	10
	8 vol	8	12
Cartwrighti harmon. Evang. 4to		1	6
Catalogus sanctorum 4to		5	12
Catalogus lib in Academia Bodleiana 1620 4to		1	7
Chemnitij Loci Communes fol		4	4
Ejusdem Harmonia		9	2
Ejusd. Exam. Concil. Trid.		8	24
Centur Magdeburg fol	1 vol	10	16
	2 vol	10	17
	3 vol	10	18
	4 vol	10	19
	5 vol	10	20
	6 vol	10	21
	7 vol	10	22
Chronicon Regnor. Aquilonar. fol		5	28

		Class	Librorum
Chrysostomi opera lat. fol	1 vol	7	13
	2 vol	7	14
	3 vol	7	15
	4 vol	7	16
Clemantis Alexand. opera fol		7	24
Clusij Historia Aromatum 4to		1	10
Compilatio Decretaliis Graec folio		6	3
Concilia per Binnius folio	1 vol	10	8
	2 vol	10	9
	3 vol	10	10
	4 vol	10	11
	5 vol	10	12
Concordantiae Lat. fol		8	3
Concordantiae Hebr. fol		8	4
Crooke's Anatomy fol		11	2
Cyrilli Alexand. opa Lat. fol.		7	17
Catena Graecorum patrum in jobi		2	22
Collectorae Niceta			
< Chrysostomi opera in 8 volumes			
ex ... Saviliana >			
Critici sacri 9 vol	1 vol	1	20
fol.	2 vol	1	21
	3 vol	1	22
	4 vol	1	23
	5 vol	1	24
	6 vol	1	25
	7 vol	1	26
	8 vol	1	27
	9 vol	1	28
A Concordance made in Edward 6th tyme		5	16

[Col. 2]

		Class	Librorum
Calvini Lexicon juridicum fol.		5	15
Cameronis opera		11	28
Chrysostomi opera in	1 volume	12	25
8 vol. ex editione savil.	2 volume	12	26
	3 volumes	12	27
	4 volumes	12	28
	5 volumes	12	29
	6 volumes	12	30
	7 volumes	12	31
	8 volumes	12	32

		Class	Librorum
D			
[Col.1]			
J Damasceni opera fol.		6	23
Drayton's Polyalbion fol.		5	9
Drawdii Bibliotheca 4to	1 volume	2	10
	2 volume	2	11
Durandus in sententias fol.		8	19
E			
Effigies et Elogia Theol reform folio		5	15
Epithanij opera Graec	1 vol	6	21
collat	2 vol	6	22
Eusebii Historia Eccles folio		1	16
F			
[Col. 1]			
Foxe's martyrology fol.		10	1
Fulgentij opera 8vo		1	12
Forsteri Lexicon Heb.		4	13
Filiucij moralia fol.		4	14
Fulk on the Rhemists Test. fol.		9	33
Funcij Chronologia		12	43
G			
Gesneri Bibliotheca fol		7	12
Gregorij magni opera fol		7	12
Gerardi Loci Communes	1 vol	4	8
	2 vol	4	9
	3 vol	4	10
	4 vol	4	11
Harmonia Evangel		11	19
Harmonia passionis		9	3
Gregorius de valentia		2	23
< Gualteri opera in 12 vol >			
Gomarus in 3 vol	1 vol	12	40
	2 vol	12	41
	3 vol	12	42

		Class	Librorum
Gualtheri opera 12 vol			
	In Isaiam	12	50
	In prophetes minores	12	51
	In St Math.	12	52
	In St Marcum	12	53
	In St Luc.	12	54
	In St joannem	12	55
	In Acta Apost.	12	56
	In Romanos	12	58
	In Corinth. 1 & 2	12	57
	In Galat.	12	50
Ejusd	Hom. aestivales	12	60
	Hom. Hyemales	12	61

H

		Class	Librorum
Halensis Summa fol.	1 vol	8	14
Ejusdem	2 vol	8	15
Ejusdem	3 vol	8	16
Hemingius in Epistolas fol.		2	17
Ejusdem opuscula fol.		4	6
Heroologia Anglicana fol.		5	6
Hieronimi opera fol.	1 vol	7	2
	2 vol	7	3
	3 vol	7	4
Hilarij opera folio		7	2
Historia rerum & urbis Amstelod.		5	8
Hospiniani opera fol.			
De re templis	1 vol	10	24
De re Sacram	2 vol	10	25
De re Sacram	3 vol	10	26
De Festis Christ.	4 vol	10	27
Concordia discors	5 vol	10	28
Hooker's Ecclesiasticall Polity		11	6
Hugo Cardinalis	1 vol	11	7
	2 vol	11	8
	3 vol	11	9
	4 vol	11	10
	5 vol	11	11
	6 vol	11	12
Hieron ab Oleastro		2	19

		Class	Librorum

I

		Class	Librorum
King James his workes		11	1
Illyrici clavis Scriptura		8	9
Ejusd Glossa in Novum Test.		5	7
Ejusd Catalogus testium		10	14
Irenij opera		7	28
Junij opera theologica	1 vol	3	7
	2 vol	3	8
Ejusd. Anotat. in Biblia 4o		2	3
Justini Martyris opera		7	2
Justiniani Cod. lib. 9 fol		6	1
Ejusdem institutiones 12o		4	12
Josephi opera Graec Lat. fol		5	16
Dr Jackson's works	1 vol	4	27
	2 vol	4	28
	3 vol	4	29

K

		Class	Librorum
Kircheri Concordantia Gr. Heb. 4o			
Ejusdem	1 vol	2	8
	2 vol	2	9

L

		Class	Librorum
Cornelius a Lapide			
In Pentatuchum fol		2	8
In 4 Prophet majores fol		2	9
In 12 Prophet minores fol		2	10
In Ecclesiasticum fol		2	11
In Epistolas Pauli fol		2	12
In Acta Apostol. fol		2	13
In Proverbia fol		2	14
In Evangelia		2	15
Lavater			
In Job Pro. Eccles. Ezech.		3	5
In Jos. Jud. Paralip. Esther.		3	6
In Nehemiam et Esdram 4o		1	3
Dr de Lawnes translation of the English Liturgy Gall. 4o		2	12

		Class	Librorum
Leiturgia Belgica in Gr. Ling. Converse 4o		2	1
Legenda in fol		5	11
Lorichij thesaurus scriptura fol.		4	7
Lyra cum glossa ord. in Pentateuchum			
	1 vol	3	1
In Jos etc lib histo	2 vol	3	2
In Job etc	3 vol	3	3
In Prophetas fol.		3	4
Lyra absque glossa fol	1 vol	6	5
fol	2 vol	6	6
Lutheri opera	1 vol	3	14
	2 vol	3	15
	3 vol	3	16
	4 vol	3	17
	5 vol	3	18
	6 vol	3	19
	7 vol	3	20
Lipsij opera	1 vol	12	63
	2 vol	12	64
	3 vol	12	65
	4 vol	12	66
	5 vol	12	67
	6 vol	12	68
	7 vol	12	69
	8 vol	12	70
Ludolphus de vita Christi fol		6	21

M

	Class	Librorum
Maldonatus in Evangelia fol.	2	16
Marini arca Noe fol.	8	5
Marloratus in Novum Testamentum fol.	8	1
Petrum Martyris Loci communes fol.	4	5
Martyris commentarii In Romanos fol.	9	26
In librum Regum	9	27
In librum Samuelis	9	28
In Genesin	9	29
In Epis. ad Corin	9	30
In Judices	9	31

		Class	Librorum
Martins defence of Priests marriages		1	8
Melancthonis opera fol	1 vol	9	13
	2 vol	9	14
	3 vol	9	15
	4 vol	9	16
Mollerus in Psalmos		9	17
Musculi Loci communes fol.		4	3
Ejusd Comment In Math. Fol		9	18
In Corinth		9	19
In Genesin		9	20
In Psalmos		9	21
In Epist. ad Collos. Philip Thess. Tim.		9	22
In Epist ad Gal. et Ephes.		9	23
In Isaiam		9	24
In S. Johannem		9	25
Minshaei Dictionarium		8	1
Ejusd. Emendatio &t		8	2
Martinij Lexicon		8	11
Pagnini Thesaurus Ling. Heb. edit J. Mercerus et alios		6	20

N

		Class	Librorum
Newman's Concordance fol.		7	10
Navarij Enchiridion 8vo		4	10
Nicetae Catena Graecorum Patrum in Beatum job		2	26

O

		Class	Librorum
Hieronimi Oleastri Com. in Pentateu fol.		2	19
Origenis opera Lat. fol	1 vol	7	26
	2 vol	7	27
Oecumenij opera Graec Lat			
	1 vol	2	20
	2 vol	2	21

P

[Col. 1]

	Class	Librorum
Pagnini Epitome Thesauri Heb. Graec	1	13
Ejusdem Thesaurus Ling S. fol	6	20

		Class	Librorum
Pelargi Bibliotheca 4to		1	5
Peretius de divinis et Apostol. Tradit		10	23
Perkins his workes fol	1 vol	11	14
	2 vol	11	15
	3 vol	11	16
Piscatoris Commentarii in 4to et 8vo			
In Nov. Testament		3	1
In Psalmos		3	2
In Jobum et Eccles.		3	3
In Isajam		3	4
In Proph. minores		3	5
In Jeremiam		3	6
In Ezechielem et Dan.		3	7
In Proverbia et Cantica		3	8
In Paralip.		3	9
In Lib. Regum		3	10
In Lib. Samuelis		3	11
In Librum Josuam et Jud.		3	12
In Leviticum Num. et Deut.		3	13
In Exodum		3	14
In Genesin		3	15
Polani opera varia in fol. 4to et 8vo			
Syntagma theol.		4	1
Commentar In Ezechielem 4to		4	1
In Danielem		4	2
In Hoseam		4	3
Symphon. Cathol.		4	4
De morte incarnatione et resurrec. Christi, et in 13: 1o Psalm		4	5
De methodo concionandi		4	6
Mellificium		4	7
De ratione leg. Scrip. et in Psalmos		4	8
De eterna dei Prodest Syllogi disputat.		4	9
Polydori Virgilii history. Angl. fol.		5	5
Plinij historia naturalis fol.		5	2
Plutarchi vitae Lat.		5	3
Prosperi opera 8vo		1	14
Psalterium Gr. et Lat. 12 vo		4	13
Purchas his pilgrimage 1st pt.		5	4
Pererij Comment in Genesin		12	73

		Class	Librorum
[Col. 2]			
Parei opera	1 vol	11	17
	2 vol	11	18
	3 vol	11	19
Math. Paris		4	15
Philo Judeus Gr. Lat.		2	25
Photij Bibliotheca		6	24
[Col. 1]			
R			
Ravanelli Bibliotheca fol.		8	7
Rosini Antiquitates Rom. fol.		5	13
Reveti opera	1 vol	11	20
	2 vol	11	21
	3 vol	11	22
Raymundi Martini pugio fidei		5	19
S			
Salmeronis Commentar. in totio Novum Testamentum fol.			
	1 vol	3	21
	2 vol	3	22
	3 vol	3	23
	4 vol	3	24
	5 vol	3	25
	6 vol	3	26
	7 volume	3	27
Scapulae Lexicon fol.		17	8
Scaliger de Emendat. temporum fol.		11	4
Sculteti medulla patrid 4to		1	4
Speed's History & Mapps fol.		5	1
Stella in Lucam fol.		2	18
Schindleri Lexicon Pentaglotton		6	11
Summa Syluestrina		12	71
Smidij Concordantiae Graec. Fol.		6	14
Suidae opera Gr. Lat. 2 vol fol.		6	12
			13
Sanctius in libros Regum		12	2
In lib. Jobi		12	4
In Isaiam		12	5

		Class	Librorum
In Jeremiam		12	6
In Ezech. et Danielem		12	7
In minores prophetas		12	8
In libros Apocryph. Ruth		12	3
Esdram et Nehem.			
In Cantica Canticorum		12	9
In Act. Apostol.		12	10
Sylburgij Etymologicon Magnum		12	44
Sigonii opera in 5 vol.			
	1 vol	12	15
	2 vol	12	16
	3 vol	12	17
	4 vol	12	18
	5 vol	12	19
Stephani Thesaurus Grae lingua			
	1 vol	11	23
	2 vol	11	24
	3 vol	11	25
	4 vol	11	26
	5 vol	11	27
Seneca opera			
Sylvij (Aeneae) opera fol.		10	5

T

Tertulliani opera fol.		10	29
Theophilacti opera Gr. Lat. fol			
	1 vol	6	17
	2 vol	6	18
Tremellij Biblia 4to		2	3
Tolleti casus conscien. 8vo		4	11
Tostati opera 14 vol.			
In Genesin		12	11
In Exodum		12	12
In Leviticum		12	13
In Numeros		12	14
In Deuteronomium		12	14
In Librum joshuae		12	15
In Librum judicum		12	15
In Librum Ruth		12	15
In Sammueleni		12	16
In Librum Regum		12	17

		Class	Librorum
In Paralep.		12	18
In Sanctum Math. vol. 1		12	19
In Sanctum Math. vol. 2		12	20
In Sanctum Math. vol 3		12	21
In Sanctum Math vol 4		12	22
Index operis		12	23
Index Quaestionum		12	24

V

Vatabli Annotationes in Biblia		1	10
	1 vol	1	11
	2 vol	1	1
Vigueirij institutiones 4to		1	1
Viti Historia Britann. Insul. 4to		1	14
Vasquez in Thomam Aqui. 7 vol.			
	1 vol	12	33
	2 vol	12	34
	3 vol	12	35
	4 vol	12	36
	5 vol	12	37
	6 vol	12	38
	7 vol	12	39

W

Weems his workes 4to	1 vol.	2	5
	2 vol.	2	7
Whitakeri praelectiones		8	23
Willet's Synopsis Papismi fol.		8	25
Weckeri Antidotarium 4to		12	72
Willet on Genesis		2	24

Z

Zanchij opera theologica			
	1 vol	3	11
	2 vol	3	12
	3 vol	3	13
Zuingeri theat. vitae humanae			
	1 vol	6	7
	2 vol	6	8
	3 vol	6	9
	4 vol	6	10

Register of Librarians

John Collinges	February 1657
John Whitefoot	January 1659
Robert Harmer	January 1661
George Cock	January 1663
John Smith	January 1665
Thomas Morley	January 1667
Benjamin Snowden	January 1670
Nicholas Norgate	January 1672
Benedict Riveley	January 1674
John Watson	January 1675
John Ellsworth	January 1678 (died in office)
John Connold	August 1678
Thomas Studd	January 1680
William Cecil	May 1681
Steven Painter	March 1683 (paid a forfeit to stand down)
John Whitefoot	March 1683
John Jeffery	March 1684
John Shaw	February 1686
John Pitts	January 1688
Peter Burgess	April 1690 (resigned in August)
William Adamson	August 1690
John Graile	January 1693
John Richardson	December 1694
Joseph Ellis	January 1697
Isaac Girling	February 1699
Thomas Clayton	February 1700
John Barker	February 1701
Edward Riveley	January 1703
Joseph Brett	January 1705
John Havett	January 1707
William Herne	March 1709
Samuel Jones	February 1711
Francis Fayerman	January 1713
John Clarke	February 1714
John Brand	February 1716

Samuel Salter	February 1720
John Fox	May 1722 (resigned in June)
John Morrant	June 1722
Benjamin Mackerell	June 1724
William Pagan	February 1732

By 1699 the librarian seems to have had to pay 9s. for serving two years. These payments continued at least until February 1711. Clearly, some librarians found the payment onerous. Samuel Jones, whose period of office ended in January 1713, did not settle his debt until March.

There appears to have been no formal record of any meetings in the Library between October 1730 and December 1731, which may be related to a simmering controversy over Benjamin Mackerell retaining the post of librarian for no less than eight years. On 6 December 1731 the under librarian, Peter Scott, was asked to deliver an ultimatum to Mackerell that the members intended having an election the following day, 'the time for such election being long since lapsed'. Significantly, Mackerell's name does not reappear in the minutes after that date.

Chronological Conspectus of Places of Printing

[This index is based exclusively on the works listed in the catalogue of c.1707]

1481	Nuremberg	71		1568	Zurich	301
1493	Nuremberg	208		1569	Basle	92
1496	Nuremberg	68		1569	Basle	149
1496	Vensice	69		1569	Zurich	298
1496	Nuremberg	70		1570	Paris	102
1498	Basle	27		1570	Basle	62
1504	Basle	181		1570	Basle	146
1514	Lyon	58		1570	Basle	151
1514	Lyon	59		1570	Basle	202
1514	Lyon	87		1570	Zurich	294
1514	Lyon	88		1572	Antwerp	2
1518	Paris	93		1572	Zurich	292
1519	Nuremberg	60		1572	Zurich	299
1519	Cologne	74		1572	Zurich	302
1519	Nuremberg	86		1572	Paris	186
1530	Basle	94		1573	Zurich	295
1534	Basle	51		1574	Basle	337
1535	Basle	84		1575	Geneva	139
1535	Basle	108		1575	Lyon	81
1536	Cologne	106		1576	Zurich	300
1545	Basle	101		1578	Geneva	135
1545	Zurich	120		1578	Basle	150
1545	Basle	147		1580	Frankfurt	50
1549	Cologne	168		1582	Geneva	32
1550	Basle	103		1582	Frankfurt	49
1550	London	63		1582	Zurich	156
1551	Basle	179		1583	Basle	52
1556	Basle	112		1583	Zurich	291
1558	Basle	152		1583	Zurich	293
1559	Basle	288		1584	Basle	114
1560	Geneva	214		1585	Zurich	28
1561-74	Basle	249		1585	Geneva	130
1562	Basle	105		1585	Leiden	296
1562	London	96		1585	Leiden	297
1562-74	Basle	167		1586	Strasbourg	18
1564	Basle	45		1586	Zurich	29
1564	Basle	104		1586	Geneva	41
1566	Basle	95		1586	Paris	90
1567	Basle	97		1586	Zurich	191

1587	Lyon	124	1603	Heidelberg	40
1587	Basle	199	1603	Zurich	169
1588	Lyon	20	1604	Cologne	35
1589	Geneva	136	1604	Basle	72
1590	Zerbst	177	1604	Cologne	121
1591	Geneva	137	1604	Basle	240
1591	Frankfurt	286	1604	Frankfurt	287
1592	Geneva	140	1605	Cambridge	24
1593-7	London	180	1605	Geneva	33
1593	Heidelberg	99	1605	Wittenberg	34
1593	Frankfurt	289	1605	Neustadt	192
1593	Frankfurt	290	1605	Nassau	233
1593	Lyon	336	1606	Augsburg	85
1594	Heidelberg	66	1606	Heidelberg	155
1594	Heidelberg	285	1606	Cologne	163
1595	Geneva	134	1606	Cologne	188
1595	Geneva	141	1606	Basle	236
1595	Zurich	154	1606	Basle	239
1595	Lyon	201	1606	Cologne	303
1596	London	161	1606	Antwerp	329
1597	Geneva	133	1607	Geneva	37
1597	Franeker	174	1607	Cologne	189
1598-	Douai	200	1607	Frankfurt	216
1602			1607	Nassau	231
1598	Geneva	31	1608	Heidelberg	30
1598	Zurich	170	1608	Paris	125
1599	Heidelberg	2	1608	Geneva	166
1599	Basle	38	1608	Zurich	173
1610	Geneva	126	1608?	Frankfurt	193
1599	Basle	145	1608	Basle	235
1599	Heidelberg	153	1609	Mainz	8
1600	Geneva	138	1609	Freiburg	42
1600	Basle	148	1609	Paris	91
1600	Basle	243	1609	Cologne	203
1600	Basle	244	1610	Paris	23
1601	Wittenberg	142	1610	Geneva	157
1601	Basle	237	1610	Amsterdam	197
1601	Wittenberg	284	1610	Nassau	230
1602	Hague	61	1610	Antwerp	235
1602	Zurich	171	1611	Paris	16
1602	Paris	305	1611	London	48

1611	Amsterdam	55	1615	Venice	259
1611	Paris	111	1615	Venice	260
1611	Basle	143	1615	Venice	261
1611	Basle	144	1615	Venice	262
1611	Basle	165	1615	Venice	263
1611	London	207	1615	Venice	264
1611	Nassau	229	1615	Venice	265
1611	Nassau	234	1615	Venice	266
1611	Basle	242	1615	Venice	267
1612	Cologne	7	1615	Venice	268
1612	Pont à Mousson	17	1615	Venice	269
1612	Frankfurt	73	1615	Venice	270
1612	Geneva	160	1615	Venice	271
1612	Cologne	162	1615	Vencie	272
1612	Zurich	172	1615	Antwerp	330
1612	London/	182	1616	Wittemberg	39
	Cambridge		1616	Leiden	100
1612	London	190	1616	London	175
1612	Nassau	222	1616	London	218
1612	Nassau	223	1616	Nassau	228
1612	Basle	238	1616	Leiden	255
1613	Cologne	26	1616	Mainz	317
1613	London	56	1616	Mainz	319
1613	Amberg	241	1617	Antwerp	19
1613	Eton	273	1617	London	54
1613	Antwerp	328	1617	London	109
1614	Douai	123	1617	Geneva	213
1614	Geneva	127	1617	Nassau	227
1614	London	128	1617	Mainz	321
1614	Nassau	225	1617	Mainz	322
1614	Nassau	226	1617	Antwerp	332
1614	Cologne	325	1618	Antwerp	82
1614	Antwerp	331	1618	Paris	96
1614	Antwerp	333	1618	Cremona	129
1614	Antwerp	334	1618	Geneva	132
1615	Hanover	36	1618	Nassau	221
1615	Basle	116	1618	Leiden	256
1615	Braunschweig	131	1619	Rouen	247
1615	London	158	1619	Leiden	257
1615	London	176	1619	Mainz	311
1615	Nassau	224	1619	Mainz	318
1615	Nassau	232	1619	Mainz	323
1615	Leiden	258	1620	Basle	4

1620	Leiden	164	1633	London	215
1620	Oxford	195	1634	Geneva	77
1620	Mainz	312	1635	Paris	14
1621	Nassau	220	1636	Paris	78
1621	Leiden	254	1636	London	79
1621	Antwerp	274	1636	London	107
1621	Antwerp	275	1637	London	22
1621	Antwerp	276	1638	Wittenberg	75
1621	Antwerp	277	1640	Paris	25
1621	Antwerp	278	1640	London	47
1621	Antwerp	279	1640	Basle	250
1621	Antwerp	280	1643	London	118
1621	Mainz	308	1644	Amsterdam	281
1622	Paris	10	1644	Amsterdam	282
1622	Paris	98	1644	Amsterdam	283
1622	Cologne	122	1646	Rotterdam	184
1622	Mainz	310	1647	Frankfurt	183
1623	Bremen	119	1650	Geneva	115
1623	Leiden	251	1651	Paris	80
1623	Mainz	315	1652-60	Rotterdam	185
1624	Mainz	316	1655-7	London	5
1625	Frankfurt	217	1656	London	204
1625	Leiden	253	1657	Frankfurt/	43
1625	Mainz	314		Hamburg	
1625	Lyon	324	1657	London	204.1
1627	London	83	1658	Geneva	187
1627	London	110	1658	London	219
1627	Amsterdam	194	1659	London	327
1627	Harderwijk	211	1660	London/	6
1628	Münster	65		Oxford/	
1628	Leiden	252		Cambridge	
1629	Cologne	46	1669-76	London	306
1629	Basle	117	1672	London	326
1629	Geneva	178	1673	London	64
1629	Mainz	320	1675	Oxford	209
1630	Paris	9	1678	Paris	304
1630	Paris	11	1680-2	Oxford	206
1631	Paris	13	1688	Cambridge	209.1
1631	Paris	15			
1631	Paris	21			
1633	Lyon	12			
1633	Paris	44			
1633	London	159			

Index

Authors and places of publication listed in the Donation Book and the Catalogue are not covered. For the latter see Appendix Two.